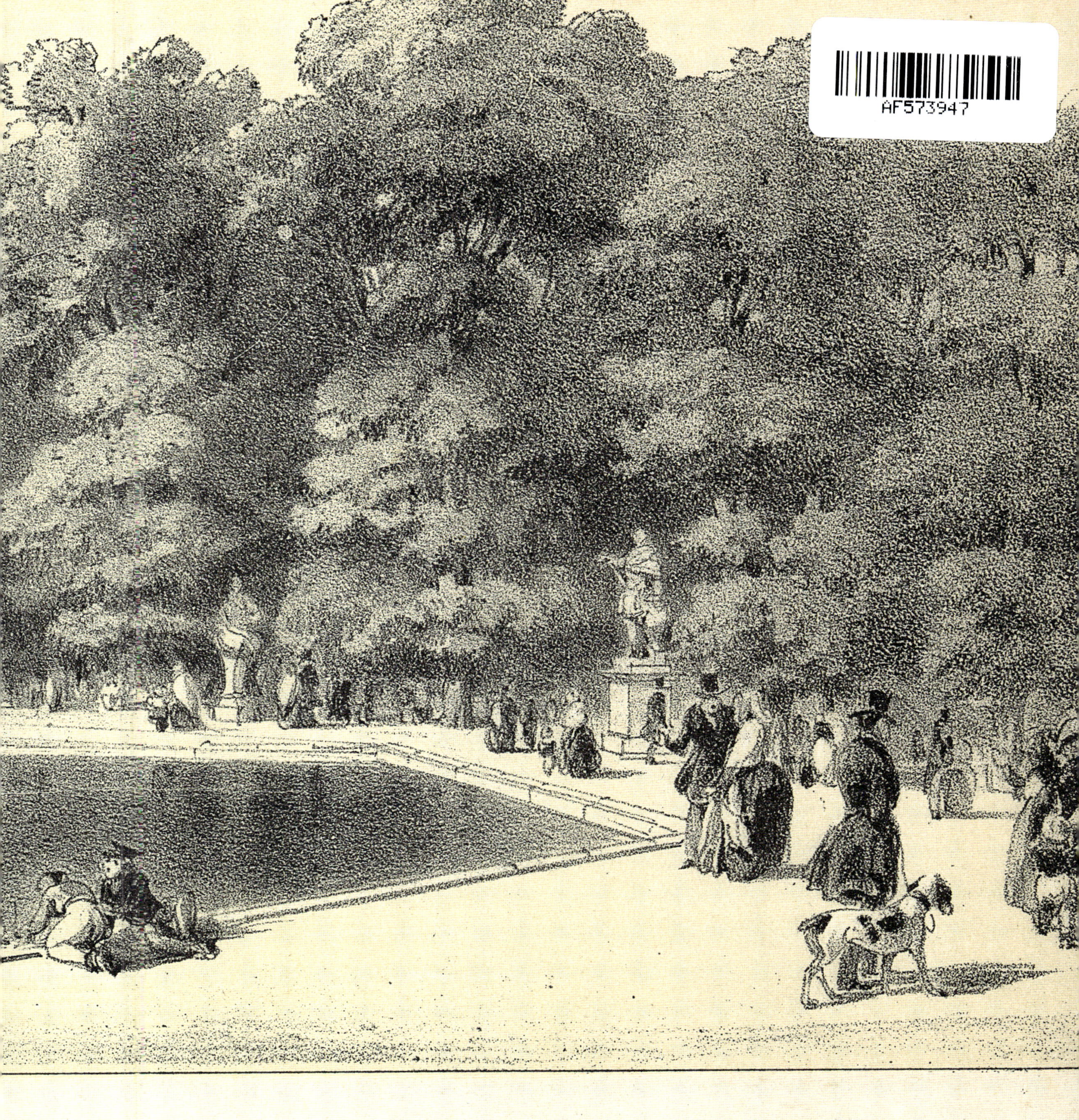

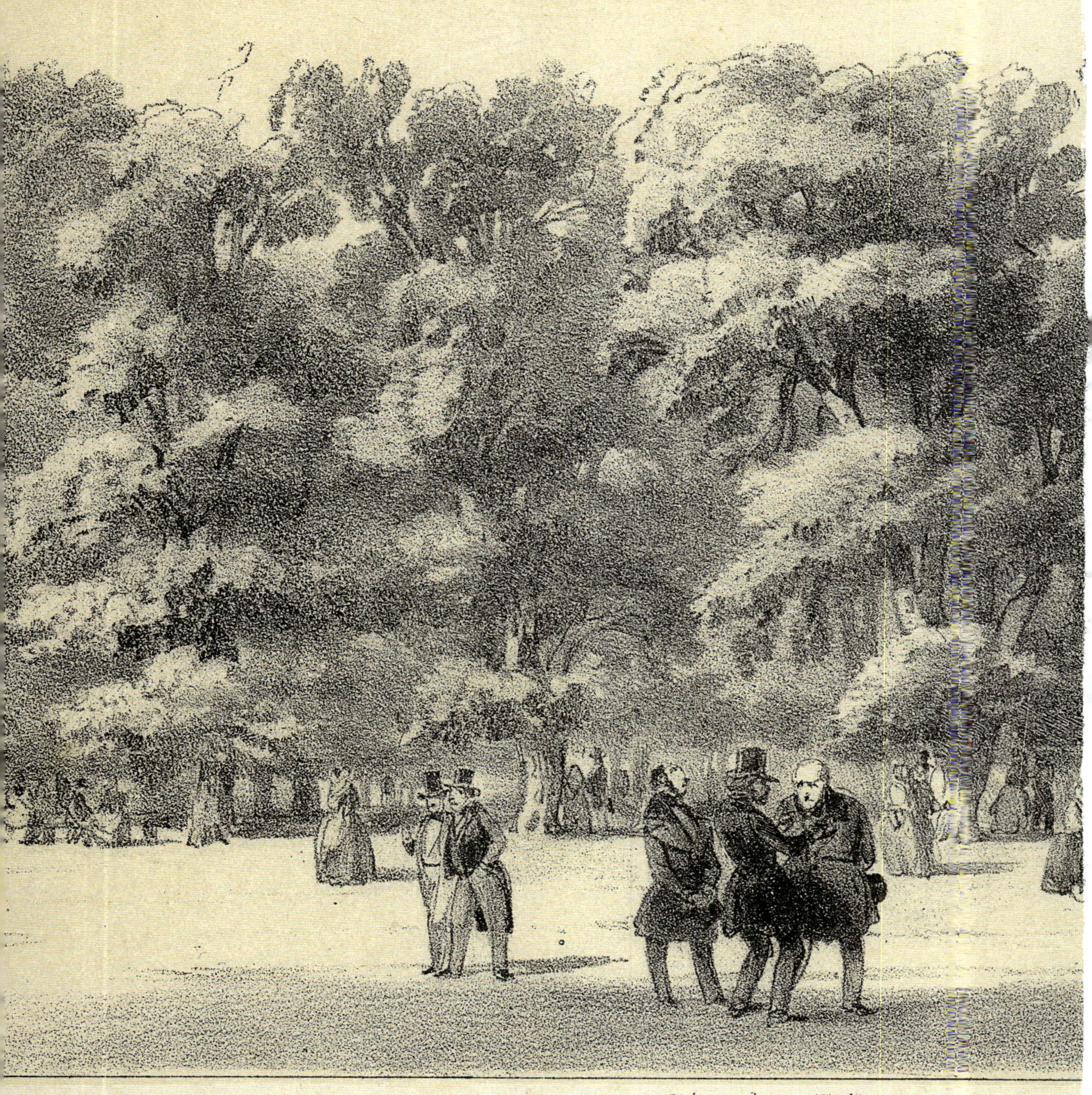

Allée des Tuileries

Public Parks, Private Gardens

PARIS TO PROVENCE

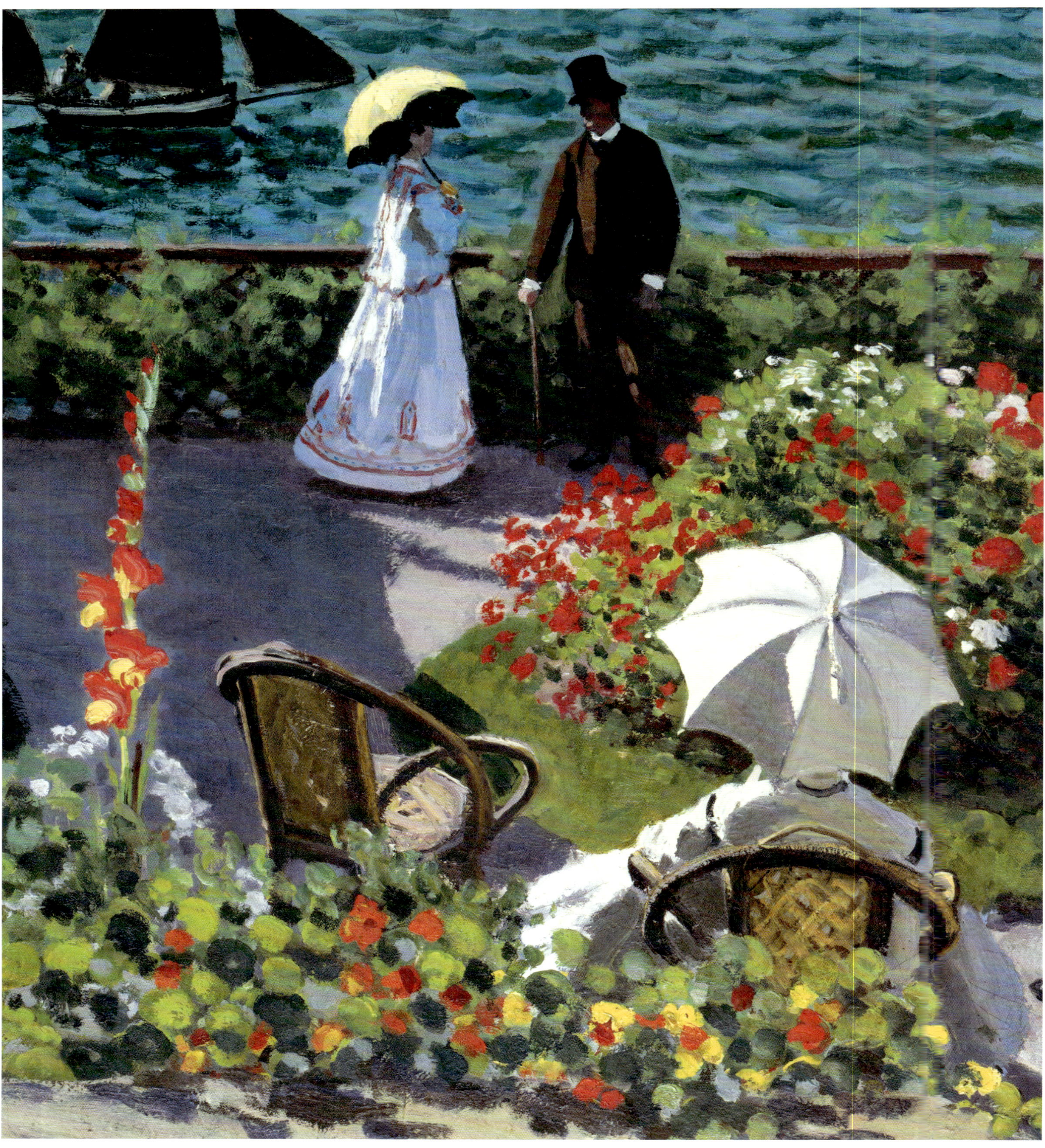

Public Parks, Private Gardens

PARIS TO PROVENCE

Colta Ives

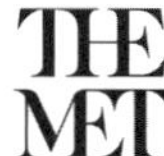

The Metropolitan Museum of Art, New York

DISTRIBUTED BY YALE UNIVERSITY PRESS, NEW HAVEN AND LONDON

This book is published in conjunction with "Public Parks, Private Gardens: Paris to Provence," on view at The Metropolitan Museum of Art, New York, from March 12 through July 29, 2018.

The exhibition is made possible by the Sam and Janet Salz Trust, the Janice H. Levin Fund, and The Florence Gould Foundation.

The catalogue is made possible by the Janice H. Levin Fund and the Doris Duke Fund for Publications.

Published by The Metropolitan Museum of Art, New York
Mark Polizzotti, Publisher and Editor in Chief
Gwen Roginsky, Associate Publisher and General Manager of Publications
Peter Antony, Chief Production Manager
Michael Sittenfeld, Senior Managing Editor

Edited by Cynthia Clark and Emily Walter
Designed by Susan Marsh
Production by Sally VanDevanter
Bibliography and notes edited by Jean Wagner
Image acquisitions and permissions by Josephine Rodriquez-Massop

Photographs of works in the Metropolitan Museum's collection are by the Imaging Department, The Metropolitan Museum of Art, unless otherwise noted; new photography is by Kathy Dahab, Heather Johnson, Paul Lachenauer, and Juan Trujillo. Additional photography credits appear on p. 204.

Typeset in Filosofia Opentype by Matt Mayerchak
Printed on Tatami White 135 gsm
Separations by Alta Image, London
Printed and bound by Ofset Yapimevi, Istanbul

JACKET ILLUSTRATIONS:
(front) Claude Monet, *The Parc Monceau*, 1878 (Fig. 46); (back) Eugène Atget, *Jardin du Luxembourg*, 1902 (Fig. 44)

ENDPAPERS:
Details from A. Provost, *Panorama of the Champs-Elysées*, ca. 1845–50 (Fig. 61)

FRONTISPIECES:
p. ii, Detail of Claude Monet, *Garden at Sainte-Adresse*, 1867 (Fig. 88)
p. vi, Detail of Camille Pissarro, *The Garden at the Tuileries on a Winter Afternoon*, 1899 (Fig. 41)
p. xii, Detail of Eugène Cuvelier, *Fontainebleau Forest*, early 1860s (Fig. 28)
p. 2, Detail of Claude Monet, *Water Lilies*, 1919 (Fig. 102)
p. 6, Detail of Auguste Garneray, *Interior of the Hothouse at Malmaison*, ca. 1810 (Fig. 14)
p. 24, Detail of Georges Seurat, *Study for "A Sunday on La Grande Jatte,"* 1884 (Fig. 65)
p. 70, Detail of Alfred Stevens, *The Glass Ball*, ca. 1875 (Fig. 94)
p. 108, Detail of Edouard Manet, *The Monet Family in Their Garden at Argenteuil*, 1874 (Fig. 113)
p. 126, Detail of Edgar Degas, *A Woman Seated beside a Vase of Flowers (Madame Paul Valpinçon?)*, 1865 (Fig. 137)
p. 164, Detail of Edouard Vuillard, *Garden at Vaucresson*, 1920; reworked 1926, 1935, 1936 (Fig. 95)
p. 168, Detail of Eugène Atget, *Versailles—Cour du Parc*, 1902 (Checklist)
p. 192, Detail of Adolphe Braun, *Rose of Sharon*, ca. 1854 (Fig. 127)

FIRST PRINTING

The Metropolitan Museum of Art
1000 Fifth Avenue
New York, New York 10028
metmuseum.org

Distributed by
Yale University Press, New Haven
yalebooks.com/art
yalebooks.co.uk

Library of Congress Cataloging-in-Publication Data

Names: Ives, Colta Feller, author. | Clark, Cynthia, editor. | Walter, Emily, editor. | Metropolitan Museum of Art (New York, N.Y.), issuing body, host institution.
Title: Public parks, private gardens : Paris to Provence / Colta Ives ; edited by Cynthia Clark and Emily Walter.
Description: New York : The Metropolitan Museum of Art, [2018] | Published in conjunction with "Public Parks, Private Gardens: Paris to Provence," on view at The Metropolitan Museum of Art, New York, from March 12 through July 29, 2018. | Includes bibliographical references and index.
Identifiers: LCCN 2017055373 | ISBN 9781588395849 (hardcover)
Subjects: LCSH: Parks in art—Exhibitions. | Gardens in art—Exhibitions. | Landscape painting, French—France—Paris—19th century—Exhibitions. | Landscape painting, French—France—Provence—19th century—Exhibitions. | Impressionism (Art)—France—Exhibitions. | Post-impressionism (Art)—France—Exhibitions.
Classification: LCC N8234.P3 I94 2018 DDC 709.03/46--dc23
LC record available at https://lccn.loc.gov/2017055373

ISBN 978-1-58839-584-9

Contents

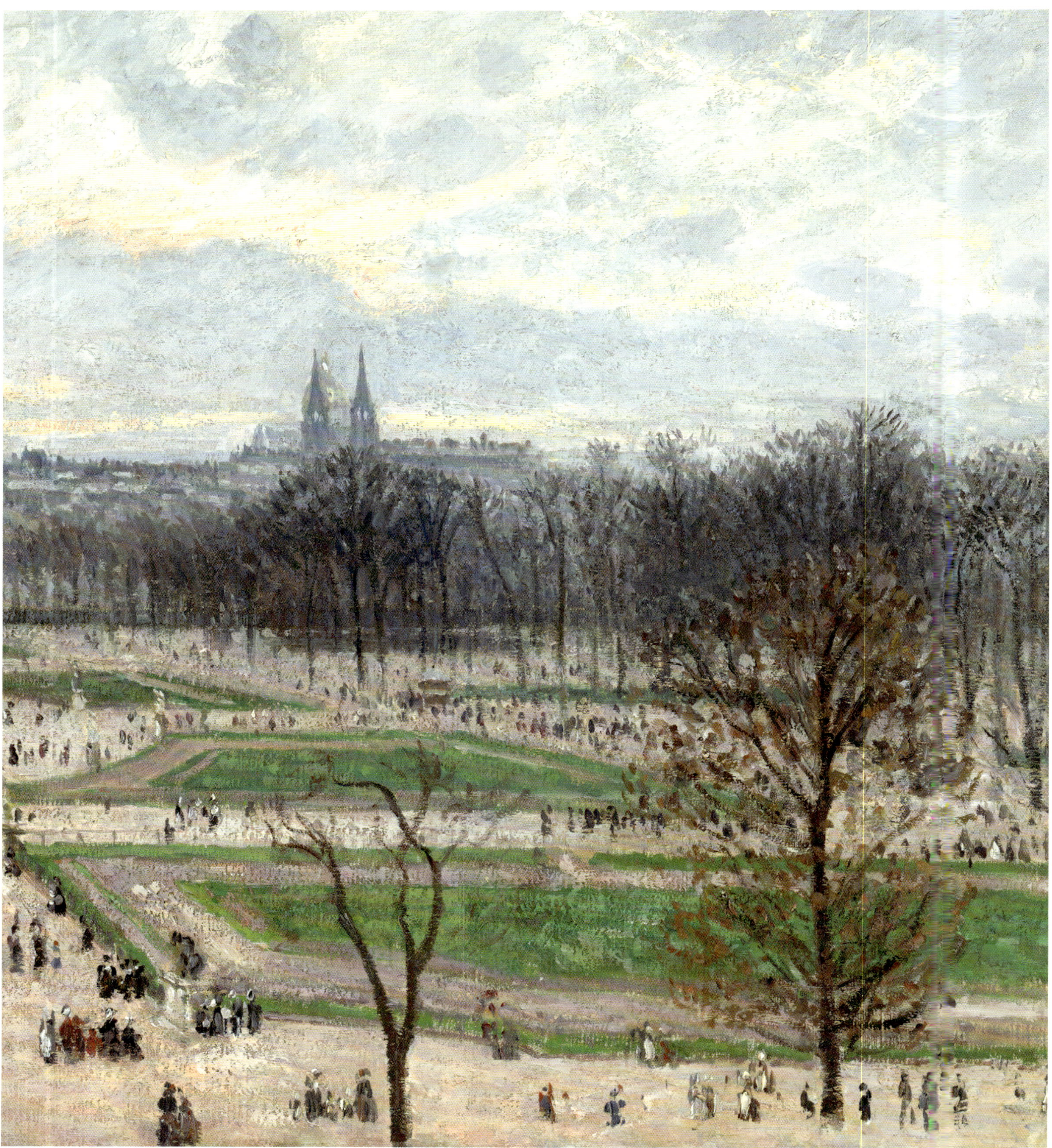

Foreword

ALTHOUGH THE METROPOLITAN MUSEUM, founded in 1870, first opened its doors to the public on Fifth Avenue in midtown Manhattan, it established its permanent home a decade later in an oasis of greenery, New York's Central Park. Like many of the world's museums situated in the surrounds of splendid parks or botanical gardens, The Met settled into a landscape of lawns and trees, walkways and flowers, in a companionable union of nature and art.

Central Park, America's first major landscaped public park, constructed between 1858 and 1873, constitutes one of the major landmarks in urban planning achieved during the nineteenth century. It is also the offspring of horticultural and landscape design developments in England and in France, where Central Park's architect, Frederick Law Olmsted, studied the grand urban green spaces then under construction in Paris.

The richness of The Met's own collection makes it possible to present the story of the horticultural developments that reshaped much of the landscape of France during the nineteenth century and played a significant role in contemporary art and life. Indeed, the popularity of pleasure gardens and floral motifs during this period is evidenced throughout the pictorial and decorative arts, most arrestingly in the paintings of the Impressionists and Post-Impressionists.

The extraordinary phenomenon of the greening of France during the nineteenth century and its impact upon the artists of the period is presented in this book and in the accompanying exhibition by two Museum curators who have collaborated previously on exhibitions presenting the work of Francisco

Goya, Edgar Degas, Paul Gauguin, and Vincent van Gogh: Susan Alyson Stein, Engelhard Curator of Nineteenth-Century European Painting, and Colta Ives, Curator Emerita. In organizing the present project, they have enjoyed the dedicated assistance of Research Associate Laura D. Corey and the support of many individuals, both inside and outside The Met, including staff members from the seven curatorial departments whose works anchor the exhibition and friends of the Museum who have kindly parted with key supplemental works from their private collections.

Neither this presentation nor this book could have been realized without the generosity of our donors. We are grateful to the Sam and Janet Salz Trust and The Florence Gould Foundation for making possible the exhibition. We thank the Janice H. Levin Fund, which supported both the exhibition and this catalogue, and has demonstrated an enduring commitment to the Museum's special exhibitions. Finally, we wish to recognize the Doris Duke Fund for Publications, which has ensured the success of this and so many scholarly volumes at The Met.

DANIEL H. WEISS
President and Chief Executive Officer

Acknowledgments

ENJOYING A COLLABORATIVE RELATIONSHIP of longstanding, we—the author of this book and the curator of the accompanying exhibition—gratefully recognize the valuable participation of the many individuals who became engaged in our work. We extend profound thanks to those who contributed their knowledge and time, their encouragement and direction, and often the loans of treasured objects in their care.

Research for this project began most conveniently with access to the archives of the Museum's Department of European Paintings and to the holdings of the Thomas J. Watson Library (Kenneth Soehner, Arthur K. Watson Chief Librarian). The Mertz Library of the New York Botanical Garden also provided extraordinary resources with the aid of Susan Fraser, Vice President and Director; Vanessa Sellers; Stephen Sinon; and Daniel Atha. In Paris, the author benefited from visits to the library of the Société Nationale d'Horticulture de France, assisted by Emmanuelle Royon, and consultation with Marie-Hélène Bénetière, Chargée de Mission Parcs et Jardins, Ministère de la Culture et de la Communication. Authors named in the extensive bibliography of selected references appended to this book merit special notice for their investigations of horticultural history and its connections with the visual arts, particularly Clare A. P. Willsdon, who has carefully examined the floral occupations of the Impressionists.

The Metropolitan Museum's own vast art collection has provided innumerable works related to the horticultural boom in France during the nineteenth century. Within the seven curatorial departments represented in the exhibition, many staff members generously sustained this project. In the Department of European Paintings, Keith Christiansen, John Pope-Hennessy Chairman, offered unfailing support and Research Associate Laura D. Corey devoted tireless attention to the accuracy of details in this publication and to all aspects of the organization of the exhibition; we also enjoyed the assistance of Katharine Baetjer, Jane R. Becker, Rebecca Ben-Atar, Lisa Cain, Alison R. Hokanson, Theresa King-Dickinson, Patrice Mattia, John McKanna, Asher E. Miller, and Rachel Robinson. In the Department of Drawings and Prints, we are grateful for the collegial participation of Nadine M. Orenstein, Drue Heinz Curator in Charge, Ashley Dunn, David del Gaizo, Harrison Jackson, Ricky Luna, Allison Rudnick, Femke Speelberg, Perrin Stein, Elizabeth Zanis, and Mary Zuber; in the Department of Photographs, Jeff L. Rosenheim, Joyce Frank Menschel Curator in Charge, Beth Saunders, and Predrag Dimitrijevic; in the Department of Modern and Contemporary Art, Sheena Wagstaff, Leonard A. Lauder Chairman, Cynthia Iavarone, and Sabine Rewald, Jacques and Natasha Gelman Curator; in the American Wing, Elizabeth Mankin Kornhauser, Alice Pratt Brown Curator of American Paintings and Sculpture; in the Department of European Sculpture and Decorative Art, Luke Syson, Iris and B. Gerald Cantor Chairman, and Denny Stone; and in the Robert Lehman Collection, Dita Amory, Curator in Charge, and Manus Gallagher.

This publication was produced under the direction of Mark Polizzotti, Publisher and Editor in Chief, and Michael Sittenfeld. It has profited from the thoughtful and informed editing of the late Emily Walter as well as from the efforts of Cynthia Clark, who pruned and weeded its text and saw the manuscript along its path to the printer; Jean Wagner ably vetted and edited all bibliographic elements of the book. Susan Marsh created the graceful and ingenious design of this volume, whose production was skillfully managed by Peter Anthony, Sally VanDevanter, and Josephine Rodriguez-Massop.

The organization of the exhibition was overseen by Quincy Houghton, Deputy Director of Exhibitions, and our dedicated project manager, Christine D. McDermott. Daniel Kershaw and Kamomi Solidum directed the exhibition's handsome installation design and graphics. Other staff members made valuable contributions to the project: Jennifer Bantz; Melissa Bell; Linda Borsch; Barbara J. Bridgers; Paul Caro; Ferida Coughlan; Martha Deese; Reagan Duplisea; Kate Farrell; Charlotte Hale; Jason Herrick; Heather Johnson; Daniel Koppich; Bryan Martin; Christopher Noey; Kendra Roth; Marina Ruiz-Molina; Fred Sagers; Katherine Sanderson; Robin Schwalb; Marjorie Shelley,

Sherman Fairchild Conservator in Charge, Paper Conservation; Marianna Siciliano; Hyla Skopitz; Elizabeth Stoneman, and Wendy Walker.

Although conceived to showcase The Met's collection, the exhibition has been wonderfully enriched with loans from supporters of the institution whom we recognize most gratefully for their generosity: Graham Arader, Lawrence J. Ellison, Marc and Cathy Lasry, Mark K. Morrison, and other private collectors who chose to remain anonymous.

For assistance and expertise at pivotal points in this project's development we wish also to thank Morgan Beckwith, Andrew Engel, Ronald Fein, Ay-Whang Hsia, Carmel Mahon, Jack Mascharka, Jeffrey Munger, Jill Newhouse, Lilian and Dieter Noack, Alison Oscar, Emily Rafferty, Fabienne Ruppen, Amanda Shore, Elizabeth Szancer, and Jayne Warman.

COLTA IVES
Curator Emerita

SUSAN ALYSON STEIN
Engelhard Curator of Nineteenth-Century European Painting

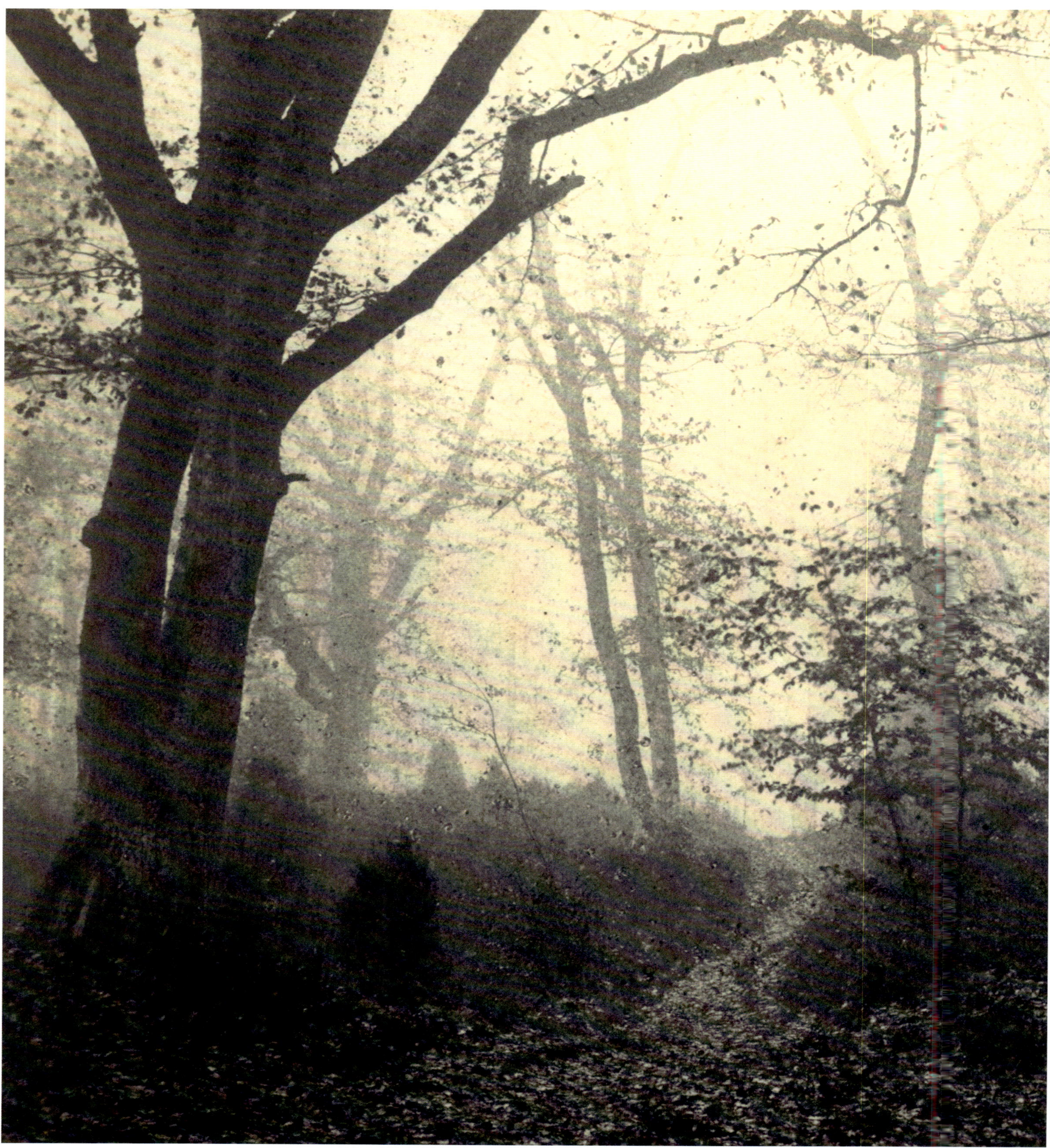

Public Parks, Private Gardens

PARIS TO PROVENCE

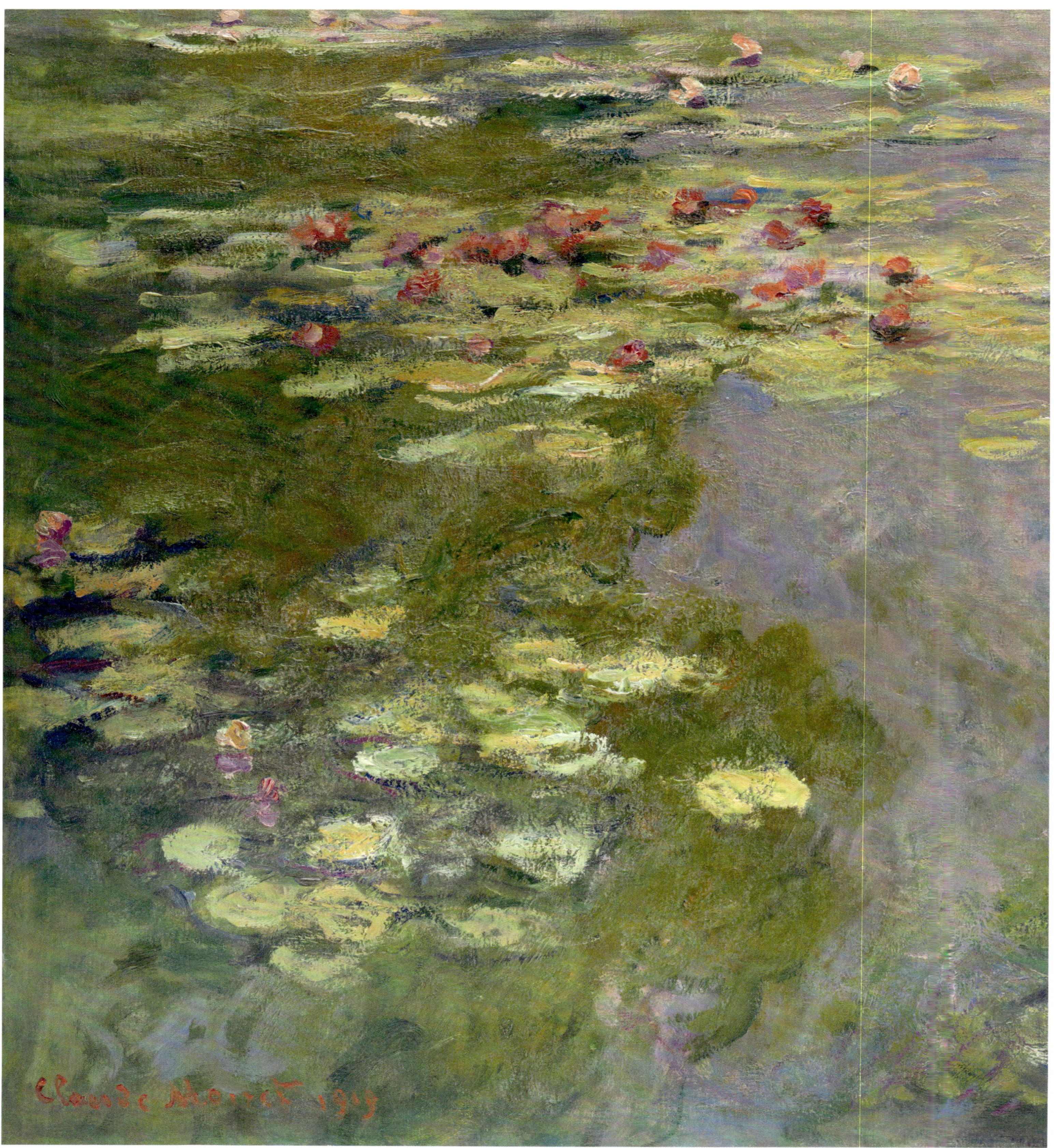

The Green Wave

DURING THE AGE OF DISCOVERY that began in the fifteenth century, Europeans sailed across distant seas to foreign lands, returning to their own shores laden with treasures, many of which were exotic plants. By the mid-eighteenth and well into the nineteenth century, as such voyages multiplied, an unprecedented flood of novel floral material was carried homeward by exploring travelers. Among the most bountiful of the early plant-hunters' ventures were those of British botanists Joseph Banks, who accompanied Captain James Cook on his first journey to the South Pacific (1768–71), and Joseph Dalton Hooker, who sailed to regions of the Antarctic (1839–43), trekked the Himalayas (1847–51), and traversed the western United States (1877). Important French scientific excursions were undertaken by Nicolas Baudin to Australia (1800–1803) and Victor Jacquemont to India (1829).

The Prussian naturalist Alexander von Humboldt examined flora as well as all manner of natural phenomena in Latin America, Mexico, and the United States between 1799 and 1804. In his travels through varying elevations, latitudes, and longitudes he came to recognize connections between nature's varied forms. Upon his return to Europe Humboldt established a base not in his native Berlin but in Paris, a city he knew to be a vital center of scientific inquiry, where he chose to deposit his cargo and publish reports supporting his theory of an all-encompassing web of life. To the Jardin des Plantes, the world-renowned national botanical garden in Paris founded in the seventeenth century under Louis XIII (r. 1610–43), Humboldt and his expedition

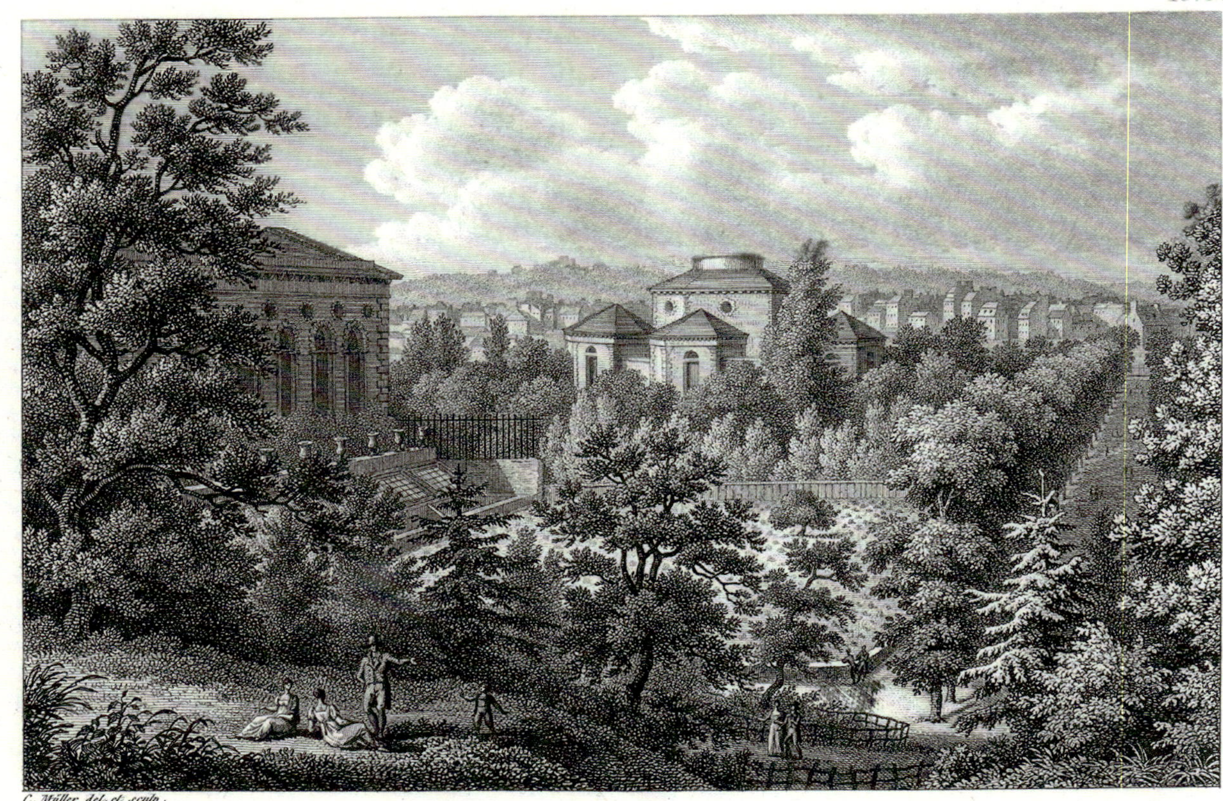

FIG. 1. Henri Charles Müller. "View of the Jardin des Plantes," from René Jean Durdent, *Vues et description du Jardin des Plantes* (Paris, 1813). Aquatint. The Metropolitan Museum of Art, New York

partner, the Frenchman Aimé Bonpland, brought some sixty thousand plant specimens, including six thousand different species, of which nearly two thousand were new to European botanists (fig. 1).[1]

It is no doubt due to the discovery abroad of diverse plants (and animals) that during the Age of Enlightenment, beginning in the mid-seventeenth century, new ideas arose about the nature of both life and landscape as evidence of a vast creative power. Fascination with nature's mysteries in turn inspired disciplined investigations between about 1770 and 1840 that led to the advancement of botany as a unique science, distinct from the age-old consideration of plants solely as herbal medicine. This development was enhanced by the observations of Antoine Laurent de Jussieu, who published the first natural classification of flowering plants, *Genera plantarum*, in 1789, adhering to the binomial nomenclature of genus and species established during the 1750s by the Swedish botanist Carl Linnaeus. It was not long before the cultivation of ornamental flora became regarded as a viable and also educational pursuit to be enjoyed by more than a privileged few.

With the variety of available plants vastly increased and with interest in their cultivation strengthened, the nineteenth century proved to be a great age for horticulture. Plant propagation and hybridization arose as commercial industries, while the art of garden design burgeoned into a significant practice. Amateur gardening, formerly a luxury, now presented itself as an affordable, popular pastime for a growing middle-class population, especially when train travel provided city dwellers with easy access to country plots.

As many rural areas became blighted by factories and cities bristled with construction projects, nature's gifts of light, air, and greenery gained currency. To address the tensions of urban life and concerns for public health, plans for recreational outdoor spaces were widely discussed and implemented in America and in Europe — most notably in France, where at midcentury the city of Paris was transformed into an ordered landscape of large parks, neighborhood garden squares, and tree-lined boulevards. An antidote to the sweeping industrialization, urban crowding, and multiple upheavals that beset France between the Revolution of 1789 and World War I, the proliferation of both public parks and private gardens grounded a newfound enthusiasm for the out-of-doors as a place of leisure, renewal, and inspiration, a development splendidly celebrated by many of the century's greatest artists.

Indeed, there is no more convincing evidence of the widespread appeal of gardens, flowers, and the shared experience of public landscape than that presented in the most ingenious art works of the period. Dedicated to providing a visual account of their own modern times, avant-garde French artists, many of whom were gardeners themselves, pictured parks and gardens as distinctive scenery, vividly representative of popular contemporary life. Seeking to bring the fresh beauty of the garden indoors, they also helped to revive the practice of floral still-life painting, and in the bright colors and shapely petals of flowers from around the world they found inspiration for artistic innovation. Their unique achievements reflect the special place of botanical discovery in the history, culture, and welfare of our world.

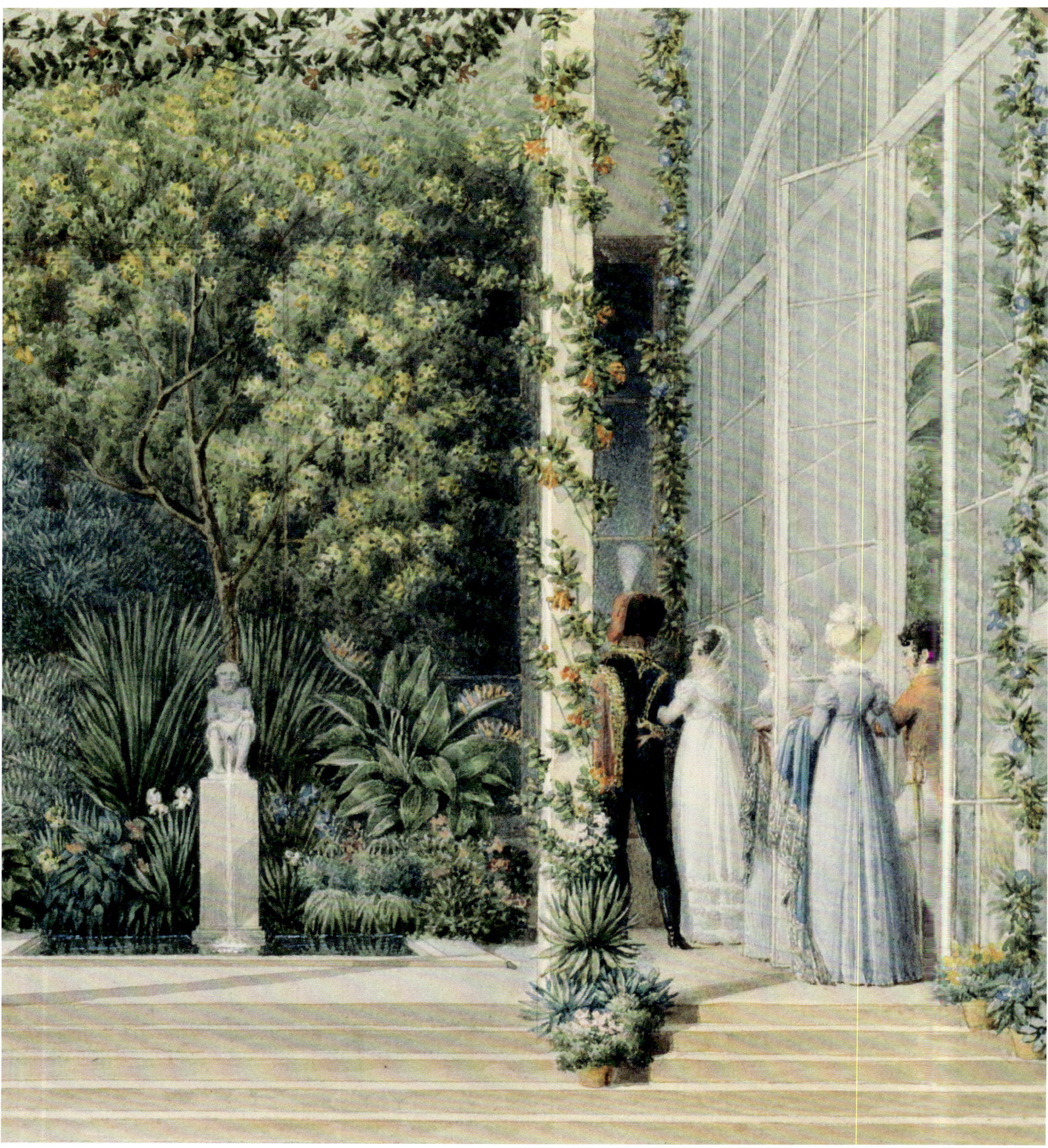

Revolution in the Garden

In the gardens of France the seeds of horticultural revolution began to germinate more than two decades before the king's palace was stormed in 1789. Not far from the regimented trees, clipped hedges, and straight walkways of the royal park at Versailles (fig. 2), libertarian ideas concerning both government and green space were being cultivated along the rolling lawns and meandering paths of private gardens. At fault in the garden were the rigid lines and severe symmetry of formal plans—seemingly "against nature"—like those created by André Le Nôtre, architect to Louis XIV (r. 1643–1715), whose magnificent landscapes were calculated to be admired mainly from the remote heights of balustraded terraces and gilded windows. At Versailles, in the final years of the ancien régime, some relief from the tight geometry of its vast formal park had been introduced with secluded groves planted in the newly fashionable irregular style, while romantic gardens designed along the fluid lines of the English Picturesque taste, strewn with pseudo-antique and rustic structures, were being installed on the palace grounds at Trianon for the pleasure of Marie Antoinette (see fig. 4). Indeed, the queen was out walking alone in her "little enchanted paradise" (still unfinished) in October 1789, only hours before Versailles fell.[1]

Although French formality had been the influential garden style in Europe during the seventeenth century, the more relaxed English manner came to predominate during the eighteenth. It was then that an increasing number of books on garden design were published in England and on the Continent, testifying to an expanding interest in this branch of the arts long practiced

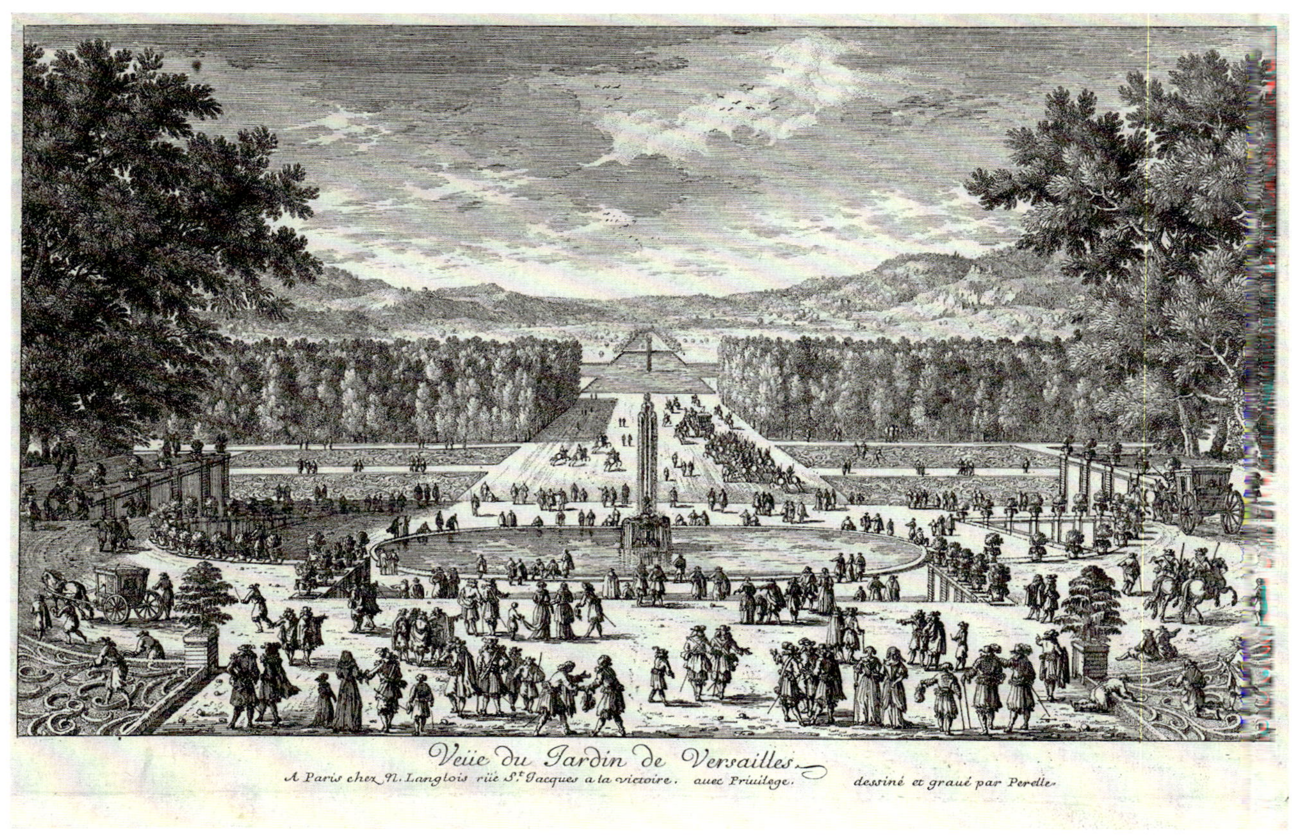

FIG. 2. Adam Perelle. *The Garden of Versailles*, 1664–68. Etching. The Metropolitan Museum of Art, New York

by both architects and painters. In France the first popular guide to estate garden improvement, *La Théorie et la pratique du jardinage* (1709) by Antoine Joseph Dezallier d'Argenville, presented a roster of classic geometric plans in the style of Le Nôtre, with occasional allowances for divergence. However, a decisive change in the tide of French taste can be seen in the more than fifteen books on the art of garden design published between 1771 and 1790 that promoted the virtues not of formal gardens but of naturalistic ones, where any sign of human intervention was disguised to pay homage to nature.[2] Several publications, like those of the cartographer Georges Louis Le Rouge, described elaborately circuitous Chinese gardens, whose "beautiful disorder" and "anti-symmetry" had been reported by the French Jesuit traveler Jean-Denis Attiret.[3] However, tastes in France generally allied with those in England, where the landscape architects William Kent, Lancelot "Capability" Brown, and Humphry Repton, among others, designed gardens that featured vast lawns, meandering paths, well-placed lakes, and stands of majestic trees.

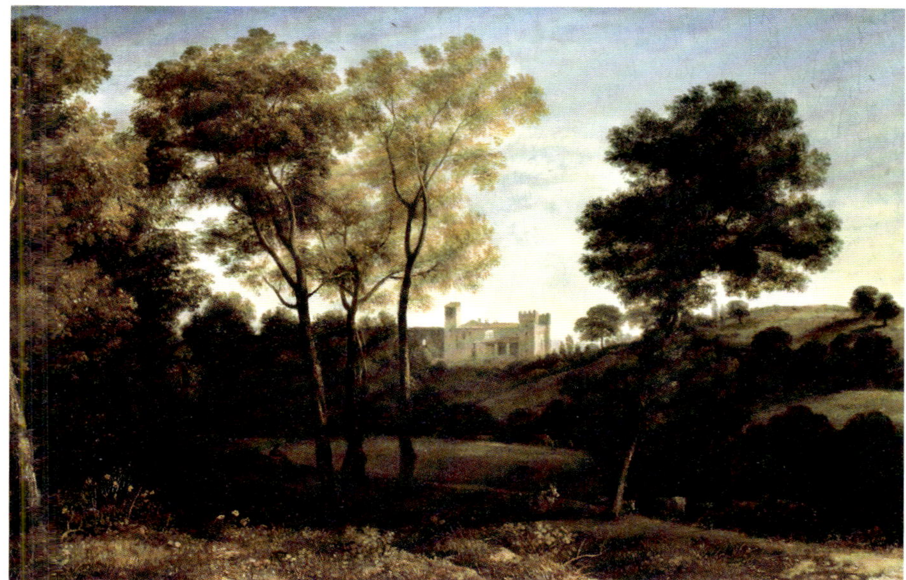

FIG. 3. Claude Lorrain. *View of La Crescenza*, 1648–50. Oil on canvas. The Metropolitan Museum of Art, New York

As the practice of landscape design evolved and received recognition as an artistic endeavor, considerable thought was brought to bear on its purposes and principles. Claude Henri Watelet (*Essai sur les jardins*, 1774) and Jean Marie Morel (*Théorie des jardins*, 1776) helped to frame the debate in France, favoring gardens based primarily on nature rather than man-made contrivances. The importance of a garden's "character" was addressed, and thematic styles such as the poetic, the romantic, and the pastoral were proposed, each entailing appropriately evocative structures that one might stroll around or enter, such as grottoes, temples, pagodas, and hermits' huts.[4]

In the first volume of his *Encyclopédie méthodique* (1788), the architectural theorist Antoine Chrysostome Quatremère de Quincy set out principles to guide designers in their consideration of both the garden's site and its purpose. These were necessary, he maintained, whether the garden was "royal," "rustic," or "public," in order "[to] satisfy our personal tastes in our gardens in as much variety and richness as is possible in painting or poetry." Quatremère's suggestion that gardens be composed like "living pictures whose subtle shades create, as in painting, an infinite variety of effects" affirmed the popularity of the Picturesque in landscape design, which sought to approximate the idealized natural scenery depicted in the work of the seventeenth-century painters Nicolas Poussin and Claude Lorrain (fig. 3).[5]

Many of the Picturesque gardens of the eighteenth century can still be

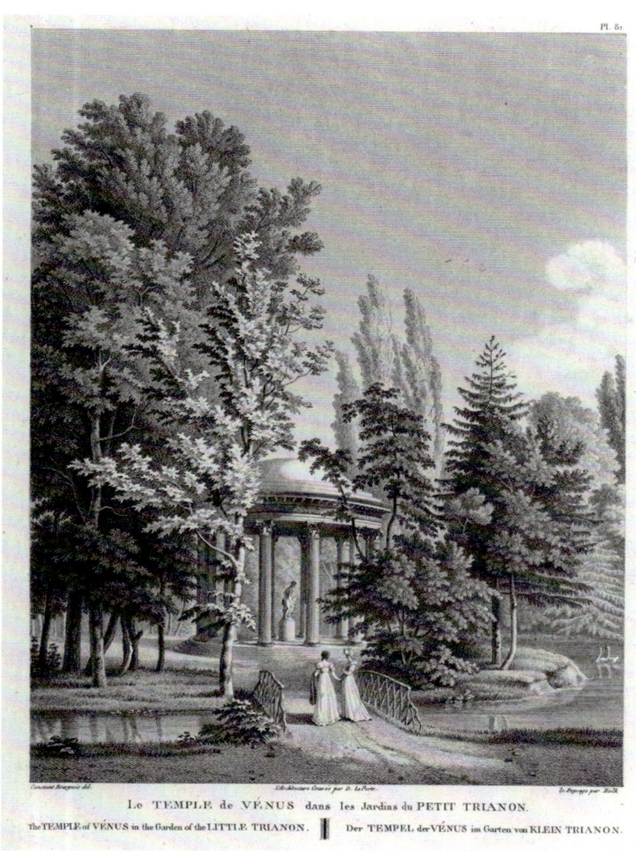

FIG. 4. Constant Bourgeois. "Temple of Venus, Garden of the Petit Trianon," from Alexandre de Laborde, *Description des nouveaux jardins de la France et de ses anciens châteaux* (Paris, 1808). Engraving. The Metropolitan Museum of Art, New York

seen in England, while in France few survived the Revolution and its aftermath. It is important to note that a number of the most outstanding French endeavors in this garden style—sometimes termed "Anglo-Chinois" because it combined both English and Chinese elements—benefited from the participation of the preeminent French artists of the day, including François Boucher and Hubert Robert, who was appointed garden designer to Louis XVI (r. 1774–92). Boucher assisted Watelet in planning his Moulin Joli (1754–72) and along with Robert provided inspiration for Marie Antoinette's romantic garden retreat at the Petit Trianon (1783; fig. 4). Robert furthermore conceived the scenery at Méréville (beginning in 1786), as he had earlier at Ermenonville (completed 1778), where the marquis de Girardin created a naturalistic refuge for the philosopher Jean Jacques Rousseau (fig. 5). Appalled by the artificiality of contemporary life and trusting only the simple inspirational laws of nature, Rousseau, himself a serious botanist, viewed the unspoiled natural order as an antidote to the corrupting influences of society. He criticized the formal garden for its pretentious contrivances and for the "false taste of grandeur" in which the stroller was "lost like a poor worm."[6] At Ermenonville, northeast of Paris, Rousseau was able to live out his final days in placid reverie within a landscape very like the one he associated with virtue in his novel *Julie; ou, La Nouvelle Héloïse* (1761), where "irregular alleys [led through] . . . flowered woods . . . [and] walkways were bordered and crossed by clear, crystalline water . . . the grass always verdant and lovely."[7]

Although much altered, two examples of the *jardin pittoresque* remain under cultivation in Paris: the Parc Monceau, not far from the city's center, and the gardens of the Bagatelle, on the edge of the Bois de Boulogne. Plantings in both were overseen by the Scotsman Thomas Blaikie, a disciple of Capability Brown, who brought the *jardin anglais* to numerous French properties between 1776 and 1834. The Parc Monceau was created for the duc de Chartres by the painter and playwright Louis Carrogis, called Carmontelle, who displayed a flair for stage design in the assortment of fanciful follies spread throughout a twenty-acre site, including tombs and sculpture, an Egyptian pyramid, a Roman colonnade, a Dutch windmill, and a Turkish tent. In 1779 Carmontelle published a lavish suite of engraved views of the garden (fig. 6).

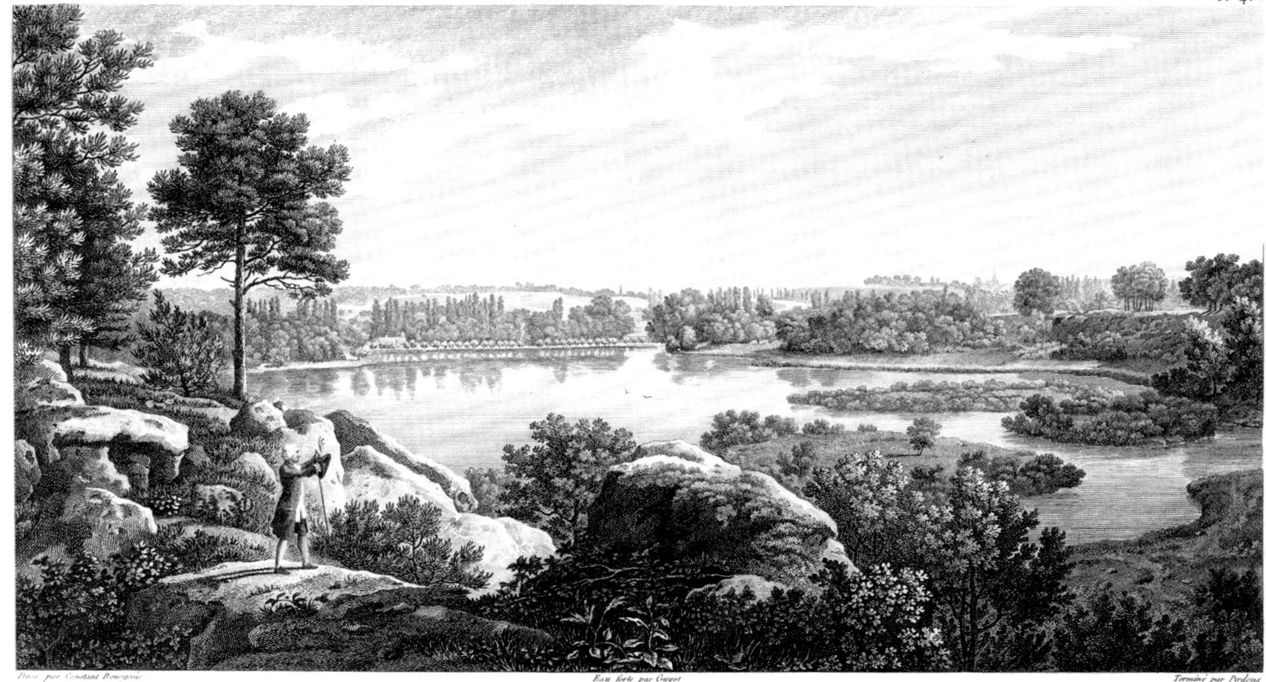

FIG. 5. Constant Bourgeois. "The Pond in the Wilderness at Ermenonville," from Alexandre de Laborde, *Description des nouveaux jardins de la France et de ses anciens châteaux* (Paris, 1808). Engraving. The Metropolitan Museum of Art, New York

FIG. 6. Louis Carrogis, called Carmontelle. "View of the Tatar Tent," from *Jardin de Monceau* (Paris, 1779). Engraving. The Metropolitan Museum of Art, New York

FIG. 7. Hubert Robert. *The Swing*, 1777–79. Oil on canvas. The Metropolitan Museum of Art, New York

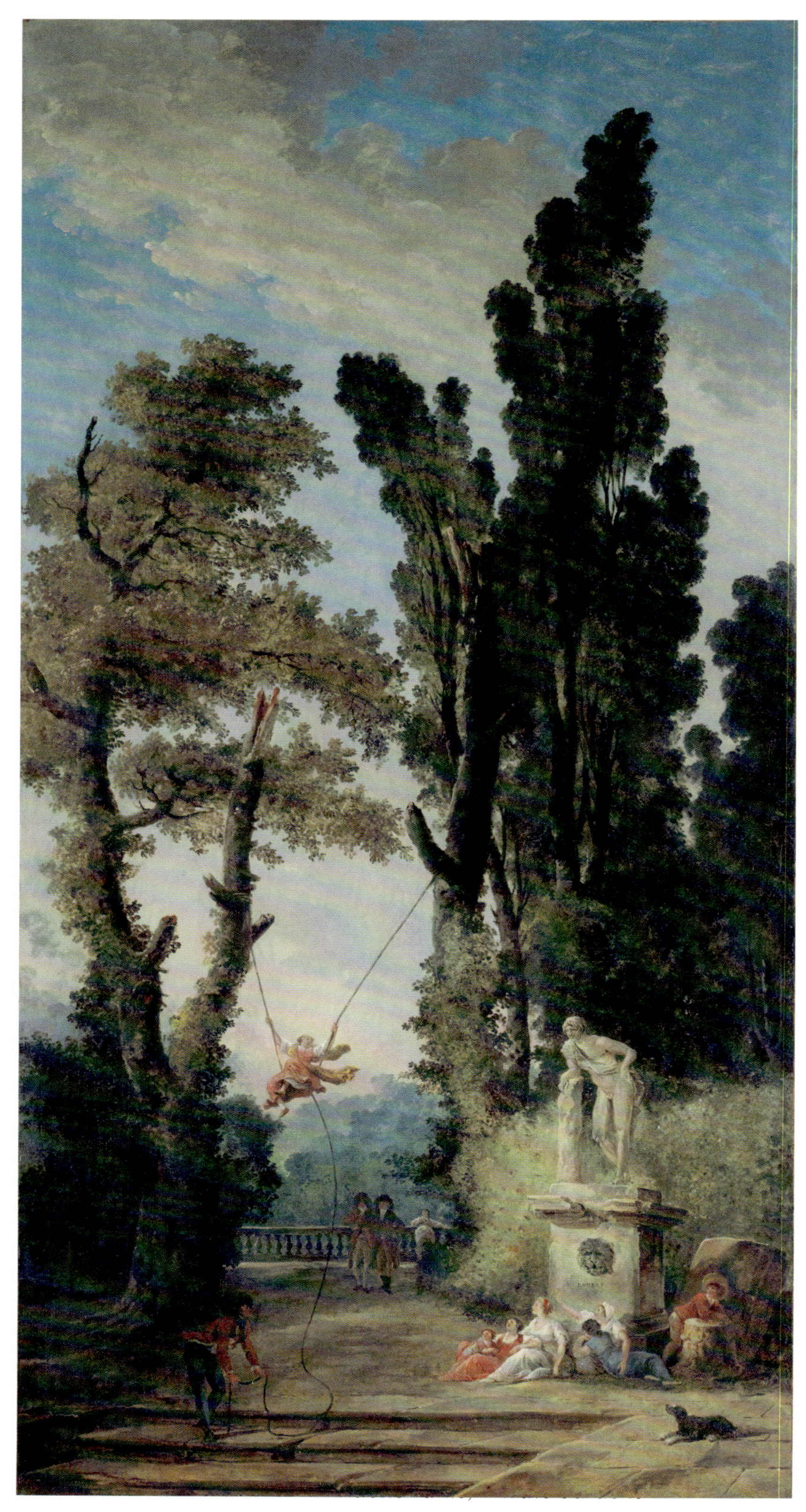

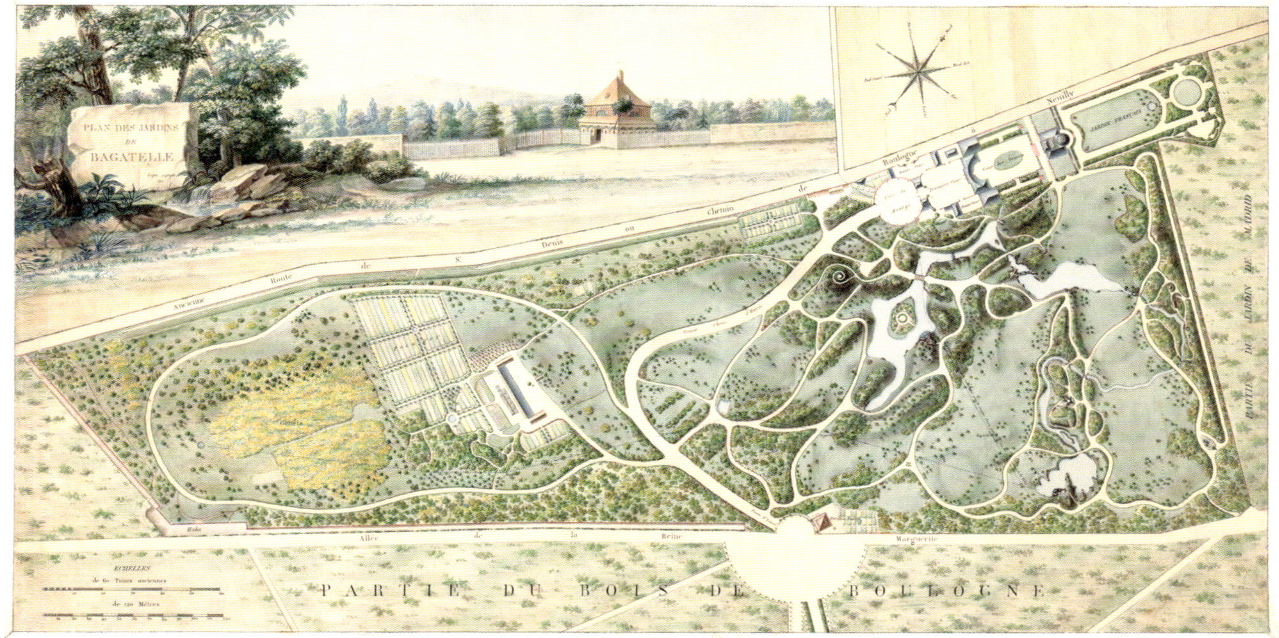

FIG. 8. Pierre Lapie. *Plan of the Garden of the Château de Bagatelle*, 1817. Pen and black ink, watercolor. The Metropolitan Museum of Art, New York

At the Bagatelle, famously built in sixty-four days on a wager between Marie Antoinette and her brother-in-law the comte d'Artois, Blaikie worked with the architect François Joseph Bélanger and Hubert Robert, who painted six outdoor scenes to decorate the château's bathing room (fig. 7).[8] To the formal *jardin français* that faced the jewel box–sized château of 1777, Blaikie added a large park in the Anglo-Chinois style (completed in 1787) that included a network of winding paths, free-form lakes, lawns, and clustered trees. The grounds were dotted with follies, such as the Swiss-style pavilion shown at the top of the garden's plan, illustrated by the cartographer Pierre Lapie (fig. 8).[9] Also shown in Lapie's watercolor are pathways bordered by flowers, an indication of the new *jardinesque* style in which flower beds were interspersed with trees and shrubs.[10]

During the Revolution a great many landscaped properties in France were destroyed or abandoned. Writing home from the ravaged country in 1802, the English traveler Francis Blagdon reported that "the great landed [French] proprietors, whom terror had induced to fly their country, have, on recovering possession of their patrimony, converted their parks into arable land. . . . No one disdains the simple title of farmer." Acknowledging France's urgent need for productive agriculture, he also observed that "the rage for ornamental gardens and pleasure-grounds is dying away."[11]

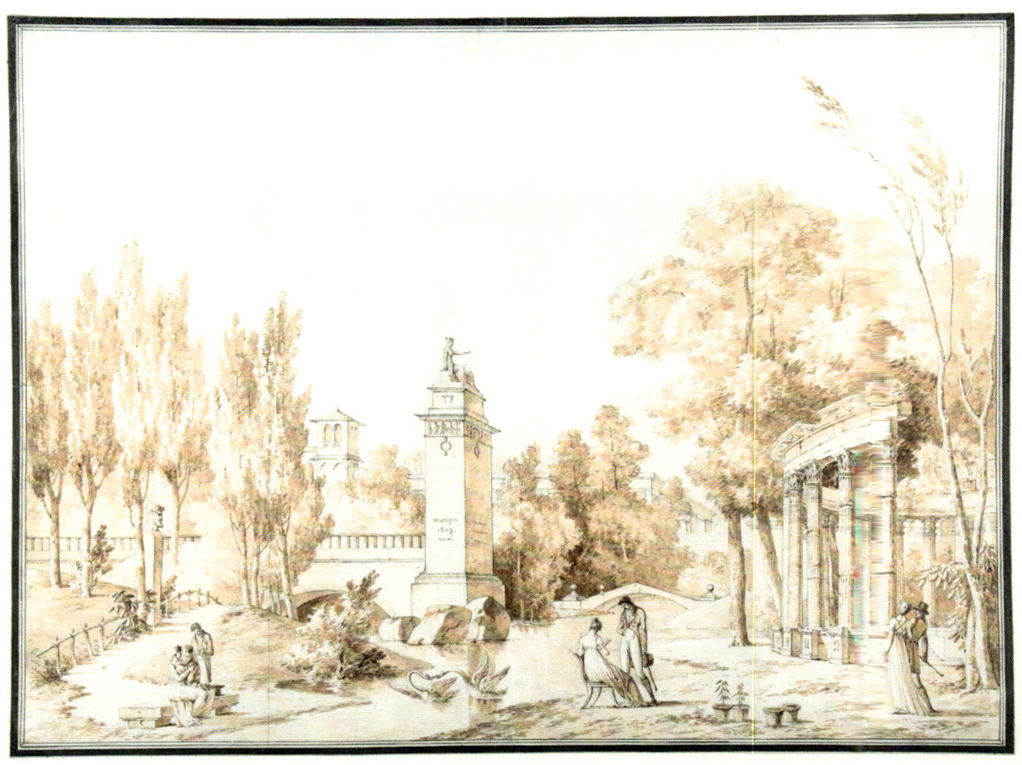

FIG. 9. Antoine Pierre Mongin. *The Progress of Love*, 1803. Brush and brown wash over black chalk underdrawing. The Metropolitan Museum of Art, New York

Nonetheless, there remained in many quarters a taste for the Picturesque garden, with its evocative monuments and sham ruins. Such romantic parks were enchantingly imagined by Antoine Pierre Mongin, whose scenic landscape designs inspired the production of panoramic wallpapers (fig. 9).[12] But new ideas were emerging among garden creators, including the painter Pierre Henri de Valenciennes, who in his "Idées générales sur les jardins" (1800) bemoaned the fussiness of overdecorated sites that made the garden look like "a dessert plate."[13] Certainly, a vision of simplicity must have been soothing to weary exiles returning to France after the Revolution to restore their country estates. The landscape artist Alexandre Hyacinthe Dunouy was commissioned to paint views of some of the tranquil parks, recently created (fig. 10).

The most extraordinary—but alas ephemeral—new garden in France during the early years of the nineteenth century was the special project of Josephine, first wife of Napoleon I (r. 1804–14; 1815) and empress of France. The Creole widow of a guillotined general, Josephine de Beauharnais married Napoleon Bonaparte in 1796 and three years later, during Napoleon's Egyptian campaign, purchased a summer residence northwest of Paris, the

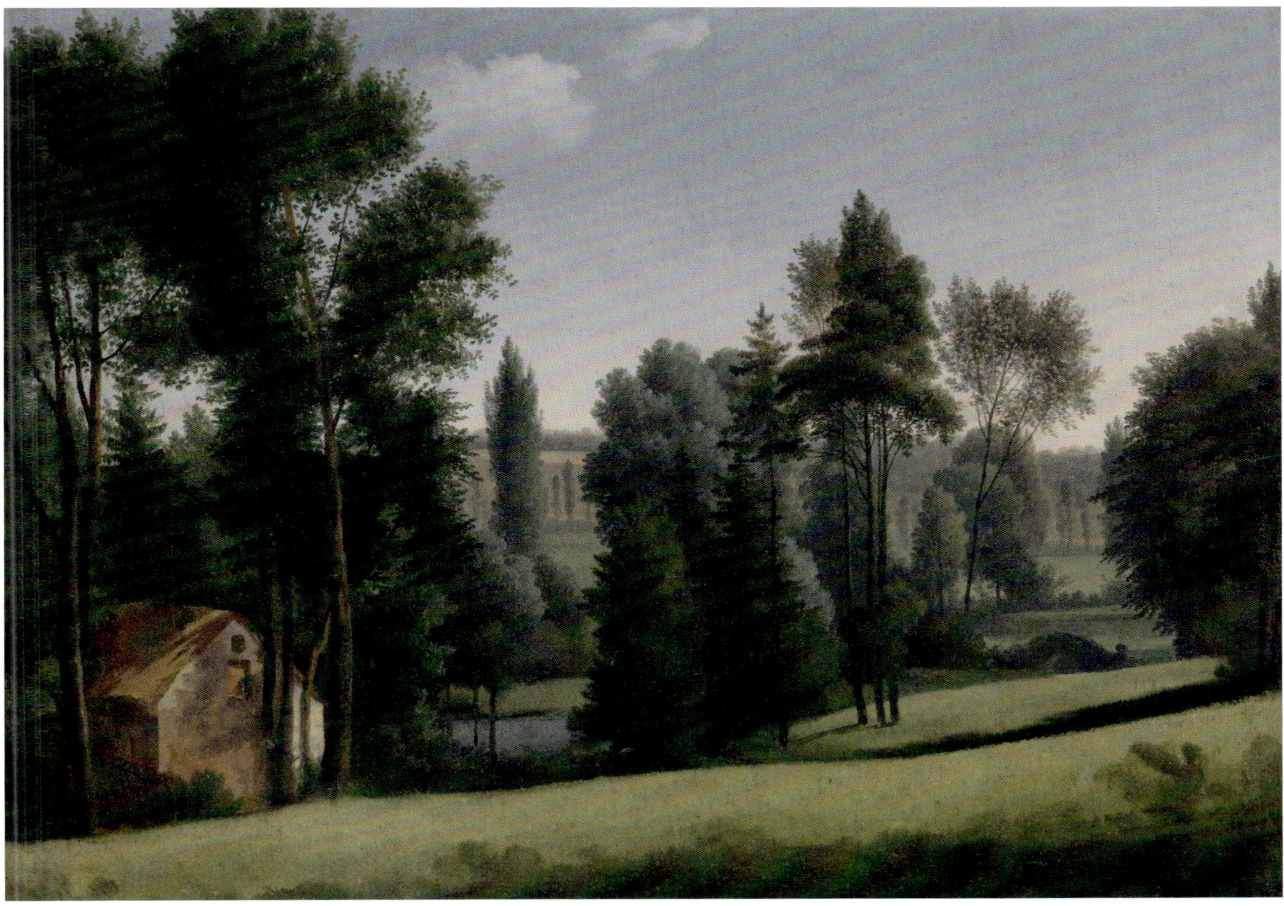

FIG. 10. Alexandre Hyacinthe Dunouy. *View in a Park*, ca. 1800–1810. Oil on paper. The Metropolitan Museum of Art, New York

Château de Malmaison. Fortuitously, Bonaparte's great military and political triumphs of 1799 provided the means required to luxuriously renovate the enormous property. The redesign of the house and grounds was assigned initially to Napoleon's favorite Neoclassical architects Charles Percier and Pierre Fontaine, but the latter's preference for formal French gardens found little favor with the consul's wife, who exhausted a succession of four designers over the course of five feverish years. In Louis Martin Berthault the newly crowned empress found a designer and landscape architect to suit her tastes. By 1808 her park of nearly 1,800 acres had achieved its final aspect.

Berthault created vast, undulating lawns planted with exotic shrubs and a marvelous variety of trees including cedar of Lebanon, ginkgo, magnolia, larch, Mediterranean hackberry, and white lime.[14] The grounds featured a small lake for boating and a stream with little waterfalls built of rocks transported from

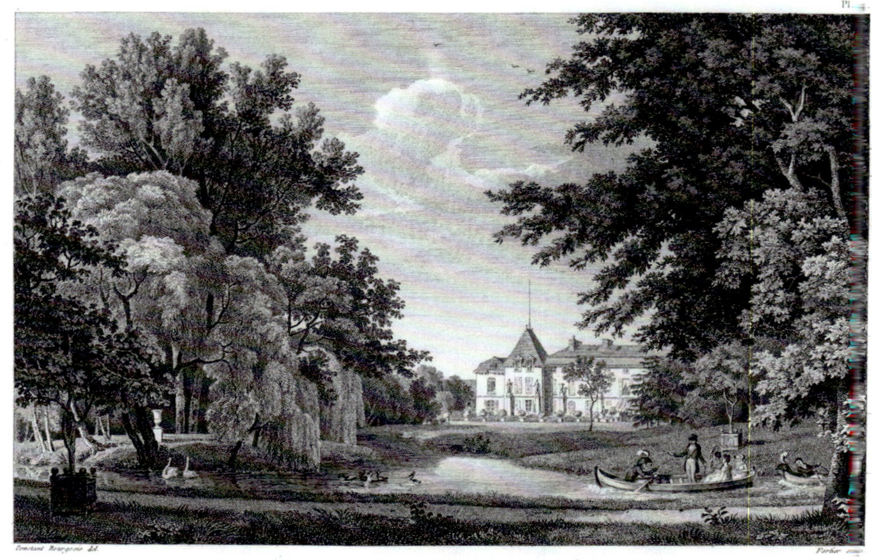

FIG. 11. Constant Bourgeois. "The Château of Malmaison, Seen from the Gardens," from Alexandre de Laborde, *Description des nouveaux jardins de la France et de ses anciens châteaux* (Paris, 1808). Engraving. The Metropolitan Museum of Art, New York

the Forest of Fontainebleau. Scattered among the plantings were statues of Apollo, Diana, and Venus, and an assortment of follies that boasted a monument to Melancholy and a Temple of Love supported by marble columns from various Parisian churches destroyed in the Revolution. In the opinion of the architect Fontaine, who visited Malmaison after its renovation, the place had become "composed of riches heaped in disorder," with "all the silliness of English gardening."[15] However, views of the estate published in Alexandre de Laborde's splendid pictorial survey of French landscape gardens of the time, *Description des nouveaux jardins de la France et de ses anciens châteaux* (1808), reveal vistas both graceful and grand (fig. 11).

Unquestionably, the most significant structure at Malmaison was the tremendous glasshouse, more than 150 feet long, built on plans by Jean Marie Morel in 1804–5 as a gallery for the empress's collection of exotic flowers, shrubs, and trees from around the world (see figs. 13, 14). Josephine, who had been raised on the island of Martinique, where her wealthy family owned a sugar plantation, may have developed an early interest in tropical flora that became sharpened when, at the age of sixteen, she arrived in France to discover a whole new panoply of vegetation.

In midlife, as a titled woman of means passionate about plants, Josephine became a major participant in the great age of botanical discovery. Conferring with the most prominent scientists and nurserymen of her day, she made her glasshouse a famous site for the collection and cultivation of exotic flora. There, among more than two thousand imports, nearly two hundred plants flowered for the first time in France, including the tree peony, purple magnolia, hibiscus, phlox, camellia, and dahlia.[16] So great was Josephine's authority that when the important survey and scientific expeditions to Australia led by Nicolas Baudin returned to France in 1803 and 1804, the national botanical garden—the Jardin des Plantes—gave her first choice of specimens, both floral and animal.[17] Kangaroos, emus, black swans, ostriches, and other zoological wonders joined Malmaison's menagerie, as eucalyptus, acacia, bottlebrush, and banksia entered the glass conservatory. A renowned extravagance, Josephine's collection of "exoticks" was satirized in an English cartoon illustrating the day's leading politicians sprouting up as potted plants, including the Prince Regent (later George IV), who shone as the "Royal Sunflower" (fig. 12).[18]

Roses, too, arrived at Malmaison from across the seas. Josephine (named Marie Josèphe Rose at birth) wished to raise all known varieties. Of the more than two hundred fifty species said to have been cultivated in her care, most were supplied by the nursery of the English specialist John Kennedy, whose shipments, despite the fact that England and France were at war, were allowed

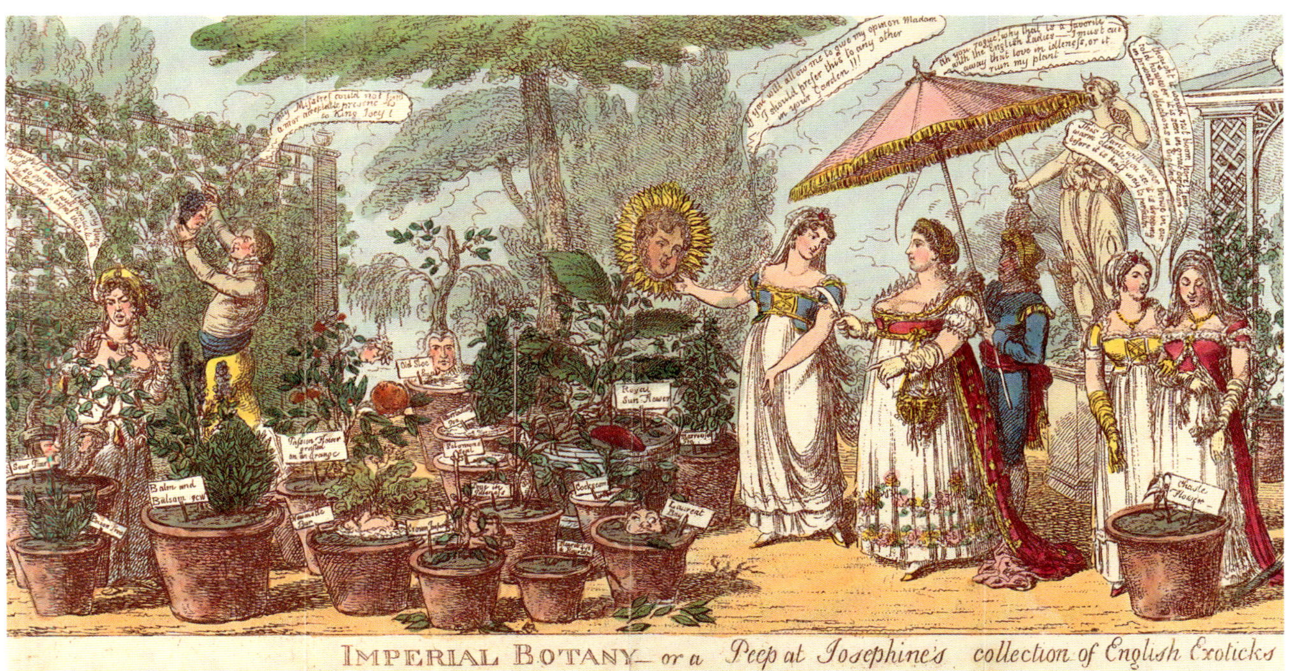

FIG. 12. Attributed to Charles Williams or George Cruikshank. *Imperial Botany—or a Peep at Josephine's Collection of English Exoticks* (detail), 1814. Hand-colored etching. The Metropolitan Museum of Art, New York

passage through blockades. Thus Kennedy, an important source of Chinese imports, was able to provide Josephine with *Rosa odorata*, the uniquely scented reblooming tea rose, in 1809, just a year after its first flowering in Europe. Within a short time the empress had built the largest *roseraie* in all of France, guided largely by the expertise of the country's foremost amateur rose grower, André du Pont, who is remembered for having begun the modern hybridization of roses through an innovative technique of hand-pollination.

Homage to Josephine as patroness of the horticultural arts — a gardener who not only raised plants but also supported botanists and their research — is paid in a drawing by François Gérard that depicts the goddess Flora placing a garland of flowers around a mounted bust of the empress (fig. 13). In the background stands the Grande Serre Chaude (Great Hothouse), in which all but the most hearty of Josephine's imported plants (such as her Himalayan rhododendrons) were exhibited in pots and brought outside for display when in bloom. Much more than a practical facility for growing exotic species, the glasshouse adjoined majestic salons for the reception of guests (fig. 14).

FIG. 13. François Gérard. *Allegory of Empress Josephine as Patroness of the Gardens at Malmaison*, ca. 1805–6. Watercolor and pen and black ink over black chalk. The Metropolitan Museum of Art, New York

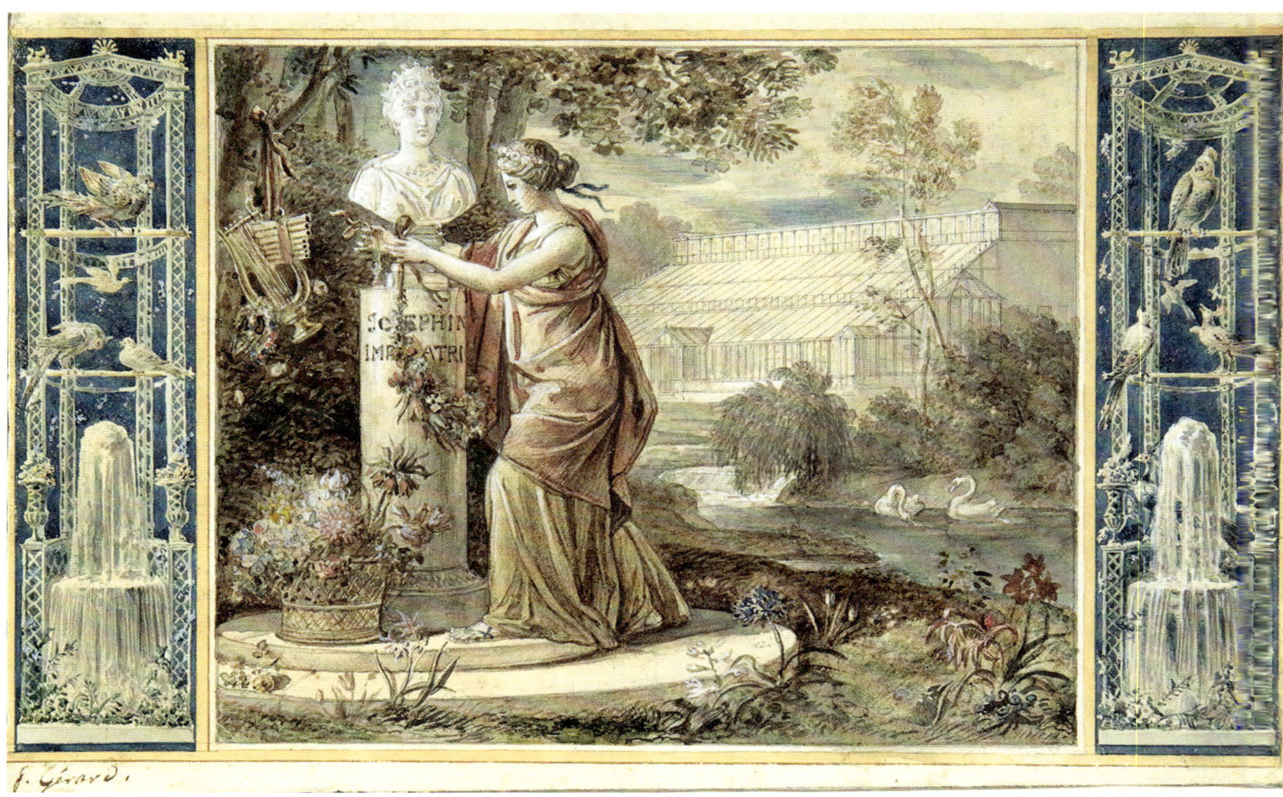

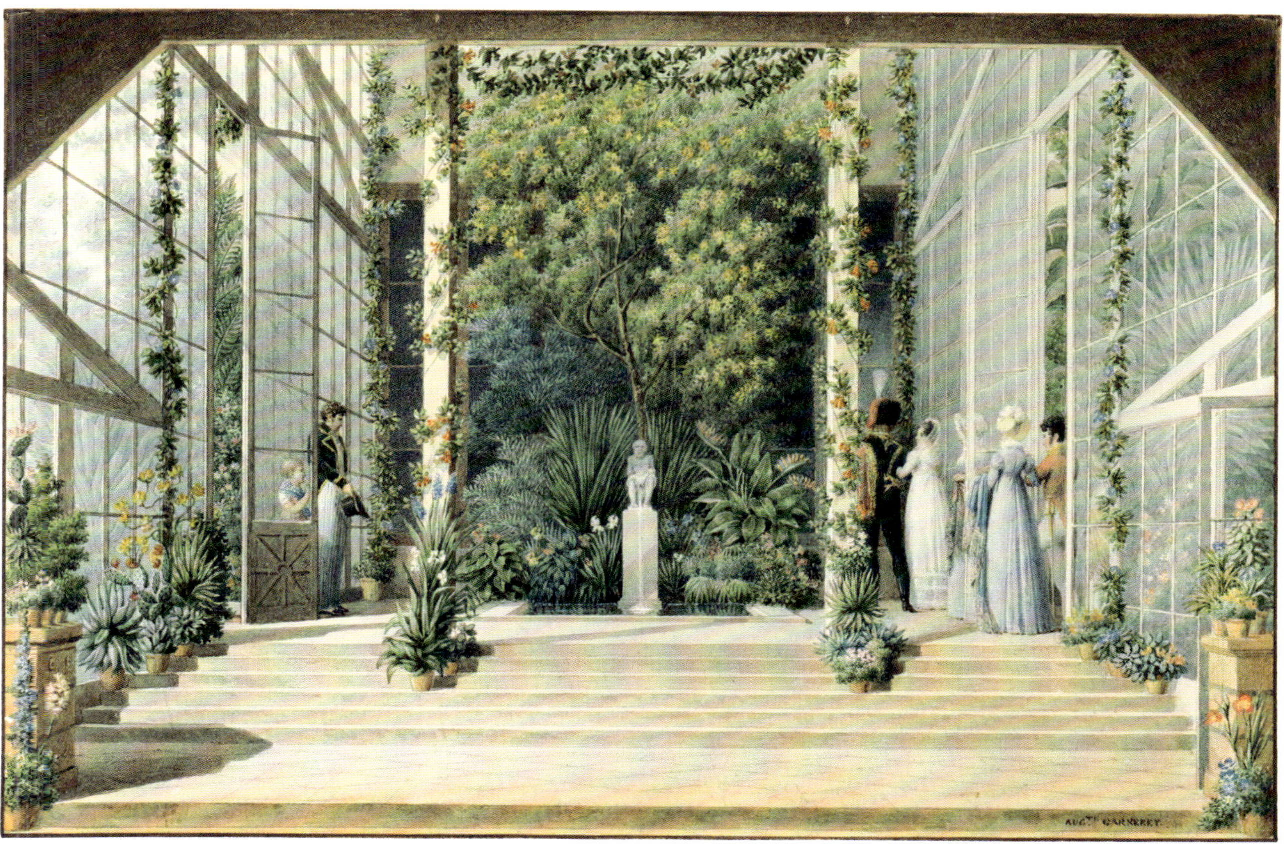

FIG. 14. Auguste Garneray. *Interior of the Hothouse at Malmaison*, ca. 1810. Watercolor. Musée National des Château de Malmaison et Bois-Préau, Rueil-Malmaison

Josephine's customary displays of fresh flowers within the interiors of Malmaison undoubtedly stimulated new fashions in household decoration. Percier and Fontaine, in their design book of 1801, introduced lavish plans for jardinières, inspiring other decorators to create elaborate planters in the Neoclassical style (fig. 15). One of the loveliest of these to survive was designed in 1812 as a table centerpiece for Josephine by Louis Martin Berthault, Malmaison's garden architect and the decorator of the glasshouse (fig. 16).[20] To further enhance Josephine's dinner table, a richly gilded dessert service ornamented with exotic botanical motifs was ordered from the Royal Porcelain Factory in Berlin during the city's occupation by the French.[21]

In 1809 Napoleon divorced Josephine, citing her inability to produce a son and heir. He allowed her to remain at Malmaison and to retain her rank and title, supplying her with a generous allowance "[to] have as much planting done as you like."[22] Less than five years later, after Napoleon had been exiled to the island of Elba, Josephine succumbed to pneumonia. With her death,

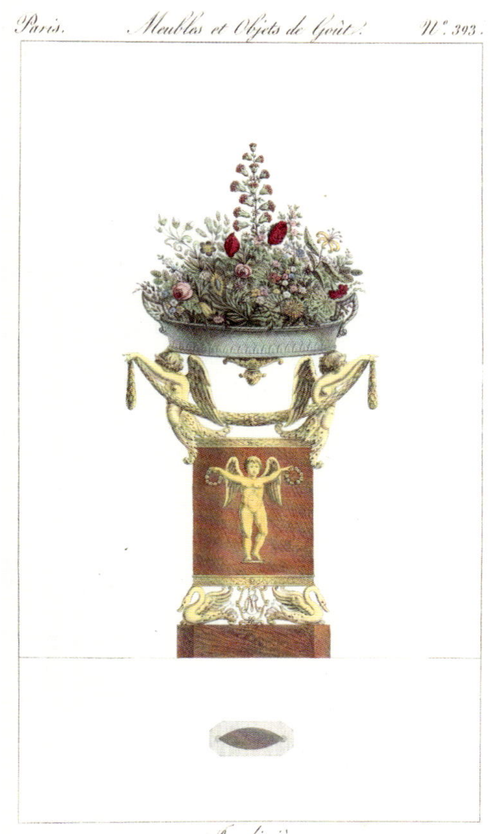

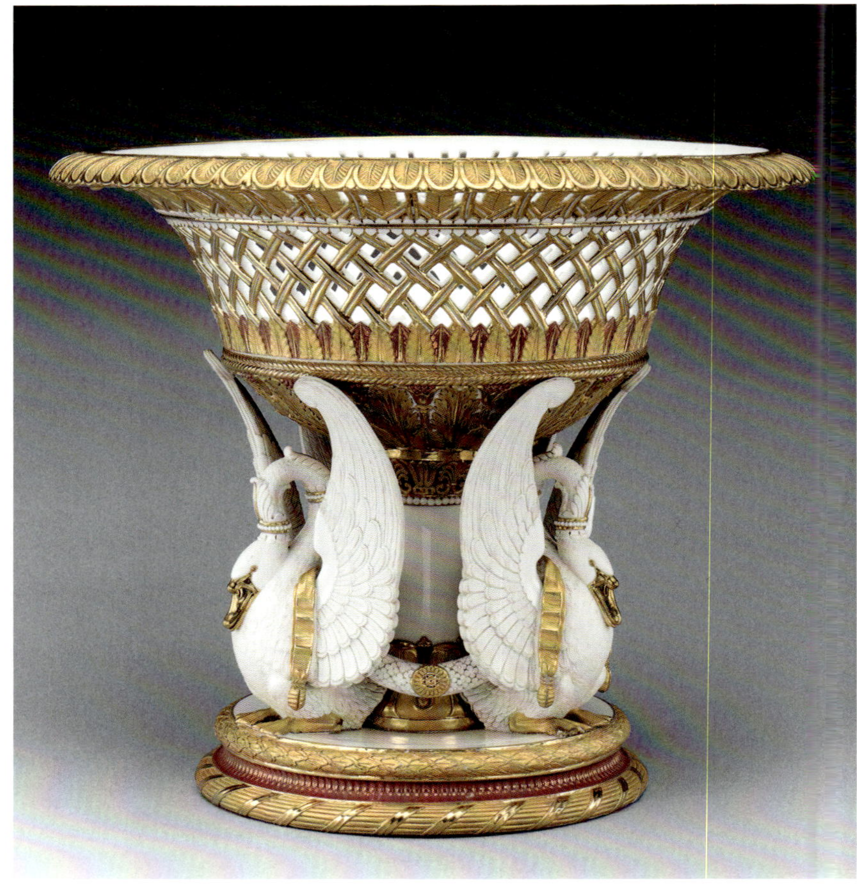

FIG. 15. Jardinière, from Pierre de La Mésangère, *Collection de meubles et objets de goût* (Paris, 1806–18). Hand-colored engraving. The Metropolitan Museum of Art, New York

FIG. 16. Louis Martin Berthault. Fruit or flower basket, designed 1812; Sèvres Manufactory, 1823. Hard-paste porcelain. The Metropolitan Museum of Art, New York

Malmaison, often vacant, fell into disrepair. The removal of the glasshouse in 1826 marked the end of Josephine's treasured assembly of frost-tender plants. Much of its history, however, had been secured by her foresight in assigning the care and cataloguing of her collection to the noted botanists Etienne Pierre Ventenat and Aimé Bonpland, veteran of the renowned scientific expeditions undertaken by Alexander von Humboldt. Furthermore, Josephine commissioned the Flemish-born French artist Pierre Joseph Redouté, formerly floral draftsman to Marie Antoinette, to pictorially document each of her rare specimens. Captured by Redouté in exquisite detail and at the freshest moment of bloom, Josephine's extraordinary flowers are now prized among the great masterpieces of botanical art.

The first group of Redouté's floral illustrations was published in 1802 in *Les Liliacées*, a suite of engravings after Redouté's watercolors that by 1816

FIG. 17. Pierre Joseph Redouté. Crown Imperial (*Fritillaria imperialis*), from *Les Liliacées* (Paris, 1802–16). Colored stipple engraving. Private collection

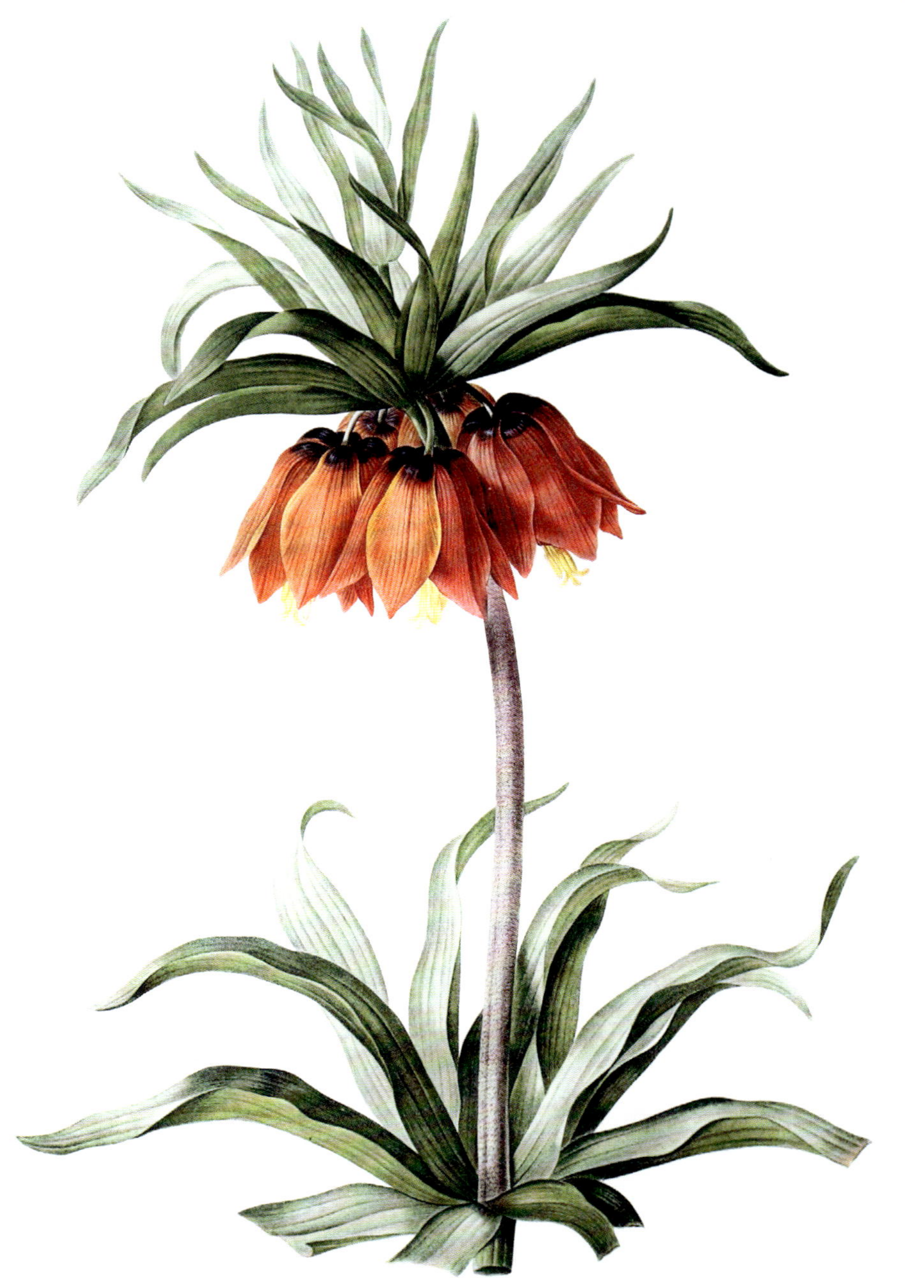

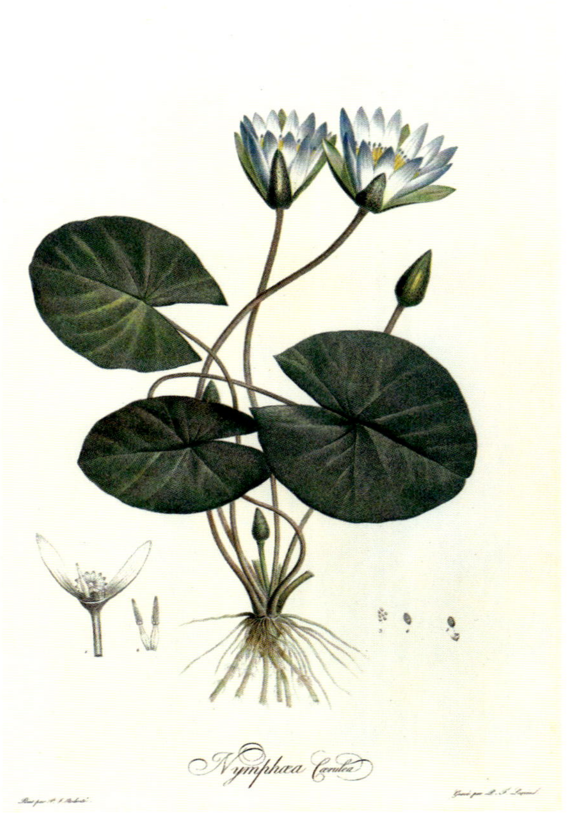

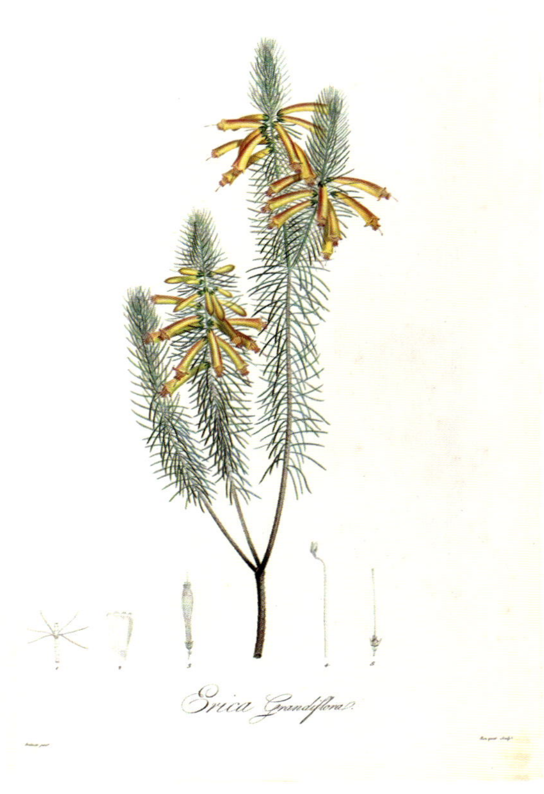

FIG. 18. Pierre Joseph Redouté. *Nymphaea caerulea*, from Etienne Pierre Ventenat, *Jardin de la Malmaison* (Paris, 1803–4). Colored stipple engraving. New York Botanical Garden

FIG. 19. Pierre Joseph Redouté. *Erica grandiflora*, from Aimé Bonpland, *Description des plantes rares cultivées à Malmaison et à Navarre* (Paris, 1813). Colored stipple engraving. New York Botanical Garden

totaled 486 color prints, including Josephine's candelabra lily (*Brunsvigia josephinae*) from the Cape of Good Hope and the Crown Imperial (*Fritillaria imperialis*), native to southwestern Asia (fig. 17). Many of the most exotic plants in the empress's collection appeared in the 120 engravings of Ventenat's *Jardin de la Malmaison* (1803–4; fig. 18) and in illustrations to Bonpland's *Description des plantes rares cultivées à Malmaison et à Navarre* (1813; fig. 19).[23]

Redouté's best-known work, *Les Roses*, with 168 color plates and text by Claude-Antoine Thory, was published between 1817 and 1824, after Josephine's death. Among the roses depicted were those that she, herself, had named: 'Le Grand Napoléon,' 'La Belle Sultane,' and 'Cuisse de Nymphe Emue' (Thigh of an Aroused Nymph). Both Josephine and Redouté may be credited with the increasing popularity of roses as garden plants during the nineteenth century. Their legacy is honored in the fragrant 'Souvenir de la Malmaison' (dating from 1844) and the pink ruffled bloom of 'L'Impératrice Joséphine' (originally named *Rosa turbinata*; fig. 20).

FIG. 20. Pierre Joseph Redouté. *Rosa turbinata*, from Pierre Joseph Redouté and Claude-Antoine Thory, *Les Roses* (Paris, 1817–24). Colored stipple engraving. Private collection

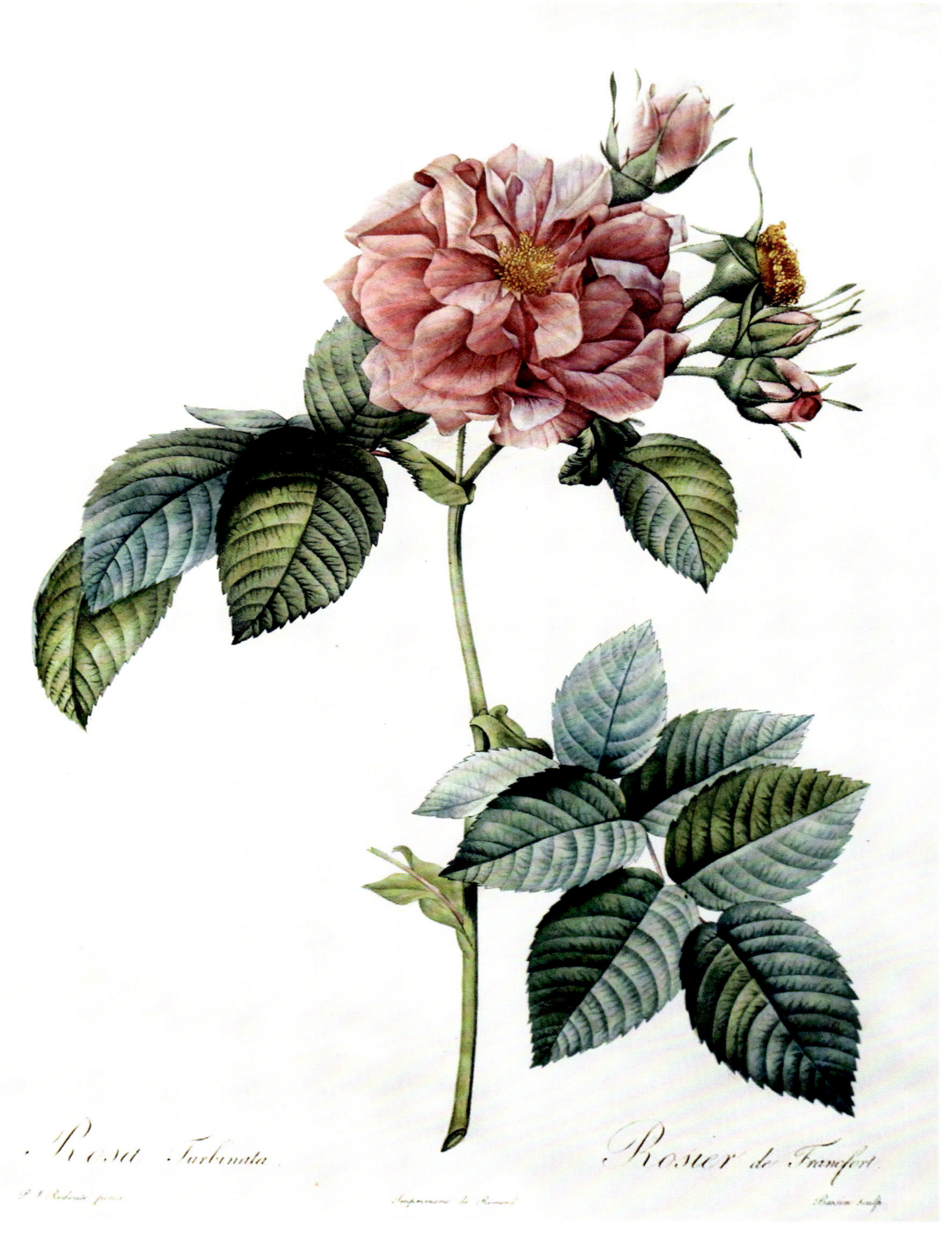

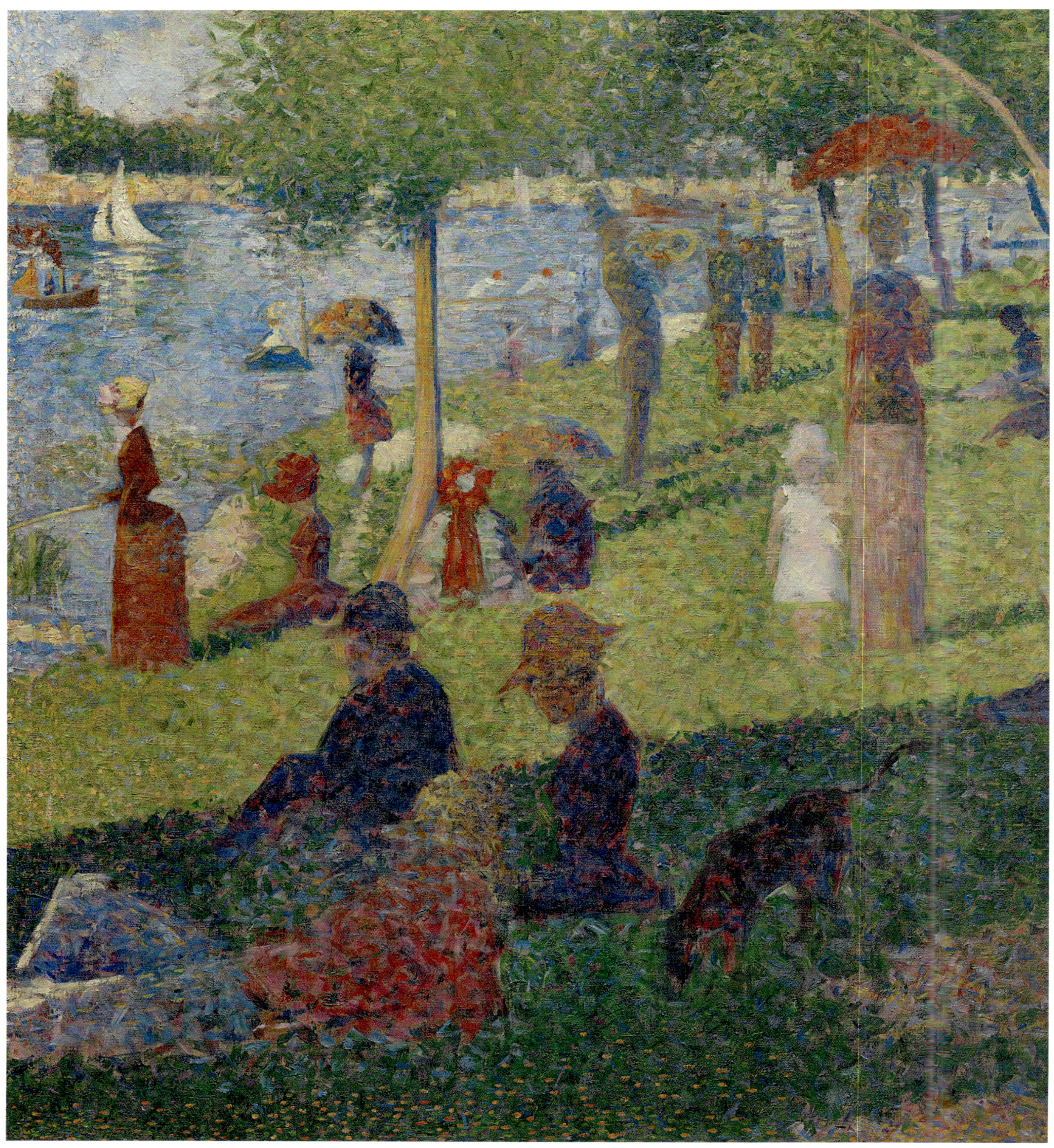

Parks for the Public

In France as in England and America, the dedication of large tracts of land to the common enjoyment of the out-of-doors marked the nineteenth century as the great era of public parks. The Industrial Revolution moved thousands of workers from farms to factories, uprooting them from familiar rural landscapes and creating an acute need to provide an experience of fresh air and natural scenery for growing populations of urban dwellers. There were grave concerns for public health; in France, deadly cholera epidemics that killed thousands of Parisians in 1832 and 1849 increased the sense of urgency. The first publicly financed park in England, designed by Joseph Paxton at Birkenhead, opened in 1847. Five years later, when Napoleon III (r. 1852–70) became emperor of France, he began to implement the first city plan to integrate a large network of publicly funded parks.

For centuries, in Paris and its surrounds pleasure gardens and parks had been designed for aristocrats and royalty; in the nineteenth century these areas were fully opened to the public. There followed the development of green spaces purposefully designed for the recreation and welfare of the general populace. Carrying out perhaps the most ambitious urban-renewal project of modern times, Napoleon III and his commissioner Baron Haussmann transformed the city of Paris by opening up broad tree-lined avenues and establishing more than thirty new public parks and neighborhood squares, while renovating old gardens dating from France's ancien régime. The obvious benefits of this vast undertaking to both the social and economic well-being of the French capital helped to inspire the creation of urban green spaces around the globe.

The Parks of the Ancien Régime

One of the most immediate results of the French Revolution was the transfer of lands owned by the monarchy to its citizens. Previously, royal gardens and hunting grounds had been available to the public only infrequently, on occasions when these guarded areas were not in use by the court. After 1789, as one garden historian rejoiced, "the pleasures of the king became the pleasures of the people."[1]

The fall of the monarchy left the royal palace and park at Versailles deserted and dilapidated. The once magnificent 2,000-acre garden designed by Le Nôtre for Louis XIV in 1661, renamed the "jardin national," was more or less officially opened to the public, though it suffered greatly from neglect. There was talk of "plowing up the park" by none other than Charles Delacroix, government administrator and presumed father of the great Romantic painter Eugène Delacroix. Plans were proposed to convert the parterres into vegetable plots, fruit trees were planted around the drained Grand Canal, and the woods were logged for timber.[2]

Further deterioration of the park was detained when Napoleon Bonaparte, likely under the guidance of his Neoclassical architect Pierre Fontaine, began to take an interest. He set a small sum aside for the restoration of the gardens and the Trianon, which he and his family used briefly as a private residence.[3] After Louis XVI's younger brother Louis XVIII (r. 1814–20) succeeded to the throne, he added a new "jardin du roi" to the formal Versailles plan. Its hybrid design, which combined both irregular and geometric elements, was created by Alexandre Dufour, who recalled that the Bourbon king ordered the garden's trees and flowers to be planted by hired paupers.[4]

The vast water basins and spectacular fountains at Versailles remained its most outstanding attractions and no doubt helped to secure care for the surrounding greenery. Evidently, to the American painter John Vanderlyn, who visited the park during the crisp autumn days of 1814 in preparation for his 165-foot-long panoramic view of the palace and gardens, the lawns and allées viewed from the expansive terrace appeared in good order (fig. 21). By then, new trees planted in bosquets had reached some maturity and alterations carried out during the period of the First Empire had simplified the lines of the garden markedly.

The legendary palace landscape continued to age with a minimum of maintenance until, under the Second Empire (1852–70), a campaign of restoration was activated by Napoleon III, who valued Versailles as an impressive

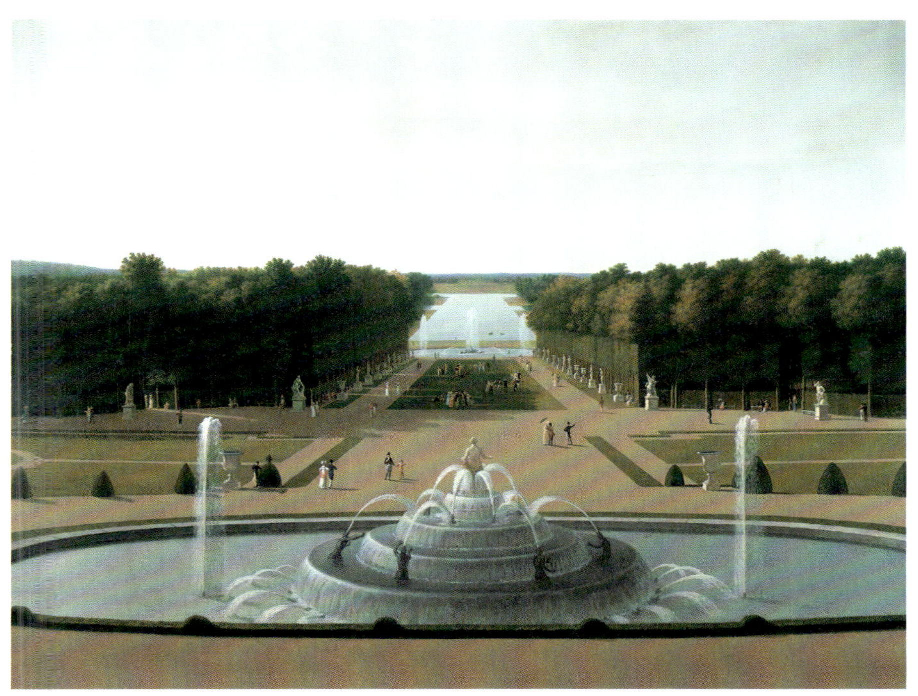

FIG. 21. John Vanderlyn. *Panoramic View of the Palace and Gardens of Versailles* (detail), 1818–19. Oil on canvas. The Metropolitan Museum of Art, New York

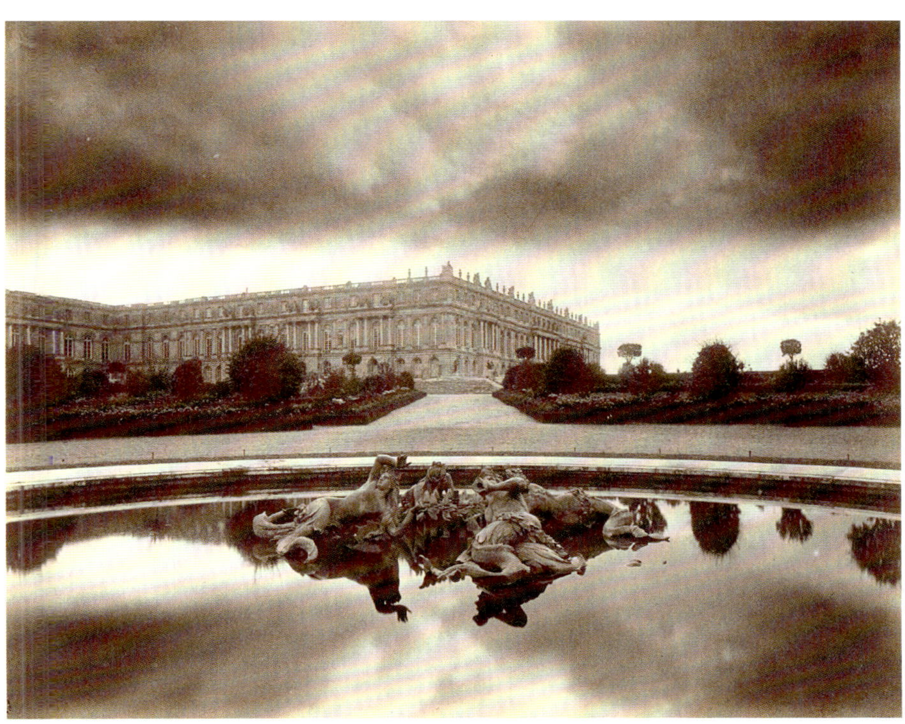

FIG. 22. Eugène Atget. *The Palace at Versailles, Late October Evening, Cloud Effect, View from the North Parterre*, 1903. Albumen silver print from glass negative. The Metropolitan Museum of Art, New York

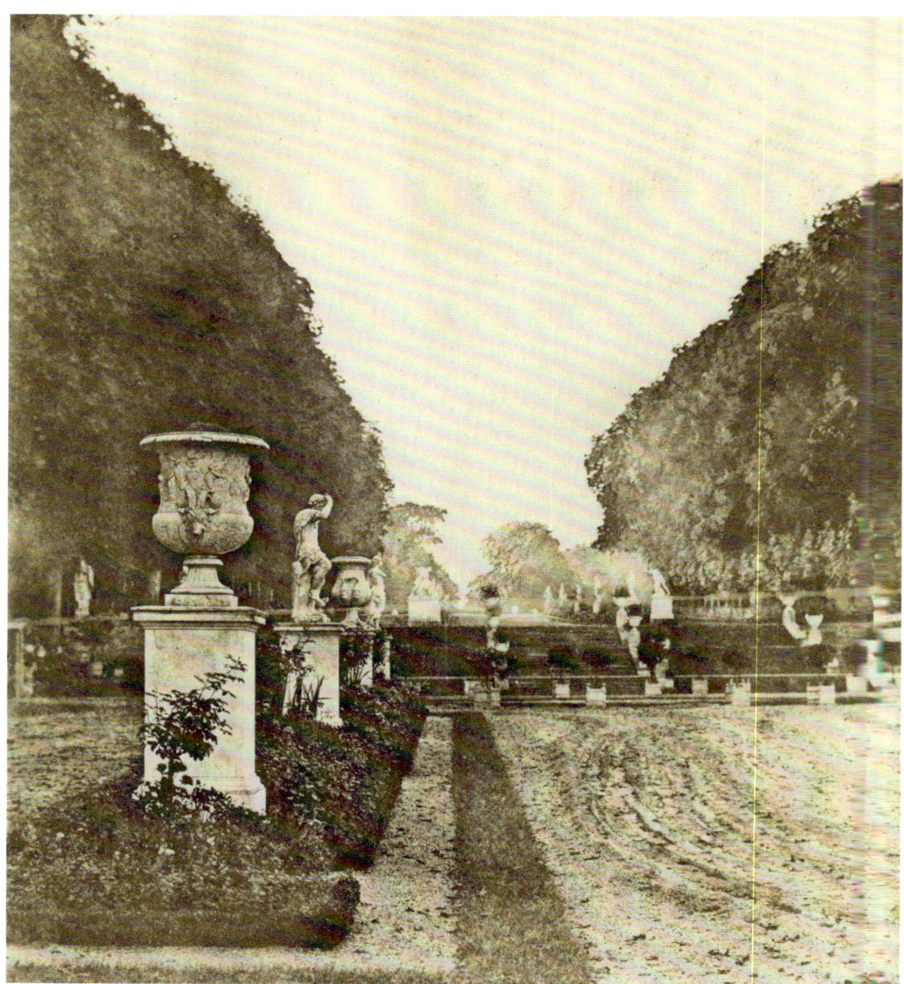

FIG. 23. Henri-Victor Regnault. *Gardens of Saint-Cloud,* before 1855. Salted paper print from paper negative. The Metropolitan Museum of Art, New York

backdrop for celebrations. A display of fireworks amid the splashing fountains was the highlight of the party held there in 1855 for Queen Victoria of England and her family. Later, a replanting of the garden, supervised by the architect and designer Charles-Auguste Questel, extended from 1863 to 1880.

As one of the most celebrated gardens in the world, the park at Versailles was, throughout the nineteenth century, an enormously popular tourist destination, despite disruptions in its care and the disapproval of critics like William Robinson, founding father of the English "wild" garden. His 1869 guidebook to the parks, gardens, and promenades of Paris bemoaned the "bald formality," the "general dreariness" of its "interminable . . . spreads of gravel, grass, [and] stumpy clipped yews," and its "water basins, with their squirting pipes."[5] A profoundly nostalgic response to the yawning site is felt in later views by the most sensitive photographer of old Paris, Eugène Atget, for whom Versailles, with its faded grandeur, held a deep resonance (fig. 22). He worked there from 1901 until the year before his death in 1927.

Napoleon III also entertained Queen Victoria at the imperial seat at Saint-Cloud, outside Paris, where both he and, earlier, his uncle Napoleon I often took residence. Although the palace was destroyed in 1870 during the Franco-Prussian War, the majestic park designed by Le Nôtre (about half the size of the garden at Versailles) survives still, inviting visitors to enjoy its fountains, canals, and broad avenues of sculpture and clipped trees (fig. 23). To update the geometric plan laid out in the seventeenth century, a free-form garden *à l'anglais* was added in the 1820s.

The largest acquisition of parklands by the French people following the Revolution was the Forest of Fontainebleau, over 40,000 acres of hunting grounds that had been used by royals since the eleventh century. Adjoining the palace and former hunting lodge, this rough and varied terrain 35 miles south of Paris, with its woodlands, massive rocks, and plateaus, was exalted in the nineteenth century as a model of unspoiled nature.

Napoleon I, who once ridiculed the gardens at Versailles as mere "bankers' follies," declared, "My own garden is the Fontainebleau forest."[6] His architect Pierre Fontaine was like-minded. In 1813, despairing of "the stupidity of those people who waste their fortune making little lakes, little rocks, little rivers," Fontaine declared the Forest of Fontainebleau "my own English garden . . . and I want no other."[7] The dramatic beauty of the site's topography and aged, unspoiled vegetation was a matter of French pride and soon attracted artists dedicated to painting out of doors, in changing conditions of weather and light, in their desire to capture the marvels of nature through direct experience (fig. 24). The forest thus became an inspiration for a groundswell of naturalistic landscapes in the 1830s, leading eventually to the light-infused paintings of the Impressionists in the 1860s.[8]

Camille Corot is believed to have made some of his first plein-air paintings at Fontainebleau in the spring of 1822; after excursions in sunny Italy, he often returned to the forest to capture the cool light of the north (fig. 25). In his precise study of the contrasting verdant and rocky aspects of the Fontainebleau landscape, he was followed in the 1830s and 1840s by Théodore Rousseau, Narcisse-Virgile Diaz de la Peña, Antoine-Louis Barye, Gustave Courbet, and a host of other artists who stationed themselves around Barbizon and Chailly, villages within and near the forest.

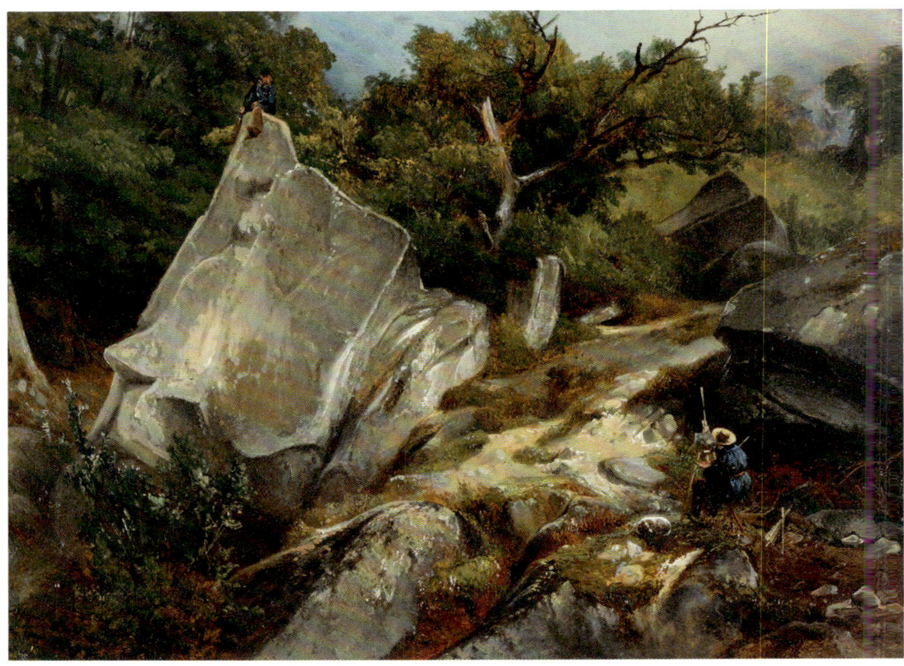

FIG. 24. Augustin Enfantin. *An Artist Painting in the Forest of Fontainebleau*, ca. 1825. Oil on paper, laid down on canvas. Private collection

Of all the artists at Fontainebleau, Rousseau became the most passionately dedicated. Intensely observant and strongly influenced by the seventeenth-century Dutch masters, he focused his gaze on the forest's varied terrain over a period of four decades (fig. 26). In 1852, as self-appointed guardian, he petitioned Napoleon III for its protection. Protesting widespread commercial logging and the wholesale planting of nonnative pine trees to be harvested for timber, Rousseau asked that the area be spared further intervention, in particular "these old trees which for artists are the source from which they derive their inspiration, their joys, and their future, and which are for all visitors, venerable souvenirs of past ages."[9] The extraordinary result of his petition was an imperial decree in 1861 that set aside some 4,000 acres of the forest as a *partie artistique*, the first nature preserve in history.[10]

It was not long after photography was invented in France that photographers too began to visit Fontainebleau, setting up their cameras before the woodland's great trees.[11] Gustave Le Gray was one of the earliest to arrive, in 1849, and the first of his profession to employ waxed-paper negatives rather than heavy glass plates. The lighter material made excursions into the woods less cumbersome, shortened exposure time to about twenty minutes, and produced tonally rich pictures, dreamy and reverent. Trained as a painter, Le Gray

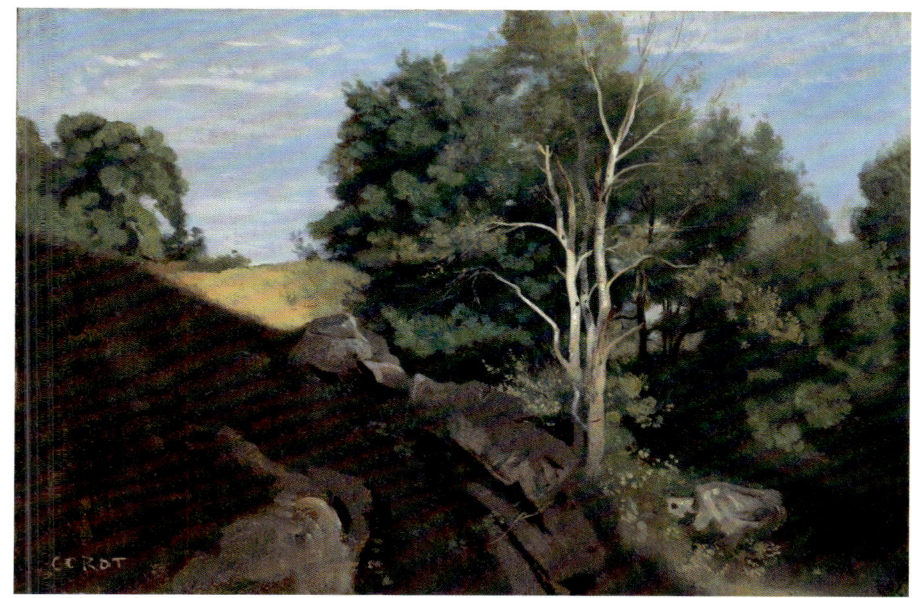

FIG. 25. Camille Corot. *Fontainebleau: Group of Trees on the Flank of a Rocky Hillside*, ca. 1845–50. Oil on canvas. Louis-Dreyfus Family Collection

FIG. 26. Théodore Rousseau. *The Edge of the Woods at Monts-Girard, Fontainebleau Forest*, 1852–54. Oil on wood. The Metropolitan Museum of Art, New York

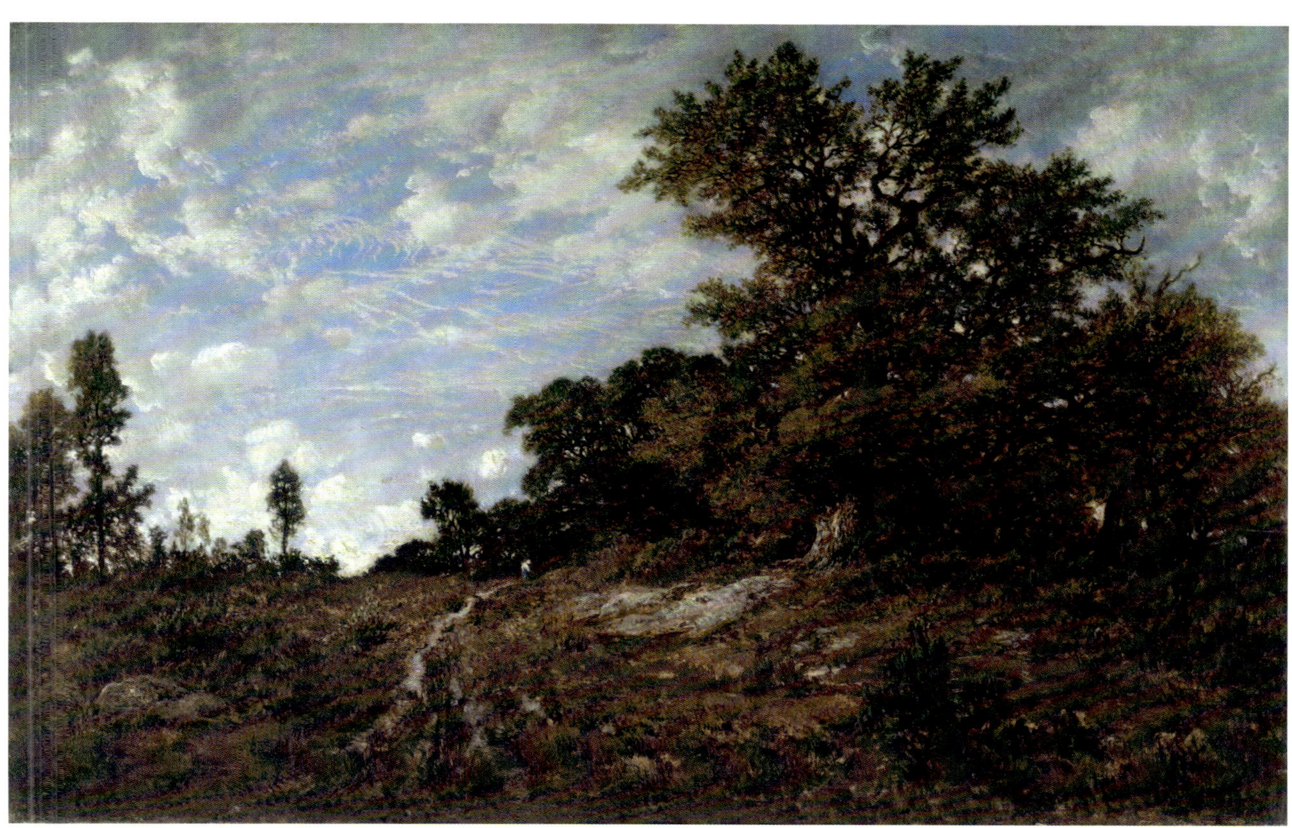

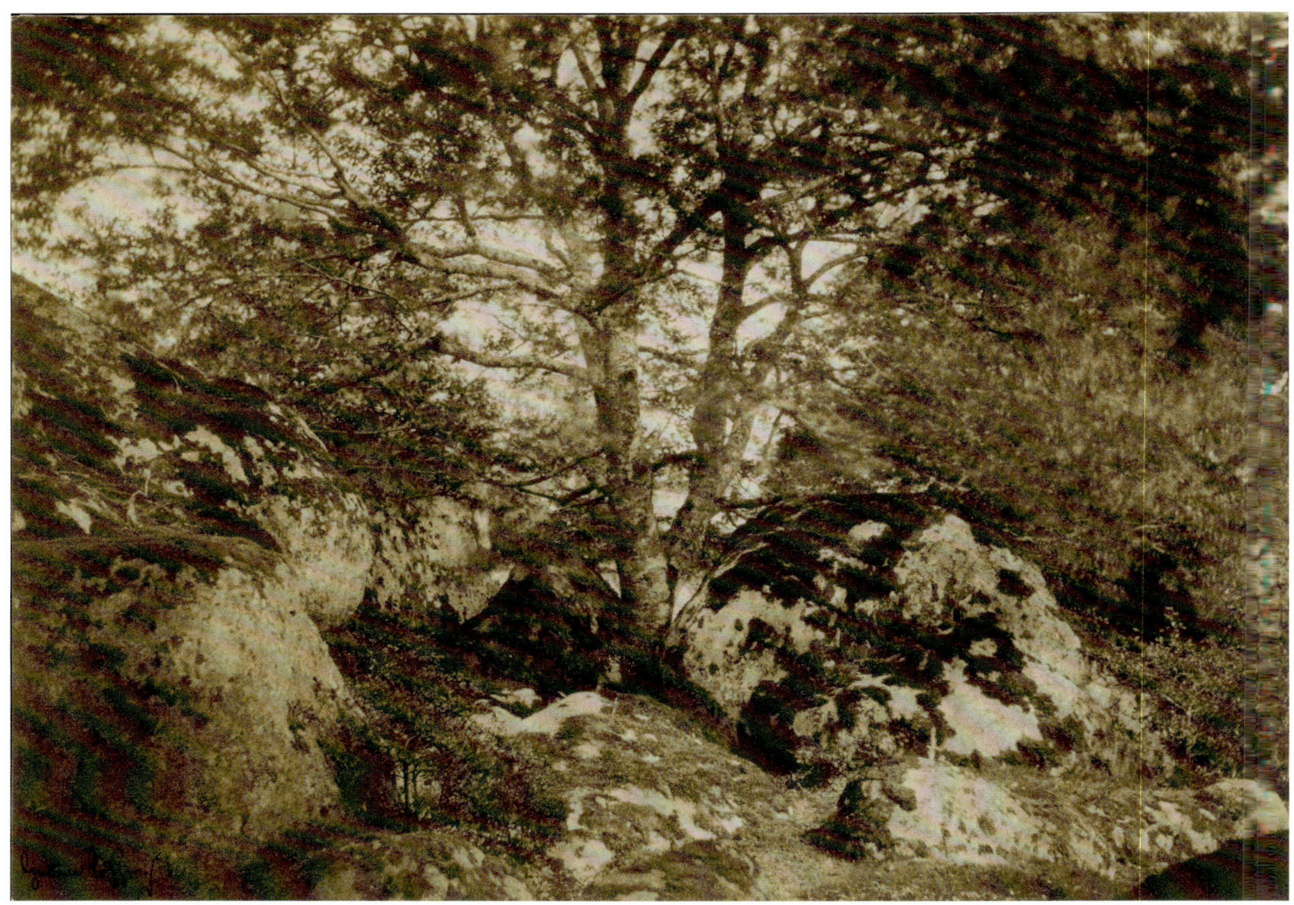

FIG. 27. Gustave Le Gray. *Oak Trees and Rocks at Fontainebleau Forest*, 1849–52. Salted paper print from paper negative. The Metropolitan Museum of Art, New York

was entranced by Fontainebleau's evocative scenery and worked patiently to capture its lichen-covered rocks and gnarled oaks contoured by dark shadows and shafts of light. Along with Charles Marville and Eugène Cuvelier, who photographed the forest with similar sensitivity during the 1850s and 1860s, Le Gray blazed a trail that would lead to the camera's acceptance as an instrument of art (figs. 27, 28).

No longer the haunt solely of privileged huntsmen and foraging peasants, Fontainebleau by midcentury had become a popular tourist site. *Galignani's New Paris Guide* of 1839 recommended a visit: "The journey is performed very easily by means of the steamers which go thither every day, and no one who makes the excursion can fail to be delighted with it."[12] In 1840 train lines from Paris to the vicinity opened, and by 1849 one could travel there directly by rail in little more than an hour.

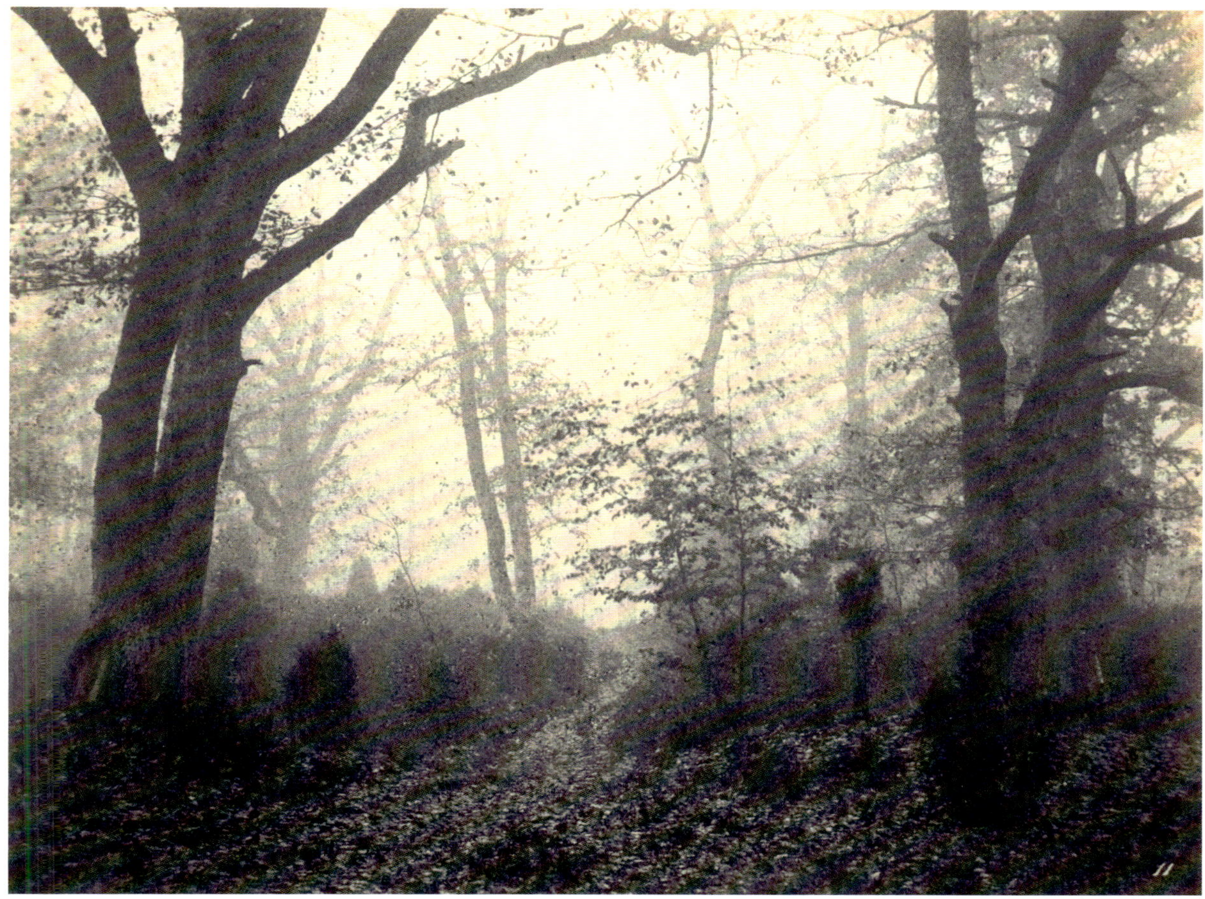

FIG. 28. Eugène Cuvelier. *Fontainebleau Forest*, early 1860s. Salted paper print from paper negative. The Metropolitan Museum of Art, New York

One individual more than any other could claim credit for the extraordinary surge in Fontainebleau traffic. Claude François Denecourt, a veteran of Napoleon's army who turned his love of the forest into a career, published the first of his more than three dozen guides to Fontainebleau in 1839. The most popular, *L'Indicateur de Fontainebleau*, had appeared in seventeen editions by the time of the author's death at the age of eighty-seven in 1875.

Denecourt, who could be described as the inventor of the modern hiking trail, also devised a system of painted blue arrows that directed walkers to the most arresting vistas, rocks, and ancient oak trees, which he labeled with names derived from history and mythology, such as Charlemagne, Goliath, and Neptune.[13] His detailed itineraries and maps made even the most remote corners of the forest accessible to all. The great writers of France, among them George Sand and Stendhal, were guided by them, and Gustave Flaubert, in

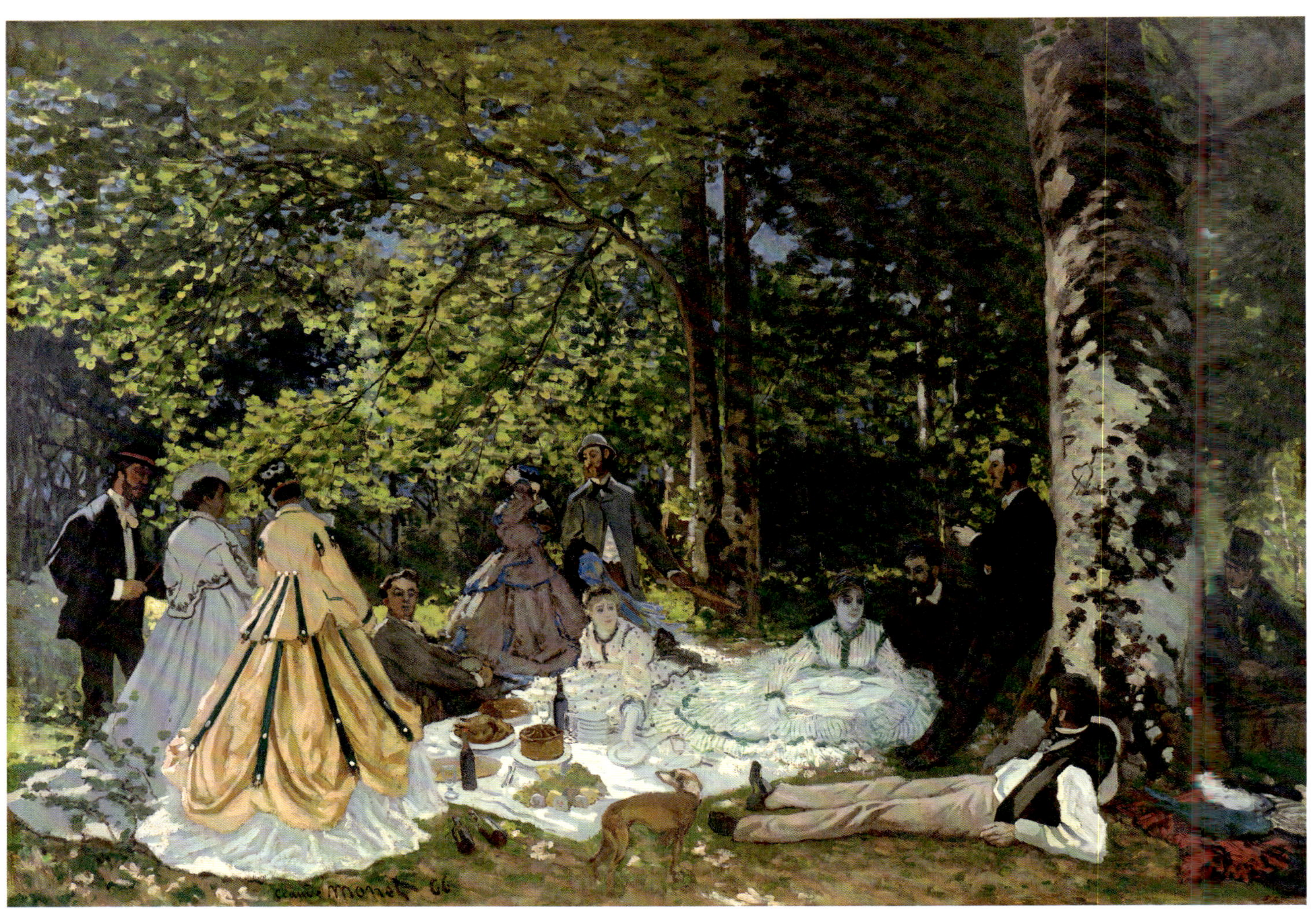

FIG. 29. Claude Monet. *Le Déjeuner sur l'herbe*, 1865. Oil on canvas. Pushkin State Museum of Fine Arts, Moscow

his *L'Education sentimentale* (1869), included many descriptive passages that bring the woodlands to life. Some visitors to Fontainebleau, however, took Denecourt to task for taming and commercializing the forest with too many signs and arrows. George Sand complained, "The surroundings have become a bit too like a pleasure garden."[14]

Indeed, the forest appears to have been valued as a highly agreeable place for a picnic and is celebrated as such in a painting by Claude Monet, which he intended to display at the Salon of 1866. Inspired by Edouard Manet's *Le Déjeuner sur l'herbe* of 1863, Monet, in a picture nearly four times larger than Manet's, endeavored to glorify a moment from everyday life on a scale usually reserved for the grand events of history and myth. Although he ultimately abandoned the huge canvas, later damaged and now in fragments, his preliminary oil sketch describes a sumptuous luncheon party at Chailly in the leafy, sun-dappled shade of a fine old beech (fig. 29).[15] Monet's future wife, Camille, was part of the gathering, as was the artist Frédéric Bazille, who in 1863 had joined Monet, Renoir, and Alfred Sisley on their first painting expedition to Fontainebleau. In preparation for his ambitious picture Monet had studied the dramatic shapes and shadows formed by one of Fontainebleau's most frequently painted and photographed trees, the Bodmer Oak (fig. 30), named for the nineteenth-century Swiss landscapist Karl Bodmer, who often made it his subject.

Having planted *arbres de la liberté* (liberty trees) during the revolutions of 1789 and 1848, the people of France regarded majestic trees as realizations of the persistent power of nature and as silent witnesses to history. Old French trees, as well as the exotic new imports being introduced into the country's gardens and parks, were of such interest that the popular *Magasin Pittoresque* began in the 1830s to feature regular articles on examples of note. Throughout the nineteenth century artists not only privileged trees as the subjects of their pictures but also helped to preserve them. Michallon studied beeches and the woods of the Bois de Boulogne (fig. 31). Rousseau protected the oaks and beeches at Fontainebleau. Monet hindered the cutting of poplars

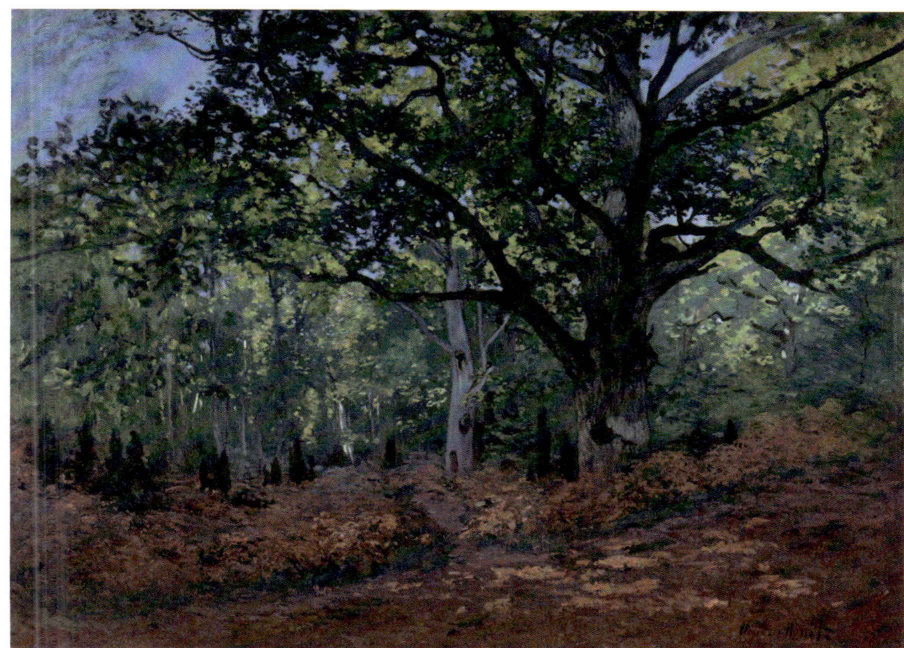

FIG. 30. Claude Monet. *The Bodmer Oak, Fontainebleau Forest*, 1865. Oil on canvas. The Metropolitan Museum of Art, New York

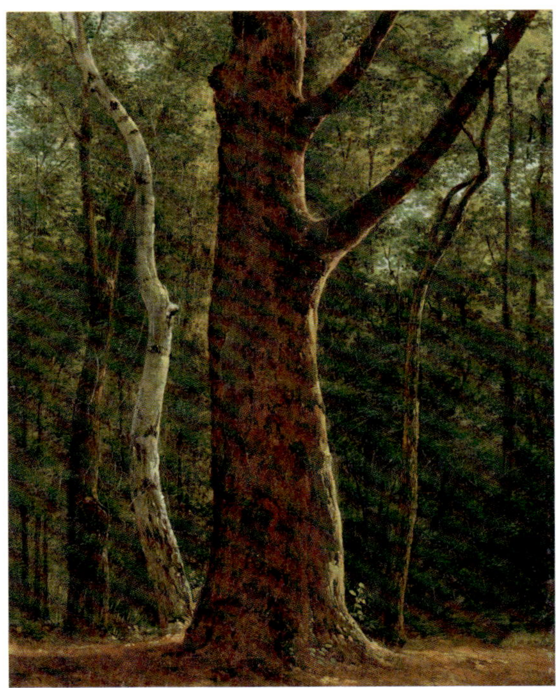

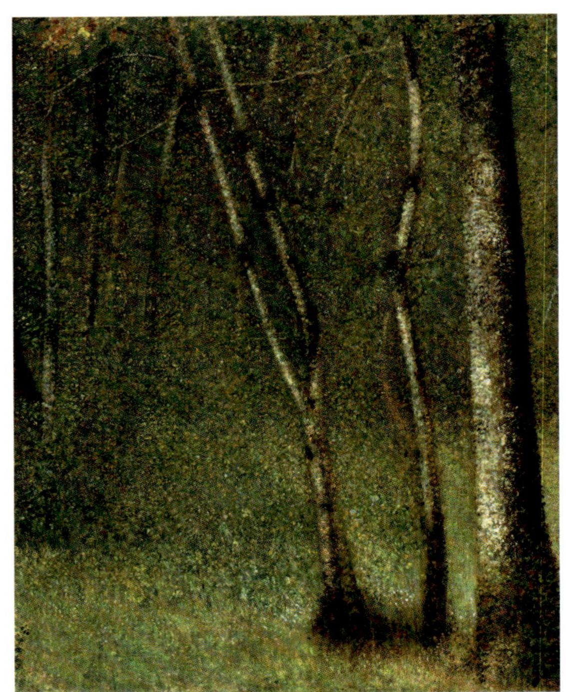

FIG. 31. Achille-Etna Michallon. *Beech Tree*, by 1817. Oil on canvas. The Metropolitan Museum of Art, New York

FIG. 32. Georges Seurat. *The Forest at Pontaubert*, 1881. Oil on canvas. The Metropolitan Museum of Art, New York

along the Seine. Seurat painted saplings in the forest at Pontaubert (fig. 32). In Provence, Van Gogh honored cypresses, Renoir rescued olive trees, and Cézanne memorialized old pines.

In Paris the Jardin des Plantes (formerly the Jardin du Roi) became a popular place to appreciate extraordinary trees, especially after the publication in 1803 of a guide to its grounds, galleries, and hothouses. Founded as a medicinal herb garden in the seventeenth century by Guy de la Brosse, physician to Louis XIII (r. 1610–43), and greatly enlarged during the eighteenth century by the plant collection formed by Louis XV (r. 1715–74), it developed into a renowned center for the study of botany, sending scientists on far-flung plant-hunting expeditions. By the beginning of the nineteenth century its gardeners had under cultivation 3,600 species of foreign plants, including the still-standing cedar of Lebanon that the naturalist Bernard de Jussieu in 1734 famously carried there in his hat (fig. 33).[16] The ever-increasing regiments of trees installed throughout Paris during the nineteenth century in the parks and squares and in rows along the boulevards helped to define the city's structure while providing shaded walkways and cleaner air for its rapidly expanding population.

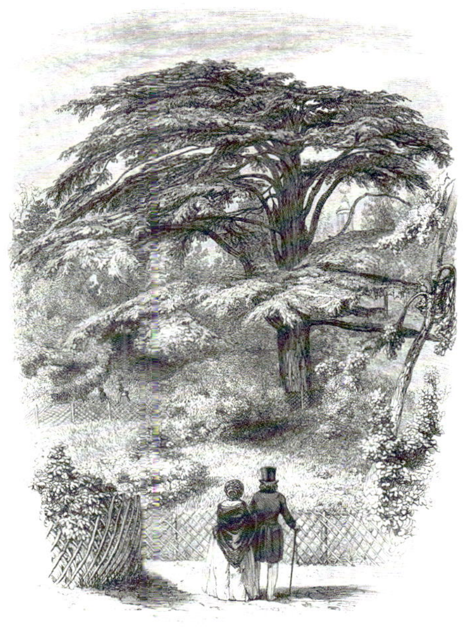

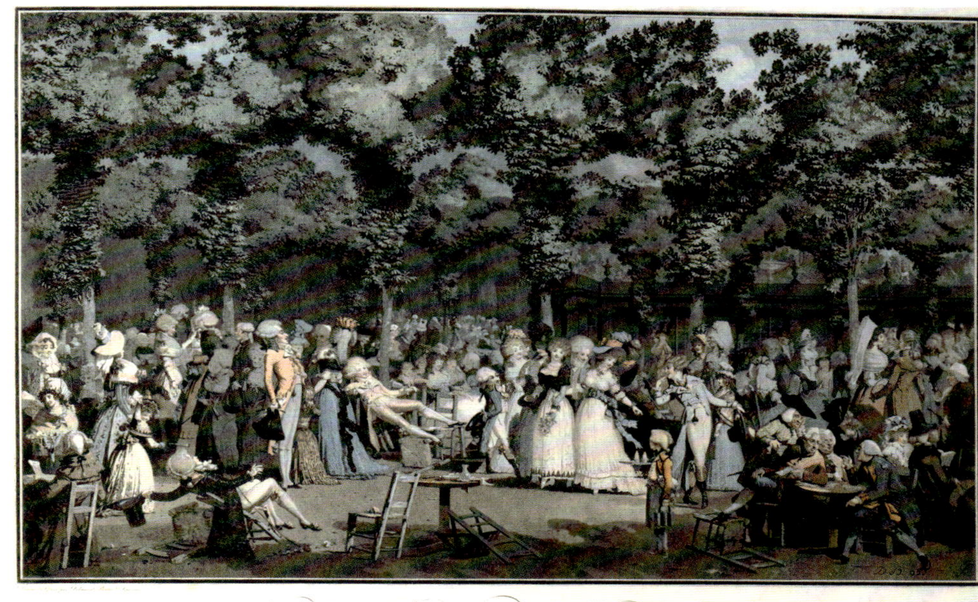

After the fall of the monarchy the urban parks of the Tuileries and Luxembourg palaces attracted growing numbers of visitors. The smaller garden of the old Palais-Royal, dating back to the seventeenth century, had been opened to the public in 1784 after the duc d'Orléans installed apartments and shops around the rows of leafy linden trees. With boutiques, cafés, refreshment kiosks, and gambling rooms, the site continued to attract a large, often unsavory crowd, having become a haunt of ne'er-do-wells and prostitutes (fig. 34). Elsewhere in Paris during the early years of the nineteenth century, prosperous city dwellers could enjoy outdoor greenery in posh garden cafés—the Jardin Turc and the Café Chinois—as well as large theme gardens (*jardins-spectacles*) in converted estates, forerunners of today's amusement parks; the last of these, the Nouveau Tivoli, closed its doors in 1833. Landscaped entertainment spots continued to proliferate throughout the century, often incorporating terraces for dancing and outdoor stages. Enduring still is the Closerie des Lilas, modeled on the Moorish palace of the Alhambra, which opened in 1847 with a dance floor and a garden swing nestled among bushes of lilacs.

The oldest and grandest garden in the heart of Paris, on land previously occupied by tile workshops (*tuileries*), dates back to 1561, when it was

FIG. 33. François-Louis Français. "Cedar of Lebanon," from Pierre Boitard, *Jardin des Plantes* (Paris, 1842). Engraving. The Metropolitan Museum of Art, New York

FIG. 34. Louis Philibert Debucourt. *The Public Promenade*, 1792. Etching, engraving, and aquatint printed in color. The Metropolitan Museum of Art, New York

commissioned by Catherine de' Medici, who wished to adorn the proposed Tuileries Palace with fountains and grottoes in the style of the Italian Renaissance. A century later Louis XIV commanded the garden's complete redesign by the architect of the park at Versailles, André Le Nôtre, who installed within an area of more than 60 acres a stately, geometric arrangement of circular basins, trees, lawns, and flower beds placed symmetrically along a broad central path (fig. 35). Although said to be one of the first public gardens in Europe, the Tuileries before the Revolution was a closely guarded enclave, open only to the upper echelons of society. At the patrolled gate, entrance was denied to domestic servants, soldiers, and "people in rags" or "livery."[17] Thus it was with an air of triumph that the dramatist and writer Louis-Sébastien Mercier declared in 1798: "For a crown, one buys the privilege of thronging with the multitude these magnificent gardens that one could not enter. . . . This was no small pleasure for an enemy of the Ancien Régime."[18]

In 1793, while the palace of the Louvre was opened to the public as the Central Museum of Arts, the adjacent gardens of the Tuileries were eyed as planting grounds for apple trees and beans under a decree meant to relieve severe food shortages.[19] It was not until the Directory (1795–99) that damages sustained during the Revolution were fully addressed. The park's central walkway was widened and the northern terrace extended. A pocket-sized guide for the *promeneur aux Tuileries*, published in 1798, delivered a rhapsodic appreciation of the "imposing grandeur" of the central allée, as well as the "happy disorder, close to nature" of the wooded areas, where dead trees had been replaced.[20] The book's author, Louis Philipon de La Madelaine, devoted most of his praise and illustrations to the fifty-five park sculptures, many of which had been added to the parade of statues on pedestals installed during the reign of Louis XV (fig. 36). Once the garden had been made fully accessible to the public, Napoleon I directed the architect-designers Percier and Fontaine to frame it along the newly opened rue de Rivoli with an elegant iron grille surmounted by gilt spearheads and flower-filled vases. To the elms and chestnuts planted during the ancien régime, bosquets of linden were added and eight hundred orange trees set out in boxes from May to October.[21] In 1801 the English traveler Francis Blagdon could report that the garden, "the most magnificent in Paris . . . is now kept in much better order than it was under the monarchy."[22]

With its spacious walkways, sparkling fountains, and lawns lined with small Persian lilacs the gardens of the Tuileries became the perfect arena in which modern Parisians might stroll, to see and to be seen. There were chairs

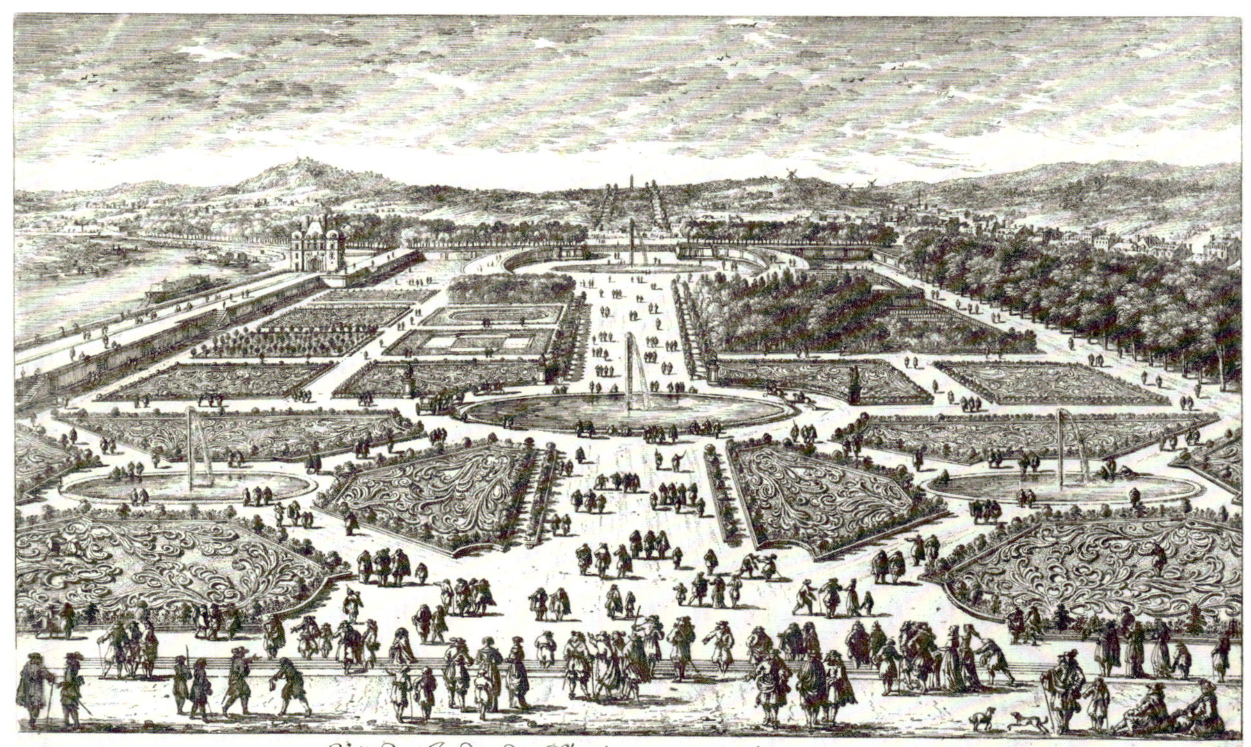

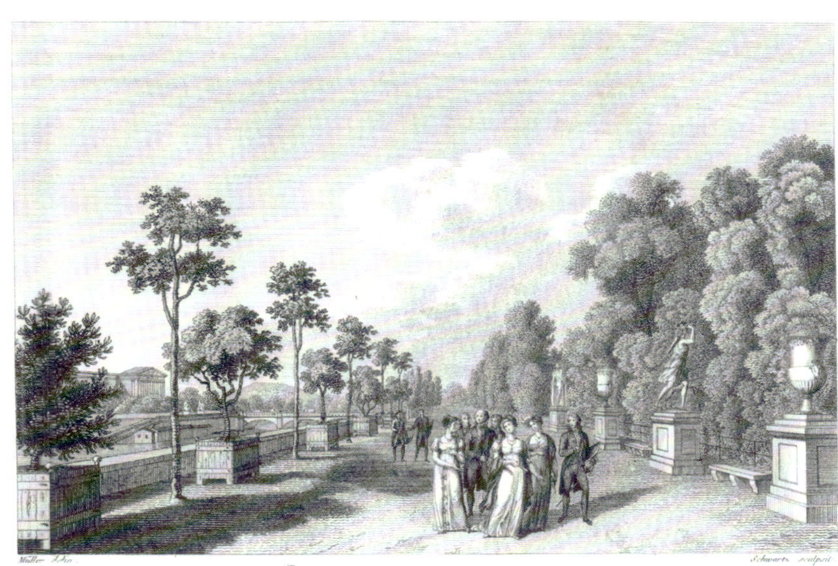

FIG. 35. Adam Perelle. *Jardin des Tuileries*, 1680. Etching. The Metropolitan Museum of Art, New York

FIG. 36. Henri Charles Müller. "The Waterfront Terrace, Jardin des Tuileries," from J. Philibert, *Promenades de Paris* (Paris, 1812). Etching and aquatint. The Metropolitan Museum of Art, New York

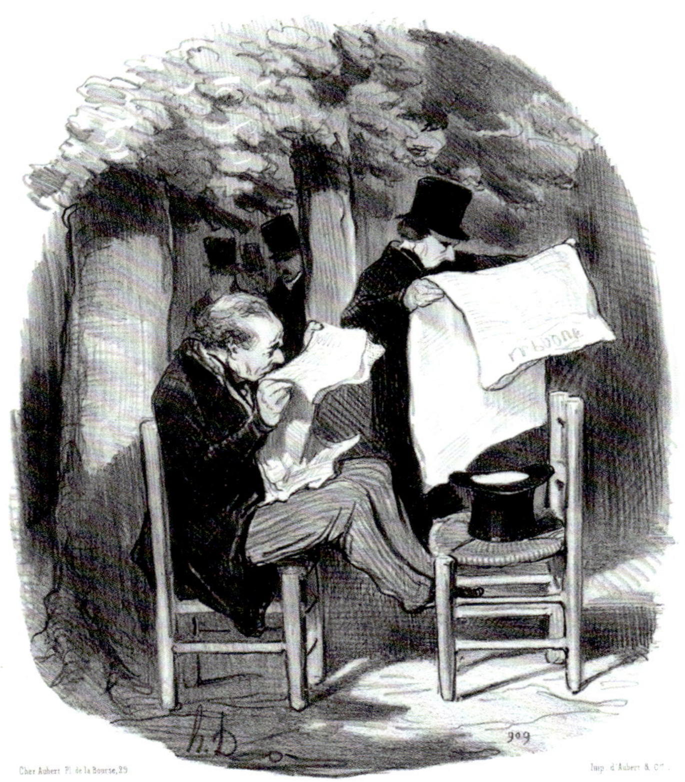

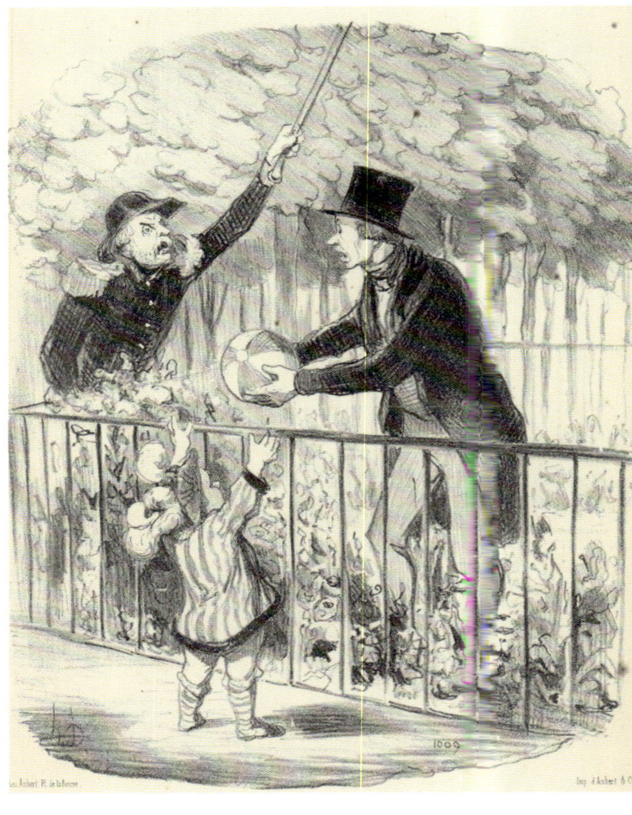

FIG. 37. Honoré Daumier. "What the Bourgeoisie Call a Minor Distraction," from *Le Charivari*, August 30, 1846. Lithograph. The Metropolitan Museum of Art, New York

FIG. 38. Honoré Daumier. "But I assure you that this is his ball and I am his father . . . ," from *Le Charivari*, February 25, 1847. Lithograph. Private collection, New York

for hire, refreshment booths, and the popular restaurant Véry on the Terrasse des Feuillants. The young poet in Balzac's *Lost Illusions* (1837–43), making his way there for dinner, admired the "fashionable crowd, the lovely women with their admirers, men of fashion, walking in couples, arm in arm, greeting one another with glances as they passed . . . [like colorful] birds on this gilded perch."[23] Honoré Daumier, the keenly observant chronicler of urban life, could picture the average Frenchman, as well as himself, making the most of the park's pleasant amenities, perhaps its shady groves or the children's play areas, where toy balls inevitably strayed into nearby flower beds, much to the annoyance of the park's uniformed guards (figs. 37, 38).[24]

From the time of the Revolution and throughout the nineteenth century, the park served as the venue for festivals and celebrations, some held exclusively for the country's rulers, who continued to reserve areas for their personal use until the fiery destruction of the Tuileries Palace in 1871. However, the garden's primary function as the city's central playground and outdoor salon soon came to be firmly established in the lives of both the bourgeoisie,

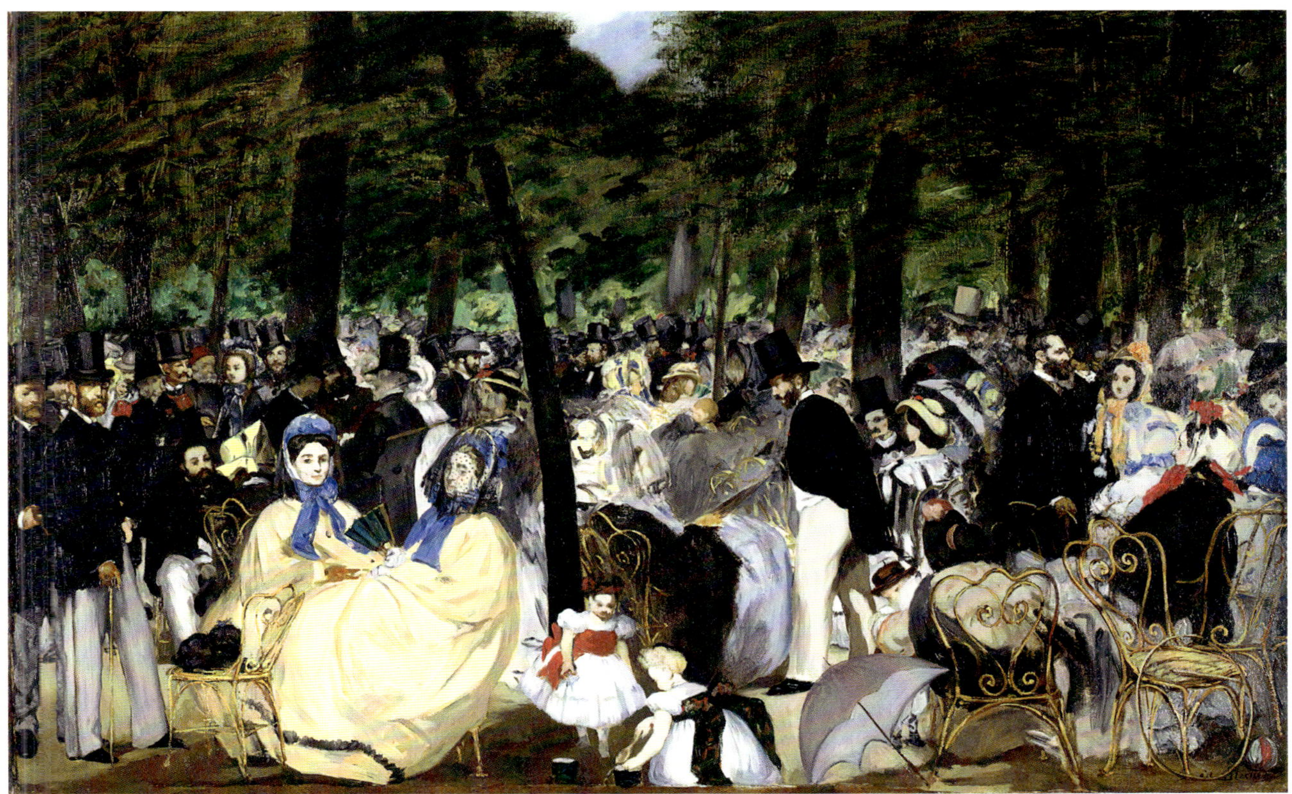

FIG. 39. Edouard Manet. *Music in the Tuileries Gardens*, 1862. Oil on canvas. National Gallery, London

who generally visited Monday through Saturday, and the working classes, whose day of leisure was Sunday.[25]

Picturing the Jardin des Tuileries in 1862, Edouard Manet recalled a crowd gathered there to enjoy an afternoon concert by a military band (fig. 39). The image startled the artist's contemporaries because it portrayed nothing of great import, although the throng of smartly dressed Parisians chatting and milling about included a number of personages, among them Charles Baudelaire, Jacques Offenbach, Théophile Gautier, and Manet himself.

At the height of the Impressionist period, the Tuileries was the chosen subject not only of Manet but also of Monet, Renoir, Degas, Tissot, Pissarro, and Vuillard, all of whom painted this favored open-air gathering spot from various vantage points, at different hours of the day, and in different seasons. In 1899 and 1900, during two campaigns to capture the modern landscape of Paris, Camille Pissarro took leave of the orchards and vegetable plots of his home in rural Eragny to rent rooms high above the rue de Rivoli, from which he could survey the city's boulevards and public gardens. In two series

FIG. 40. Camille Pissarro. *The Garden of the Tuileries on a Spring Morning*, 1899. Oil on canvas. The Metropolitan Museum of Art, New York

FIG. 41. Camille Pissarro. *The Garden of the Tuileries on a Winter Afternoon*, 1899. Oil on canvas. The Metropolitan Museum of Art, New York

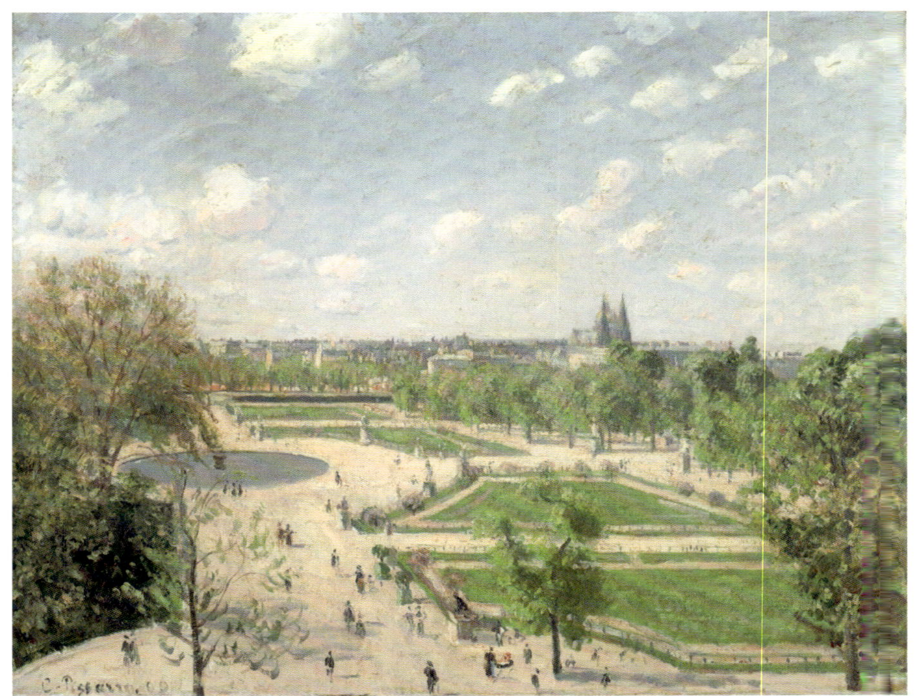

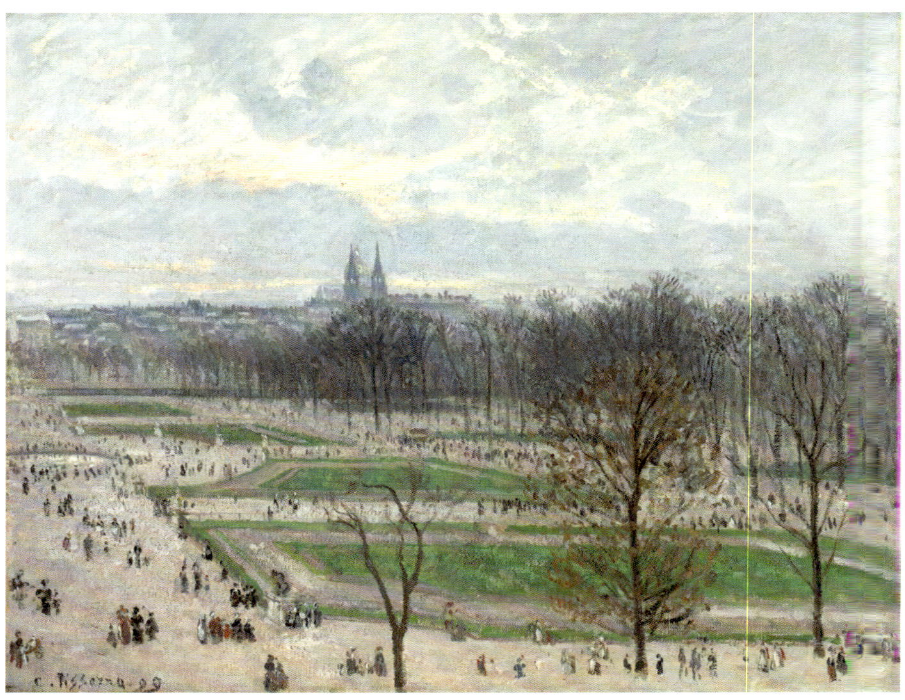

of fourteen paintings each Pissarro studied the eastern end of the Tuileries from an aerial perspective, observing seasonal changes of light and color in the grounds and in the fullness of the trees, their trunks trimmed to their crowns in the fashionable *marquise* style (figs. 40, 41). For Edouard Vuillard, who lived only two blocks from the gardens, on the rue Saint-Honoré, the geometry of the park's straight paths provided an organized field for the parade of families, children with their nannies, and scattering pigeons (fig. 42).

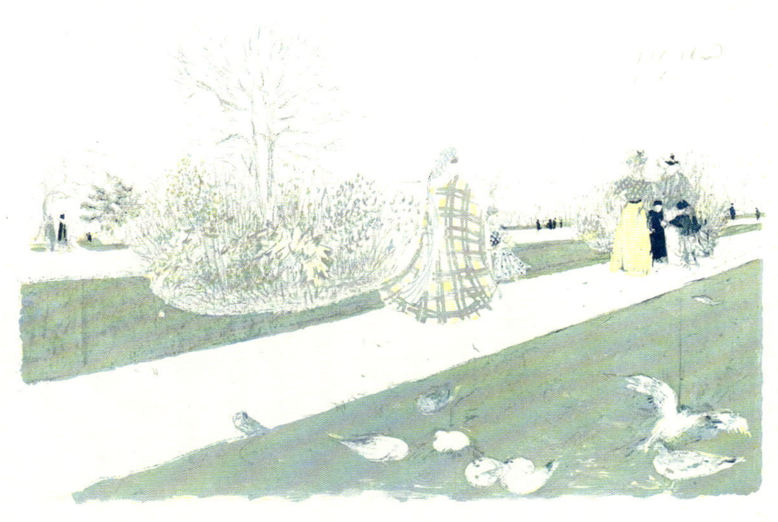

FIG. 42. Edouard Vuillard. *Jardin des Tuileries*, 1896. Color lithograph. The Metropolitan Museum of Art, New York

Somewhat smaller than the Tuileries, the gardens of the Luxembourg Palace across the Seine became national property in 1791. Designed about 1612 for Marie de' Medici, they evoked the Florentine gardens of the queen's childhood, answering a desire most perfectly satisfied in the watery grotto lined with plane trees and ivy garlands created by the Florentine fountain engineer Alessandro Francini. The garden's overall plan was centered on an octagonal basin, to which were later added elaborate flower beds in the French formal style and two raised terraces.

After years of neglect by later French monarchs, the Luxembourg Gardens were partially restored after the Revolution, when an outer portion was enlarged in the looser English style. Julien Alexandre Hardy, the chief gardener for over forty years, started breeding roses soon after his appointment in 1817 and by the 1850s had established an illustrious collection of more than 1,800 species.[26] Camellias, orchids, and fine tropical ferns later filled the conservatories, as did "the largest collection of vines ever accumulated," relocated at midcentury to the capacious hothouses of the renovated Bois de Boulogne.[27]

Parisians developed a special affection for the Luxembourg Gardens, a sentiment that found expression in Victor Hugo's *Les Misérables* (1862): "The Luxembourg . . . was delicious . . . flower-beds sent balm and dazzlement into the light. . . . All was grace and gayety . . . the grand silence of happy nature filled the garden. . . . The breeze formed undulations in the magnificent enormity of the chestnut trees. It was splendid."[28] To the mostly upper-class residents of the neighborhood and to members of the Senate then occupying the Luxembourg Palace, there was cause for alarm when Baron Haussmann in 1865 decided to appropriate large sections of the garden

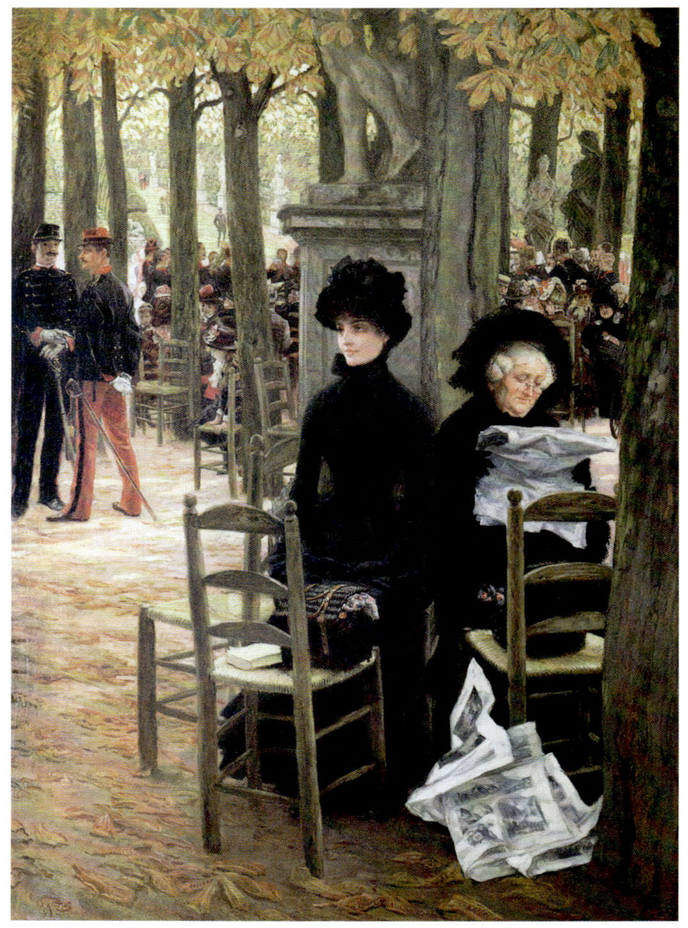

FIG. 43. James Tissot. *Sunday in the Luxembourg Gardens*, 1883–85. Oil on canvas. Private collection

for urban development. This was but one of the numerous objections that met Haussmann's sweeping projects. The sacrifice of the area known as the *pépinière*, a nursery created at the time of the Revolution, mobilized public protest and inspired Guy de Maupassant's short story "Menuet" (1882), dedicated to a "dear garden of bygone days, with its labyrinth of paths . . . and the graceful detours of its hornbeam hedges."[29] In 1848 Louis Philippe (r. 1830–48) added statues of French queens and female saints to the park's broad gravel terraces, popular meeting grounds on Sunday afternoons. There, James Tissot pictured Parisians assembled under a canopy of autumn chestnut leaves (fig. 43), and, decades later, the photographer Eugène Atget captured the stark beauty of bare trees in the cold light of winter on the all-but-abandoned terraces (fig. 44).

FIG. 44. Eugène Atget. *Jardin du Luxembourg*, 1902. Albumen silver print from glass negative. The Metropolitan Museum of Art, New York

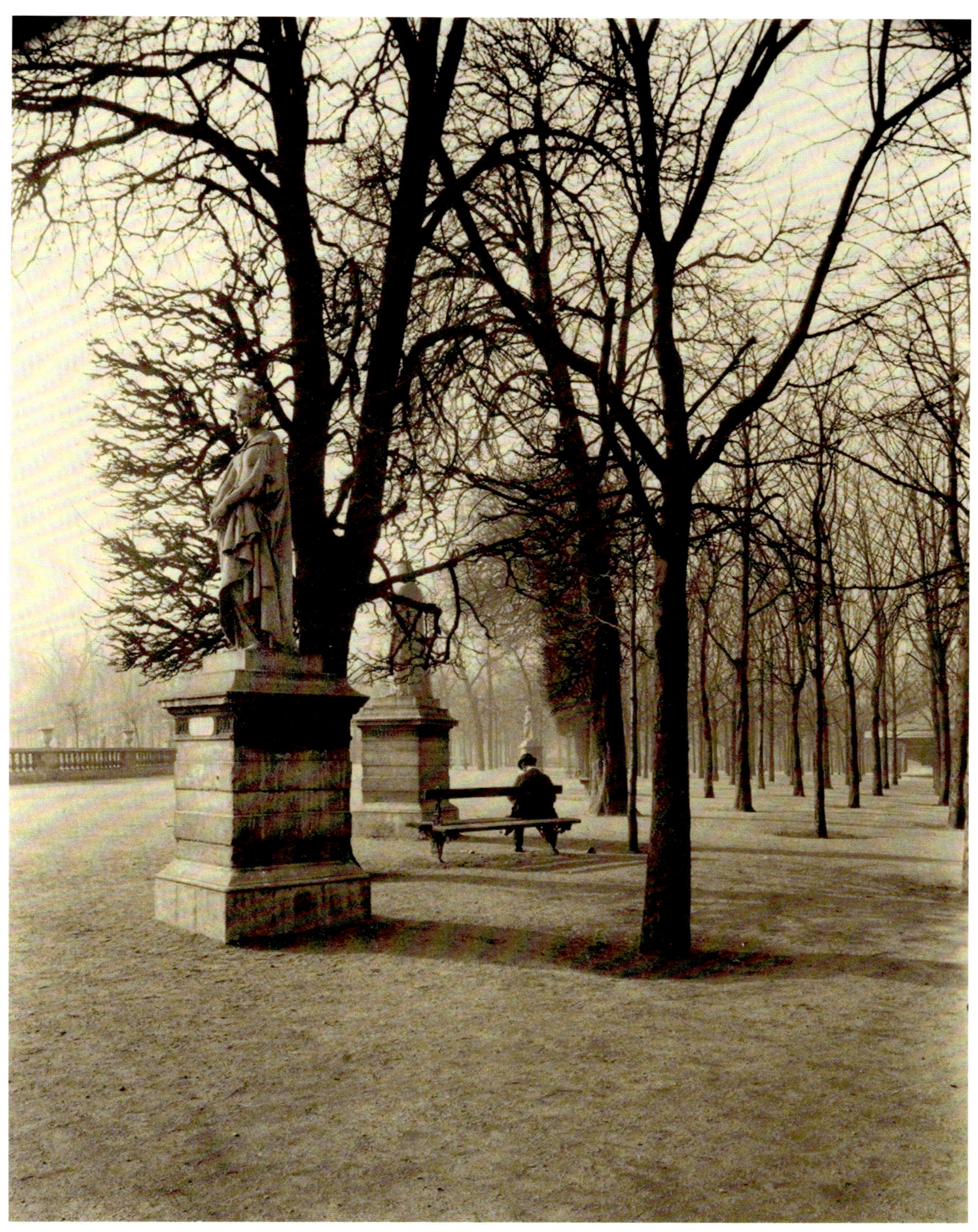

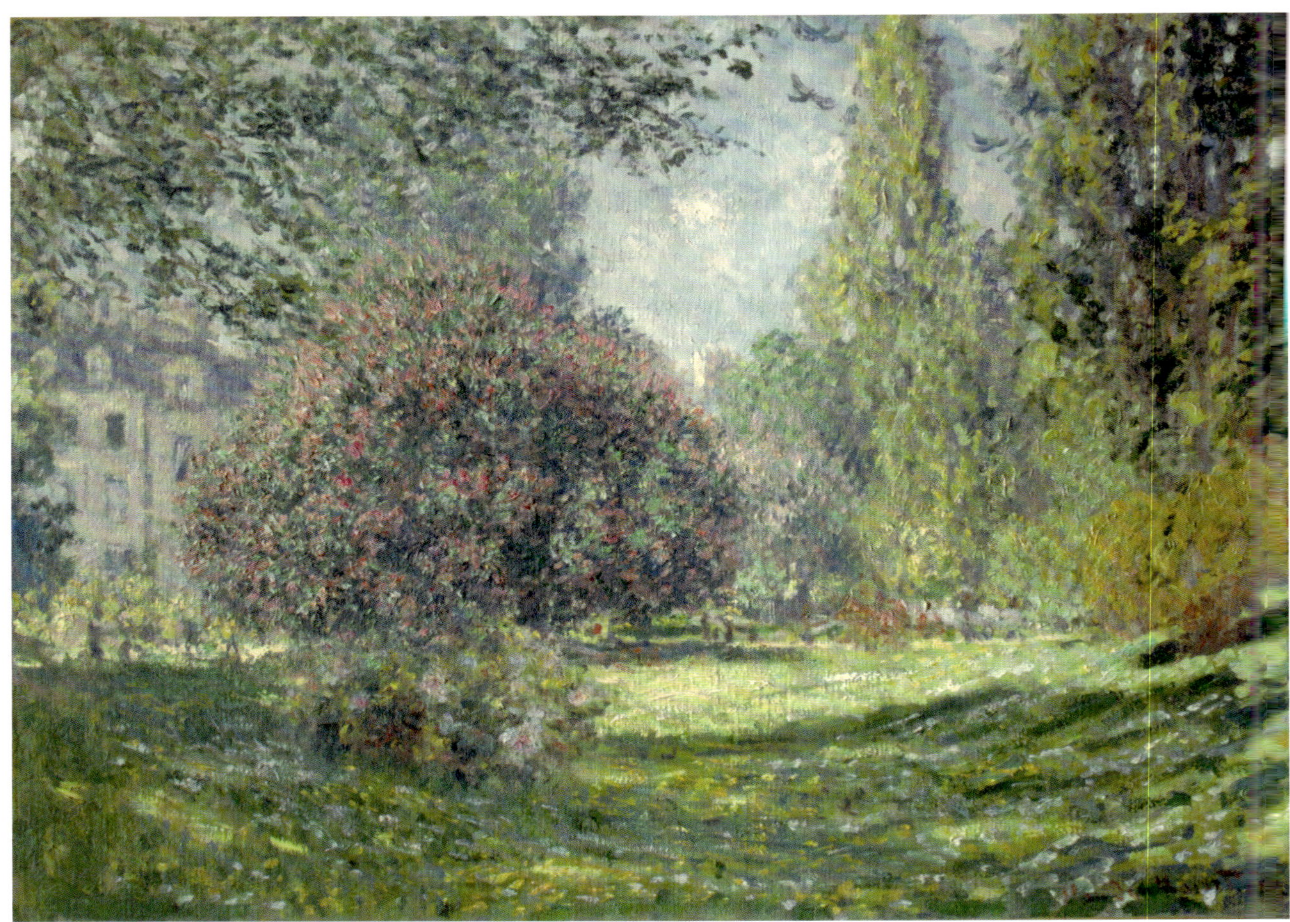

FIG. 45. Claude Monet. *Landscape: The Parc Monceau*, 1876. Oil on canvas. The Metropolitan Museum of Art, New York

FIG. 46. Claude Monet. *The Parc Monceau*, 1878. Oil on canvas. The Metropolitan Museum of Art, New York

Among the surviving gardens of old Paris the most intimate is the Parc Monceau, nestled amid the fashionable town houses at the northern edge of the city. One of the earliest and most influential gardens in France to be designed in the "irregular" English style, it was constructed in the 1770s as the private playground of the duc de Chartres (see p. 10). The site of public festivals during the Revolution, it gained renewed splendor about 1803–6 with improvements designed by the architect Pierre-Nicolas Bénard. The park was then opened to the public two or three days a week by ticketed admission.

During the reconstruction of Paris that took place under Napoleon III, a considerable area of the Parc Monceau was sold off for expensive building lots and the gardens were extensively redesigned. Departing from the bedding system of low-growing flowering plants commonly used in parks throughout Europe, the landscape architect and civil engineer Jean-Charles

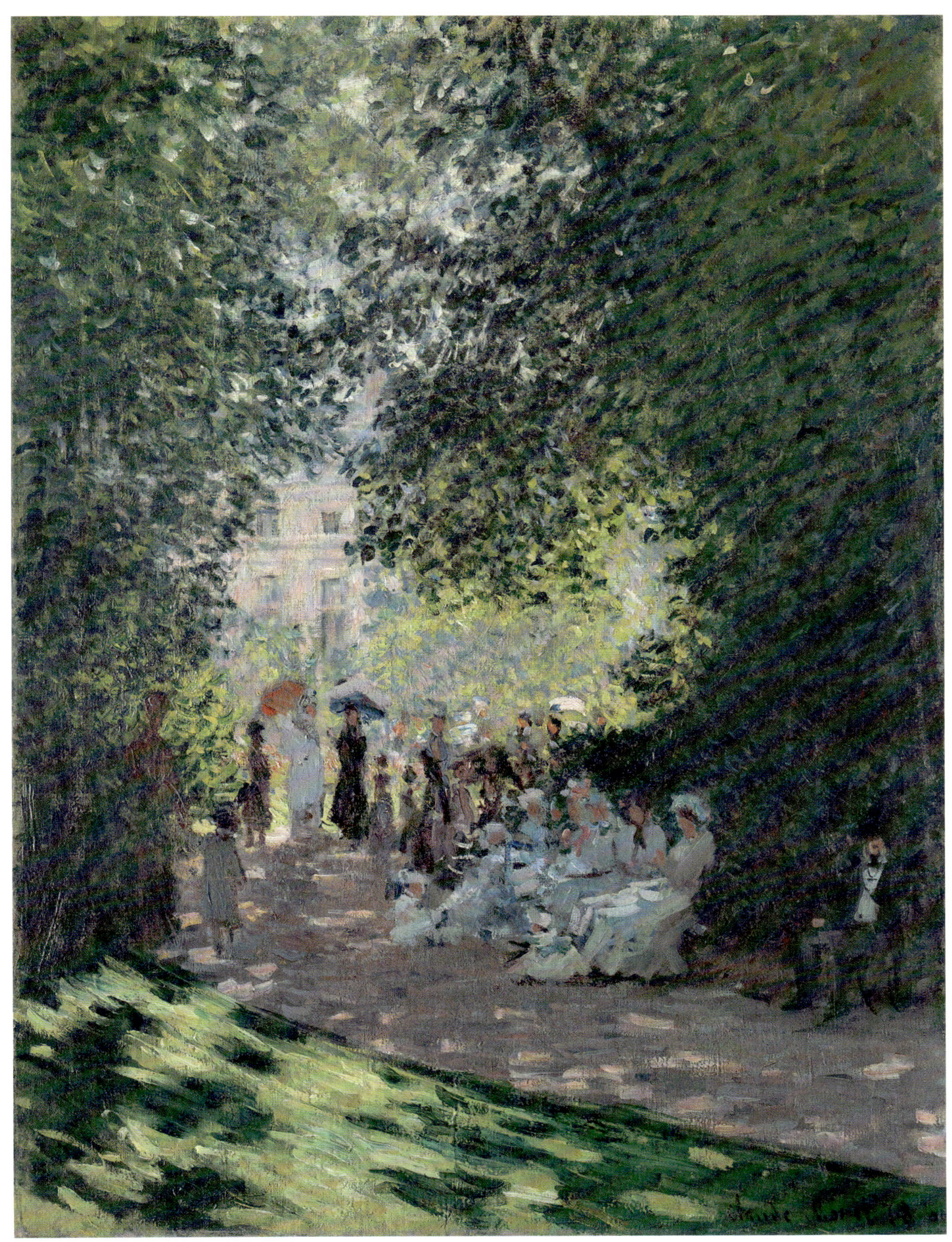

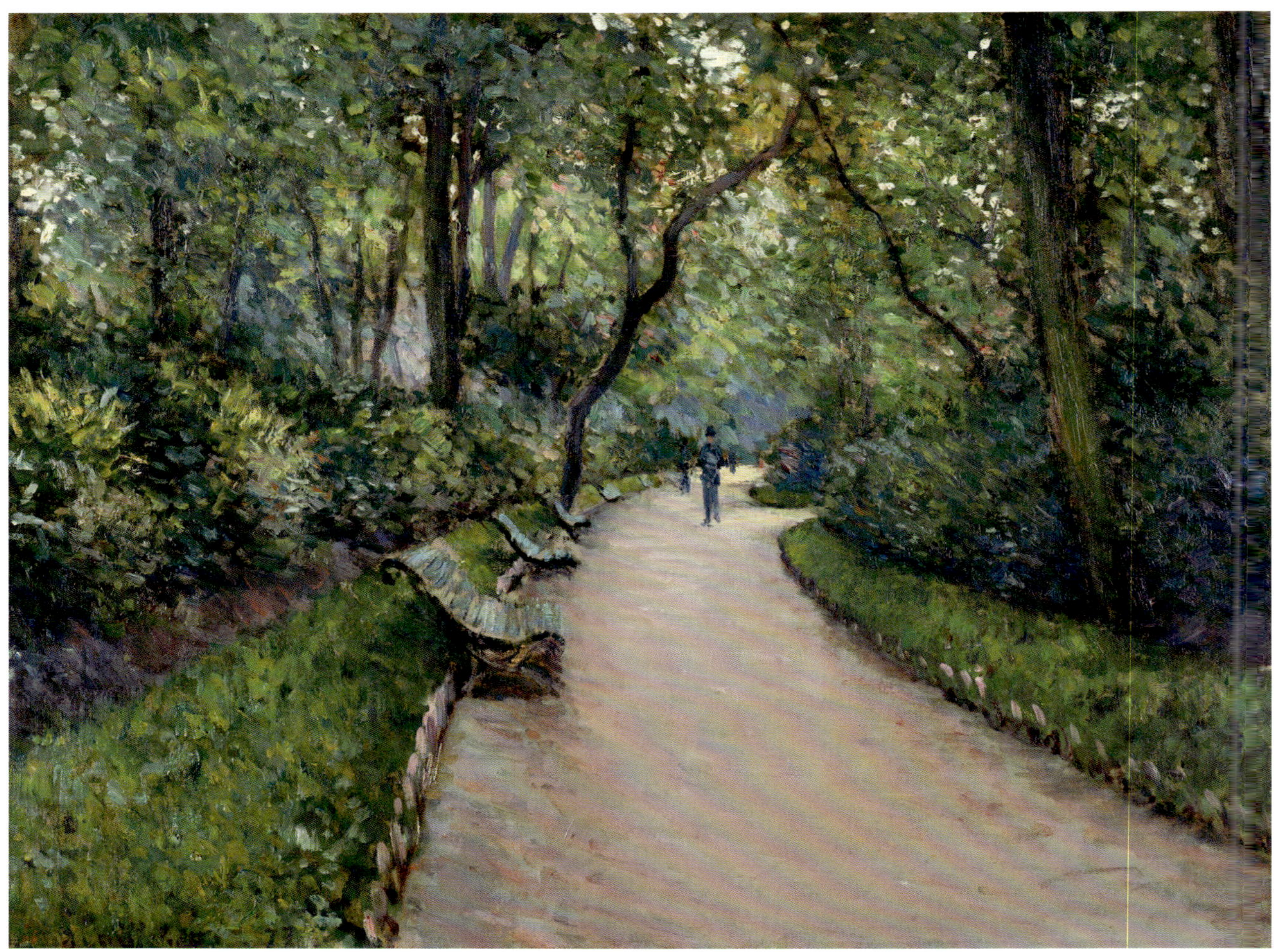

FIG. 47. Gustave Caillebotte. *The Parc Monceau*, 1877. Oil on canvas. Lawrence J. Ellison collection

Adolphe Alphand and the horticulturist and landscape architect Jean-Pierre Barillet-Deschamps introduced a variety of tropical and subtropical plants with large decorative leaves, such as tree ferns and bananas, yuccas, agaves, caladiums, and cannas, some of which were relocated to state-of-the-art municipal greenhouses during winter months.[30] After the remodeled park was inaugurated in 1861, visitors found, in a landscape transformed by tropical vegetation, relics of the follies installed by Carmontelle a century earlier.

In the decade following its modernization, Gustave Caillebotte and Monet set up their easels in the park. Both artists were avid gardeners and could well appreciate the novel renovations. Monet painted six views of the park, three in 1876 and three in 1878, when he lived only ten minutes away at 26, rue d'Edimbourg. His first Parc Monceau pictures, like the views he painted of London's Green Park (1870–71) and the Tuileries (1876), are horizontal in format (fig. 45). The second group features a somewhat unusual vertical format, possibly influenced by similarly composed landscapes in his collection of Japanese woodcut prints. In his upright landscapes Monet introduced the park's curving paths, where children and their nannies collected on sunny afternoons (fig. 46). Such gatherings may have resonated with the artist, then the father of two young boys, the second of whom was born in early spring 1878. In his painting, however, he skimmed lightly over the figures of park-goers, blending them in with enveloping vegetation, filling the canvases with little patches of color that approximated the texture of foliage and the flicker of light.

Caillebotte, who also lived in the neighborhood, painted two versions of the Parc Monceau in 1877 and 1878, one in spring and one in summer. In both instances he inserted a path to beckon viewers into the picture and a bench that invited them to linger, classic devices used by landscape artists. In Caillebotte's idealized view, the normally busy park, laden with summer foliage, is quietly reserved for the virtual visitor (fig. 47).

The Parks of Modern Paris and Beyond

During the Second Empire, as Napoleon III aspired to make the French capital the world's most beautiful city, much of Paris was planted with fresh greenery. Old gardens were renovated and new ones developed; neighborhood squares multiplied, and streets were lined with thousands of trees. To some the greening of Paris seemed long overdue. One contributor to the 1831 inaugural issue of the *Journal de l'Académie d'Horticulture* expressed dismay that the French "capital of the entire world" was "less well endowed with horticulture than even the small towns of England and Germany."[31]

A thorough renovation of urban Paris began in 1852 when Louis-Napoléon declared as a priority the revival of his uncle Napoleon Bonaparte's ambitious plans to modernize the city. Almost immediately he hired Georges-Eugène Haussmann (known as Baron Haussmann) to oversee an immense construction project with the objective of laying down a citywide network of boulevards and bringing essential services of sanitation and water supply to the ever-enlarging population; having increased from half a million in 1801 to more than two million in 1860, the citizenry of Paris would reach four million by the end of the century.[32] Recalling the splendid parks of Victorian London that he had enjoyed while in exile, Napoleon III took special interest in the creation and renovation of landscaped sites. Baron Haussmann thus dedicated himself to establishing "those verdant spaces that dispense health . . . [and] offer workers and their families places for rest and pleasure." Accordingly, he oversaw the triumphant openings of the Bois de Boulogne and the Bois de Vincennes at opposite ends of the city; the three interior parks of Montsouris, Buttes Chaumont, and the recast Parc Monceau; plus twenty-four floral urban squares and miles of wide avenues bordered by shade trees, generous walkways, and benches to offer respite to strollers and sightseers (fig. 48).[33]

A much earlier scheme known as the Artists' Plan (Plan des Artistes) very nearly came to be realized during the sweeping midcentury reconfiguration of Paris.[34] In 1793, at the time of the Revolution, a commission of artists had been set up to advise the government on the use of confiscated properties, including nearly an eighth of the land within Paris. The commission, which met regularly until its dissolution in 1797, succeeded in drawing up a comprehensive urban plan attractive to Napoleon I, who envisioned an elegant city of broad boulevards leading to grand monuments.[35] The Artists' Plan predicted improvements later made during the July Monarchy of Louis Philippe, whose prefect, the comte de Rambuteau, oversaw the redesign of the Place de la Concorde by the architect Jacques-Ignace Hittorff between 1836 and 1846, as well as the introduction of sidewalks, gas lamps, street trees, and small public gardens, like those planted around Nôtre-Dame Cathedral.[36]

The renovations of the Second Empire took place over a period of twenty years, beginning in 1853 with Napoleon III's appointment of Baron Haussmann. Establishing new municipal departments for water, roads, and architecture, the emperor also designated designer-engineer Jean-Charles Adolphe Alphand director of the Service des Promenades et Plantations, responsible for building and maintaining parks. Collaborating with the architect Gabriel Davioud and the lead horticulturist Jean-Pierre Barillet-Deschamps, Alphand oversaw a nearly hundredfold increase in property devoted to municipal parks in Paris, from 47 acres to 4,500. His commanding report on the achievement, *Les Promenades de Paris* (1867–73), described the theories and principles that guided the park projects, bringing together both French and English landscape sensibilities. The copiously illustrated two-volume publication covered all aspects of the urban parks' design, their engineering and construction, along with the cultivation and installation of more than 2,300 varieties of herbaceous plants (see figs. 50, 52). The extraordinary diversity of botanical material presented in the new public gardens was owed primarily to the horticultural enthusiasm of Barillet-Deschamps who sought to educate the public about plants from around the world. This

FIG. 48. Gustave Caillebotte. *The Boulevard Seen from Above*, 1880. Oil on canvas. Private collection

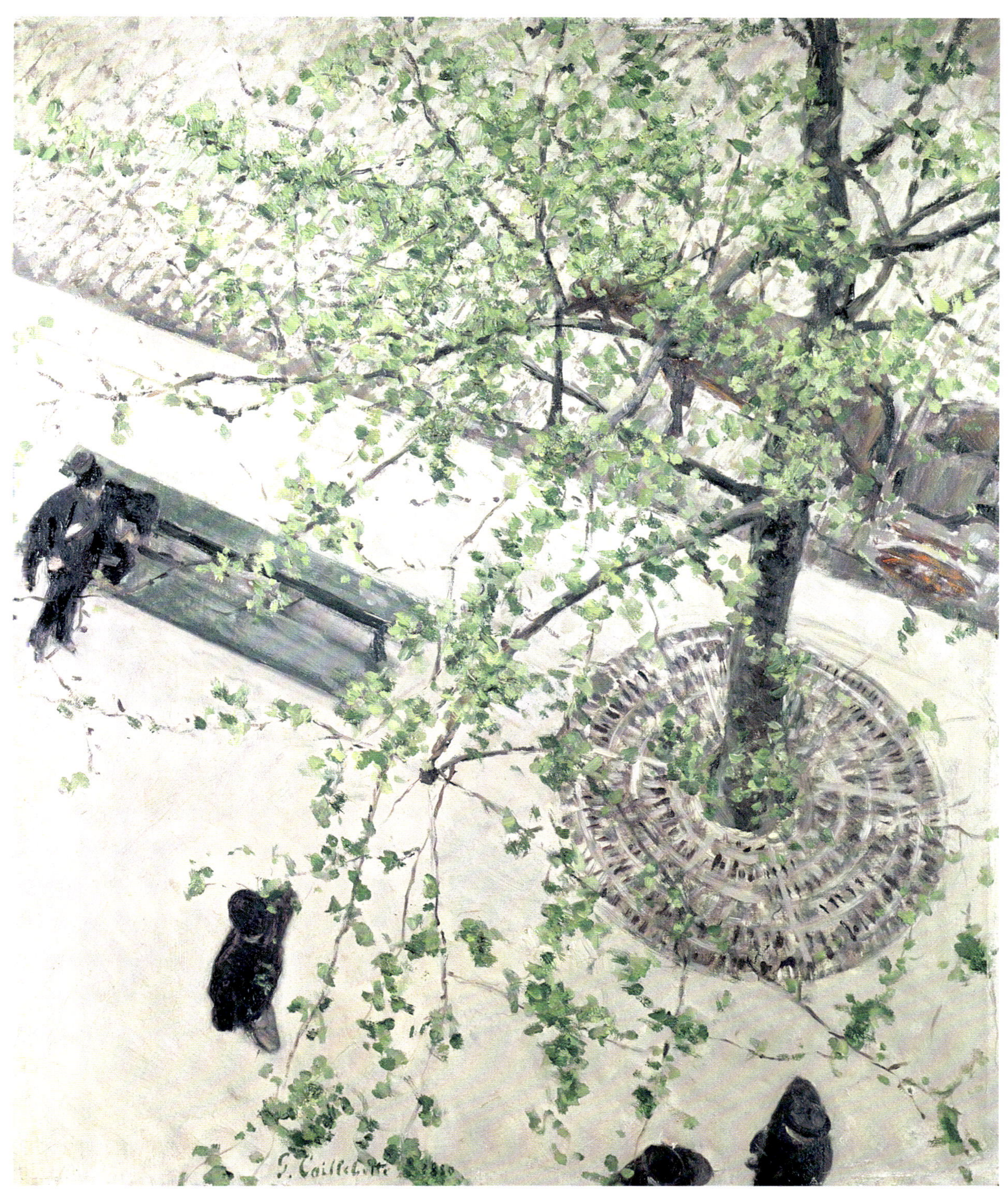

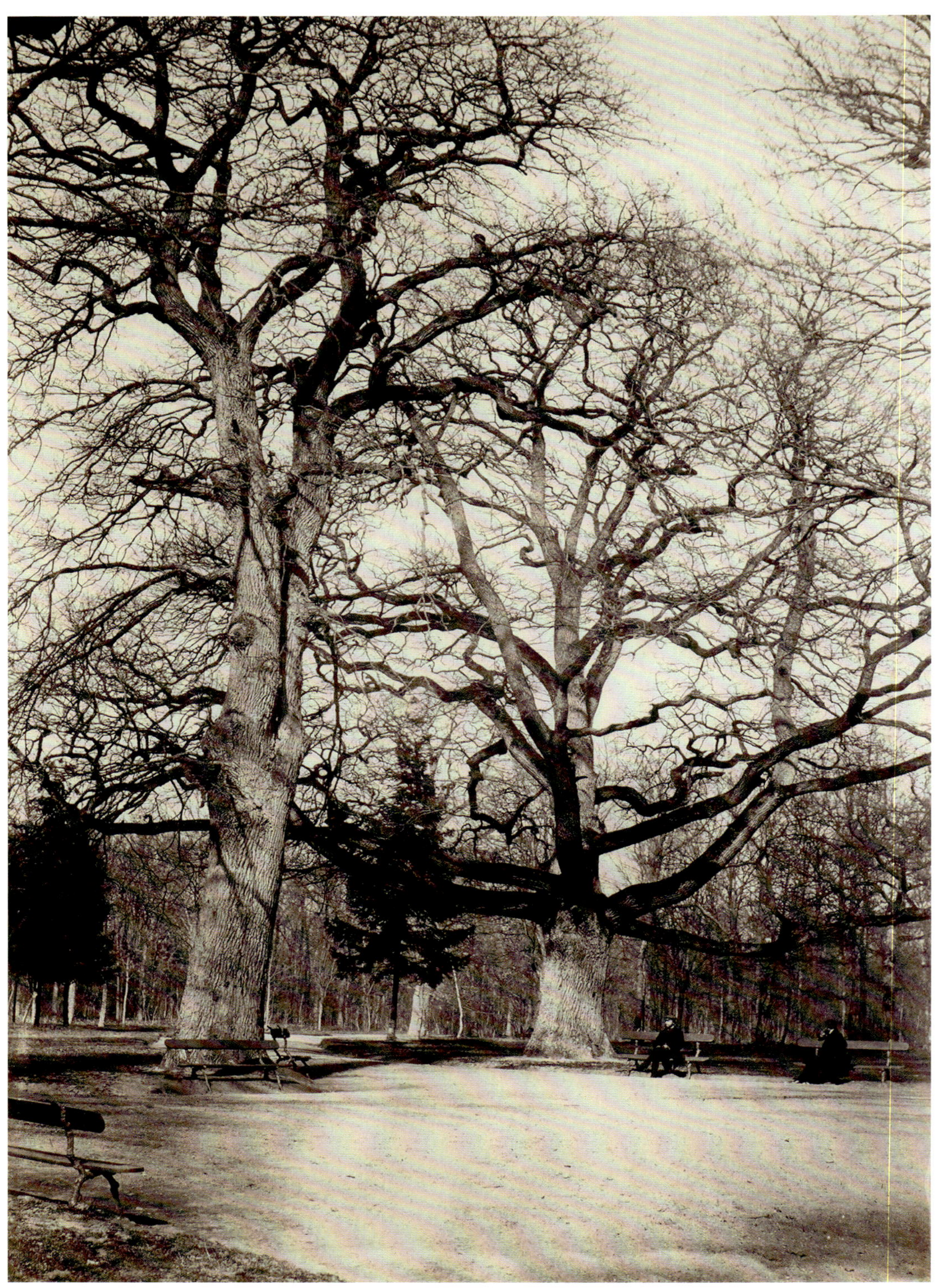

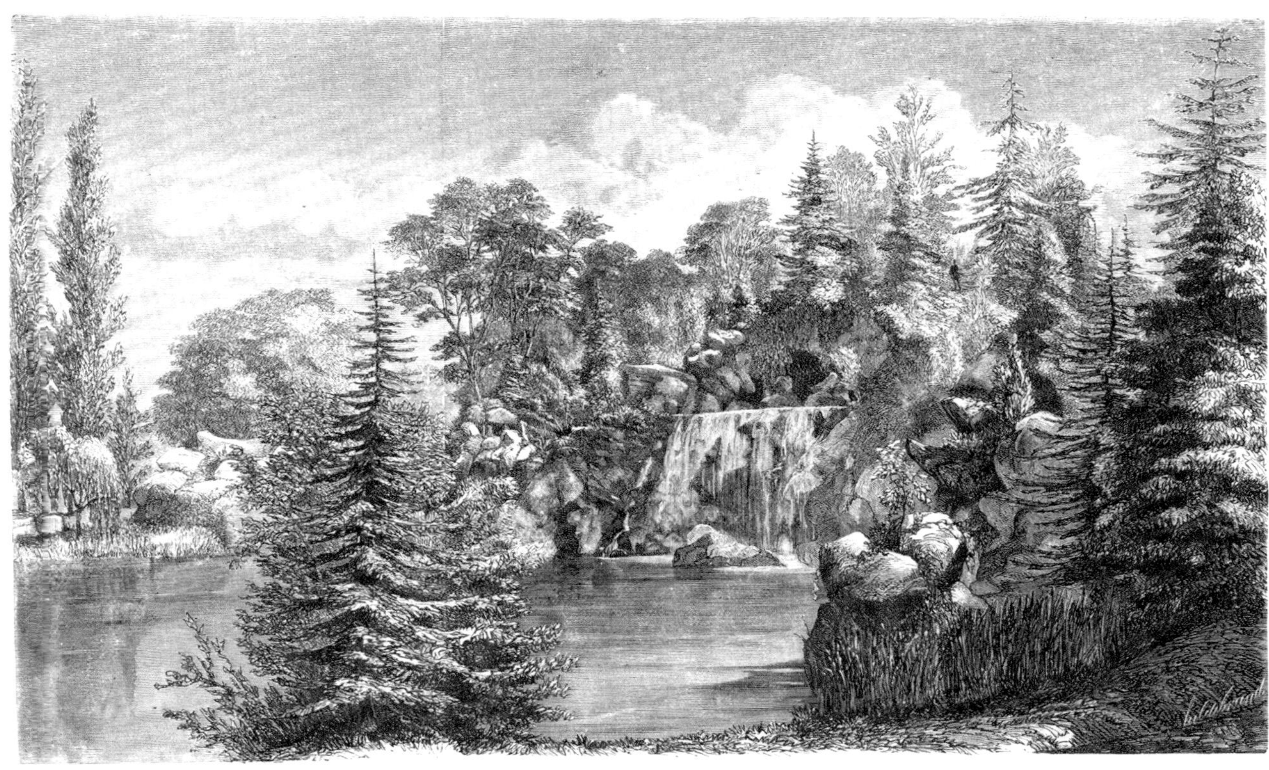

trees, shrubs, and brightly colored flowers were introduced that previously had been little known in France, among them fuschias, begonias, hibiscus, phlox, and zonal pelargoniums (now commonly called geraniums).

With a keen interest in landscape design and a desire to bring to the French the beneficial effects he perceived in large English gardens, Napoleon III focused first on the Bois de Boulogne, 2,000 acres of former royal hunting grounds at the western edge of Paris, much of it then virtual wasteland, which the emperor imagined transformed into a grand public park. The photographer Charles Marville set up a temporary studio in the Bois to photograph the renovation project while paying homage to the greatest of its old trees (fig. 49). The landscaping effort required a great deal of digging and soil shifting, the replacement of the old straight allées with new winding roads, and the insertion of elements alluding to country life: fields and trees, sculpted slopes, lakes, cliffs, grottoes, and a picturesque waterfall, the Grande Cascade, constructed of rocks transported from the Forest of Fontainebleau (fig. 50). Barillet-Deschamps planted undulating lawns dotted with flower

FIG. 50. Emile Hochereau. "The Grande Cascade, Bois de Boulogne," from [Jean-Charles] Adolphe Alphand, *Les Promenades de Paris* (Paris, 1867–73). Engraving. The Metropolitan Museum of Art, New York

FIG. 49. Charles Marville. *Bois de Boulogne*, ca. 1858–59. Albumen print. Private collection

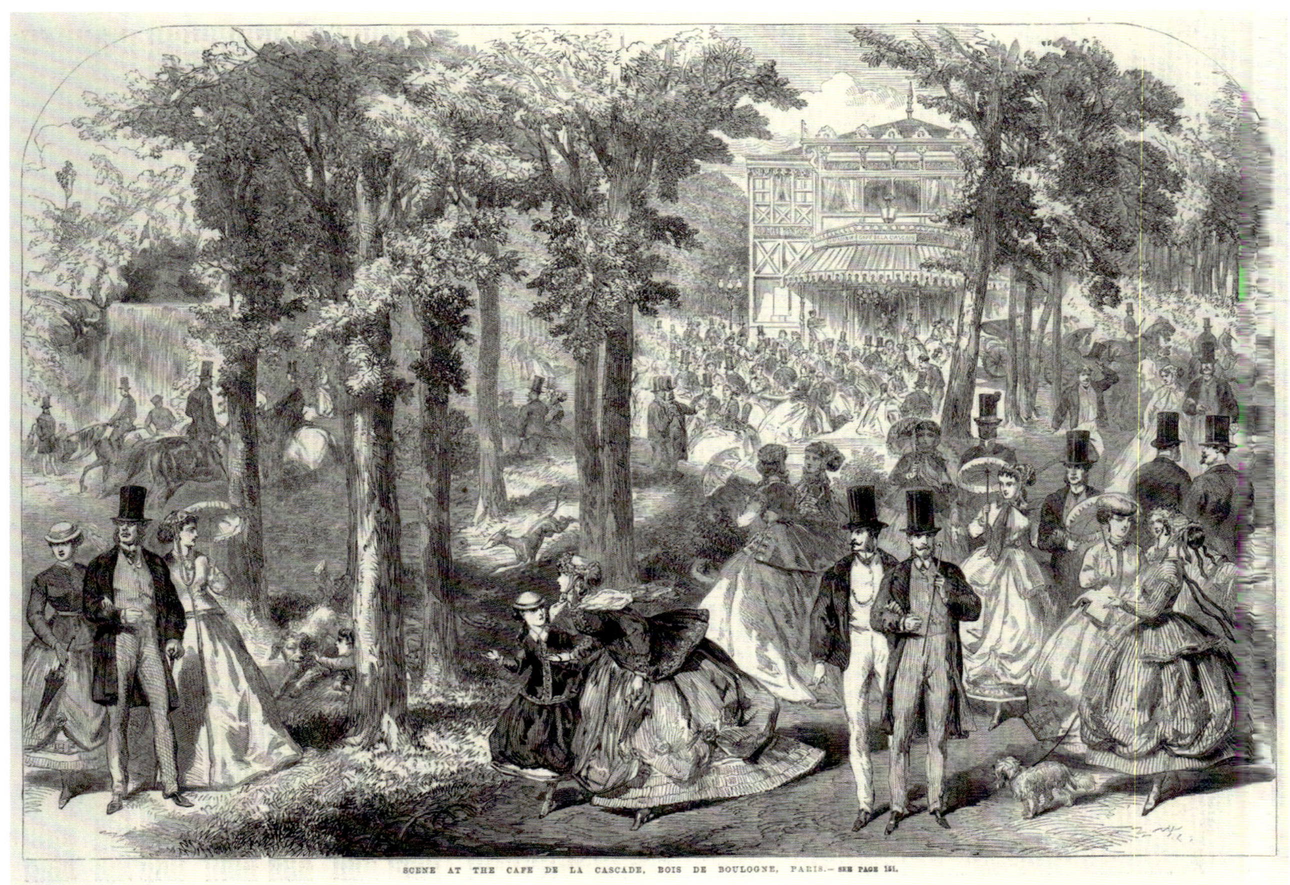

FIG. 51. "Café de la Cascade, Bois de Boulogne," from *The Illustrated London News,* August 1866. Engraving. Private collection

beds and more than forty thousand new trees, while Davioud designed cafés and kiosks, benches, and decorative ironwork that stimulated homeowners' demands for similarly ornamental garden accessories (figs. 51–53). One of the most delightful features of the new Bois de Boulogne was the Théâtre des Fleurs, an outdoor amphitheater with garden chairs for close to two thousand spectators encircled by lavish displays of flowers and evergreen shrubs. Popular with families was the Jardin d'Acclimation, a children's park with rides and a zoo. Wealthy Parisians favored afternoon carriage rides around the park lakes, a fashionable routine observed as the *tour des lacs.*

In the somewhat later and even larger project for the Bois de Vincennes (fig. 54), a plan similar to that of the Bois de Boulogne, but less contrived, was applied to the old forests: embellishments included hunting and parade grounds, a lake for boating, cascading waterfalls, and racetracks for the English sport that had only recently been introduced to France. The maréchal

FIG. 52. "Decorative Ironwork" (detail), from [Jean-Charles] Adolphe Alphand, *Les Promenades de Paris* (Paris, 1867–73). Engraving. The Metropolitan Museum of Art, New York

FIG. 53. "Garden Benches," in *Font de Fer, A. Durenne, Maître de forges* (Paris, 1877). Lithograph. The Metropolitan Museum of Art, New York

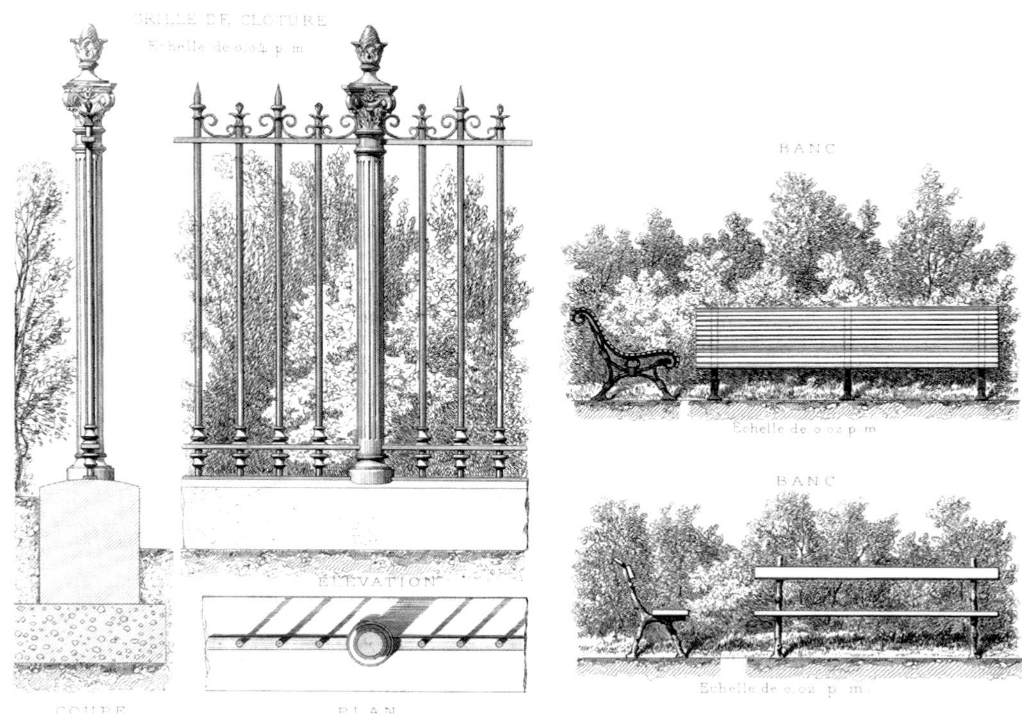

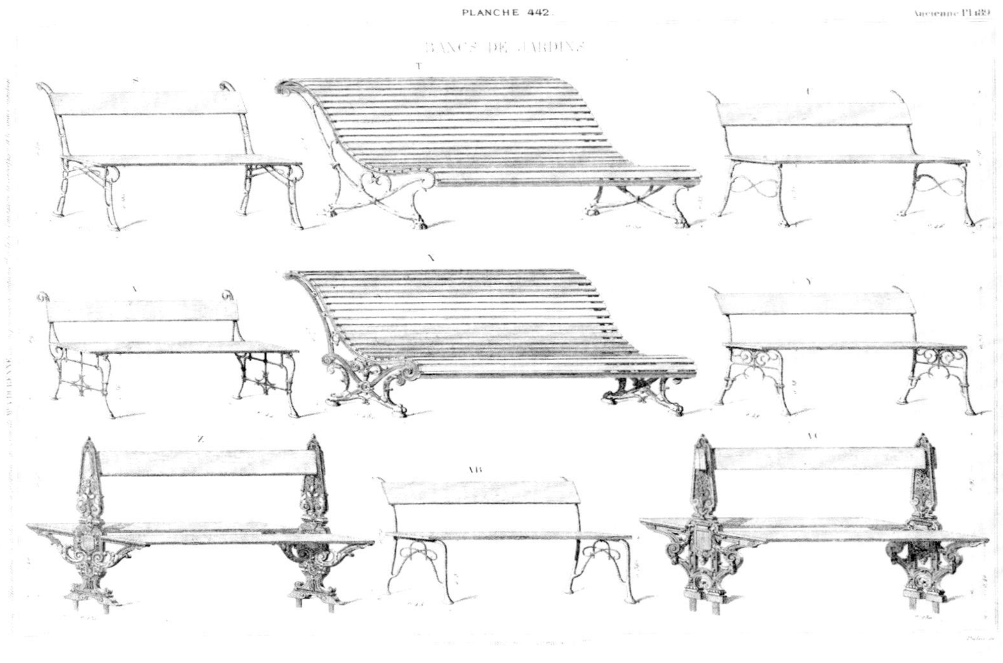

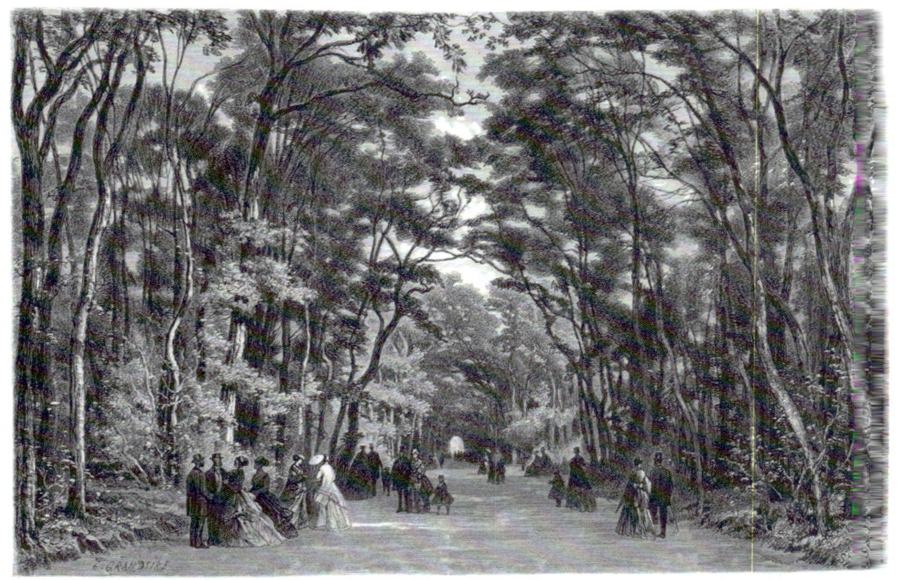

FIG. 54. Pierre Eugène Grandsire. "Route des Buttes, Bois de Vincennes," from [Jean-Charles] Adolphe Alphand, *Les Promenades de Paris* (Paris, 1867–73). Wood engraving. The Metropolitan Museum of Art, New York

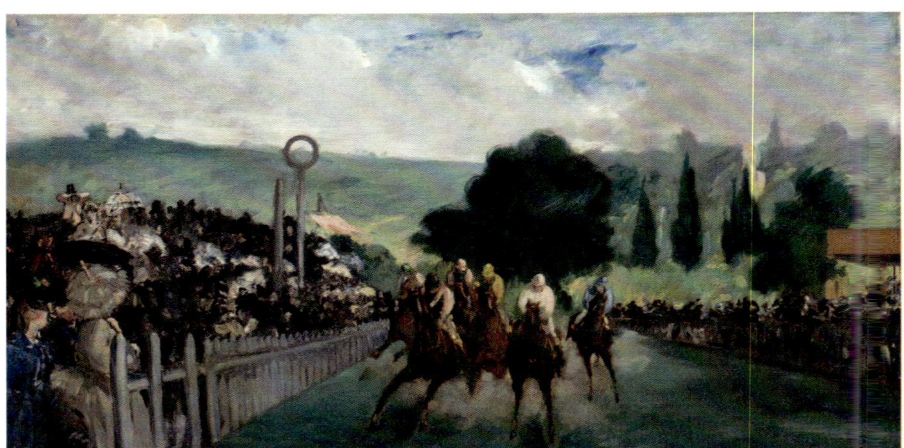

FIG. 55. Edouard Manet. *The Races at Longchamp*, 1866. Oil on canvas. Art Institute of Chicago

de Castellane in 1854 noted in his diary that twelve hundred workers were engaged in the construction work.[37] Upon its completion, large teams of maintainers were hired to tend the vast park, finding among their greatest challenges the restoration of forested areas destroyed during the Prussian army's siege of Paris in 1870, when acres of trees were cut down for firewood.

Horse-drawn carriages and horseback riders, as well as throngs of horse-racing enthusiasts, found the Bois de Boulogne a stylish spot for outings, and it quickly drew the attention of painters of contemporary life. Manet and

Degas derived particular inspiration from visits to the Longchamp track and its grassy paddocks (fig. 55), while Sisley and later Van Gogh painted strollers on the Bois's shaded paths, and Berthe Morisot pictured family excursions. Renoir portrayed equestrians riding through the trees and skaters crowding the frozen lake, where the emperor was often among the first to try the ice.[38]

Near the end of the century, for the mansion of Alexandre Natanson, a director of the prestigious art and literary journal *La Revue Blanche*, Vuillard made a decorative suite of nine near life-sized panels that recalled afternoons the Natanson children spent with their nursemaids in Paris parks (fig. 56). Designed to line the walls of the family's dining room, the paintings captured incidents played out in the spacious grounds of the Bois near their home at 60, rue du Bois de Boulogne and in the shady groves of chestnuts in the park of the Tuileries, located in Vuillard's own neighborhood.

FIG. 56. Edouard Vuillard. *Public Gardens: Conversation, Nannies, and Red Parasol*, 1894. Distemper on canvas. Musée d'Orsay, Paris

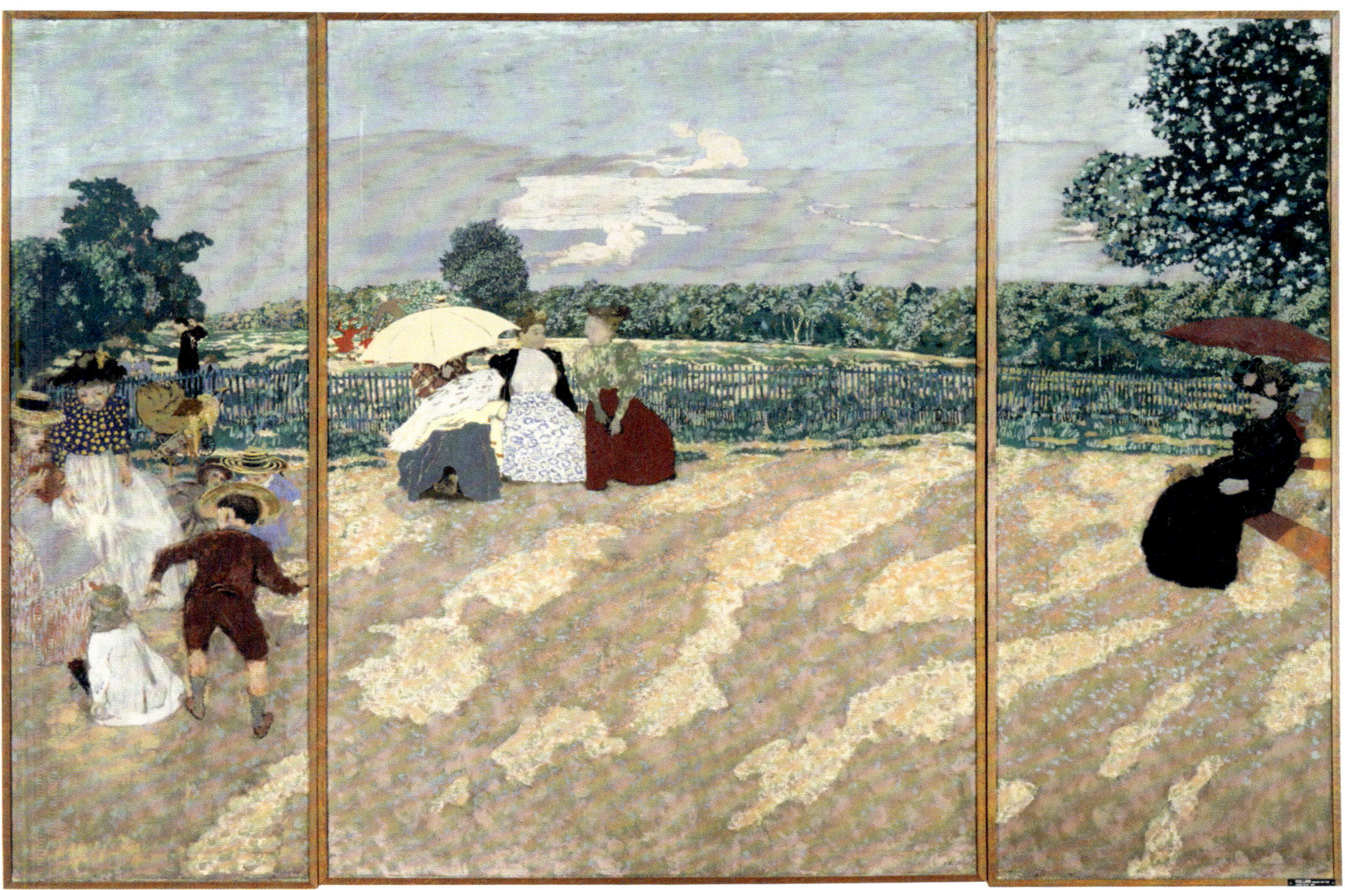

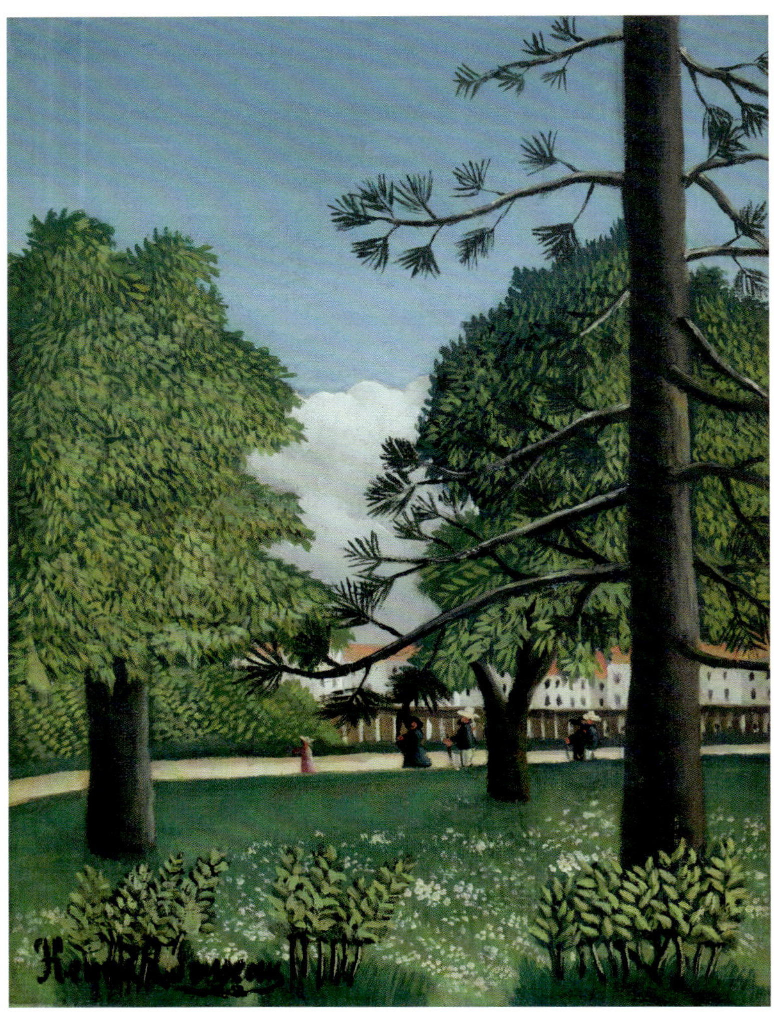

FIG. 57. Henri Rousseau (le Douanier). *Parc Montsouris*, ca. 1895. Oil on canvas. Nahmad Collection, Switzerland

Having built splendid playgrounds for the well-to-do, Napoleon III and Haussmann realized that it would be politically expedient to also provide parks for the working classes. And so, as the Bois de Boulogne in the west had as its counterpart the Bois de Vincennes in the east, the Parc des Buttes Chaumont was built in the north, with a southern equivalent in the Parc Montsouris. Among the most degraded and polluted properties in Paris, the two chosen sites had functioned earlier as stone quarries, and their renovation required complex efforts in excavation and engineering. Nonetheless, in just three years both were transformed into idealized natural landscapes incorporating the signature features of parks created by the team of Haussmann, Alphand, Barillet-Deschamps, and Davioud.[39]

The Parc Montsouris was built on land owned in large part by two railway companies whose functioning tracks had to be accommodated both above ground and below, in tunnels. Still under construction when the Post-Impressionist painter Henri Rousseau moved to Paris in 1868, the park became a favorite haunt after he took up residence in a neighborhood not far away. He admired its fine collection of exotic trees and shrubs (fig. 57), just as he marveled at the tropical greenery in the Jardin des Plantes, which grew larger than life in his surreal paintings of imagined jungles: "When I go to the glass houses [of the botanical garden] and I see the strange plants of exotic lands . . . it seems to me that I enter a dream."[40]

On the other side of the city the Buttes Chaumont, with its lofty cliff-bound island in an artificial lake (fig. 58) and inventive mixed plantings by the young landscape architect and horticulturist Edouard André, was inaugurated on April 1, 1867, the very day the Exposition Universelle d'Art et d'Industrie threw open its doors on the Champs-de-Mars. To the hundreds of thousands of visitors who came to Paris for this world's fair, Napoleon III proudly displayed a modern capital graced with tree-lined promenades and lavishly appointed parks. The occasion was marked by Manet, who painted

FIG. 58. "Le Parc des Buttes Chaumont," from *L'Univers Illustré*, ca. 1867. Engraving. Private collection

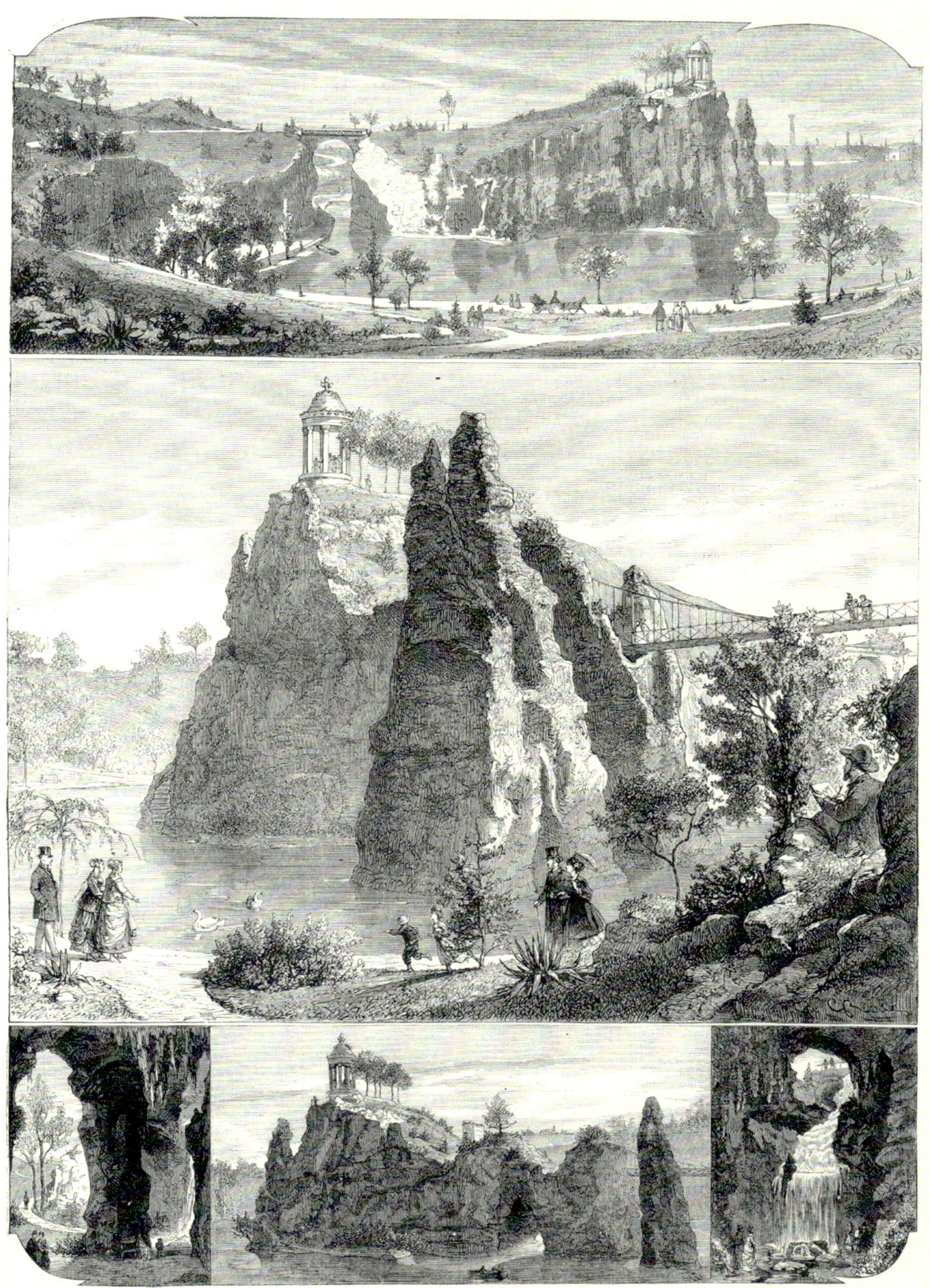

NOUVEAU PARIS. — LE PARC DES BUTTES CHAUMONT. — LE LAC, LE ROCHER CENTRAL ET LE TEMPLE DE LA SIBYLLE, LE PONT SUSPENDU, LA GROTTE AUX STALACTITES, LA CASCADE; dessin de M. G. Roux. — Voir page 374.

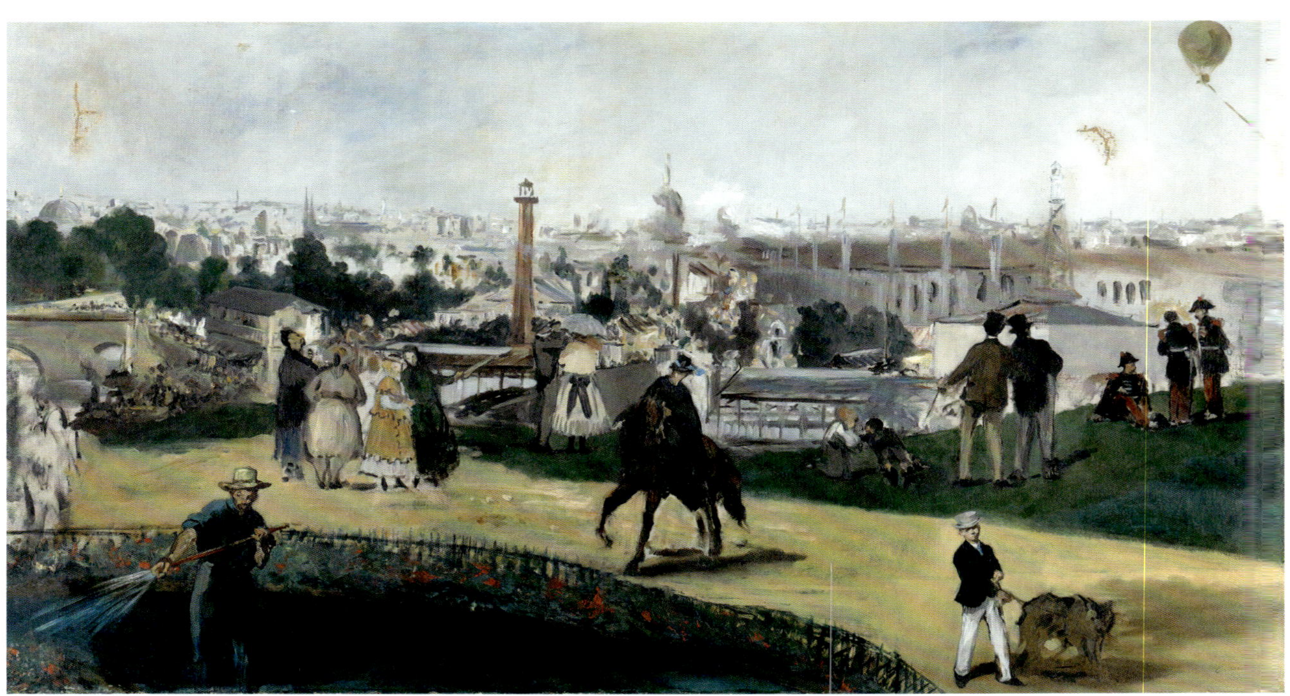

FIG. 59. Edouard Manet. *View of the 1867 Exposition Universelle*, 1867. Oil on canvas. Nasjonalgalleriet, Oslo

the exposition's main pavilion from high atop the Trocadéro, just across the Seine, where one of the city's newly planted parks could be seen receiving the attentions of a municipal maintainer armed with the latest in watering devices (fig. 59).

With a singular clarity of purpose, Napoleon III and Haussmann directed that the avenues leading to the city's public parks be built straight and wide, their axes joined at major intersections. In this way the long perspectives and roundabouts of Le Nôtre's old royal gardens, deemed too formal in design for new urban parks, were repurposed in the scheme of the city's new streets.

Among the principal boulevards and avenues of Paris the most important was the Champs-Elysées, the broad promenade laid out in 1667 by Le Nôtre as an extension of the Tuileries Gardens. The roadway named "Elysian Fields" that ran through former farmland and kitchen gardens had become a popular meeting ground by the late eighteenth century, where Parisians could find refreshment and entertainment (fig. 60).[41] Early in the nineteenth century Napoleon I envisioned the avenue as a triumphal route that would take him to a grand new palace; he commissioned the Arc de Triomphe to crown the top of the road after his victory at Austerlitz, although it remained unfinished until 1836. At that time, various plans were suggested for development of the

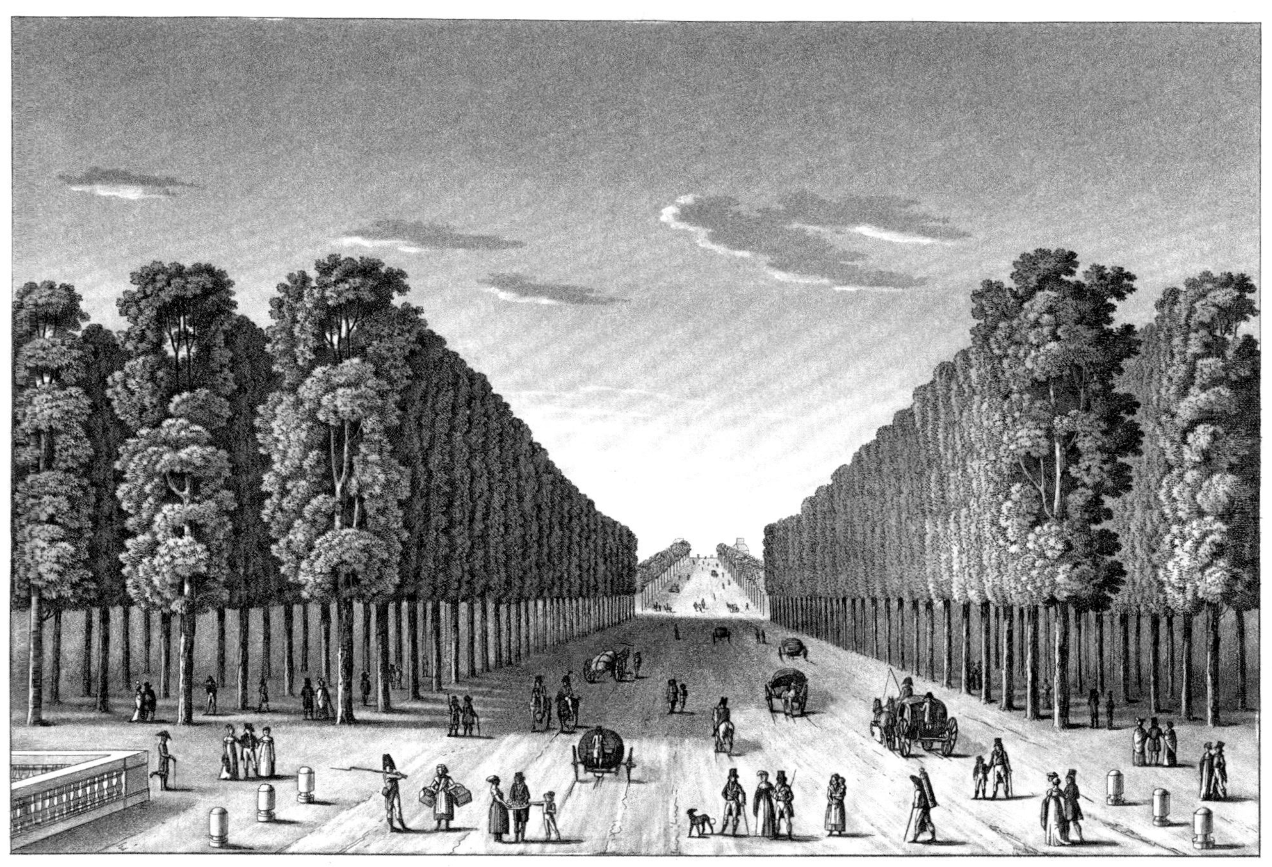

FIG. 60. *View of the Champs-Elysées in 1789*, ca. 1790. Etching and aquatint. The Metropolitan Museum of Art, New York

area, including those of the architect Jacques Ignace Hittorff, commissioned by King Louis Philippe to redesign the Place de la Concorde and gardens along the Champs-Elysées, to which were added restaurants, a large entertainment hall, several ornamental fountains, streetlights, and benches. Surveyed at midcentury in a twenty-foot-long folding panorama (fig. 61), the thoroughfare running two miles between the Tuileries Palace and the Arc de Triomphe is seen humming with traffic: carriages, horseback riders, people on foot, and dogs off the leash, the commanding route banked with tall, handsome trees. By the time Emperor Napoleon III selected the park at the base of the avenue as the site of the first Exposition Universelle in 1855, the borders of the Champs-Elysées had been made into inviting gardens embracing a variety of public entertainments.

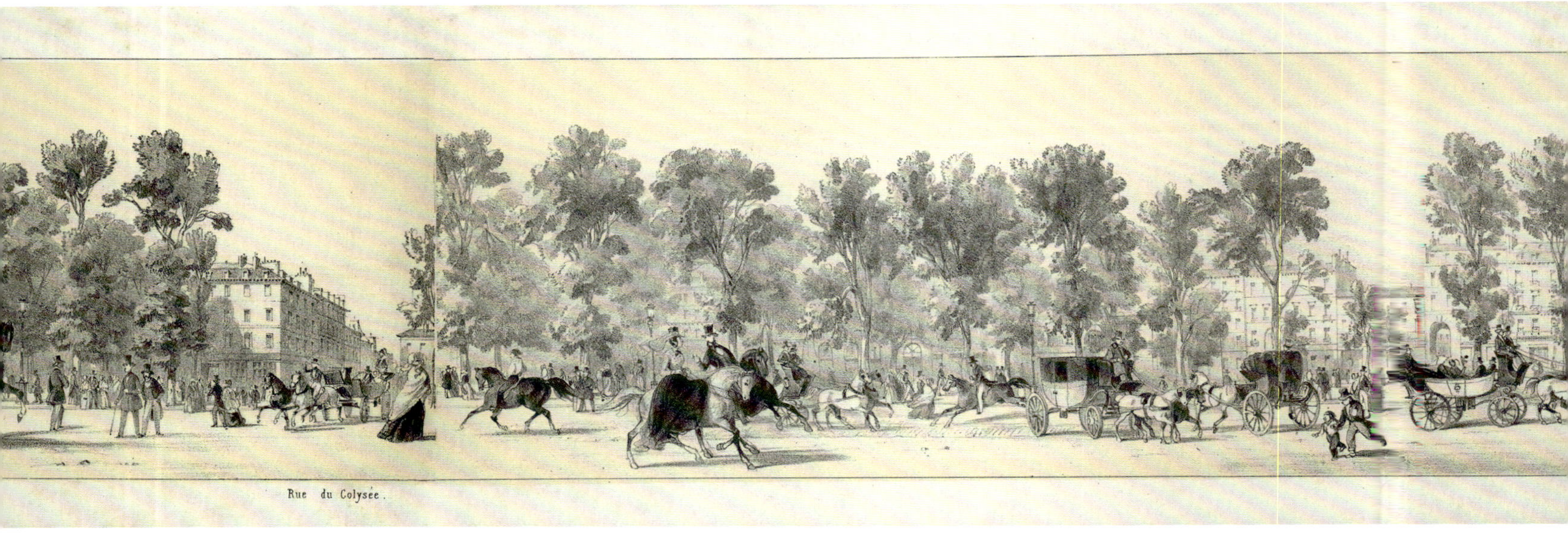

FIG. 61. A. Provost. *Panorama of the Champs-Elysées* (detail), ca. 1845–50. Lithograph. The Metropolitan Museum of Art, New York

The broad roadways called the Grand Boulevards of Paris first became known as such in 1536, when they began serving as bulwarks against invasions of the English. By 1700 they had become popular promenades, having been planted in 1660 with four rows of trees that divided the roadbed into a middle way for carriages and horses and two side paths reserved for pedestrians.[42] Under Haussmann's direction many more of the city's streets were made inviting for both walking and resting. The old elms on the Champs-Elysées were replaced with a lavish planting of Haussmann's favorite chestnut trees, and the elegant straightaway was linked to the most extravagant and impressive new thoroughfare in Paris, the Avenue de l'Impératrice, which had been ordered by the emperor to connect the traffic circle, L'Etoile, site of the Arc de Triomphe, to the reconstructed Bois de Boulogne. Often called the Avenue du Bois and today known as the Avenue Foch, the majestic roadway, 420 feet wide (three times the width of a normal boulevard), was generously embellished with trees, lawns, and beds of rare plants. Spacious and sunny, it was a fine place to stroll or to sit and watch the daily parade of horses and carriages making their way from the monumental stone arch to the entrance of the park (fig. 62).

Also among Haussmann's sweeping projects were major efforts to make the river Seine more accessible, adjoining green spaces inviting not only to Parisians but to foreign visitors as well. On visits to Paris in 1891–94 and

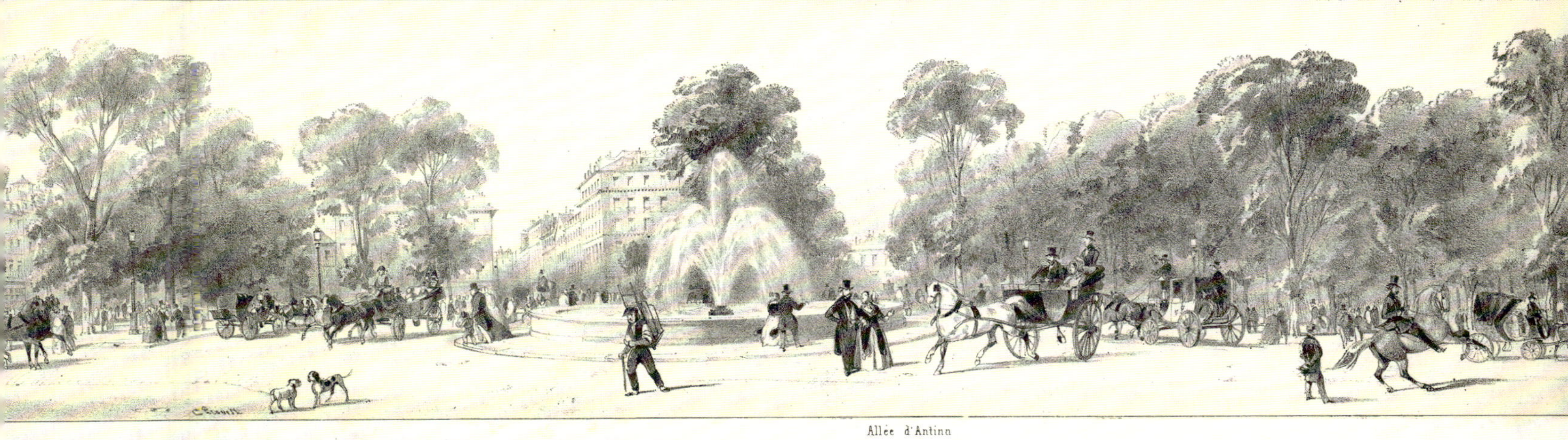

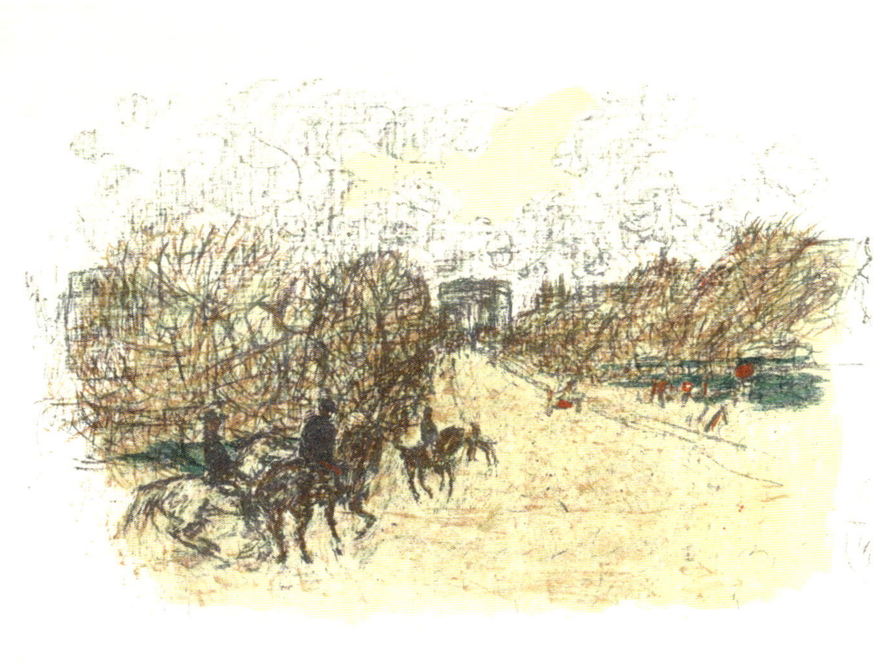

FIG. 62. Pierre Bonnard. *Arc de Triomphe*, ca. 1898. Color lithograph. The Metropolitan Museum of Art, New York

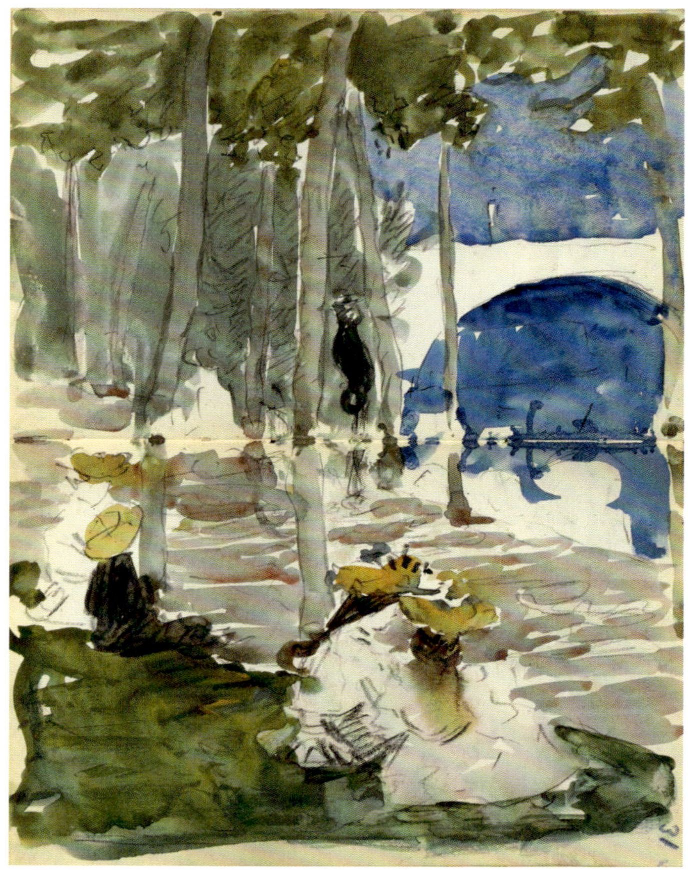

FIG. 63. Maurice Prendergast. *Paris Sketchbook*, 1891–94, leaf 30 verso–31 recto. Conté crayon, pencil, and watercolor. The Metropolitan Museum of Art, New York

again in 1907, the American artist Maurice Prendergast, a frequent painter of shorelines and parks, filled his sketchbooks with watercolors of gatherings along the boulevards, in the cafés, and in garden spots such as the one near the Quay d'Austerlitz (fig. 63).

No painting better describes the ritual that a Sunday outing in a park had become by the end of the century than Georges Seurat's view of the crowd on the Ile de la Grande Jatte (1884–86; Art Institute of Chicago). The "Island of the Egg Bowl," little more than a mile long, was set in the middle of the Seine, just outside city limits (and the Parisian park system). From its banks one might catch sight of the smokestacks and factories of Clichy. The duc d'Orléans, the future "Citizen King" Louis Philippe, had obtained the property soon after acquiring the Château de Neuilly in 1818, when his plans to renovate the château and its grounds expanded to incorporate seven islets in the Seine. Extravagant feats of dredging, fortification, and landscaping succeeded in uniting the islands

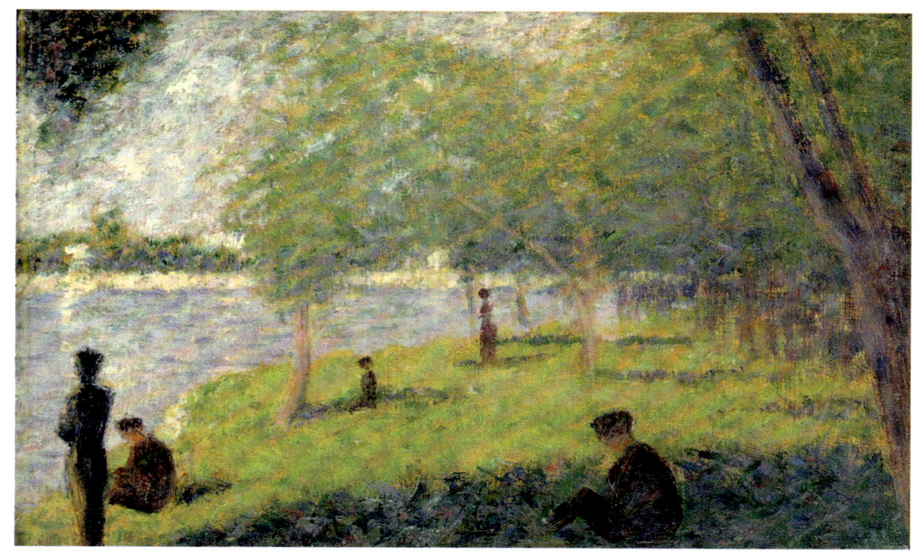

FIG. 64. Georges Seurat. *Study for "A Sunday on La Grande Jatte,"* 1884. Oil on wood. The Metropolitan Museum of Art, New York

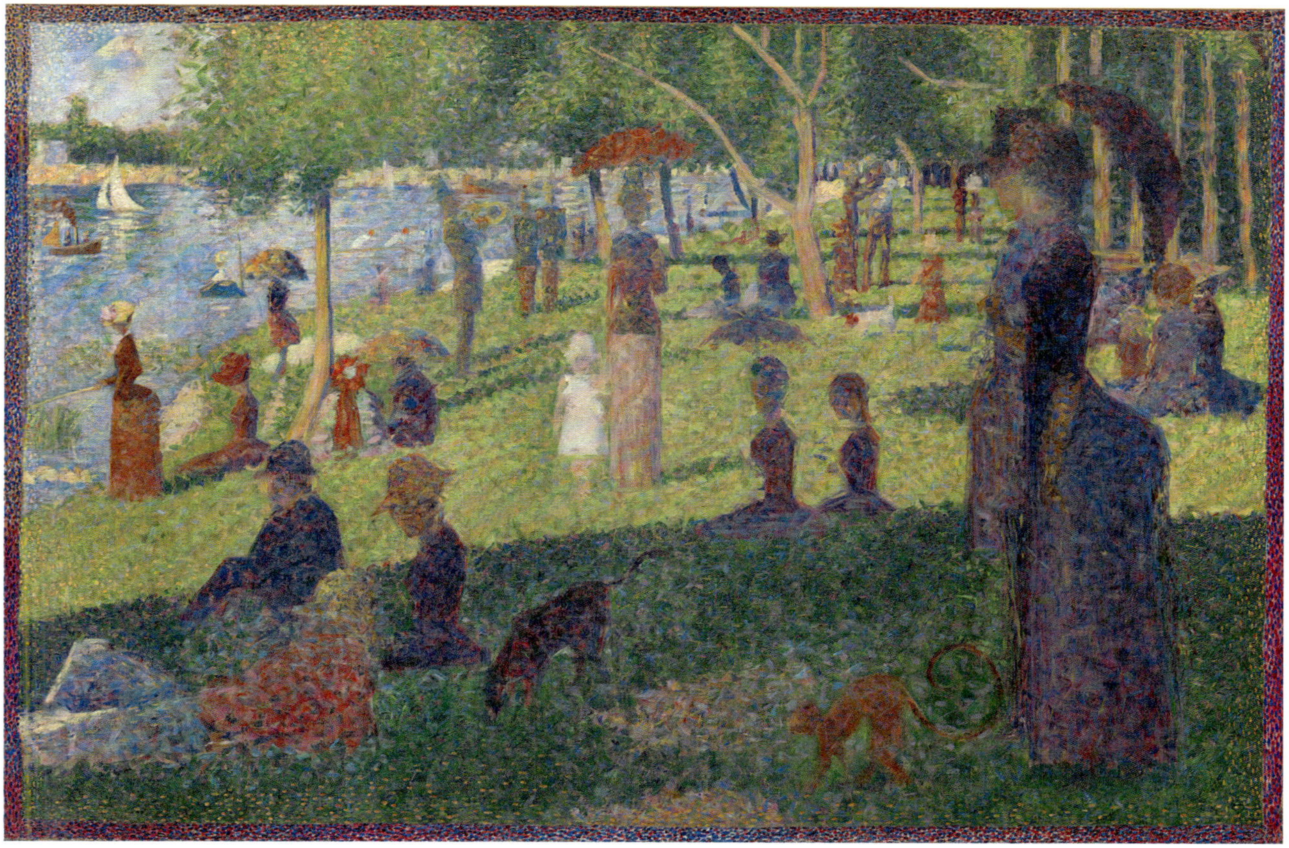

FIG. 65. Georges Seurat. *Study for "A Sunday on La Grande Jatte,"* 1884. Oil on canvas. The Metropolitan Museum of Art, New York

into a verdant park that was linked to the duc's Neuilly estate by an innovative iron bridge. At the southern tip of the island sat the Temple of Love, relocated by Louis Philippe from the Parc Monceau, where it had been erected in 1774 by his father.[43] After the park was made public and modified in the 1850s, Monet, Van Gogh, Sisley, and others set up easels on and around the Grande Jatte. It was Seurat, however, who gave us the clearest appreciation of Parisians determined to enjoy an outing where, as noted in 1886, "people take lunch on the worn-out grass, and swings, skittles, and games of toad-in-the-hole spring up in place of absent trees."[44] Working in ways that were at odds with Impressionists, who prized spontaneity in their work, Seurat instead progressed methodically through a succession of nearly sixty drawings and oil sketches (most of them but a fraction of the size of the final ten-foot-wide canvas), a process he evidently needed to perfect his vision (figs. 64, 65).

In the spectacle of Parisians in their Sunday best, Seurat realized how the public park—not so much a place to be seen, but a place in which to participate in public life—allowed for a special sort of association among city dwellers and a form of urban civility that has been characterized as "politesse de la distance."[45] Like the park of the Grande Jatte, the twenty-four pockets of greenery that Haussmann distributed throughout the city of Paris between 1853 and 1869 provided places for the shared respite, if not active recreation, of families, friends, neighbors, and outright strangers. At the end of the Second Empire the city contained seventy greened squares. Open to all, unlike the private gated parks of London neighborhoods, the squares of Paris, often woven into the fabric of family and community life, brought natural greenery and a place for leisurely regeneration within walking distance of most city dwellers. These landscaped areas were as slight as the meager plot at the foot of the Tour Saint-Jacques, whose lawns, Zola complained, "would hardly give lunch to a flock of sheep," or as accommodating as the nearly four-acre Square des Batignolles near Manet's studio, the likely site of his painting *The Railway* (1873; National Gallery of Art, Washington, D.C.), in which he pictured a child watching passing trains through the iron fencing of her playground.[46]

The Square (or Place) Vintimille in the ninth arrondissement, developed in 1859, drew the admiration of the Irish gardener William Robinson, who praised it in his 1869 guide to Paris gardens, noting that "the smallest spots in dusty cities may readily be converted into oases of verdure and sweetness."[47] When the park acquired a statue of Hector Berlioz in 1886, the square was named after the composer. Observing the active life of the site from his studio windows, the artist Edouard Vuillard made that subject a focus of multiple

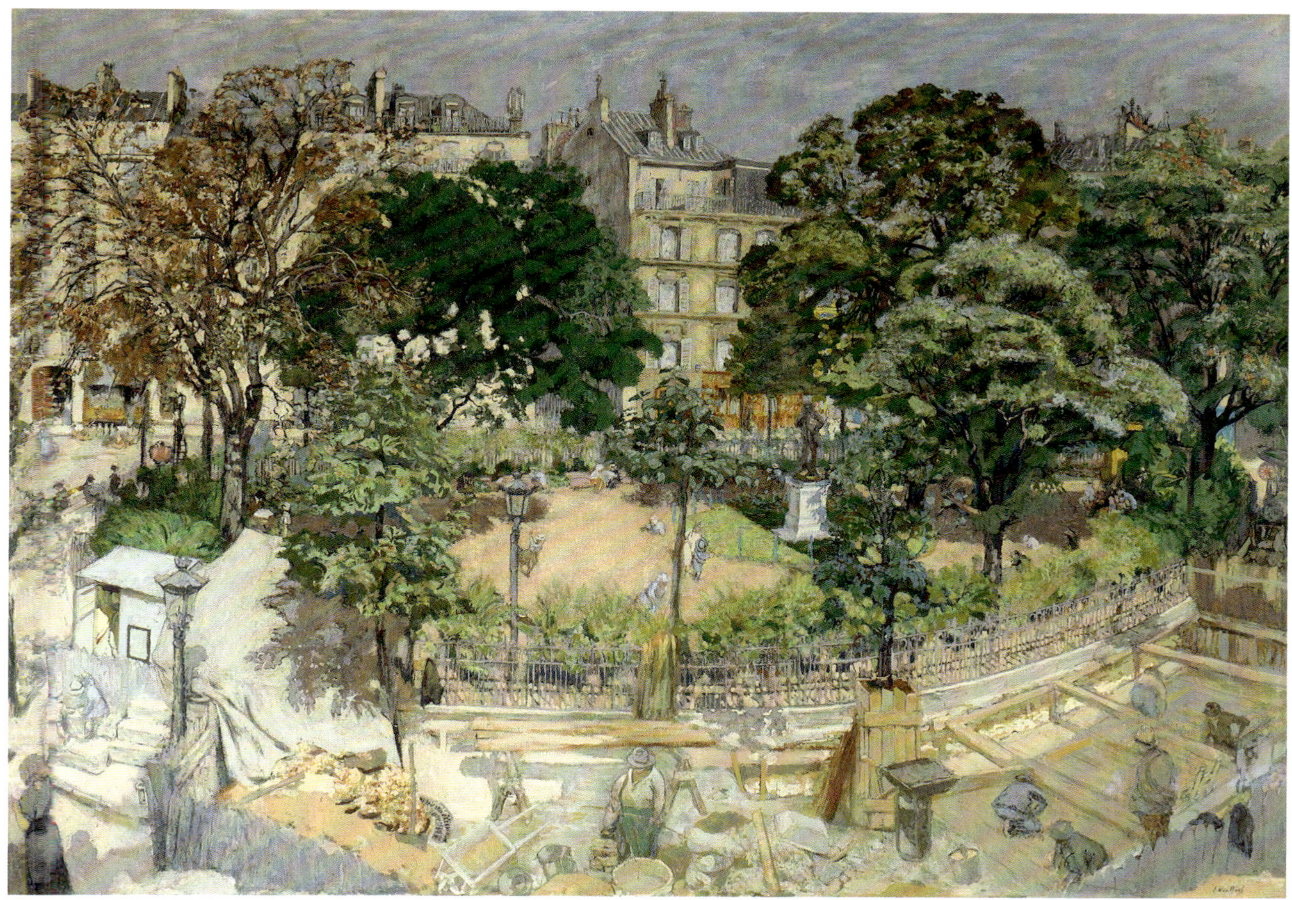

FIG. 66. Edouard Vuillard. *Place Vintimille, or Berlioz Square,* 1915–16; reworked 1923. Distemper on canvas. The Metropolitan Museum of Art, New York (promised gift)

painted projects. One of these, a five-foot-tall mural commissioned in 1915 by the industrialist Emile Lévy, included in its view the reconstruction of the broad sidewalk that encircled the park—certainly a significant event for the neighborhood (fig. 66). Designed to bring a fresh, compelling experience of the out-of-doors to the indoors, the work may have been influenced by Seurat's large painting of the park on the Grande Jatte or the lily pond murals of Monet, whom Vuillard, together with Bonnard, visited at Giverny in December 1909.[48]

The campaign in Paris for grand new parks, tree-lined boulevards, and gardenlike neighborhood squares sparked a revolution in urban planning, with the result that cities throughout France began to follow the capital's lead by initiating plans for public greenspaces. In most of the provinces of France during the second half of the eighteenth century, towns set aside land for

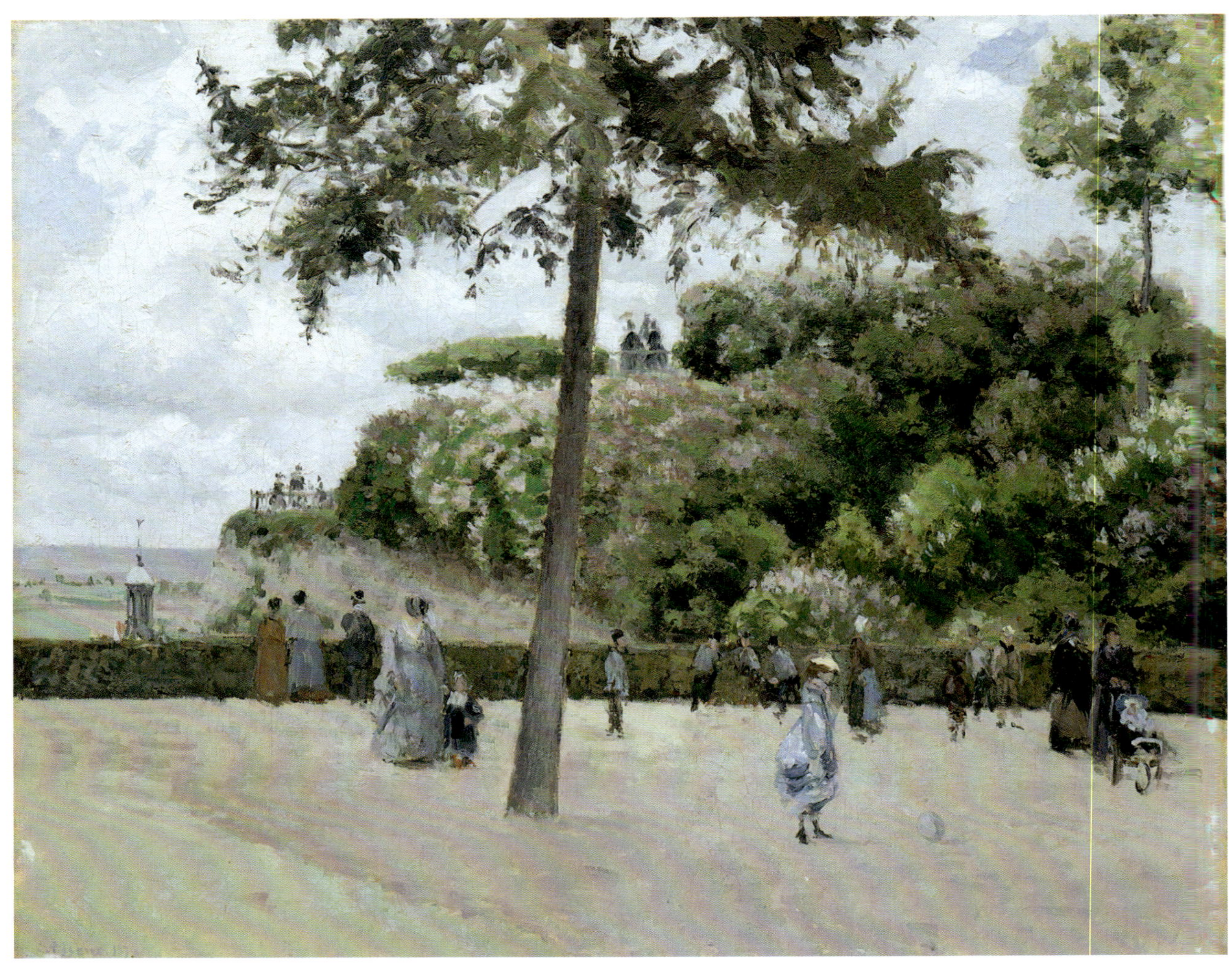

FIG. 67. Camille Pissarro. *The Public Garden at Pontoise*, 1874. Oil on canvas. The Metropolitan Museum of Art, New York

public gardens and sometimes designed urban projects that proved too ambitious to be realized.[49] During the second half of the nineteenth century, far more was accomplished. Major projects for the renovation and building of public gardens and greenhouses were launched in 1856 in Bordeaux and in Lyon, where the Parc de la Tête d'Or, encompassing 260 acres, remains the largest park in France located in the heart of a city. New parks were planted in Avignon, Lille, Nantes, Tours, as well as in Nice and in Marseille, despite the challenges posed to gardeners by the seaside climates.

Nearly every French town of any size was graced with a promenade or public garden that was to some degree like the one Pissarro painted in Pontoise

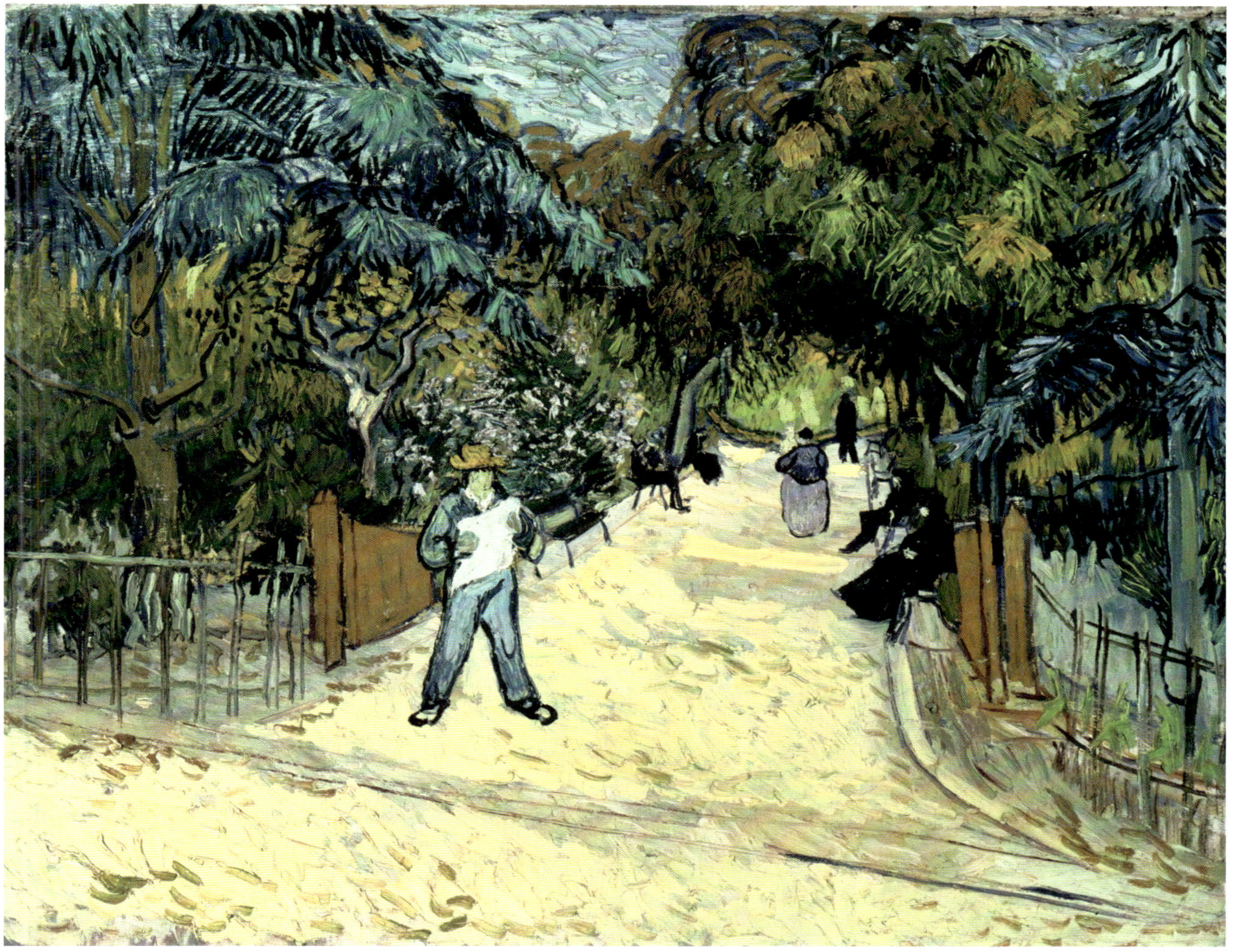

FIG. 68. Vincent van Gogh. *Entrance to the Public Gardens in Arles*, 1888. Oil on canvas. Phillips Collection, Washington, D.C.

(fig. 67). There, a stroll was a social event, while at his home nearby the artist preferred to putter among his fruit trees and cabbage patches as his wife (a former florist) cultivated a flower garden planted with iris provided by Monet. In Arles the Jardin Lamartine, inaugurated in 1872, was installed directly across the road from the house where Van Gogh rented rooms in 1888 (fig. 68). Filled with more than one hundred varieties of plants, including plane trees, firs, and flowering oleanders, the garden features in ten paintings by the artist, among them four canvases Vincent created to decorate the bedroom of his much-anticipated visitor Paul Gauguin.[50]

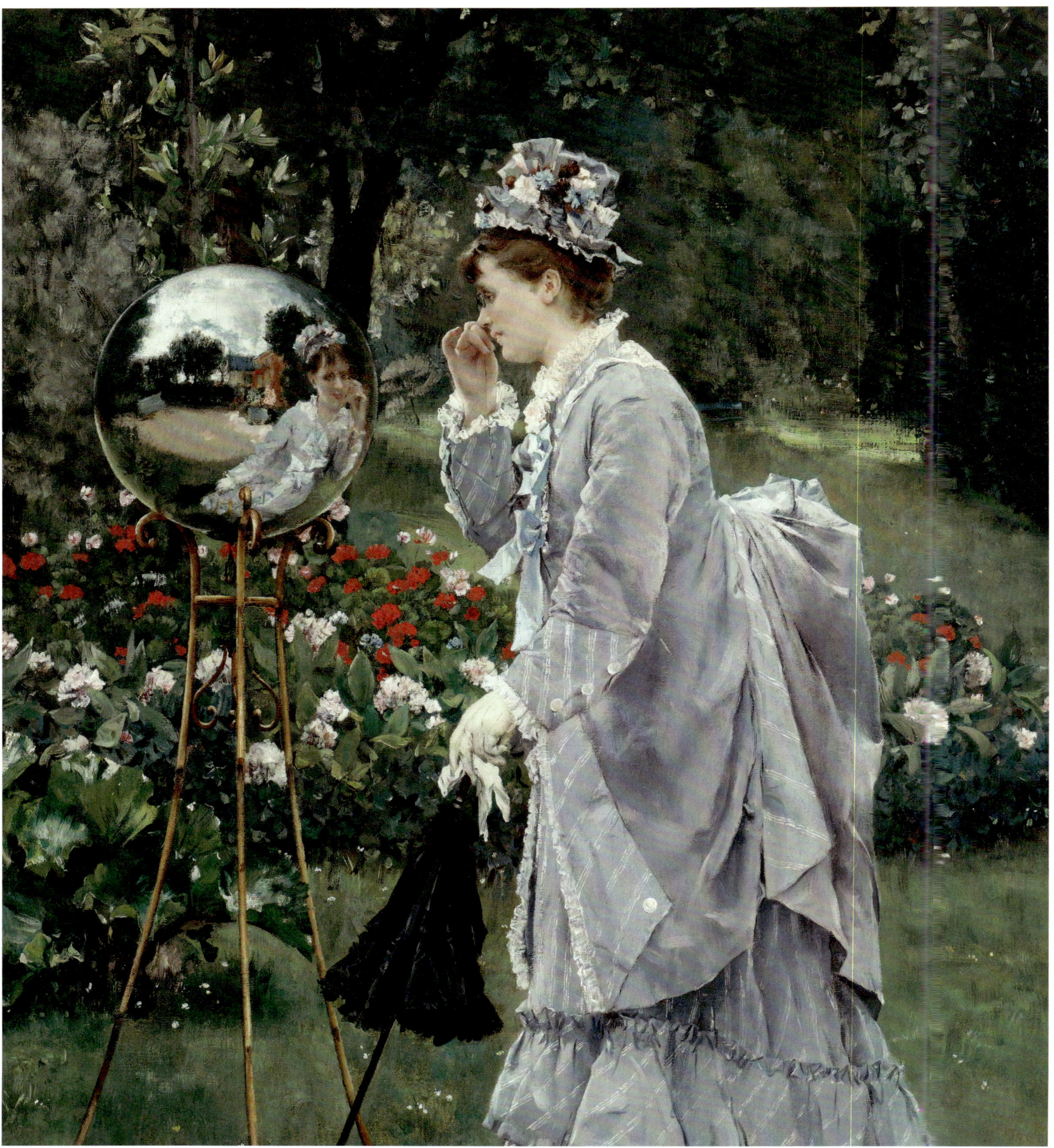

The Private Garden

An extraordinary era in the history of private gardens opens with the early years of the nineteenth century in France. Few of the grand landscaped gardens of the late eighteenth century survived the Revolution of 1789 or the effects of the subsequent abrogation of the laws of primogeniture, which until then had kept large estates intact, generation to generation. The resulting breakup of large properties made the purchase of land possible for more people than ever before. By 1820 landowners were again creating pleasure gardens for the enjoyment of family and friends, although they were, of necessity, more modest than those of the past.

Homeowners eager and able to enrich their lives with the benefits of horticulture could turn to an unpretentious handbook, *De la composition des parcs et jardins pittoresques,* first published in 1817 by J. Lalos, who wished to present a more "popular" contribution to the "science of gardens" for a wider audience, including those of modest means. Lalos advocated simplicity over the excess he found in the gardens of "maniacs" that were overrun with pavilions, kiosks, and mausoleums and where "each flower was planted in a separate pot" (fig. 69).[1]

Perhaps more inspiring to budding gardeners was Gabriel Thouin's pioneering effort to categorize garden design, *Plans raisonnés de toutes les espèces de jardins* (1820), which illustrated multiple plans intended for both city and country dwellers of "diverses classes de fortune."[2] Believing the garden to be a place of discovery and learning, Thouin considered vegetable gardens, orchards, and botanical gardens (for scientific study), while focusing mainly

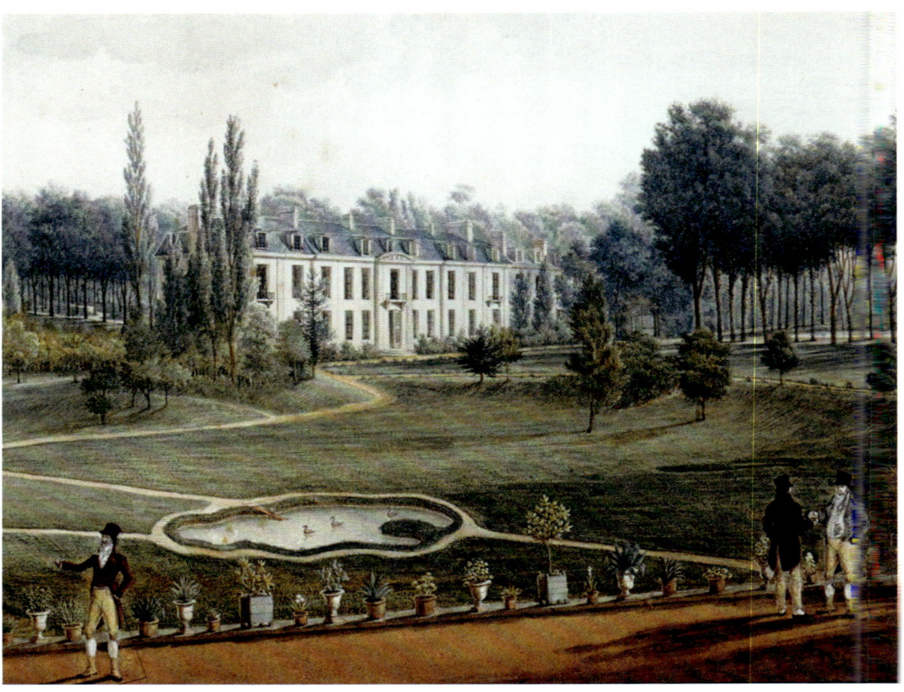

FIG. 69. Antoine Ignace Melling. *Château de Ris-Orange* (detail), 1811. Gouache. Musée de l'Ile de France, Sceaux

on pleasure gardens. These he presented in three design categories: symmetrical; thematic (described as Chinese, English, and *fantastiques*); and natural ("in imitation of the most beautiful scenes of Nature, while disguising the artifice of their making") (figs. 70–72).[3] Embellishing these plans were flower-filled lawns, flowering shrubs, and beds of flowers placed near the house, at the intersections of walkways, or next to places where one could sit. This pervasive floral presence, a relatively new garden necessity, was considered not only attractive but also beneficial to strollers, as the scent of flowers was said to be good for the health (particularly that of women) and for improving the air of stuffy apartments and insalubrious streets.

The role of flowers in the design of gardens grew enormously as the century progressed. It was the English landscape architect Humphry Repton who early in the century, had introduced the idea of situating a flower garden adjacent to the house or in a separate, designated area. The notion intensified in appeal as the variety of horticultural offerings increased and gardeners saw the benefits of putting plants directly in the ground instead of displaying them in pots. Indeed, in 1867 the historian of French gardens Arthur Mangin declared the century's greatest advance was "to have restored to the garden its first and essential function—the cultivation of flowers."[4]

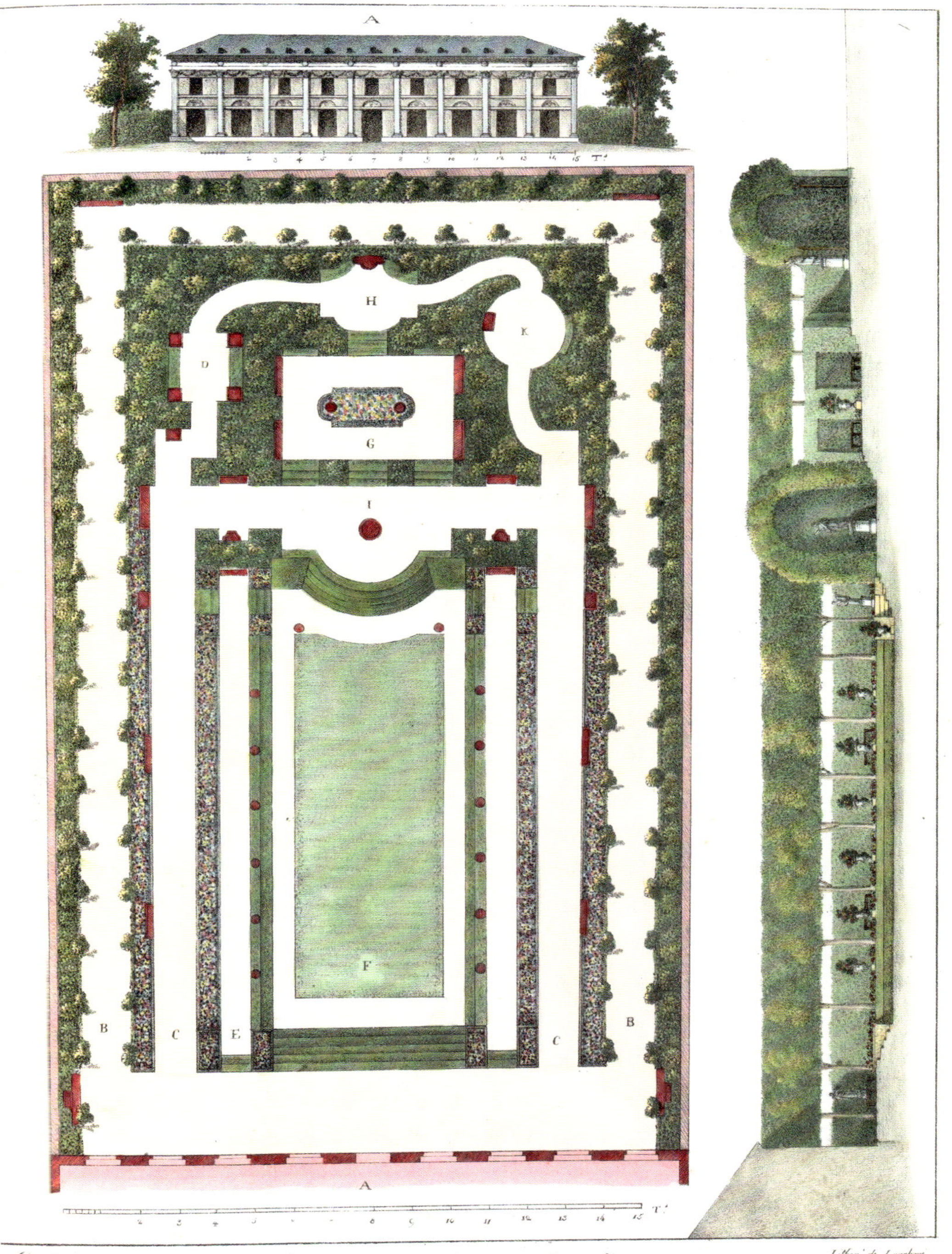

FIG. 70. Gabriel Thouin. "Symmetrical City Garden," from *Plans raisonnés de toutes les espèces de jardins* (Paris, 1820). Hand-colored lithograph. The Metropolitan Museum of Art, New York

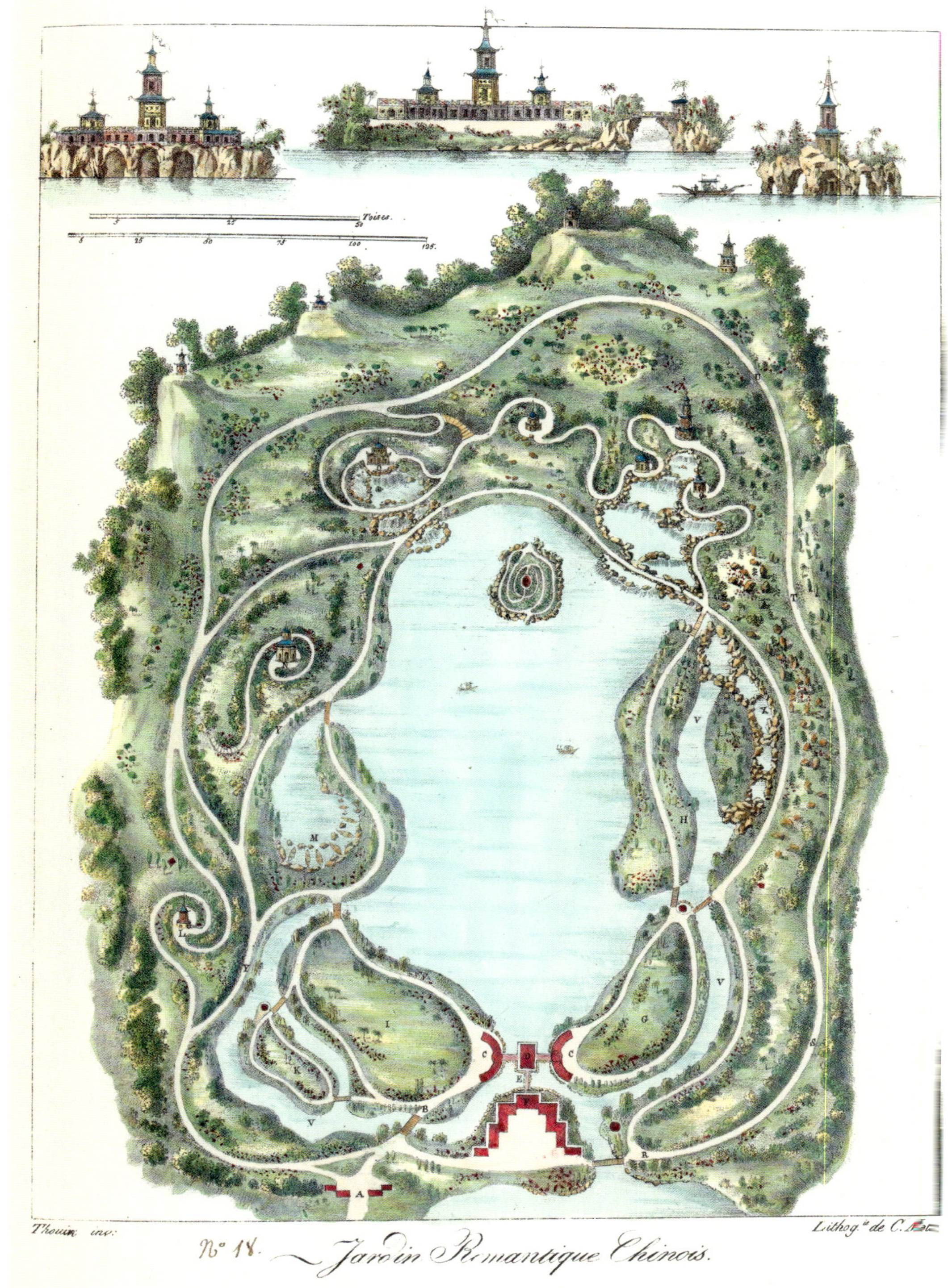

FIG. 71. Gabriel Thouin. "Romantic Chinese Garden," from *Plans raisonnés de toutes les espèces de jardins* (Paris, 1820). Hand-colored lithograph. The Metropolitan Museum of Art, New York

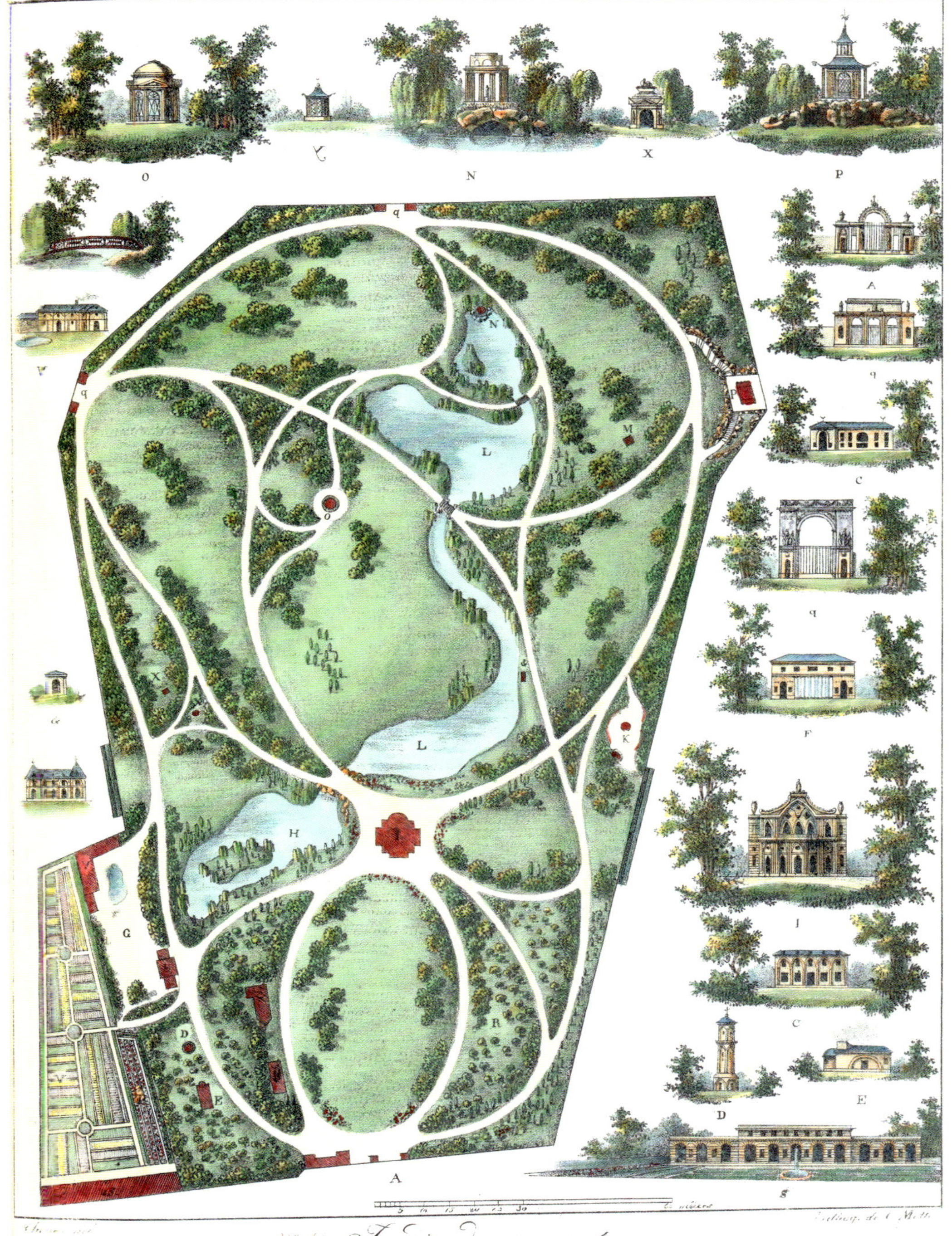

FIG. 72. Gabriel Thouin. "Pleasure Garden," from *Plans raisonnés de toutes les espèces de jardins* (Paris, 1820). Hand-colored lithograph. The Metropolitan Museum of Art, New York

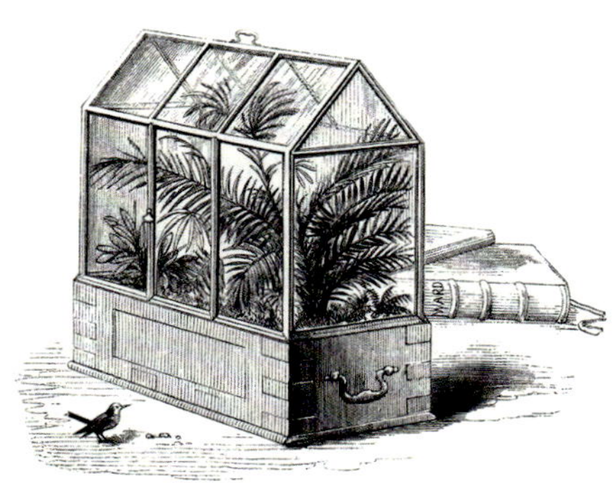

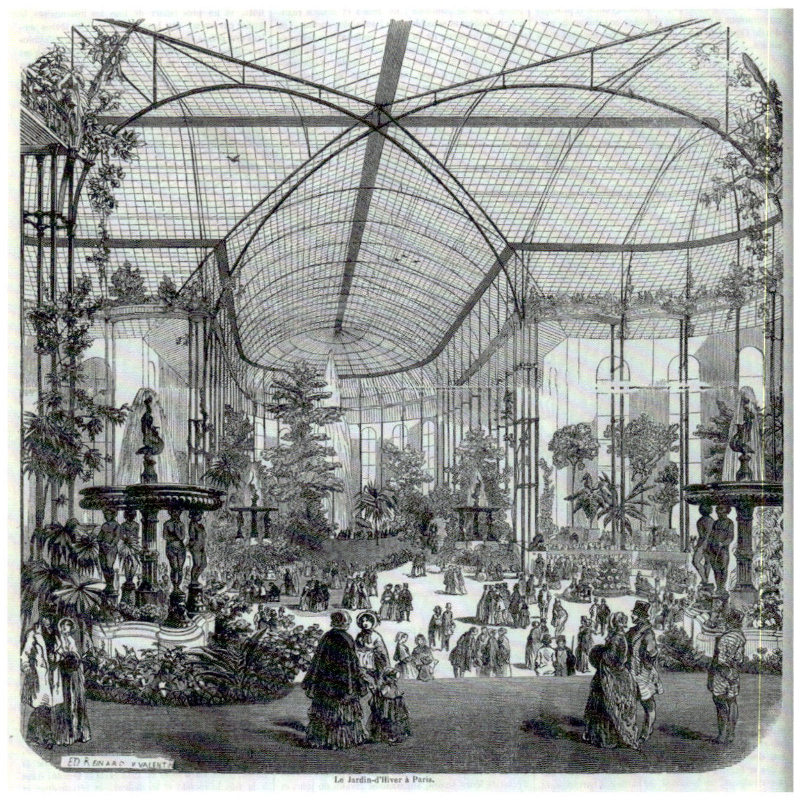

FIG. 73. "Wardian Case," from Nathaniel Bagshaw Ward, *On the Growth of Plants in Closely Glazed Cases,* 2nd ed. (London, 1852). Engraving. New York Botanical Garden

FIG. 74. "Winter Garden, Paris," from Edmond Texier, *Tableau de Paris* (Paris, 1852). Wood engraving. The Metropolitan Museum of Art, New York

As the fashion for floriculture also developed early in the century, Empress Josephine was among the trend's most influential practitioners, collecting at Malmaison hundreds of flowering plants imported from abroad (see pp. 16–18). Horticulture hunters made voyages of discovery, while the wide distribution of newly introduced plants was hastened by the proliferation of nursery gardens. By the end of the century the number of plants acclimatized to European conditions had increased a thousand times over.[5]

The transport and cultivation of exotic flowers, trees, and shrubs were made possible by the protective structure of the glass greenhouse. A feature of princely gardens since the seventeenth century, the hothouse was technologically improved in the nineteenth century with the invention of sheet glass, the wrought-iron glazing bar, and adaptable heating systems. About 1829 the British physician and explorer Nathaniel Bagshaw Ward invented a portable glass-enclosed terrarium to protect plants en route, sheltering them from salt spray while providing light and moisture from condensation (fig. 73). The so-called Wardian case that carried floral and arboreal riches from India, Australia, South Africa, and the Americas was a useful miniature version of large glasshouses like those built at Malmaison (see fig. 13) and in Paris at the Jardin des Plantes, the Jardin du Luxembourg, and the Bois de Boulogne. The widespread construction of vast iron-and-glass structures followed those first developed in 1840 by Joseph Paxton, designer of the Crystal Palace that housed London's World Exposition of 1851. Such buildings, like the magnificent glass-enclosed winter garden erected on the Champs-Elysées in 1848 (fig. 74), were often dedicated to the pleasure of people rather than the studied maintenance of tender plants.[6]

Gardening increasingly assumed the aspect of plant collecting, and the greenhouse came to be seen as a desirable extension to the ambitious gardener's home, made affordable by prefabricated cast-iron construction. Among the pages of Pierre Boitard's instructional *Traité de la composition et de l'ornement des jardins* (1825) one finds a design for a small woodland under glass, with a path running through it (fig. 75). Boitard's handbook also included plans for gates and trellises, rustic houses and furniture, pavilions, tents, and children's playthings, such as swings and a merry-go-round, while

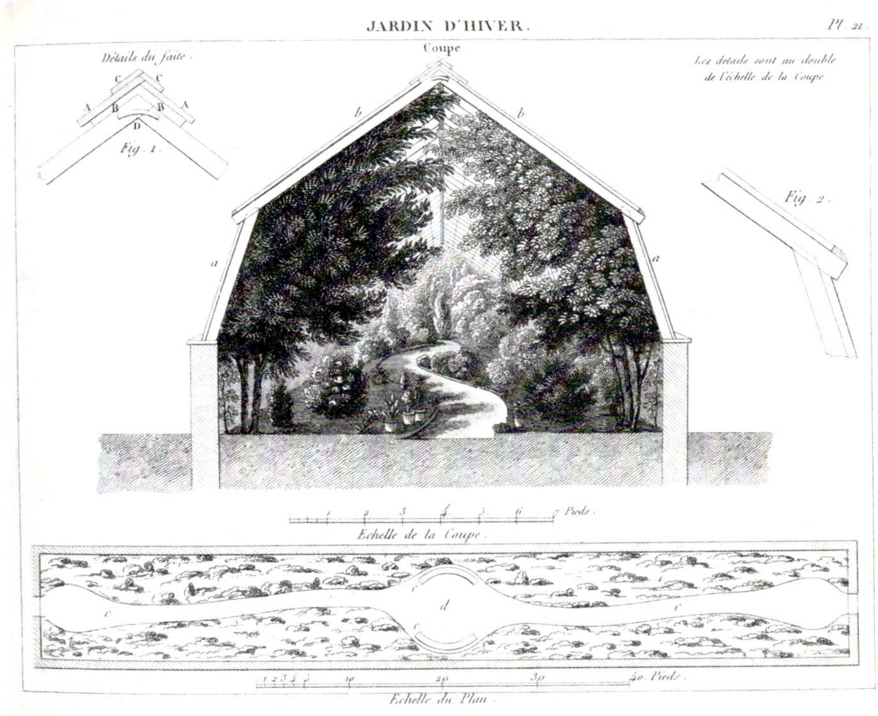

FIG. 75. "Winter Garden," from Pierre Boitard, *Traité de la composition et de l'ornement des jardins*, 3rd ed. (Paris, 1825). Etching. The Metropolitan Museum of Art, New York

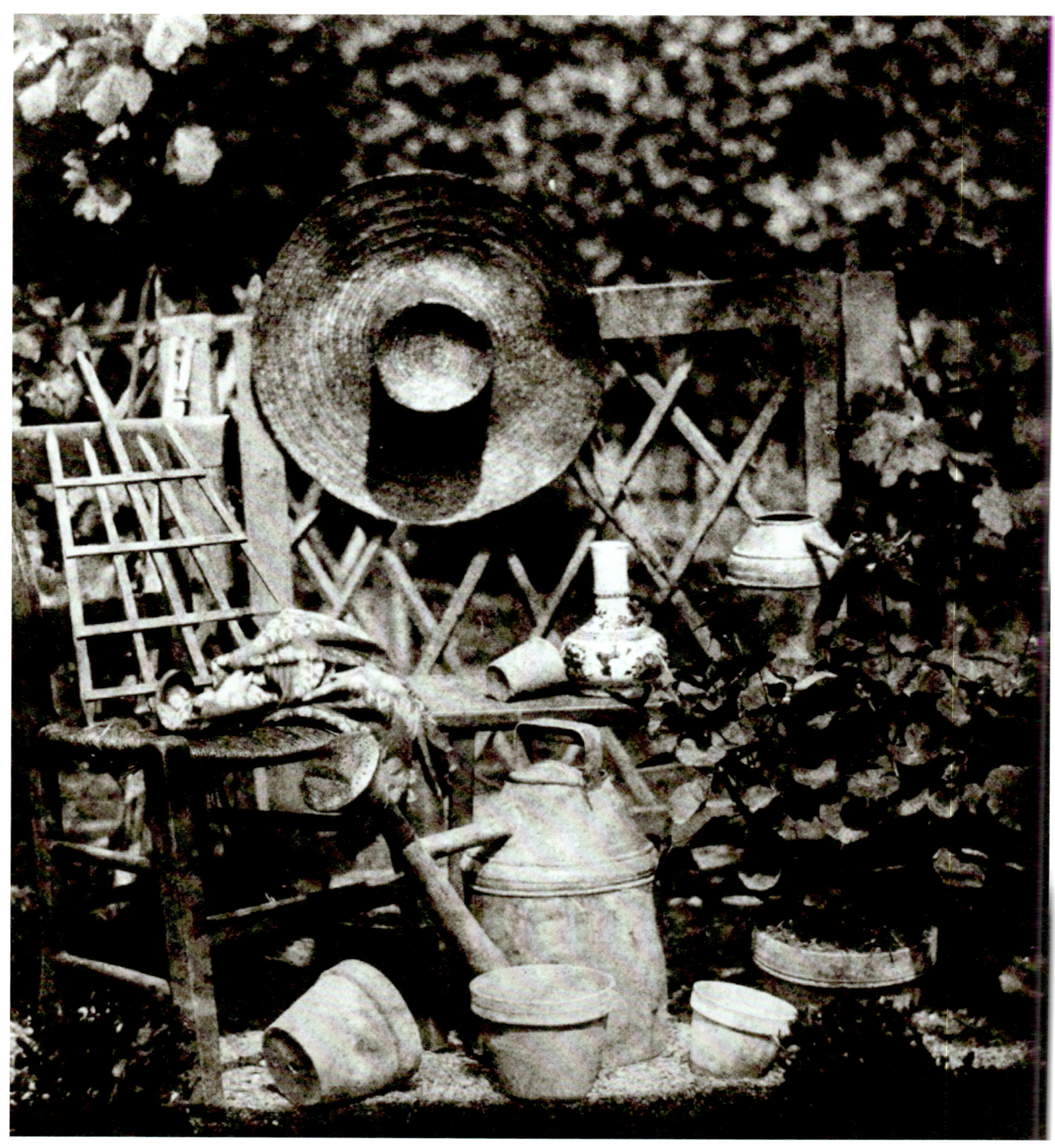

FIG. 76. Hippolyte Bayard. "In the Garden," ca. 1842, from *Bayard: XXV Calotypes, 1842–1850* (1965). Gelatin silver print. Art Institute of Chicago

offering advice on site planning and practical hints on soil preparation and planting. Gustave Flaubert cites one of Boitard's books as the garden reference turned to by the caricatured dilettantes Bouvard and Pécuchet in his caustic send-up of the bourgeoisie written in the 1870s.[7] Midcentury garden mania was but one of the various fads followed by Flaubert's amateurs, who, "dressed in blue smocks and wide-brimmed hats, gaiters to their knees, [set about] husking seeds, writing labels, arranging . . . little pots . . . [and planting] passion flowers . . . Indian lilacs, China roses, and eucalyptus, then at the height of its reputation."[8]

About 1830 a burst of activity in the founding of horticultural societies and the publication of gardening magazines can be related to further investigations in the scientific discipline of botany, introduced by Carl Linnaeus and expanded by Antoine Laurent de Jussieu in the second half of the eighteenth century (see pp. 4–5). In 1827 the Société d'Horticulture de Paris (today the Société Nationale d'Horticulture de France) was created to grant prizes, distribute medals, exhibit plants, and publish reports on horticultural advancements.[9] Two years later the *Revue Horticole; ou, Journal des Jardiniers et Amateurs* began publication. Introduced as a "resumé of everything interesting in gardening . . . in France and elsewhere," it became the leading garden magazine of the nineteenth century, eventually counting Claude Monet among its thousands of subscribers.[10] Meanwhile, the *Journal de l'Académie d'Horticulture* was launched in 1831, with practical information on plants and pests, botanical news from Calcutta and England, and pointed advice that gardeners avoid "[the] pretensions [of] bourgeois vanity" in their effort to bring their gardens into harmony with the character and size of their homes.[11]

A still-life composition of gardening equipment by the photographer Hippolyte Bayard is emblematic of the growing leisure activity that drew the French out of doors armed with sun hats and watering cans, trellises and trowels (fig. 76). Even Parisian apartment dwellers, lacking their own plots to till, carried home potted plants to tend on their windowsills (fig. 77). Special gatherings were held for horticultural enthusiasts—agricultural fairs and the Gardeners' Ball (fig. 78)—and free lectures were offered at the Jardin des Plantes and the Jardin du Luxembourg, where "an attentive class, consisting of several hundred persons" met at nine o'clock in the morning.[12]

The introduction of train service in the 1840s made travel to the suburbs faster and easier, leading to the parceling of rural land into affordable developments. Urban dwellers could now make weekend visits to their country properties and tend their own gardens (fig. 79). Eugène Delacroix spent

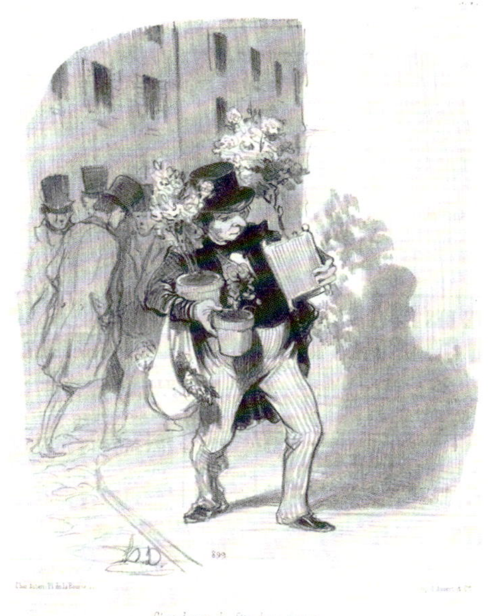

FIG. 77. Honoré Daumier. "Tomorrow Is His Wife's Birthday," from *Le Charivari*, June 18, 1846. Lithograph. The Metropolitan Museum of Art, New York

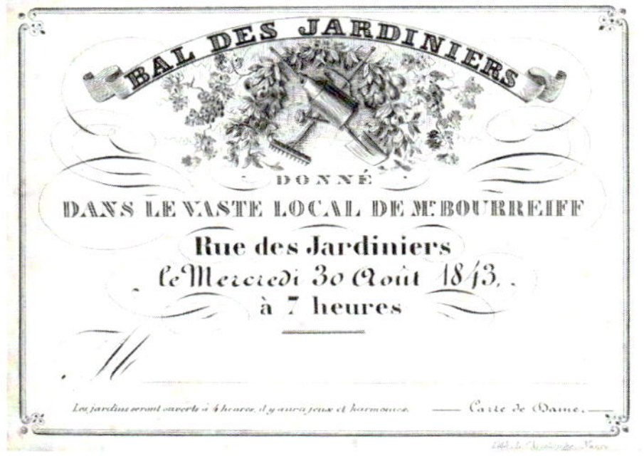
BAL DES JARDINIERS
DONNÉ
DANS LE VASTE LOCAL DE Mr BOURREIFF
Rue des Jardiniers
Le Mercredi 30 Août 1843.
à 7 heures

FIG. 78. Invitation to the Gardeners' Ball, August 30, 1843. Lithograph. The Metropolitan Museum of Art, New York

many pleasurable days with George Sand in her manor house at Nohant during the summers of 1842, 1843, and 1846. As a gift for his hostess he painted a corner of her garden, choosing a grassy spot shaded by old trees, where a stone table stood and hollyhocks bloomed (fig. 80). The scene, although devoid of people, evoked memories of times the artist had spent with the author and her lover Frédéric Chopin. Writing to Sand in June 1843, Delacroix recalled "beautiful Nohant, with its beautiful grounds"; "I see you at the table, in the garden."[13] Deeply attached to her garden, Sand displayed enthusiasm also for Parisian public parks in visits to the municipal greenhouses and to the Parc des Buttes Chaumont shortly after its opening in 1867. To the *Paris Guide* published during the year of the Exposition Universelle, she contributed an article extolling the virtues of the city's promenades, declaring Paris a showcase for that "ravishing" invention "le jardin *décoratif*."[14]

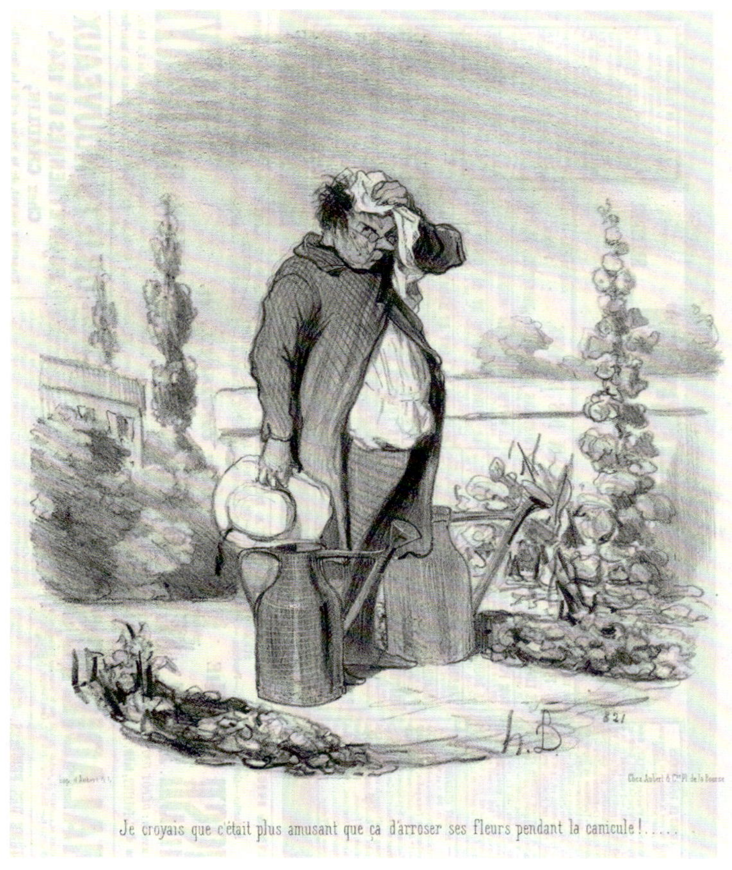

FIG. 79. Honoré Daumier. "I thought it would be more fun than this to water flowers during a heat wave!" from *Le Charivari*, December 29, 1845. Lithograph. The Metropolitan Museum of Art, New York

Delacroix began to maintain a garden of his own in 1844, after finding a desirable retreat just outside Paris in Champrosay. There, his often troubled spirits were soothed during strolls he recalled in his journal: "There was wonderful moonlight this evening in my little garden. Walked about until very late. I felt as though I could never sufficiently enjoy the gentle light on the willows, the sound of the little fountain, and the delicious scent of the plants which seem to give out all their hidden treasures at such times."[15] Later, in 1857, when he relocated his Paris studio, Delacroix purchased a house on the rue Furstenberg (now the Musée National Eugène Delacroix), mainly because it offered him a small garden in the city, which he planned to renovate and plant with roses, thyme, gooseberry bushes, and strawberries.[16]

When Delacroix visited his friend Corot in Ville-d'Avray in 1847, he probably strolled through the garden attached to the family estate. Transformed into an informal *jardin à l'anglaise* in 1799, it was ornamented with a kiosk Corot later

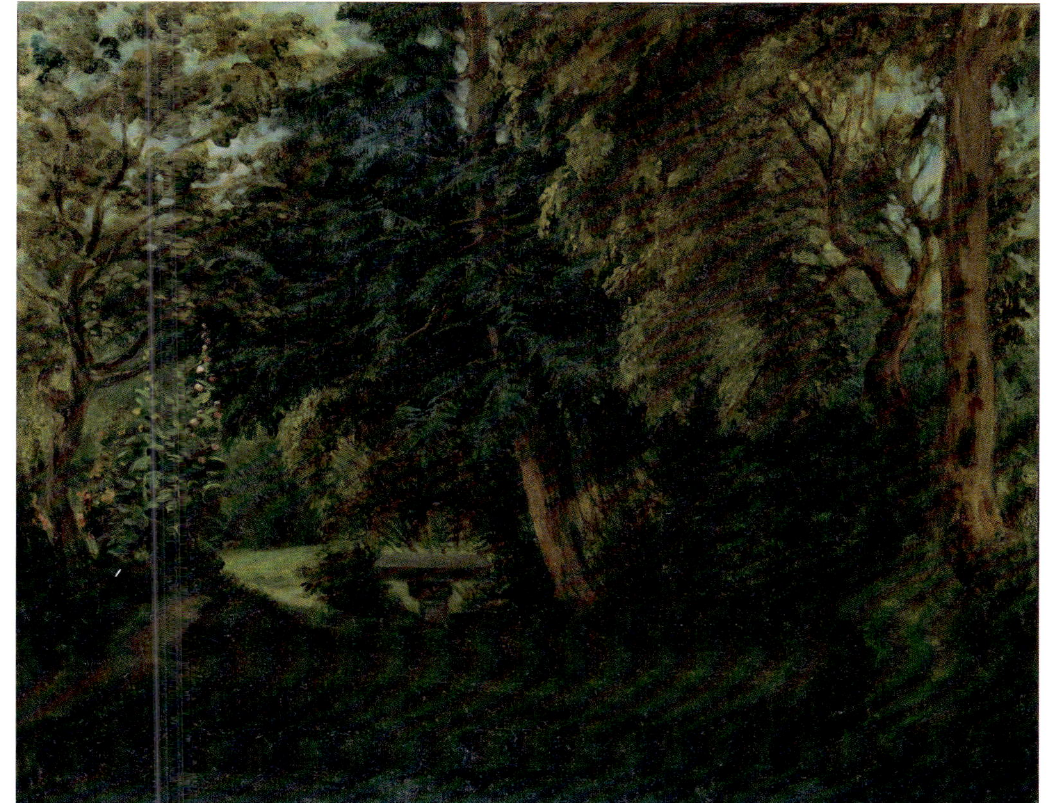

FIG. 80. Eugène Delacroix. *George Sand's Garden at Nohant*, ca. 1842–43. Oil on canvas. The Metropolitan Museum of Art, New York

decorated with paintings.[17] Although he customarily painted landscapes with broad horizons, Corot, in evident tribute to his father and mother (who died in 1847 and 1851, respectively), created an intimate picture of the garden, where his parents can be seen admiring their planting beds and the towering blooms of hollyhocks, a traditional favorite with French gardeners (fig. 81). Knowing how precious the serenity of a garden could be, especially to a busy satirist of Paris life pressured by editorial deadlines, Corot made it possible for his friend Daumier to acquire a retreat in the country, not far from his own (fig. 82).

"One of the pronounced characteristics of our present Parisian society," wrote the journalist Eugène Chapus in the 1860s, "is that . . . everyone in the middle class wants to have his little house with trees, roses, dahlias, his big or little garden."[18] Considered not only fashionable but also healthful and instructive, the garden was thought to be so beneficial that by 1879 the minister of public instruction and fine arts required every rural French school to have its own enclosed garden space.[19]

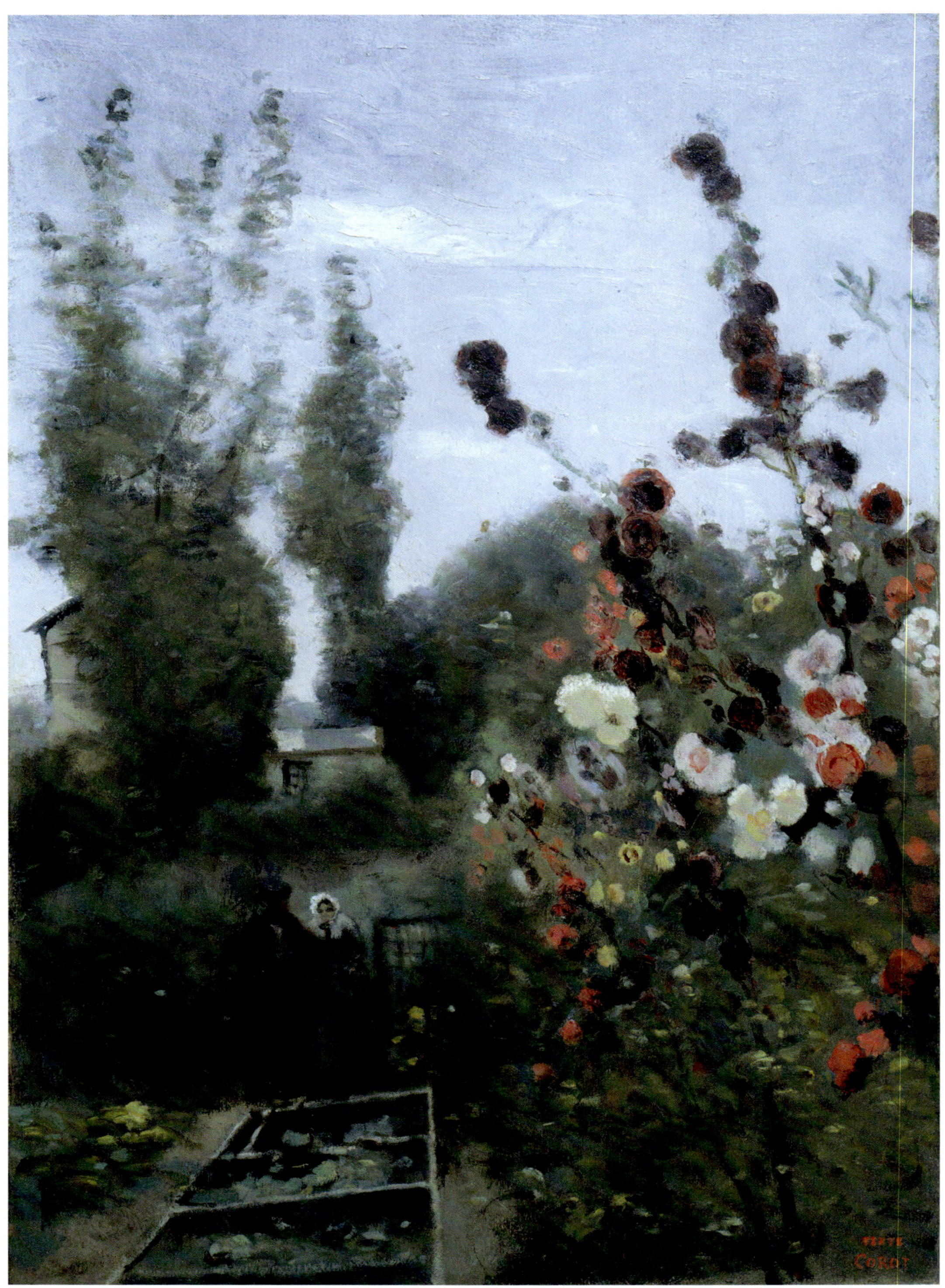

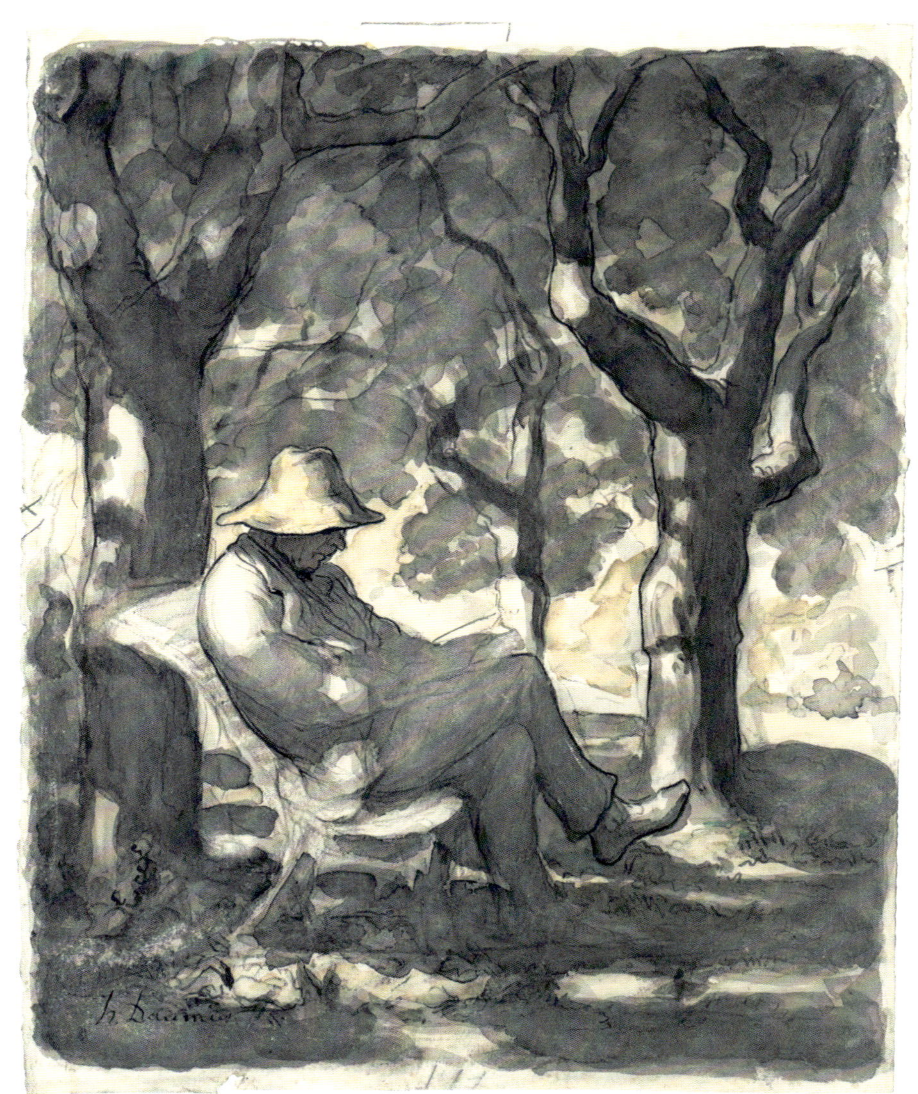

FIG. 81. Camille Corot. *Ville-d'Avray: Corot's Father and His Wife in the Garden*, ca. 1845. Oil on canvas. Private collection

FIG. 82. Honoré Daumier. *A Man Reading in a Garden*, ca. 1865. Watercolor over black chalk, with pen and ink, brush and wash, and lithograph crayon. The Metropolitan Museum of Art, New York

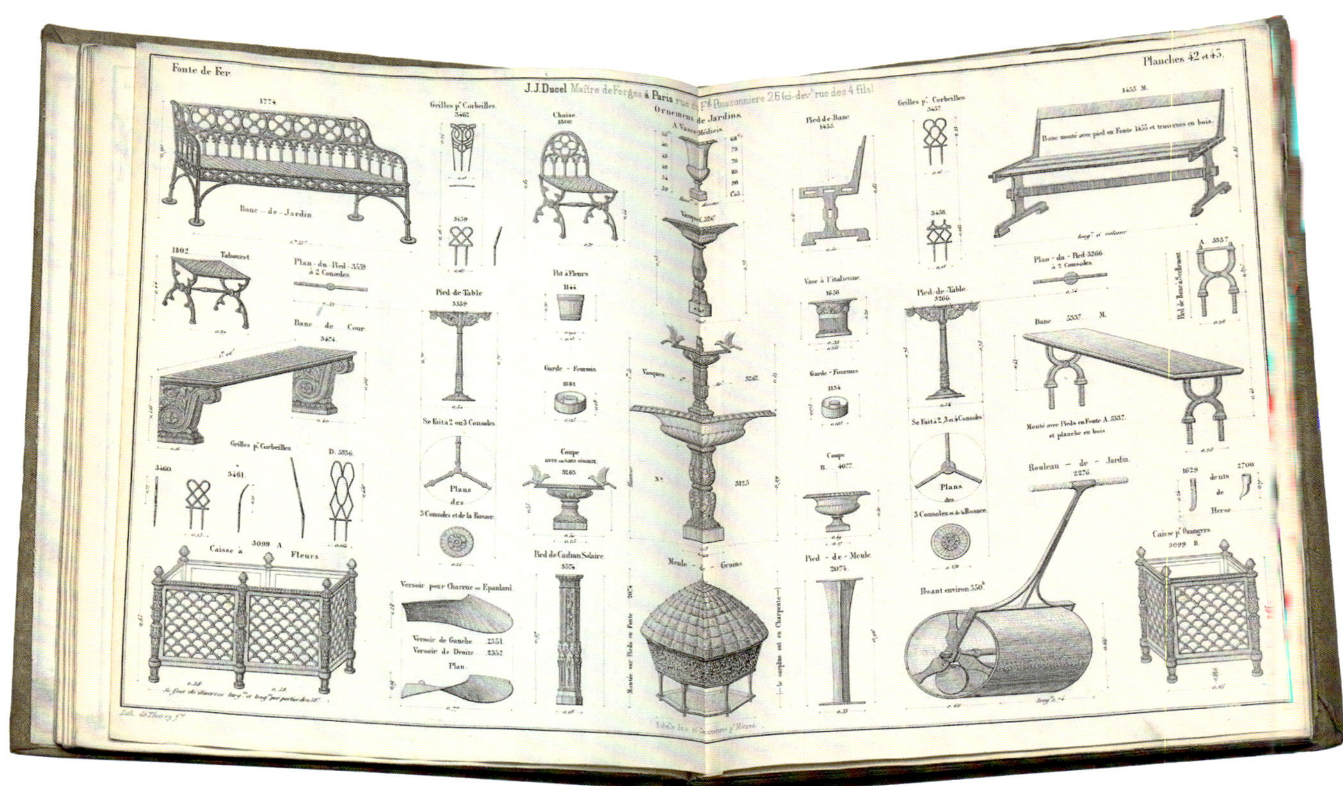

FIG. 83. "Cast Iron Garden Accessories," in *Font de Fer J. J. Ducel et Fils* (Paris, ca. 1830–50). Lithograph. The Metropolitan Museum of Art, New York

As the century progressed, an ever-expanding offering of garden manuals, periodicals, courses, and lectures became available, such as Edouard Bocquart's 1873 *Guide du parfait jardinier-fleuriste*, which included advice concerning more than seven hundred species of plants, trees, and ornamental shrubs. The amateur garden craze gave rise also to the garden tour, in which owners showed off their properties. Thus, subscribers to *Le Jardin: Journal d'Horticulture Générale* could hardly have been surprised to read in the inaugural issue (March 5, 1887): "In no other era have flowers and plants been so widely appreciated; they preside at all our ceremonies, take part in all our festivities; their use has increased a hundredfold in 20 years."[20]

To furnish the equipment essential to gardening, a whole new commercial industry was developed to supply the tools of proper horticulture, such as tillers and pruners, wheelbarrows, watering devices, and the modern reel-type lawn mower (invented in England in 1827), as well as benches and birdbaths, planters and gazebos (fig. 83). Nurseries and flower markets became active centers of business (fig. 84), some of which still operate today, among them the firms of Truffaut and Vilmorin (founded in 1743), from which Monet, Caillebotte, and Gauguin ordered seeds.

Meanwhile, garden owners cultivated ever more sophisticated tastes; for some, horticulture became a consuming passion. In the parade of bourgeois types caricatured in *Les Français peints par eux-mêmes*, published in 1840, the *horticulteur* is described as one "living among the flowers like a bee," who finds nothing so annoying as the sight of a rosebush the gardener, himself, does not own.[21]

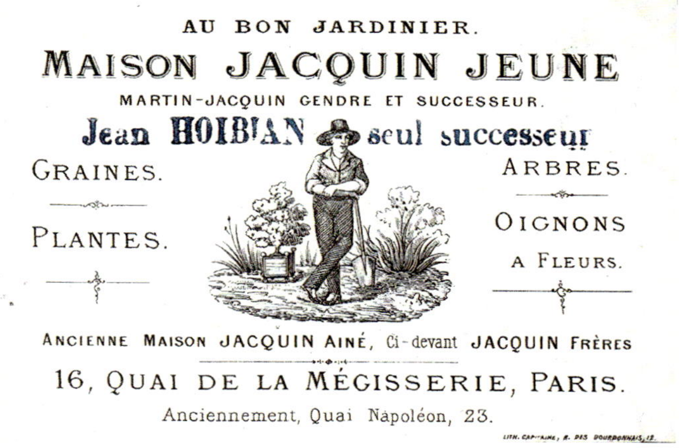

The international exhibitions held in Paris beginning in 1855 presented lavish displays of plant material from all over the world. The Exposition Universelle of 1867, housed in a huge glass pavilion constructed on the Champs-de-Mars, featured elaborate gardens both inside and out: lawns, lakes, fountains, and the rarest of flowers and trees (see fig. 59). Declared a "ravishing sight" by the *Revue Horticole*, the horticultural extravaganza was succeeded by ever-grander displays at the expositions of 1878, 1889, and 1900, when a parterre of flowers, including 32,000 square feet planted with roses, stretched from the Place de la Concorde to the Pont des Invalides.[22] In 1867 more than nine million visitors attended the Paris world's fair, which was perfectly timed to celebrate the city's brand-new parks and tree-lined boulevards, expanses that projected an image of France as a nation of progress and innovation.

Wanting to place his work before the public at the Salon of 1867, the year of the great exposition, the young Claude Monet produced his own floral display, a monumental picture in which four nearly life-size figures can be seen gathering bouquets in the garden of a suburban house (fig. 85). While updating the always popular subject of young women dallying out of doors, depicted in such pictures as Jean Honoré Fragonard's *The Swing* of a century earlier (fig. 86), Monet's *Women in the Garden* also evokes pictorial traditions of the Renaissance, with its composition centered on a leaf-crowned tree and a dance of circling maidens, seated and standing, moving and still. Monet's future wife, Camille, probably posed for three of the figures, all of whom follow the fashions of the time, as does the garden with its curving pathway, rosebushes, lawns, and flower beds. It was perhaps the chic modernity and monumentality accorded such a mundane subject, combined with the painting's lack of technical finish, that condemned it to rejection by the Salon jury. (Shortly before his death Monet retaliated for the insult, charging the French state an exorbitant sum for the picture's purchase.)

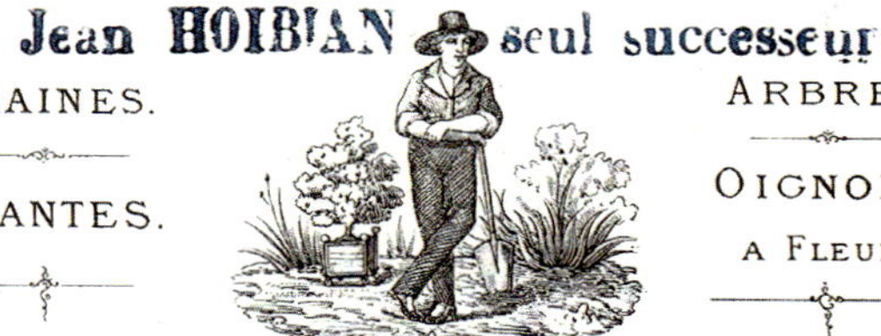

FIG. 84. Maison Jacquin Jeune. Trade card, ca. 1850. Lithograph. The Metropolitan Museum of Art, New York

OVERLEAF:

FIG. 85. Claude Monet. *Women in the Garden*, 1866–67. Oil on canvas. Musée d'Orsay, Paris

FIG. 86. Jean Honoré Fragonard. *The Swing*, 1767. Oil on canvas. Wallace Collection, London

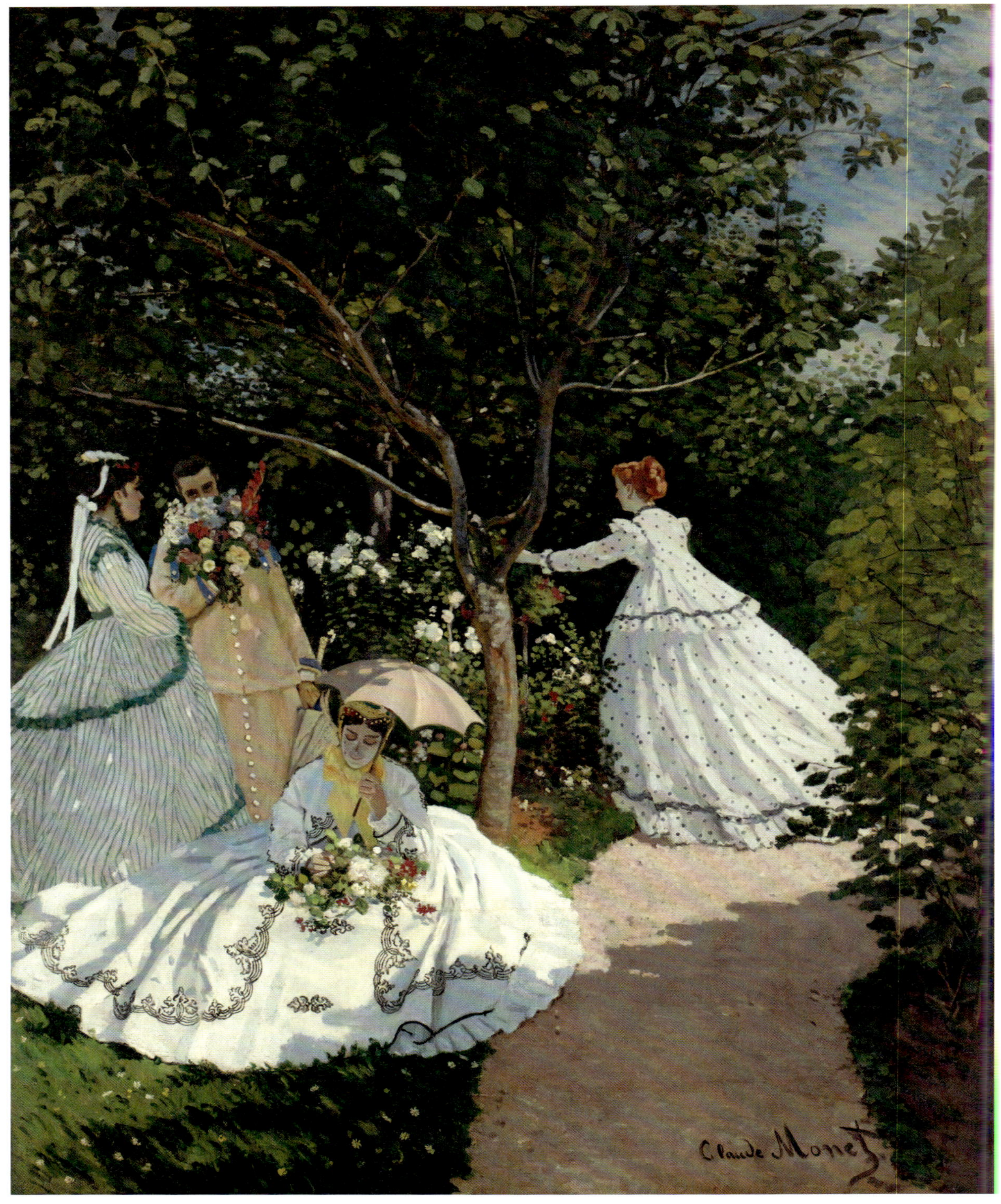
Claude Monet

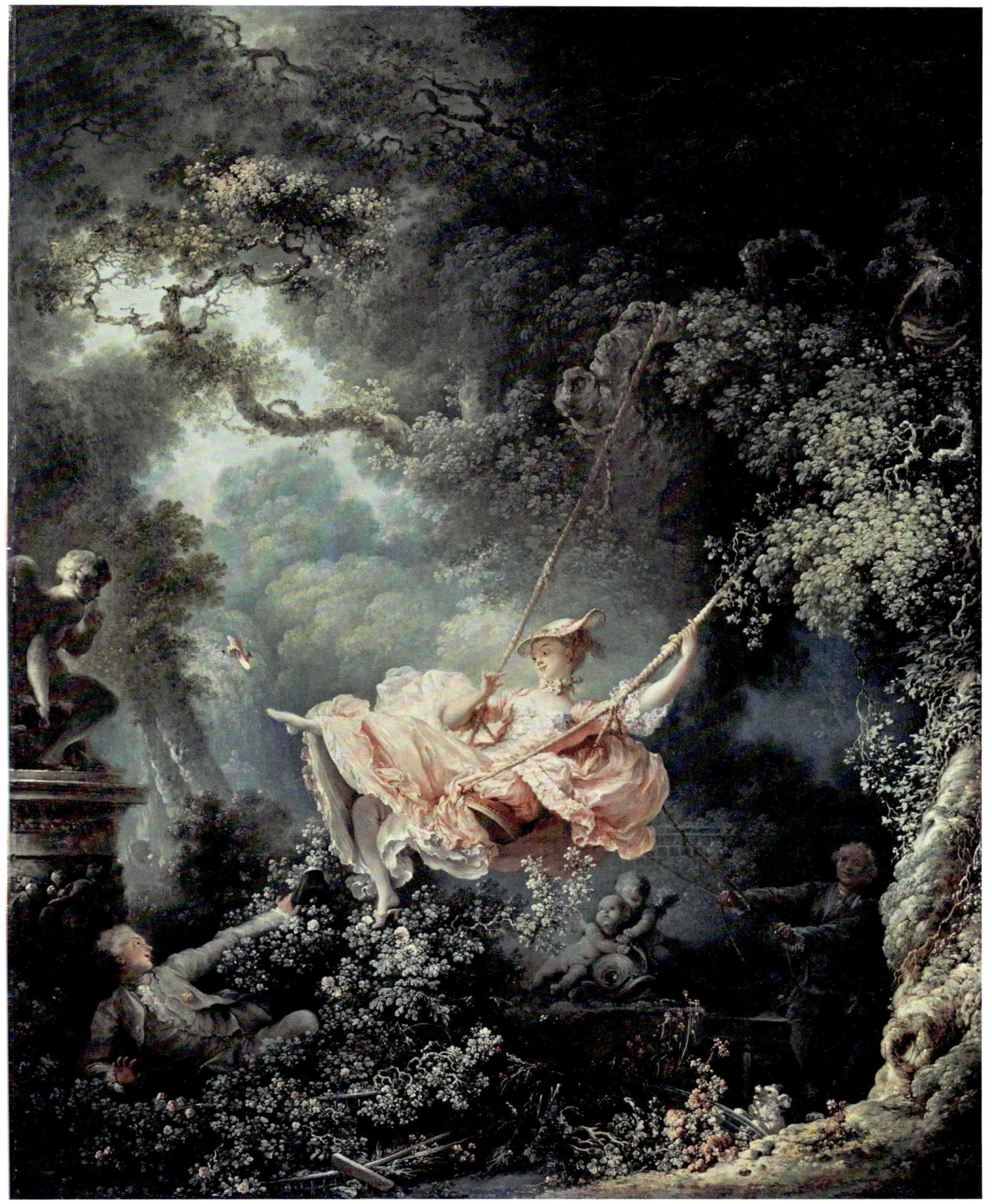

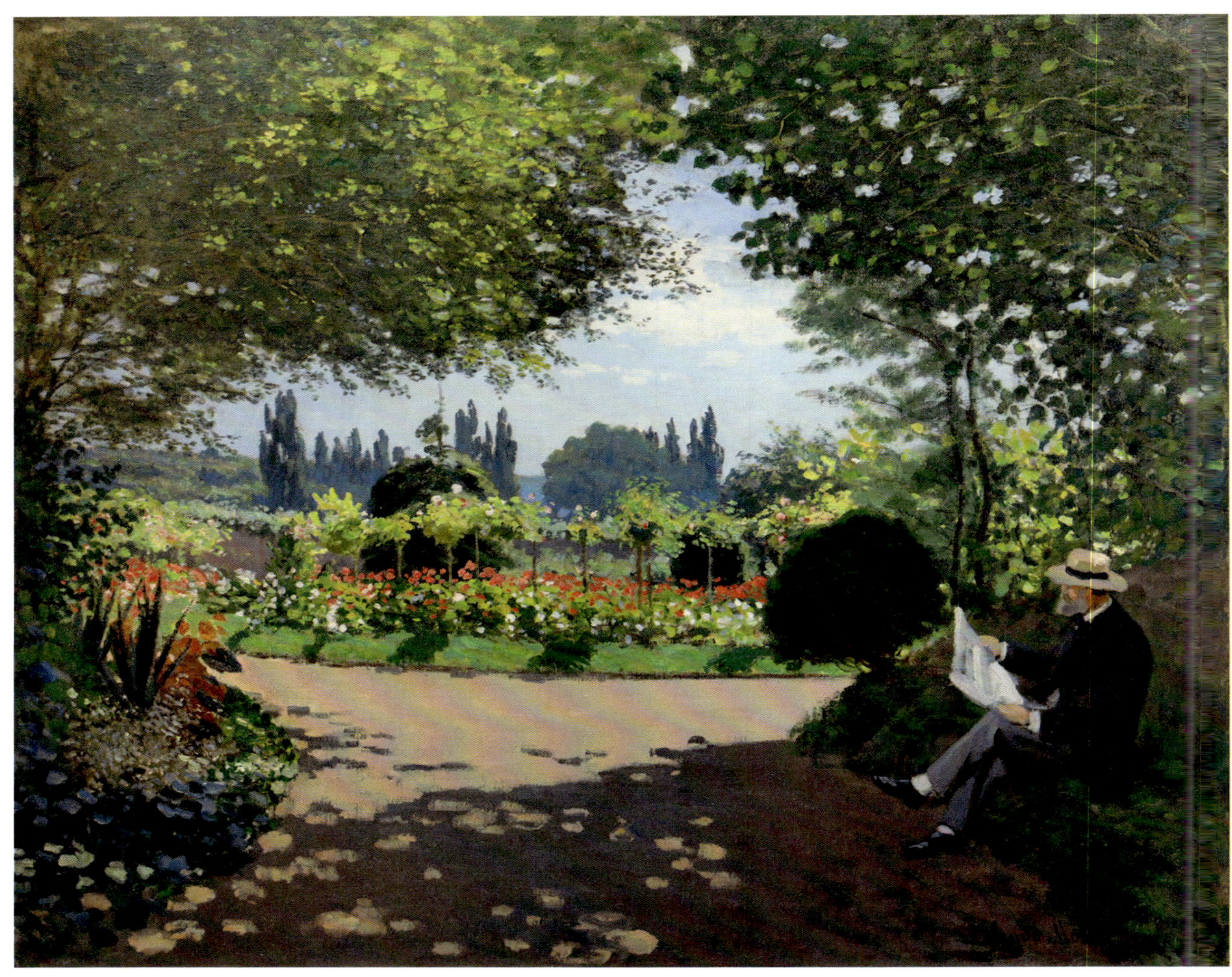

FIG. 87. Claude Monet. *Adolphe Monet Reading in a Garden*, 1867. Oil on canvas. Lawrence J. Ellison collection

Monet was in his twenties when he began setting up his easel in sunlit gardens, the most intimate of landscapes. During summer visits to his family on the coast of Normandy, he painted his aunt Lecadre's gardens in the seaside resort of Sainte-Adresse near the port of Le Havre. The manicured oasis of standard roses and bedding geraniums at the villa, Le Côteau, made a stunning setting for the artist's sidelong portrait of his father, Adolphe, a prosperous merchant (fig. 87). From a spot nearer the shore, Monet could look out on the Channel, lined with ships for which his father supplied provisions. From this height the painter took in the breezy terrace where his family was sunning amid brightly colored nasturtiums, geraniums,

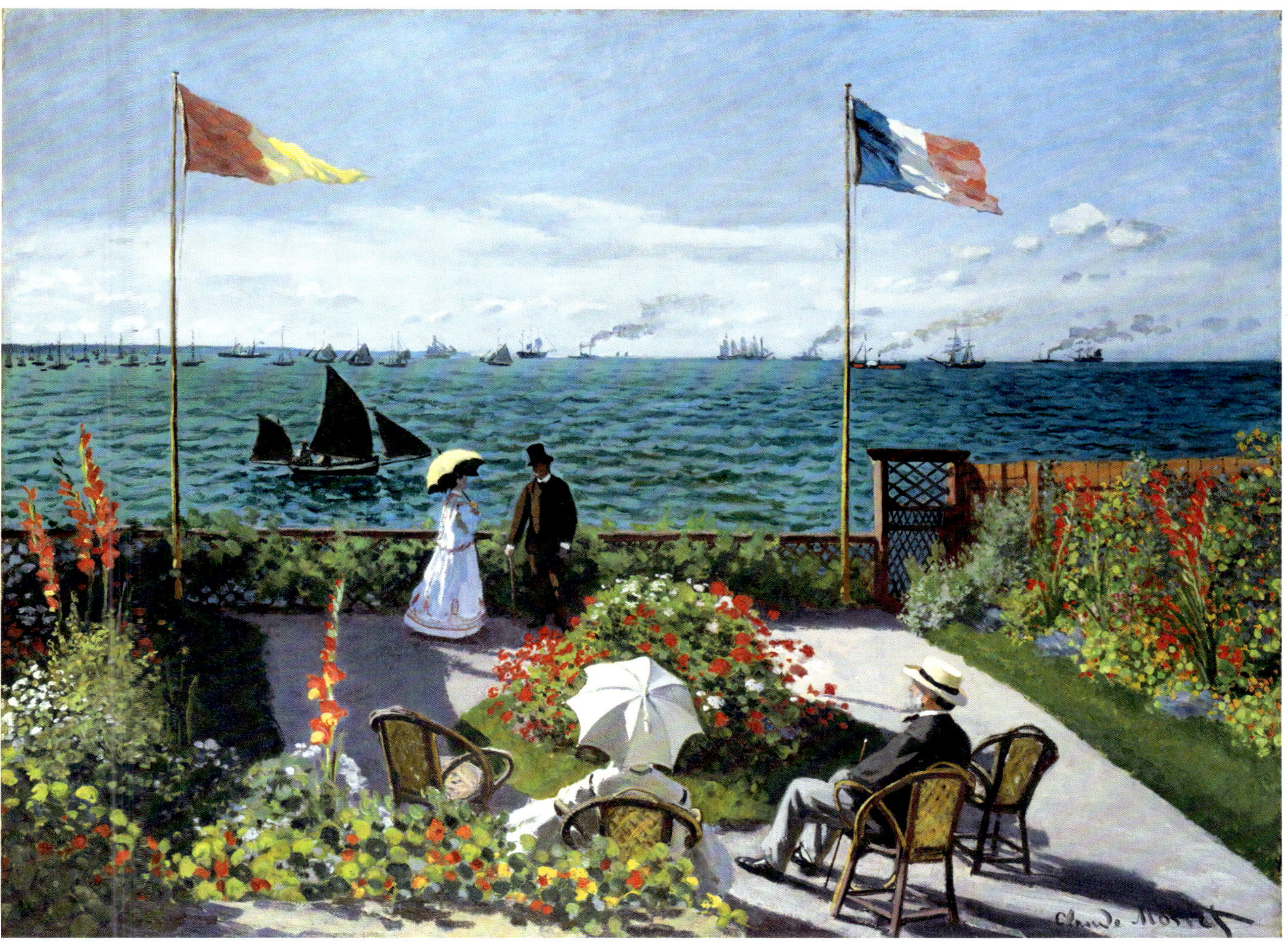

FIG. 88. Claude Monet. *Garden at Sainte-Adresse*, 1867. Oil on canvas. The Metropolitan Museum of Art, New York

and tall gladioli, South African exotica recently hybridized in France and grown extensively in the sandy soil of Le Havre (fig. 88).[23] In later years, as a gardener himself, Monet would plant the same assortment of flowers, mementos of his youth.

Monet established his own bourgeois household in two rented houses in the Paris suburb of Argenteuil between 1871 and 1876, and there he began to garden in earnest, making his own flower-filled backyards the subject of more than thirty canvases. He devoted a large plot in his first spacious garden to one of his favorite flowers, the dahlia, native to Mexico, which arrived in France in 1802 and by 1813 was in widespread cultivation. Celebrating their

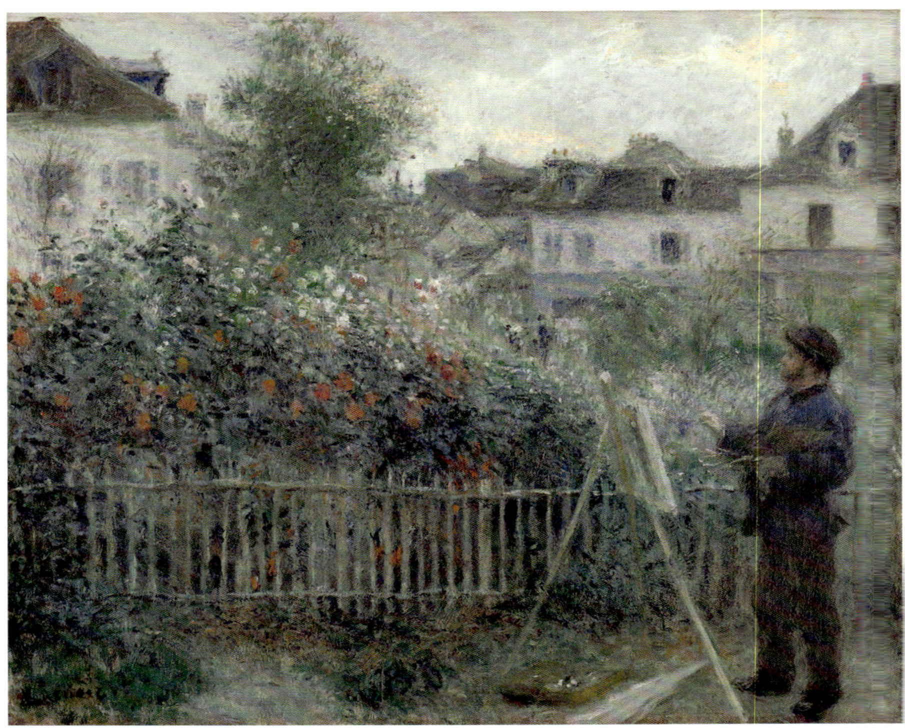

FIG. 89. Auguste Renoir. *Monet Painting in His Garden at Argenteuil*, 1873. Oil on canvas. Wadsworth Atheneum Museum of Art, Hartford

late summer flowering, Monet set up his easel to paint his dahlias at their peak, while his friend Renoir stood at his own easel nearby to capture the moment in the petal-size brushstrokes that both artists had adopted (fig. 89).

All three of the greatest garden enthusiasts among the Impressionists—Renoir, Monet, and Caillebotte—planted varieties of dahlias and traded tips on their selection and cultivation. Coincidentally, they added the brilliant colors of the tropical blooms to their palettes. Monet methodically created flowery enclosures, while Renoir enjoyed the "beautiful abandoned park" of his Montmartre studio, and Caillebotte maintained a more formal display at Petit-Gennevilliers. Each of these was a different kind of garden, but all of them functioned as open-air laboratories where the shapes, textures, and colors of plants were seen to shift in the play of light and shade.[24]

Early in the autumn of 1874 Monet moved into his second rented house in Argenteuil. The new garden would become the artist's most important pictorial motif, the subject of at least five paintings in 1875 and ten in 1876. In a walled circular space he created a central flower bed with plantings of gladioli and hollyhocks that soared above nasturtiums and geraniums to

FIG. 90. Claude Monet. *Camille Monet in the Garden at Argenteuil*, 1876. Oil on canvas. The Metropolitan Museum of Art, New York

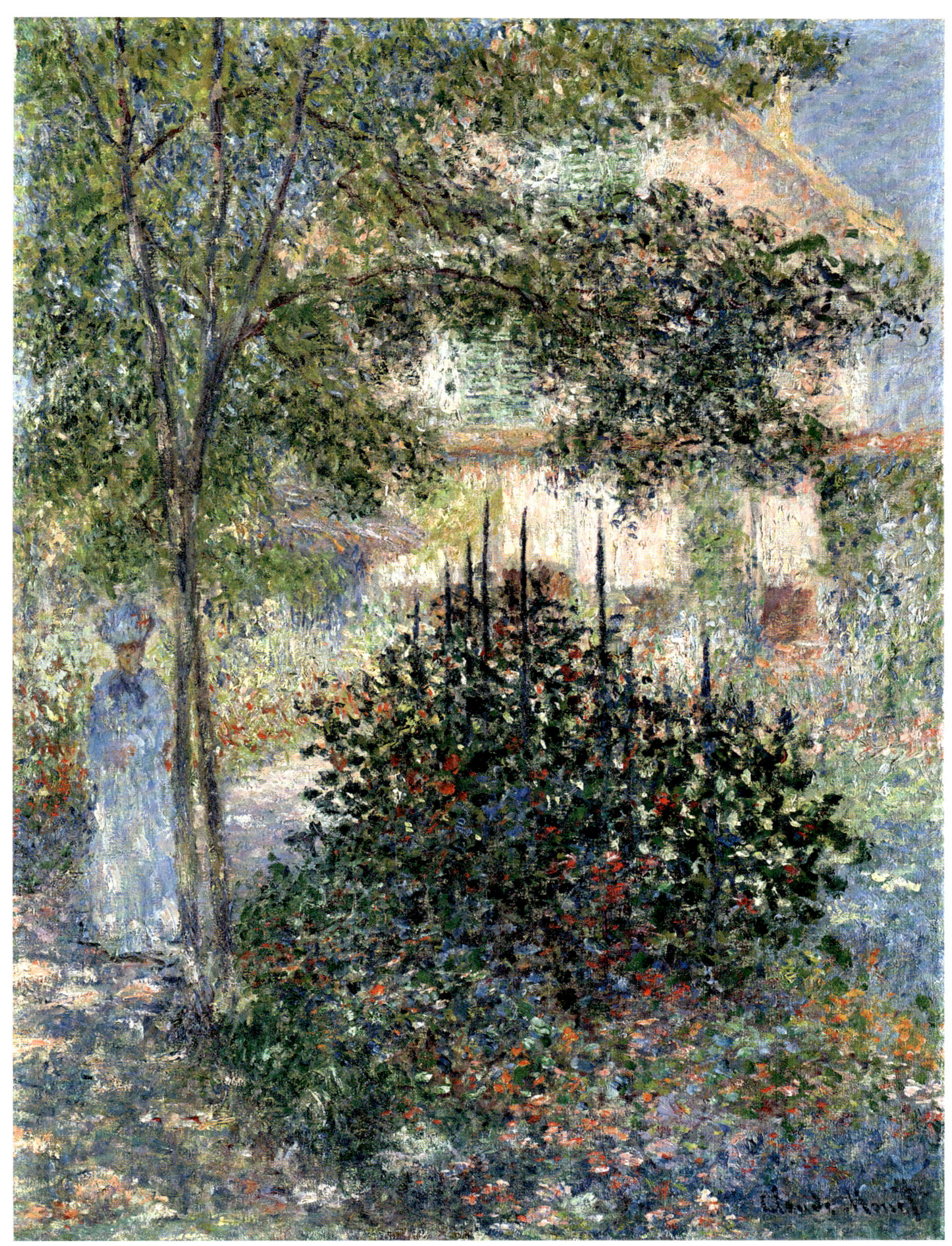

FIG. 91. Gustave Caillebotte. *Roses in the Garden at Petit-Gennevilliers*, ca. 1886. Oil on canvas. Private collection

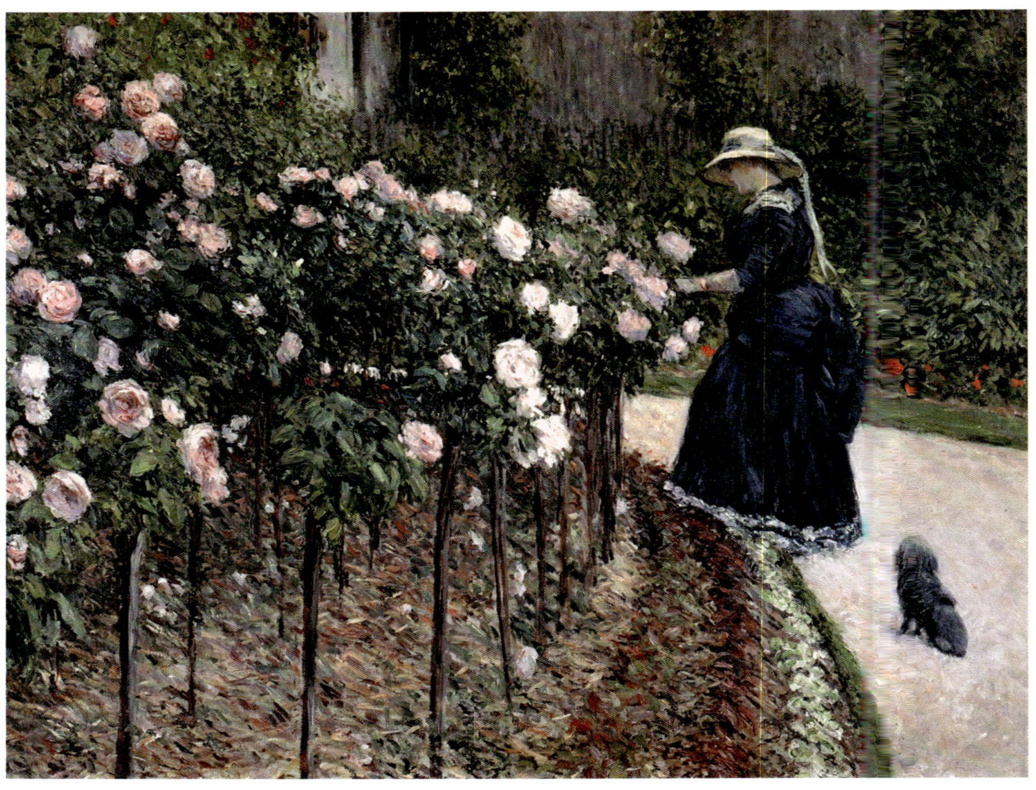

provide bursts of color at laddered levels, in accord with the current fashion for mounded combinations of annuals and perennials. The hollyhocks grew taller than Monet's wife, Camille, whose painted form dissolves in shadows, submitting to the primacy of flowers and foliage (fig. 90).

In contrast to Monet's intermingled plantings, Caillebotte's more formal garden, tended by two full-time gardeners, positioned flowers in separate beds according to their species. Caillebotte had developed his horticultural skills on his family's estate at Yerres, where he first began painting gardens. Beginning in 1881 he laid out an ambitious two-and-a-half-acre plot, much admired and no doubt inspiring to Monet, especially when the latter acquired property at Giverny.[25] In a region known for its rose nurseries, Caillebotte grew the favorite French flower in the upright standard form, then so popular, which allowed the artist's companion, Charlotte Berthier, to enjoy the sight and scent of blooms at close hand (fig. 91).[26] To provide access to taller blooms, the "parasol pruner," an ingenious implement that handily served two functions, was devised about this time (fig. 92).

The age-old association of femininity with flowers is reflected throughout the nineteenth century in images that show women as the principal players in gardens. As a popular new addition to bourgeois life the garden became an attractive setting for pictures of all kinds, including advertisements and fashion plate illustrations, where it served as a backdrop for elegant women dressed in the latest styles (fig. 93). The Belgian painter Alfred Stevens, who devoted much of his work to the private life of the "modern" Parisienne, effectively positioned models amid the greenery of his own garden ("my luxury") on the rue des Martyrs, a parklike oasis in the heart of the city with old trees and lawns, a duck pond, circular flower bed, and a glass reflecting ball (fig. 94). The site of frequent soirées gathering artists and writers, it was the spot where Manet painted *A Game of Croquet* (1873; Städel Museum, Frankfurt).[27] Like Stevens, the American painter James McNeill Whistler also took pride in his large Paris garden, which featured trees, abundant flowers, and a trellis designed by Mrs. Whistler. The artist sometimes painted, sketched, or worked on his etching plates in this outdoor studio, occasionally taking his wife as his model. It was said that "in his roses he buried his troubles."[28]

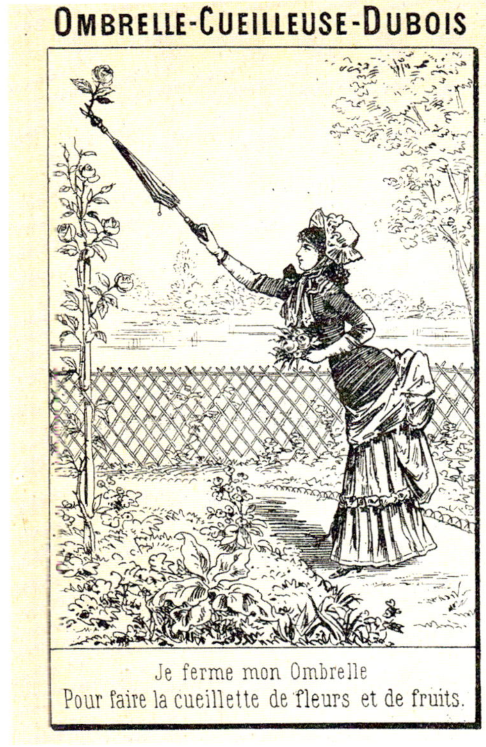

FIG. 92. *The Dubois Parasol Pruner*, 1886. Engraved card. The Metropolitan Museum of Art, New York

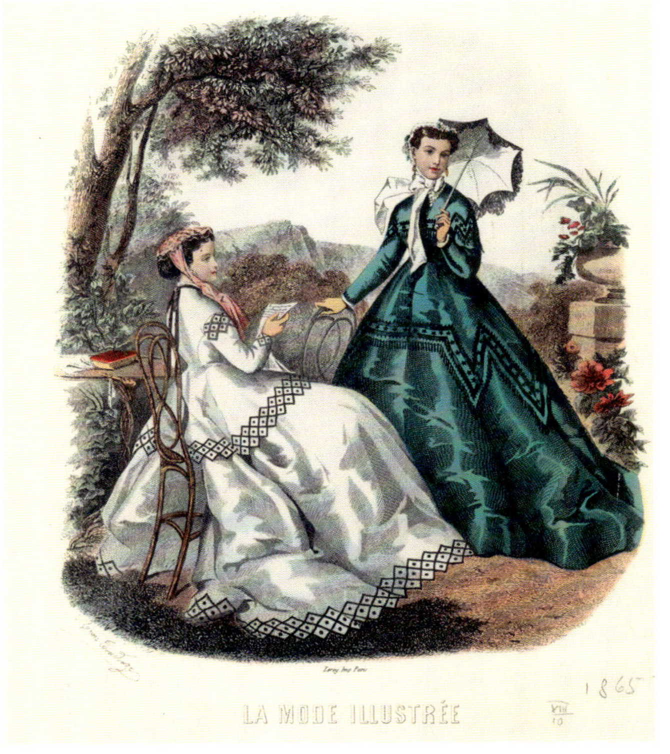

FIG. 93. "Women in a Garden," from *La Mode Illustrée*, 1865. Hand-colored engraving. The Metropolitan Museum of Art, New York

FIG. 94. Alfred Stevens. *The Glass Ball*, ca. 1875. Oil on canvas. Private collection

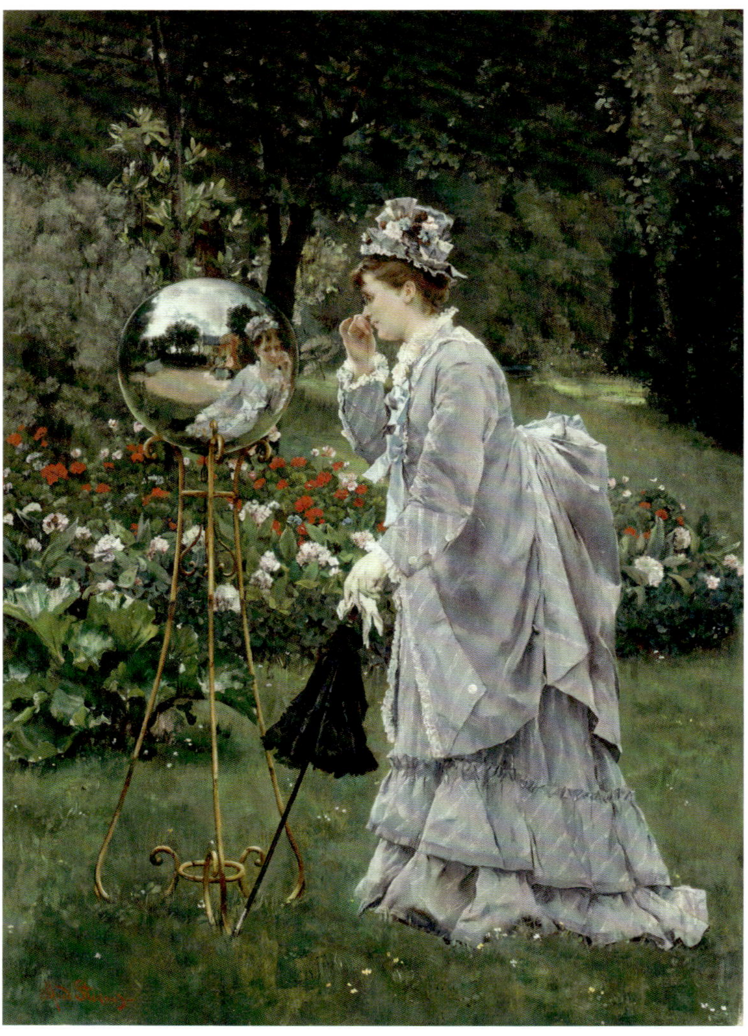

Unlike most other scientific fields, horticulture and botany became respected activities for bourgeois women, even taking a role in their education. As early as 1819 the author of *Le Langage des fleurs* (1819) promoted gardening for women as a source of both instruction and fulfillment, opening to them a "world of miracles."[29] The enormous appeal of gardens in the early twentieth century, especially to women of means, found frequent expression in the work of Edouard Vuillard. His painting of Hessel's well-tended garden at Vaucresson boasts a riot of blooms (fig. 95). Madame Hessel, wife of the art dealer Jos Hessel and a friend dear to Vuillard, often invited the artist to the couple's house in the western suburb of Paris.

FIG. 95. Edouard Vuillard. *Garden at Vaucresson*, 1920; reworked 1926, 1935, 1936. Distemper on canvas. The Metropolitan Museum of Art, New York

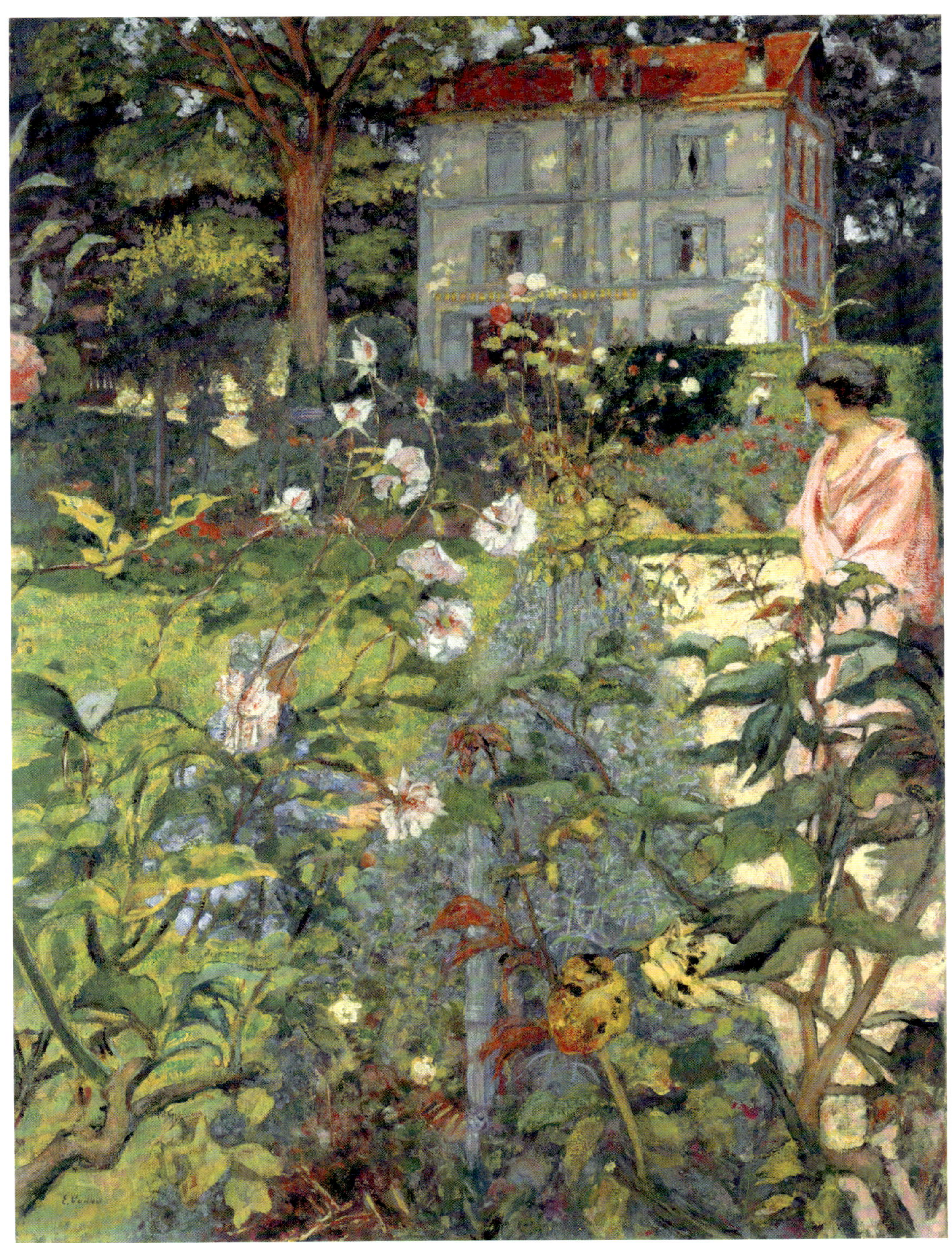

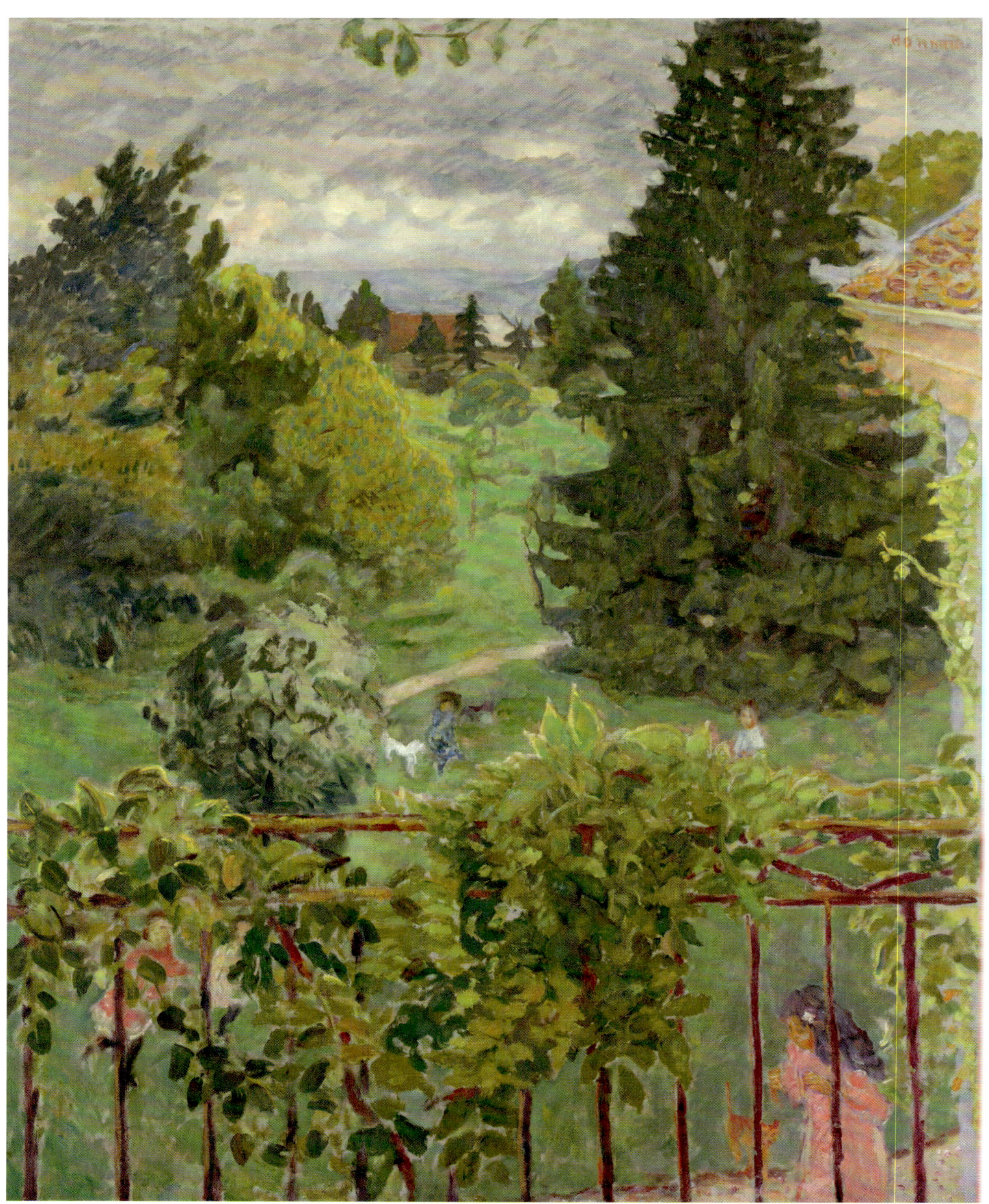

For Vuillard, and even more so for his close friend Pierre Bonnard, the garden offered an intimate place for domestic life in the open air. From the valley of the Seine to the South of France, the backyards of houses in which Bonnard resided appear in his paintings as plush playgrounds for children and animals, lovers and friends, whom the artist depicted with bemused delight. The assorted greens of vines, shrubs, and trees spread over luxuriant lawns, tilted upward like the floors of Degas's practice rooms. Often viewed from the high vantage point of a secure terrace or balcony, Bonnard's gardens, like the one at the family estate in Le Grand-Lemps, near Grenoble, were havens of peace and harmony (fig. 96).

An appreciation for the private garden moved many artists to treat green space as a place of solitude, refuge, and reverie. In 1880 Manet and his wife rented a house in Bellevue, where he was seeking treatment for his ailing leg. In his pictorial contemplation of the garden (fig. 97), the wooden bench at the center functions in the way that furniture often does in landscape paintings: the seat is empty, but, like the carafe on the iron table and the yellow jacket nearby, it suggests a narrative in which someone will soon step into the scene or someone has just left. In this case the caller may well have been Manet himself. Typical of the time with its geraniums and trellised roses, the garden has been made inviting to the viewer, although its tangled growth was annoying to Manet, who had intended to paint the more perfect gardens of nearby Versailles. "Having left [Paris] in order to do some studies in the park laid out by Lenôtre," he wrote to Eva Gonzalès on September 23, 1881, "I've had to content myself with painting only my garden, which is the unloveliest."[30]

To Paul Cézanne, the overrun formal gardens of his parents' home in Aix-en-Provence never seemed "unlovely," even as they endured years of neglect. The artist divided his time between Paris and the country estate, Jas de Bouffan, painting more than thirty views of the property over a period of some twenty-five years. Charting the symmetry of the massive chestnut trees, he sometimes included the stone washing trough and the large square pool framed by a railing that sat next to it (fig. 98). In his depictions of the cool tranquility of Jas de Bouffan, Cézanne celebrates the garden that provided refuge when he withdrew from the challenges of life in Paris.

Monet may have had ambitious plans for a large garden when he moved to a rented farmhouse in Giverny, about forty miles northwest of Paris, but in 1883 his finances could not support the effort. Only after he was able to purchase the property seven years later did his horticultural campaign begin in earnest and finally triumph in nearly six landscaped acres brimming with

FIG. 96. Pierre Bonnard. *From the Balcony*, 1909. Oil on canvas. The Metropolitan Museum of Art, New York

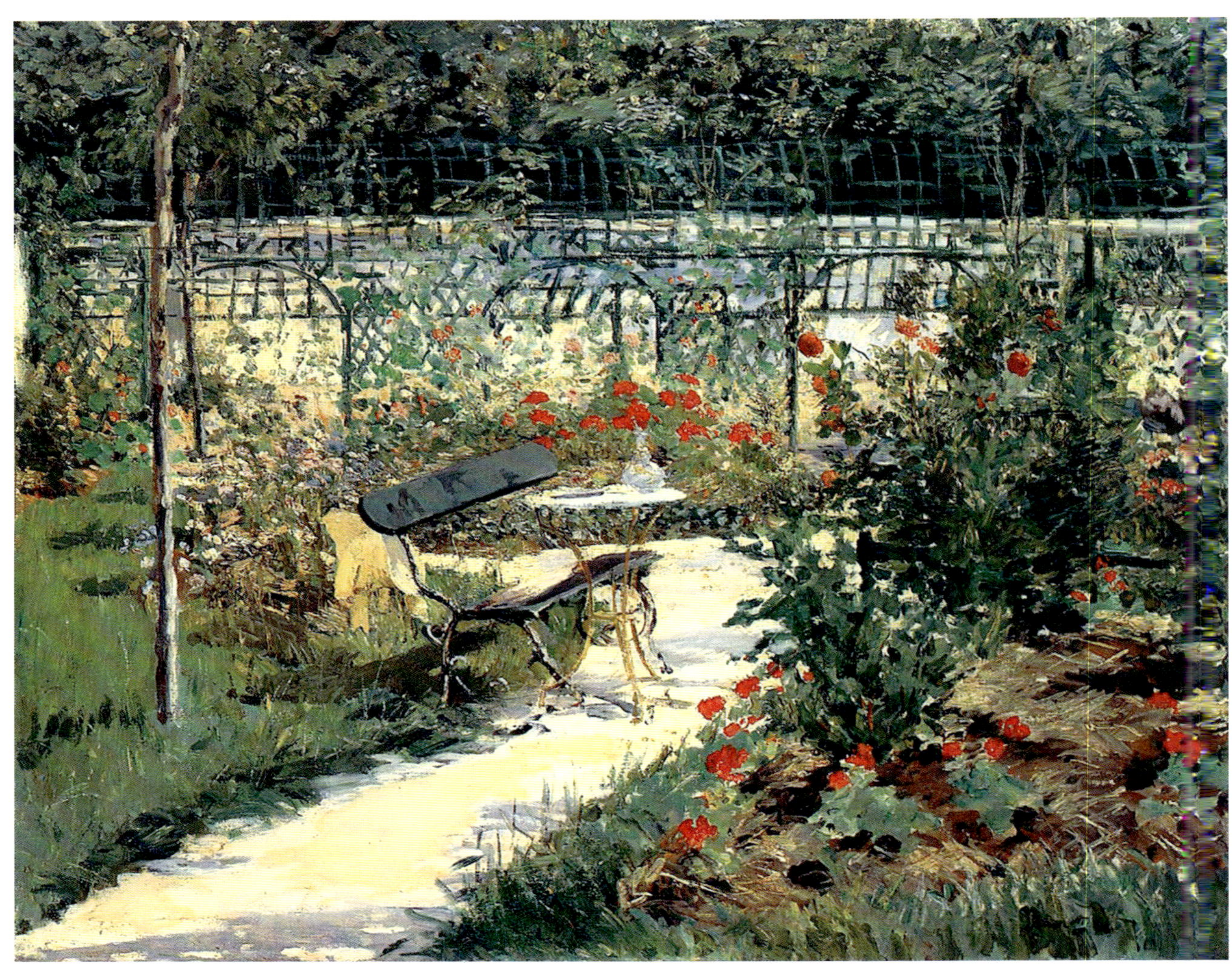

FIG. 97. Edouard Manet. *Garden Bench*, 1881.
Oil on canvas. Private collection

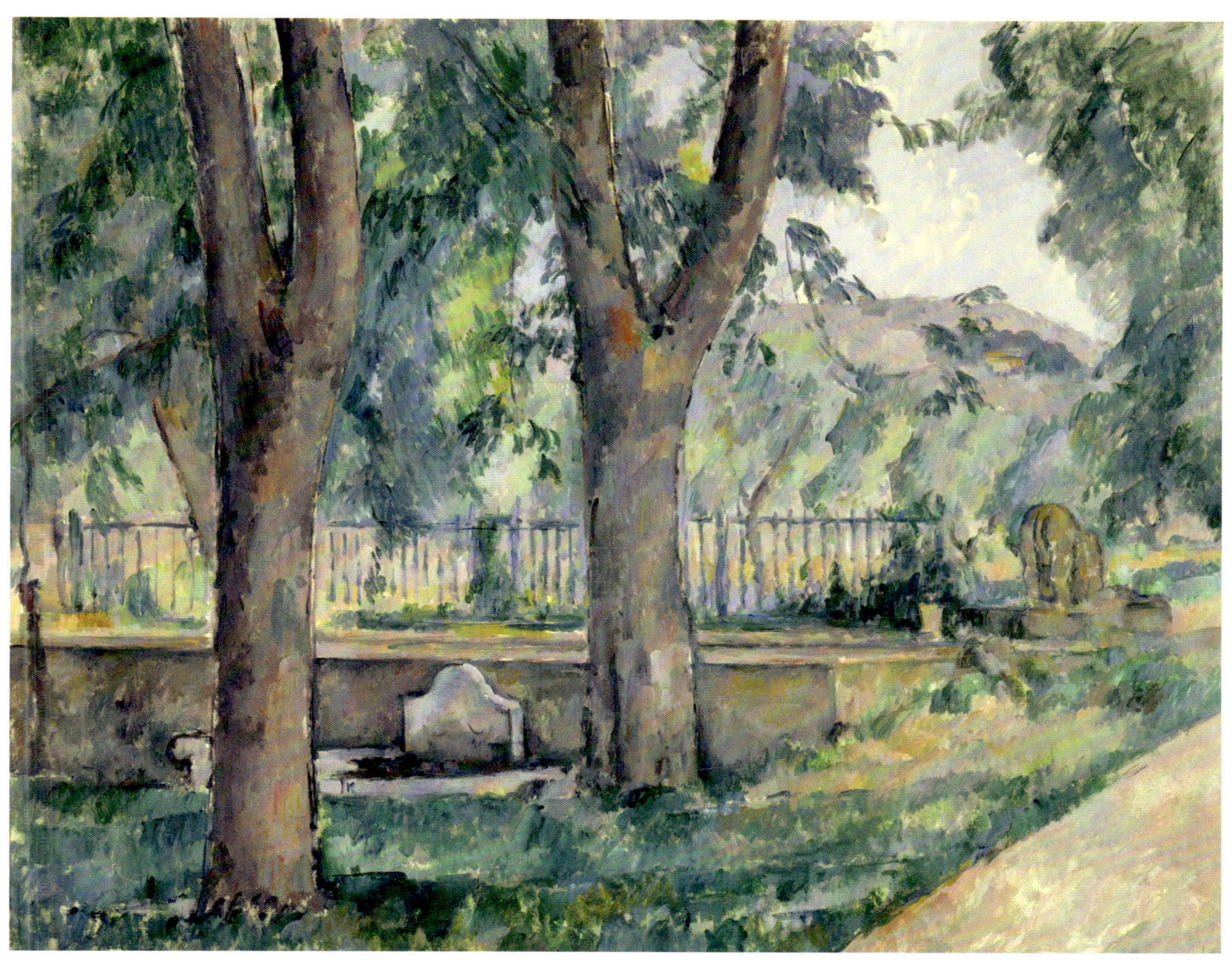

FIG 98. Paul Cézanne. *The Pool at Jas de Bouffan*, ca. 1885–86. Oil on canvas. The Metropolitan Museum of Art, New York

FIG. 99. Claude Monet. *Path in Monet's Garden*, 1902. Oil on canvas. Österreichische Galerie Belvedere, Vienna

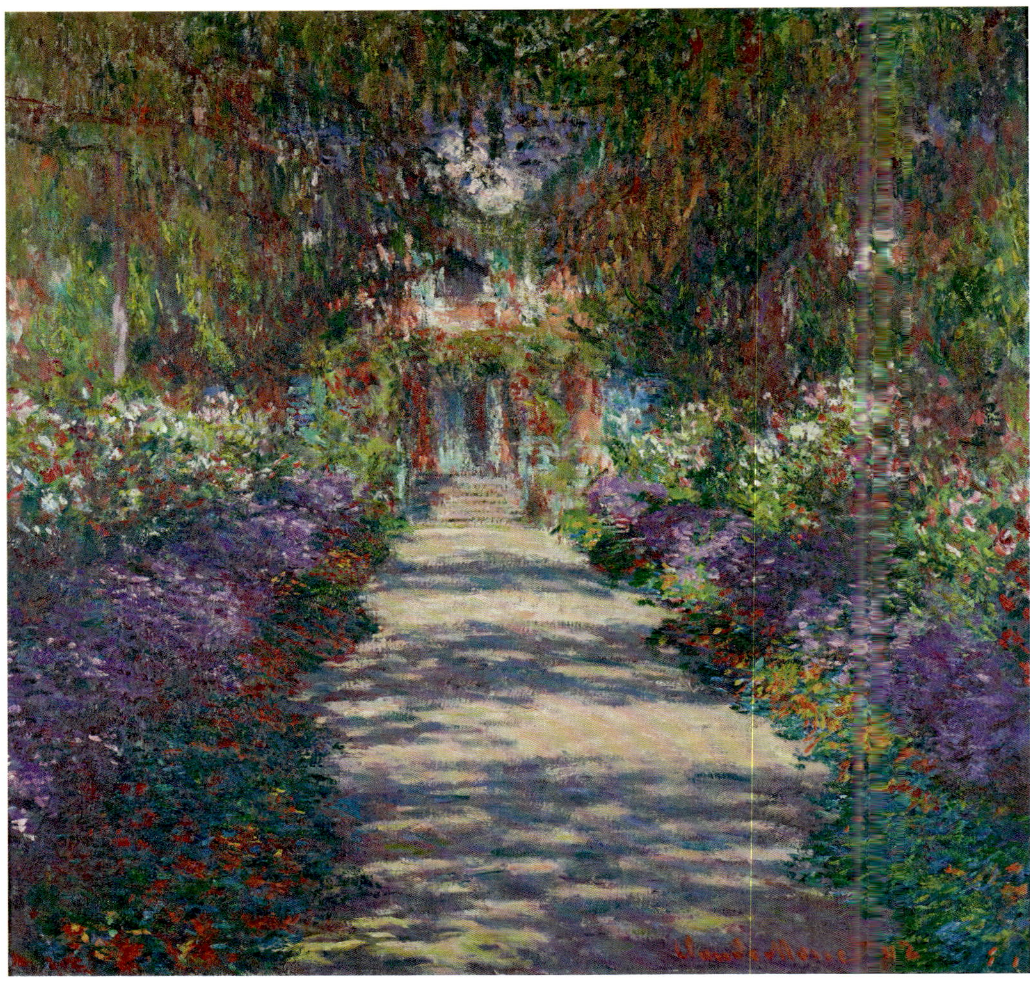

flower beds and a serene water lily pond. It was not until the mid-1890s that Monet viewed his garden as fit to paint.

In his walled garden, laid out symmetrically according to local Norman tradition, Monet liked to see flowers everywhere—left, right, overhead, and underfoot. While the gravel paths were laid straight, the borders, planted in an informal English-cottage style, blurred the edges with flowers tumbling into the walkways: poppies, peonies, irises, campanulas, and columbines in early summer; sunflowers, dahlias, daisies, and creeping nasturtiums late in the season (fig. 99). The generous planting scheme made it possible for Monet, when painting in its midst, to fill his entire canvas with color, probably keeping in mind, as he did when planting or painting, the laws of the

FIG. 100. Claude Monet. *The Path through the Irises*, 1914–17. Oil on canvas. The Metropolitan Museum of Art, New York

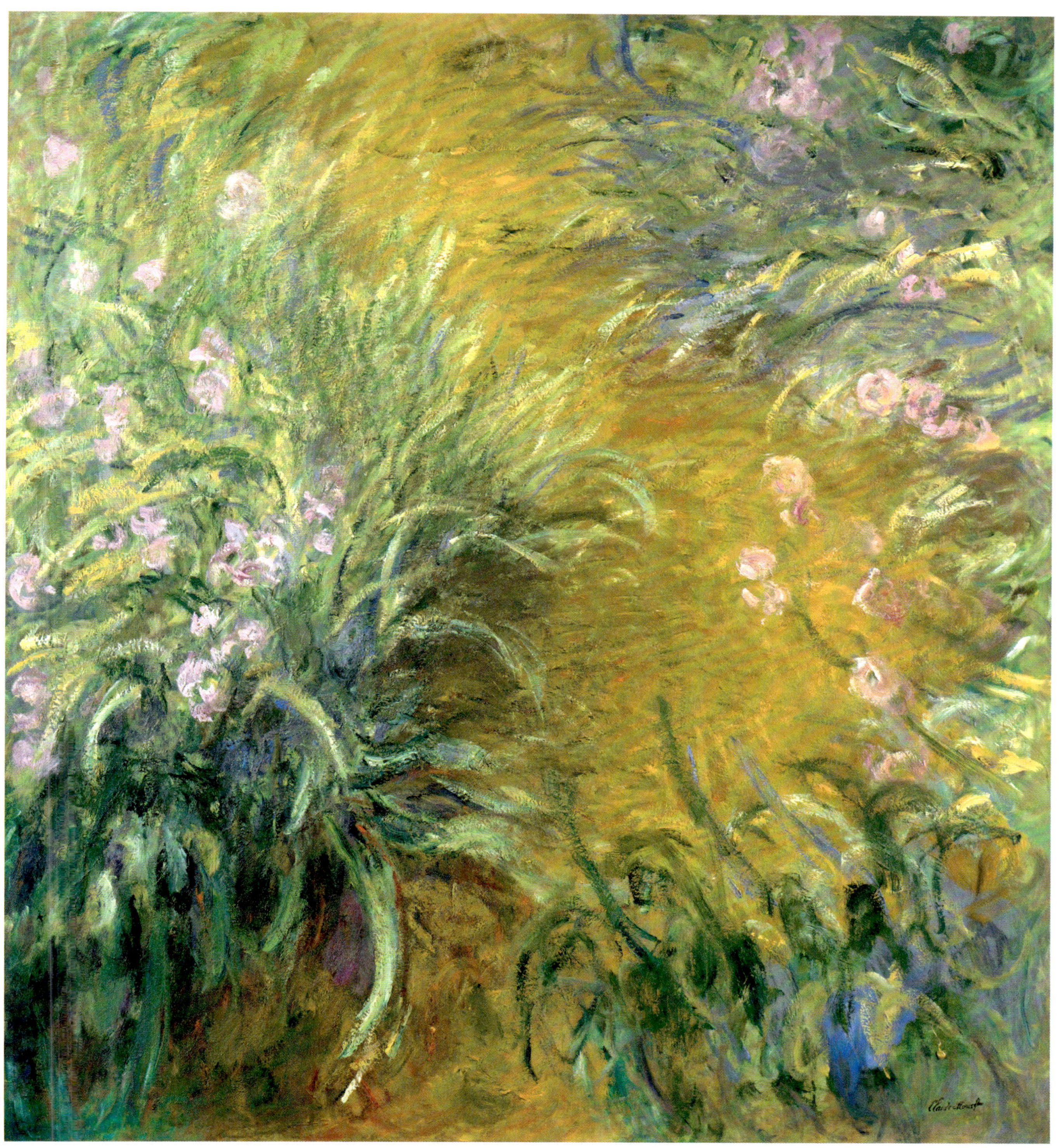

simultaneous contrast of color proposed by Eugène Chevreul, in which adjacent colors impact the viewer's perception of both. In his extensive horticultural library, Monet owned a copy of Chevreul's book, published in 1839, in which the French chemist had suggested that his color theories be applied to the arrangement of flower beds, "[to] make them more attractive."[31] As an exercise in aid of his planting design, Monet set up a sequence of "paintboxes" planted with flowers graduated in color from white to deep purple.

Toward the end of his life Monet experienced an increasingly intimate communion with his garden, and as his eyesight failed he literally drew closer to his plants, immersing himself in their opulence (fig. 100). He raised more than forty varieties of iris at Giverny, masses of bearded iris in beds up to a hundred feet long and clumps of the Japanese *Iris kaempferi* at the edges of the pond. Indeed, with the importation of many foreign species during the nineteenth century, France became the first center of systematic iris breeding, and in 1910 one of the new varieties developed was named *Madame Claude Monet*, for the artist's wife.

When the opportunity arose to expand his garden in 1893, Monet purchased a plot across the road from his house beyond the intervening railroad tracks. He filled the marshy site with a lily pond and encircled it with exotic plants much like those in a Japanese garden on display at the Paris Exposition Universelle in 1889. In addition, the artist installed a wood footbridge that arched over the water, similar to the ones pictured in his collection of Japanese prints. Perhaps recalling Hokusai's famous suite of color woodcuts, Thirty-Six Views of Mount Fuji (1826), some of which he owned, Monet continued the custom of treating subjects in series and created eighteen views of his green bridge. In the initial paintings of the sequence, the structure spans the entire width of the canvas, seemingly unsupported by any visible shoreline, and appears to float, like the lilies on the water's surface (fig. 101).

The wave of "Japonisme" that swept through France after the Tokugawa government opened its ports to trade with the West in 1854 gathered enthusiasts mainly among the avant-garde, who were struck by the novelty of a new, imported art. In addition to Monet, Albert Kahn, a wealthy Parisian banker, was also attracted to the garden art of the Japanese. After returning from a trip to Japan in the 1890s, he created a small Japanese village and garden at his home in Boulogne. Eventually including areas planted in English, French, and other styles, the garden is now a ten-acre *parc à scenes*, currently open to the public.[32]

Monet's Japanesque garden introduced a new, subtler aesthetic to Giverny, realized more in foliage than in flowers, in delicate rather than bold colors,

FIG. 101. Claude Monet. *Bridge over a Pond of Water Lilies*, 1899. Oil on canvas. The Metropolitan Museum of Art, New York

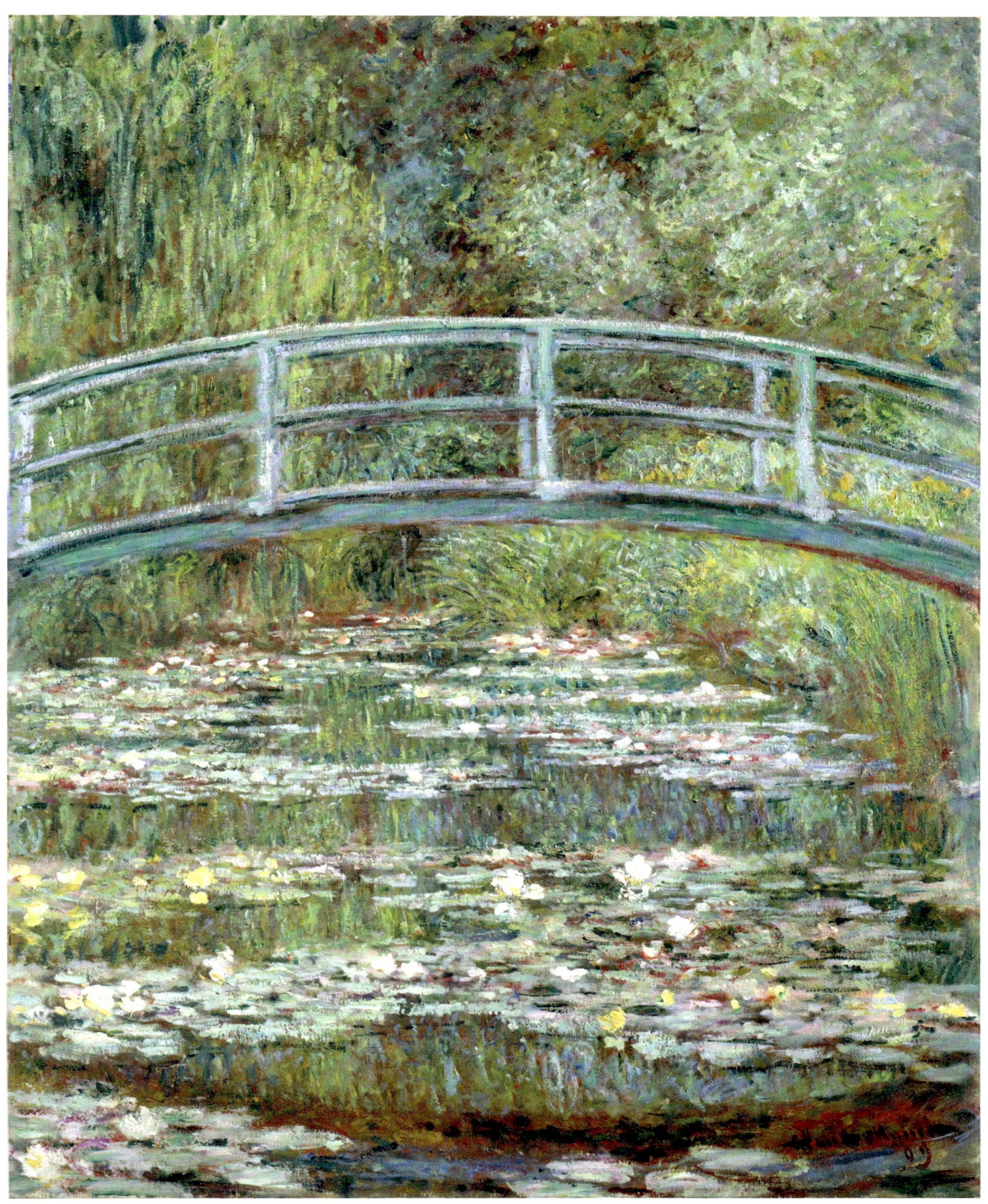

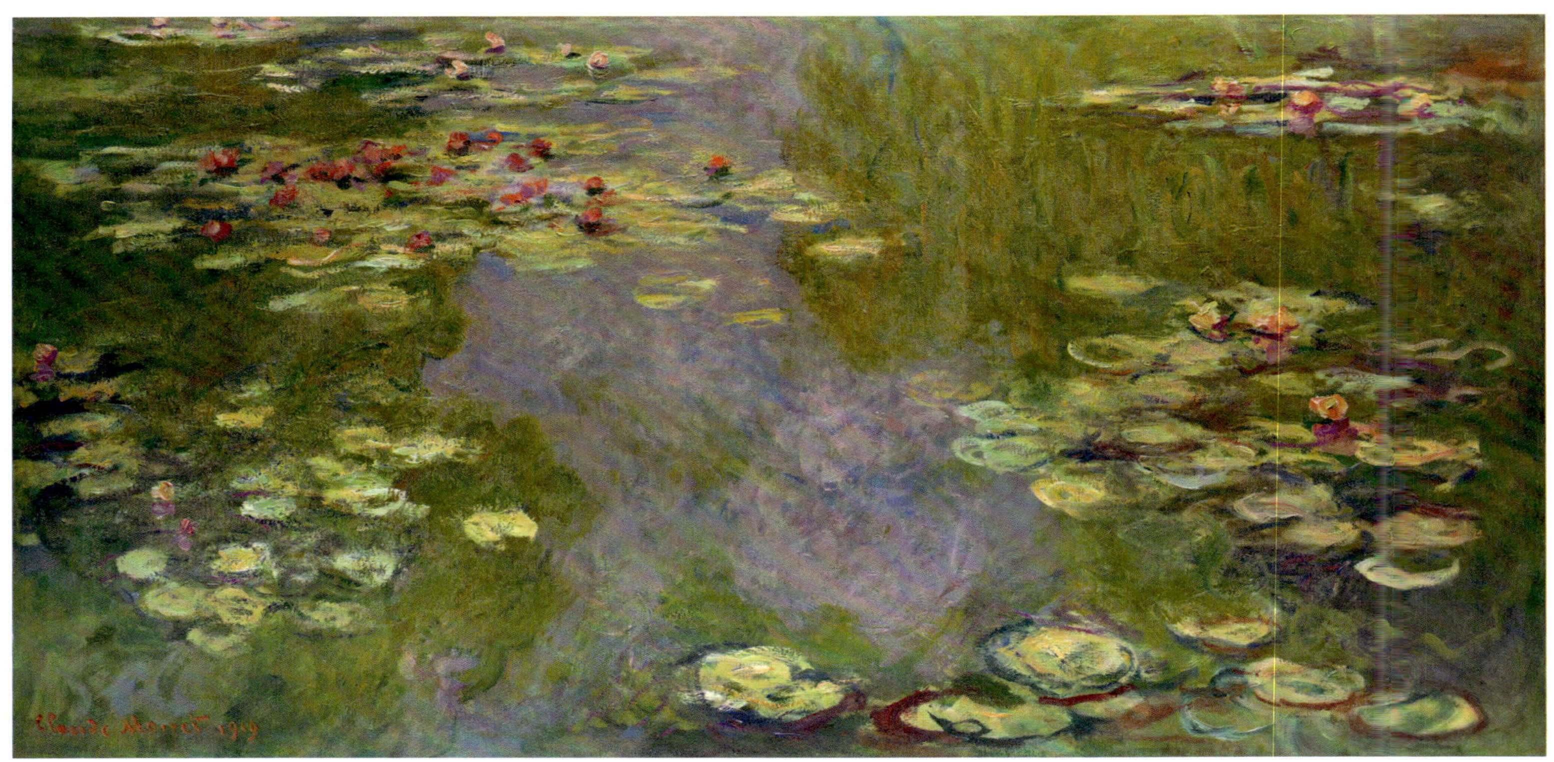

FIG. 102. Claude Monet. *Water Lilies*, 1919. Oil on canvas. The Metropolitan Museum of Art, New York

in shadows rather than sunlight. It also presented fresh horticultural challenges. To frame his pond the artist planted groves of bamboo, Japanese plum and cherry trees, and sweet coltsfoot (*Petasites japonicus*), with its enormous round leaves. When he visited the Exposition Universelle in 1889, Monet encountered a vast display of foreign plants, including exotic strains of water lily. The novel beauty of these flowers had inspired the Bordeaux nurseryman Joseph Bory Latour-Marliac to cultivate imports and to introduce a line of water lily hybrids that eventually offered gardeners more than thirty varieties, including an Egyptian pink-and-white-petaled lily.

Water lilies became a passion with Monet, and for nearly three decades the Giverny lily pond stayed the central focus of his attention. One of the six or seven gardeners usually in his employ was assigned to the pond's special care and maintenance, clearing the plants of faded blooms, aphids, and dust from the nearby road (which he eventually had paved, to eliminate the problem). Contemplating the surface of the pond from his rowboat or from the water's edge, where he often set up his easel, the artist whom Manet called "the Raphael of water" made more than two hundred water lily paintings, few of which were exhibited or released for sale during his lifetime, with a notable exception, the *Water Lilies* illustrated here (fig. 102).[33] Most of the numerous water lily pictures Monet produced over a period of more than fifteen years, however, may be seen as preparatory studies for the monumental suite of twenty-two paintings he offered to the French state after World War I as a symbol of peace. In his unprecedented mural cycle, now preserved in two oval galleries of the Musée de l'Orangerie in Paris, Monet reportedly wished to evoke the experience of a stroll around his lily pond by creating "the illusion of an endless whole, of water without horizon or shore . . . a refuge for peaceful meditation at the center of a flowering aquarium."[34]

No other artist working in the nineteenth century devoted himself so entirely to the garden as did Monet. The extent of his commitment to gardening and his understanding of its symbiotic role in his creative life may be judged by his oft-quoted comment, "My garden is my most beautiful work of art."[35] In Monet's lifelong dedication to the miraculous, fugitive sights of nature and to their realization on canvas, gardening and painting became conflated. Furthermore, the idea of the garden in and of itself as a legitimate subject for pictorial art found resonance in the modern credo articulated by Maurice Denis that a painting, before it is anything else, is "essentially a flat surface covered with colors arranged in a certain order."[36]

In work where the role of color bridges the nineteenth to the twentieth century, the Neo-Impressionist Henri-Edmond Cross followed Monet into the garden, finding light and plant life in equilibrium. In Cross's garden at Saint-Clair, in the South of France, the sun was brighter and the vegetation spikier, prompting the artist, perhaps inspired also by Van Gogh, to practice a more linear (rather than his more frequent Pointillist) application of color (fig. 103). Attentive to the individual characteristics of his semitropical plants, Cross rendered them with such vitality that human presence is unmissed.

Like Cross, Bonnard found in the Côte d'Azur colors more radiant and plant life more chaotic. The greenswards of northern France and the largely untamed grounds of his house at Vernonnet in the Seine Valley, only two miles away from Monet (whom he periodically visited), had provided relatively placid backdrops in earlier pictures (see fig. 96); in the Côte d'Azur, however, the dazzling colors and shapes of the landscape dominated. Here, Bonnard abandoned the naturalism of the Impressionists. The reality of the garden fell away, re-envisioned and re-created in arbitrary colors and forms simplified through abstraction (fig. 104).[37]

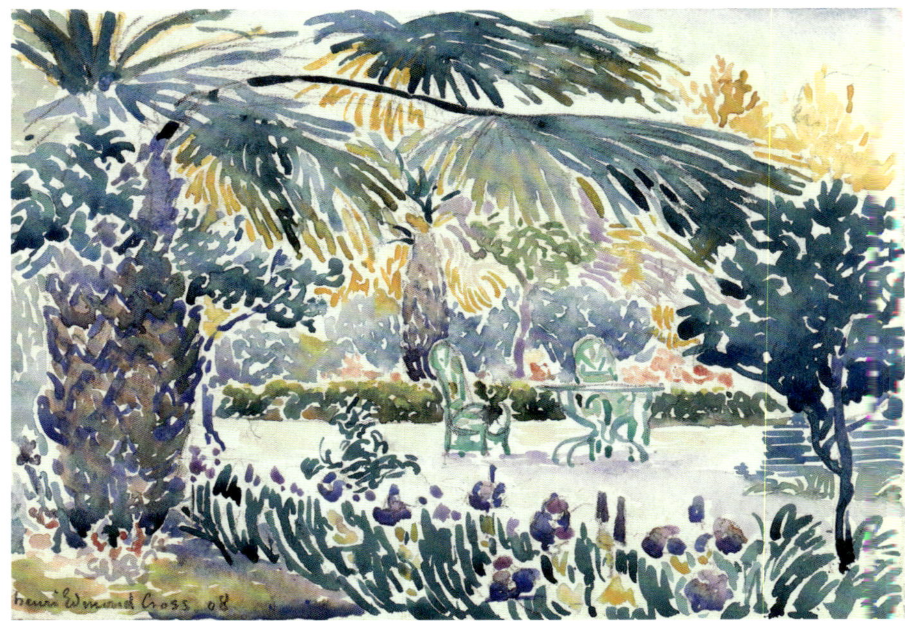

FIG. 103. Henri-Edmond Cross. *Garden of the Painter at Saint-Clair*, 1908. Watercolor over graphite. The Metropolitan Museum of Art, New York

FIG. 104. Pierre Bonnard. *Garden*, ca. 1935. Oil on canvas. The Metropolitan Museum of Art, New York

A similar divergence from the naturalistic approach in the development of garden design occurred at the end of the nineteenth century. Eclectic styles that mixed together different plants gave way to a more controlled, multicolored mosaiculture that gathered together flowering annuals in ornate patterns, rather like those introduced in the seventeenth century to the systematically "embroidered" parterres at Versailles. As nationalism took hold in France after the Franco-Prussian War of 1870, the reputation of the country's greatest landscape designer, André Le Nôtre, was restored, nearly two centuries after his death. The landscape architects Henri and Achille Duchêne oversaw renovations of the gardens at Vaux-le-Vicomte, Chenonceaux, and Courances, among other châteaus of the Louis XIV period, and in their hands the French formal garden, long a symbol of the overthrown monarchy, was revived.[38]

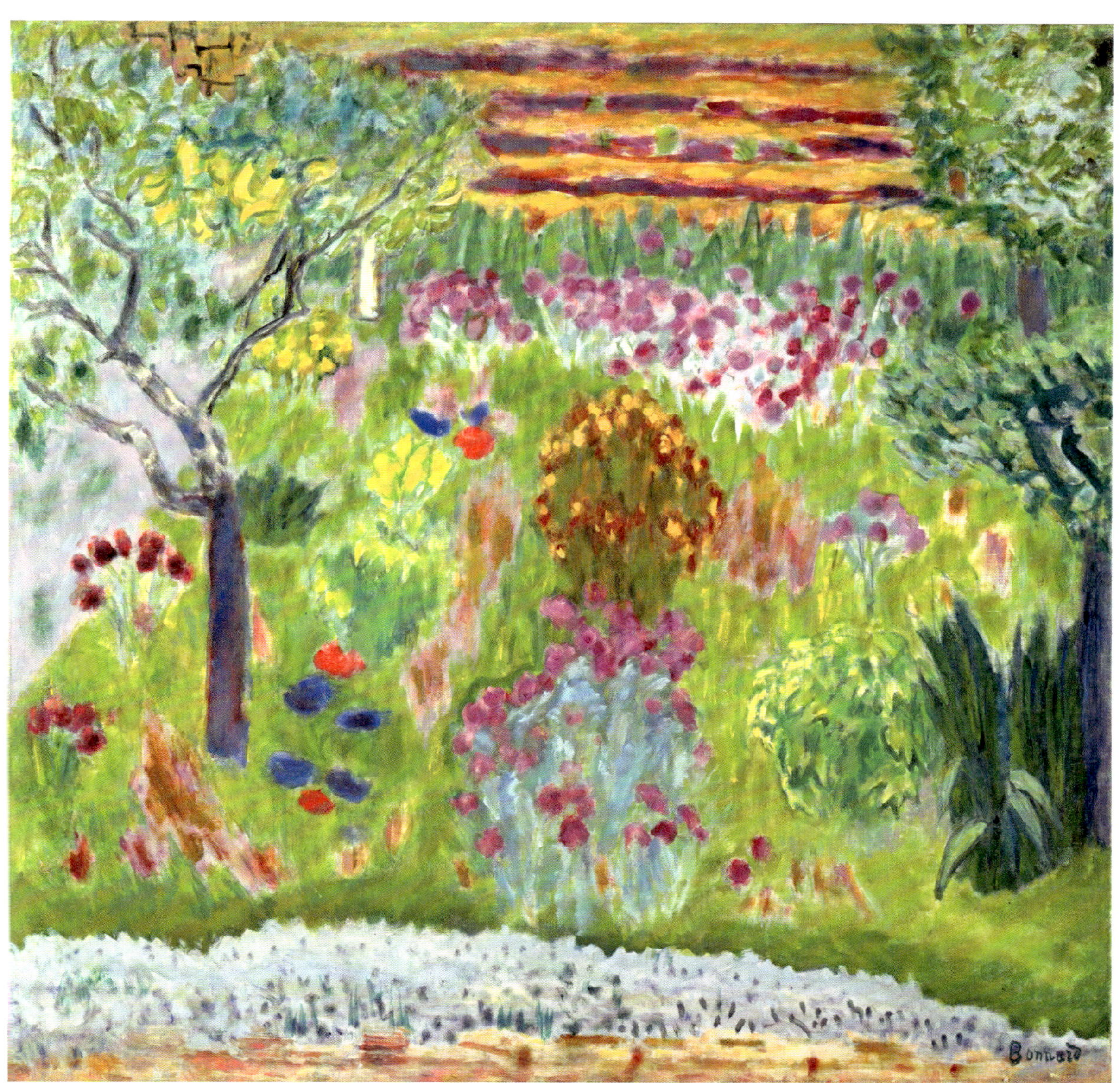
Bonnard

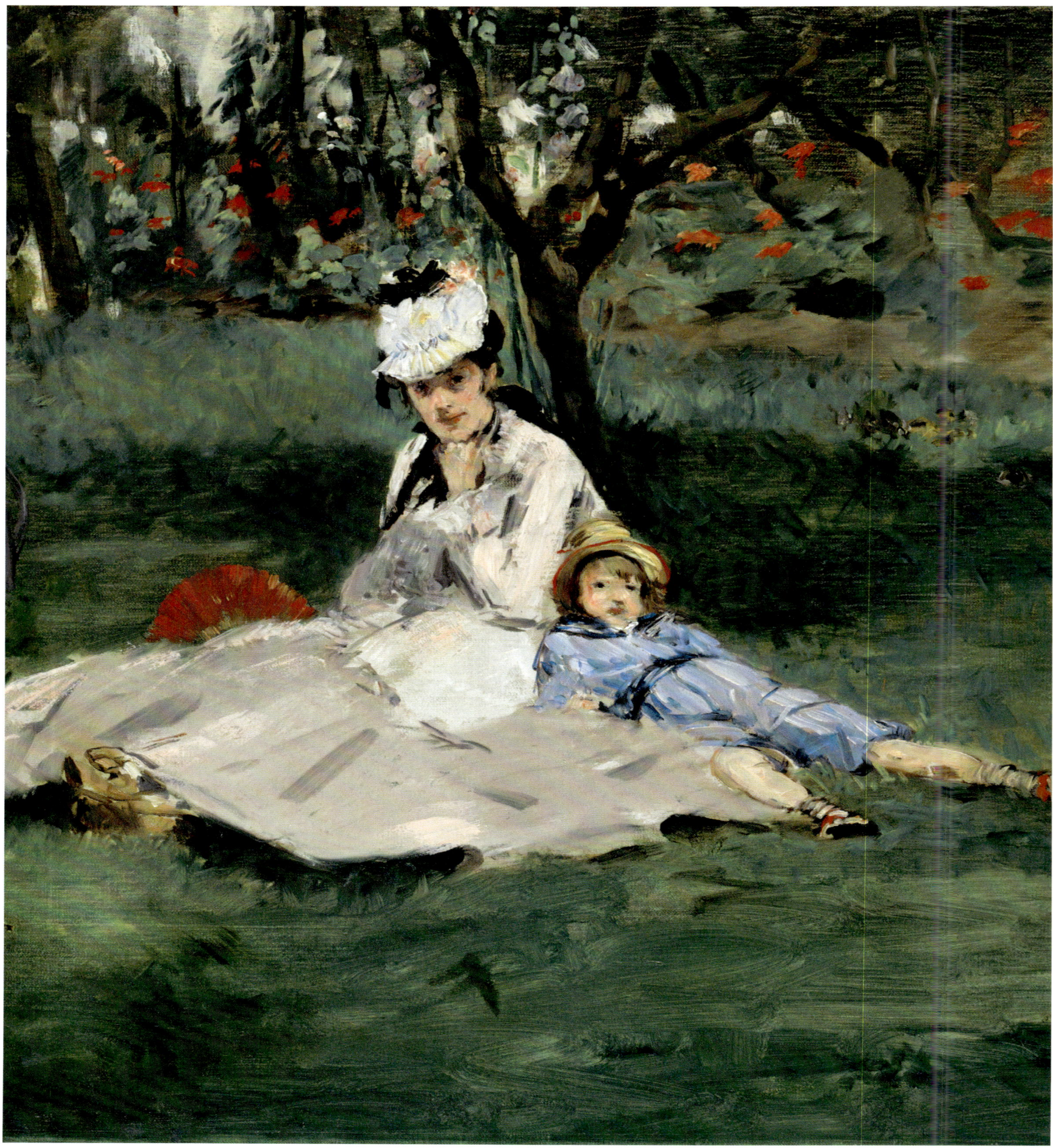

The Portrait in the Garden

Gardens have claimed a role in portraiture at least since ancient Egypt, most successfully when artists have shown as much sensitivity to the beauty of the natural world as to the characteristics of their sitters. During the eighteenth century, in particular, extravagant landscape scenery was introduced to intensify the impact of the human presence. British portraitists Joshua Reynolds, Thomas Gainsborough, and Thomas Lawrence, for example, placed their elegantly costumed subjects in the foreground of dramatic cloud-swept vistas, while French painters such as Watteau and Fragonard provided surrounds of abundant greenery; lush foliage and bountiful blooms could constitute a setting as luxurious as a palace when paying homage to a woman's beauty.

Elisabeth Vigée Le Brun, in her portrait of Marie Antoinette (fig. 105), presents the queen of France as the fashionable mistress of her garden. A corner of the vast park of Versailles was presented to her ("you who love flowers so") by her husband, Louis XVI, as "a bouquet," promising diversion and refuge from the pomp and ceremony of court life.[1] To create an environment that was more informal and carefree than the prim parterres in view of the palace, Marie Antoinette engaged the painter Hubert Robert and the architect Richard Mique to convert the area around the Petit Trianon, on the grounds of Versailles, into a landscape shaped along the lines of Chinese and English gardens, with meadows and streams, grottoes and lakes. Strolling its winding paths, the queen fussed over her flower beds, gathering blooms for bouquets, and, in her portrait, holds a richly fragrant cabbage rose (*Rosa x centifolia*), then the key component in women's perfumes.

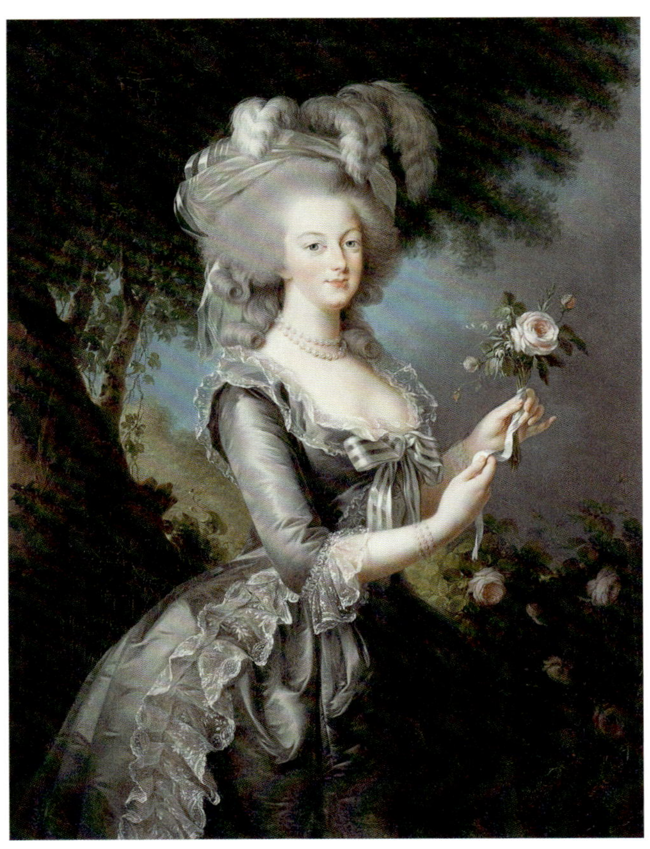

FIG. 105. Elisabeth Louise Vigée Le Brun. *Marie Antoinette with a Rose*, 1783. Oil on canvas. Collection of Lynda and Stewart Resnick, Los Angeles

Marie Antoinette was a woman much admired by Eugénie, the wife of Napoleon III. Both the queen and the later empress were devotees of fashion and shared a reputation for extravagance that made them distinctly unpopular. Eugénie reportedly made it a habit never to wear the same dress more than once and perhaps incited the kind of fashionable excess that led the emperor's mistress, Virginia Oldoini, comtesse de Castiglione, to dress for a ball as an Acacia blossom.[2] The traditional affinity between women and flowers was an especially popular theme of story and song during the mid-nineteenth century. In his fanciful illustrations to *Les Fleurs animées* (1847) Jean-Jacques Grandville imagined nearly fifty different flowers personified as prettily costumed maidens, some of whom encountered garden insects like the traitorous Japanese beetles who feigned obeisance to the Rose, Queen of Flowers (fig. 106).

It is not unlikely that Empress Eugénie aspired, in her dress, to the beauty of a flower. Her taste in luxurious attire is evident in the portrait painted of her in 1854 by Franz Xaver Winterhalter, a German artist who established himself in Paris portraying women in the finery of the Second Empire (fig. 107). Although a relatively small picture, it nonetheless has a grandeur reminiscent of late eighteenth-century portraiture; it also brings to mind contemporary fashion plates and studio photographs. Dressed in her bell-shaped gown, the empress is advantageously presented in profile, just as she is posed in a photograph of the same period that may have served as a study for the painting.[3] She is encircled by a bower of trees and flowering plants, among them the Persian lilacs that both she and Marie Antoinette favored. Perhaps meant to depict the park of the Château de Compiègne, a favorite residence of the imperial couple, or possibly the grounds at Saint-Cloud where, during the 1860s, Winterhalter's painting hung in the empress's private apartments, the background landscape instead more resembles a tired stage flat.[4] It was precisely this sort of clichéd claustrophobic scenery with its atmosphere of airlessness that the plein-air painters rejected in their desire to bring a more vibrant impression of nature to light.

Like the most advanced painters of the 1850s, practitioners of the newly invented medium of photography also traveled out of doors in pursuit of a truthful rendering of natural light. From time to time a photographer might

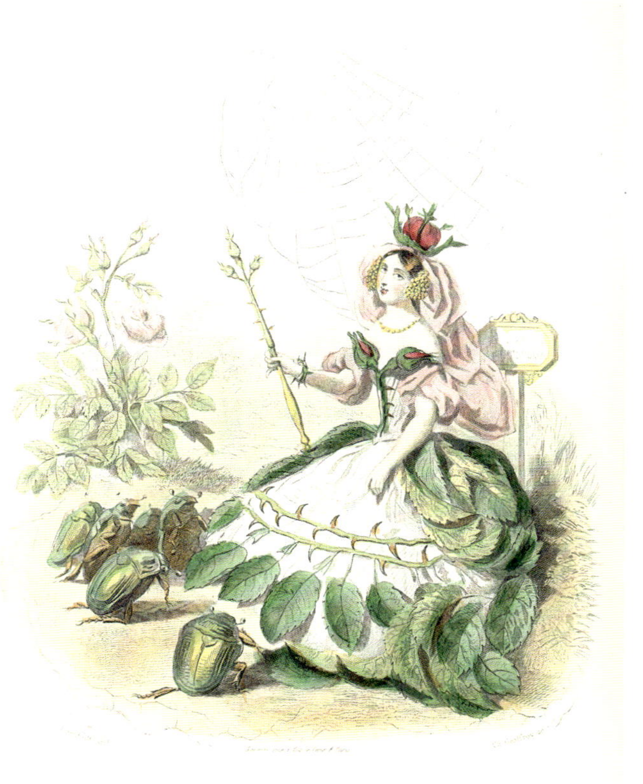

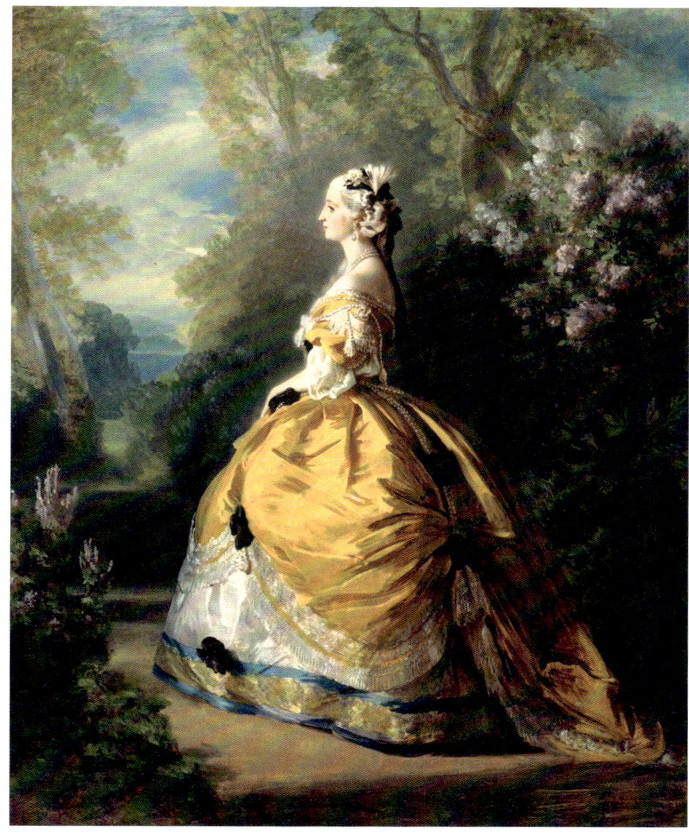

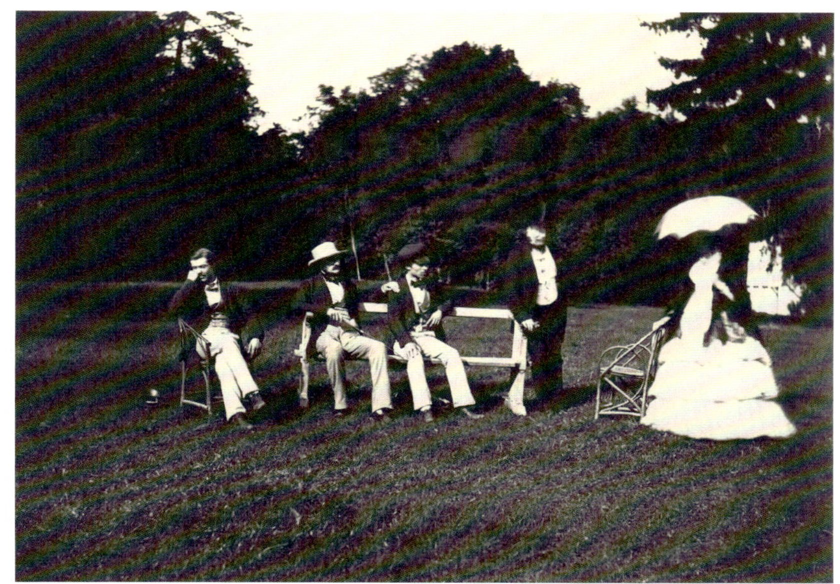

FIG. 106. Jean-Jacques Grandville. "Rose," from Taxile Delord, *Les Fleurs animées*, new ed. (Paris, 1867). Hand-colored engraving. The Metropolitan Museum of Art, New York

FIG. 107. Franz Xaver Winterhalter. *The Empress Eugénie*, 1854. Oil on canvas. The Metropolitan Museum of Art, New York

FIG. 108. Edouard Baldus. *Group at the Château de La Faloise*, 1856. Salted paper print from glass negative. The Metropolitan Museum of Art, New York

FIG. 109. Thomas Gainsborough. *Mr. and Mrs. Andrews*, ca. 1750. Oil on canvas. National Gallery, London

FIG. 110. Frans Hals. *Portrait of a Couple, probably Isaac Abrahamsz Massa and Beatrix van der Laen*, ca. 1622. Oil on canvas. Rijksmuseum, Amsterdam

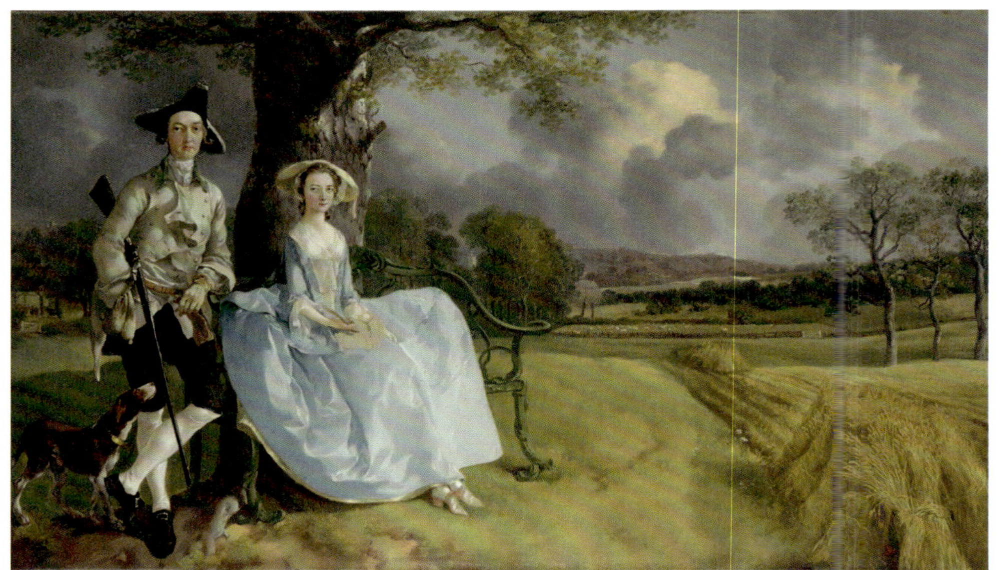

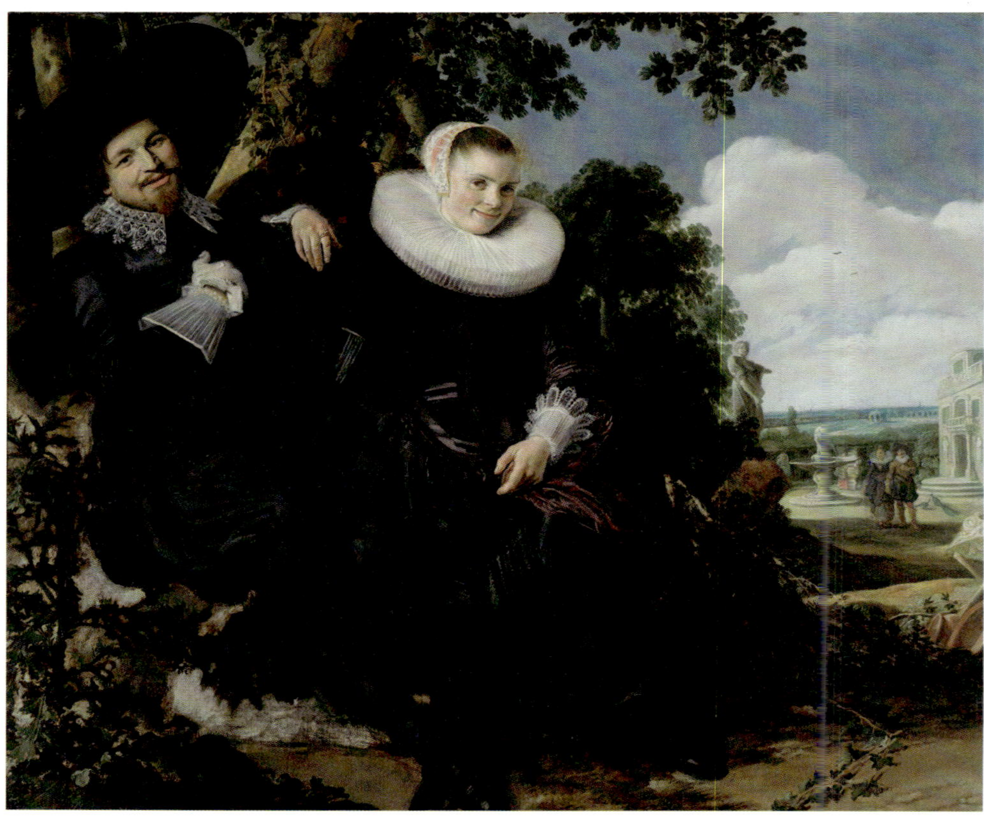

even corral a sunlit gathering of people to sit or stand still for the camera. The lawn party photographed by Edouard Baldus is one such group portrait staged in the open air (fig. 108). Although trained as a painter, Baldus would become a photographer of historic monuments and, on this occasion, had been invited to the country estate of an official in the government office where he was employed. In the photograph, one of several taken of the bureaucrat Frédéric Bourgeois de Mercey and his family, Baldus pictured his host seated on a garden bench (his eyes shielded from the sun by a white hat), his wife (shaded by a parasol), and their sons, one of whom—hatless—appears lost in reverie.[5]

Baldus's photograph adheres to the conventions of the conversation piece, fashionable in English painting of the eighteenth century, an informal portrait of two or more people, both standing and seated, usually out of doors. Such pictures, exemplified in Thomas Gainsborough's portrait of Mr. and Mrs. Andrews (fig. 109), were usually horizontal in format, allowing the artist to include a naturalistic landscape, perhaps a view of the sitters' own grounds. The conversation piece as a pictorial subject seems to have originated in the Netherlands during the seventeenth century. Frans Hals's sanguine wedding portrait of the rich merchant Isaac Massa and his bride, Beatrix, includes in the background an imaginary garden presided over by Juno, goddess of marriage (fig. 110).

A more somber mood is cast in Monet's portrait of his wife, Camille (his former model and mistress), shown seated on a bench in their garden in the Paris suburb of Argenteuil (fig. 111). In contrast to the vibrant blooms behind her, Camille wears a world-weary expression for which many have sought explanation, although hers may simply be the stilled demeanor reminiscent of sitters posed in a photographer's studio. She is joined by an attentive caller, from whom she may have received the note she holds in her gloved hand and the small bouquet beside her.[6] The top-hatted gentleman nonchalantly leaning over the bench recalls suitors in French Rococo paintings, where the garden was traditionally a site of amorous encounters. But setting the garden as a place of courtship, still customary among the Realist painters, was seldom the practice of the Impressionists.[7] Here, in one of the rare genre scenes he painted before focusing almost exclusively on landscape, Monet is perhaps exploring the old theme of the Garden of Love.

Manet, too, seems to have been revisiting pictorial tradition in a composition that is uncannily like Monet's. In his painting of Jules Guillemet and his American-born wife (fig. 112), proprietors of a fashionable shop on the rue du Faubourg Saint-Honoré, he presents the couple at close range, in the confined space of a greenhouse garden like those that wealthy Parisians of the time attached to their homes and filled with exotic plants. Such a conservatory is exhaustively described as the site of lovemaking in Zola's novel *La Curée*, published in 1871, where the hothouse disturbingly "seethed the ardent sap of the tropics" in a "furious debauch of leaves and stalks."[8]

In the more traditional presentation of the garden as *hortus conclusus*, an enclosed private space, Monet's portrait of Camille (fig. 111) includes a corner of the half-acre walled garden that the painter maintained at the first of the two houses he rented in Argenteuil. Vying for attention with the figures in the shaded foreground, the artist's sunny flower garden is admired by a woman visitor, its bright red zonal geraniums clustered in a corbeille, a basketlike arrangement of the type that had become a standard fixture in French parks. Such islands of closely packed flowers followed the English example of carpet beddings and sometimes were planted in geometric designs in the style known as mosaiculture. It was only with the large-scale cultivation of annuals in greenhouses, which began around the middle of the century, that such massed flower plantings, then at the height of their popularity, had become possible.

During the summer of 1874 Manet paid a visit to the Monet family. Finding them enjoying a leisurely afternoon in their garden, he set up his easel to paint in the open air (fig. 113), a practice he had only lately begun under the influence of the Impressionists. While Monet's depiction of the very same garden—his own—presents a formal park, Manet's resembles a common village garden, with vegetable plots and farmyard animals.

Just as Manet began to paint Camille and her son lounging on the lawn while Monet tended the flowers, Renoir arrived—and immediately borrowed materials to paint the same scene, but from a closer spot (fig. 114). Working quickly to capture the spontaneity of the moment, both painters took care to include the yard's wandering chickens, Manet placing the rooster, hen, and chick as avian counterparts to Monet's family. Monet, too, made a picture that day, of Manet painting in the garden; the location of that canvas is unknown.[9]

In the 1870s and 1880s not only Monet but also Manet, Caillebotte, and Berthe Morisot painted members of their families, young and old, in the garden. During the eighteenth century children had begun to appear more frequently in European paintings, where they served as reminders of the carefree innocence of youth, sometimes in the context of the domestic garden, a natural extension of the home. In the most winning of these portraits like

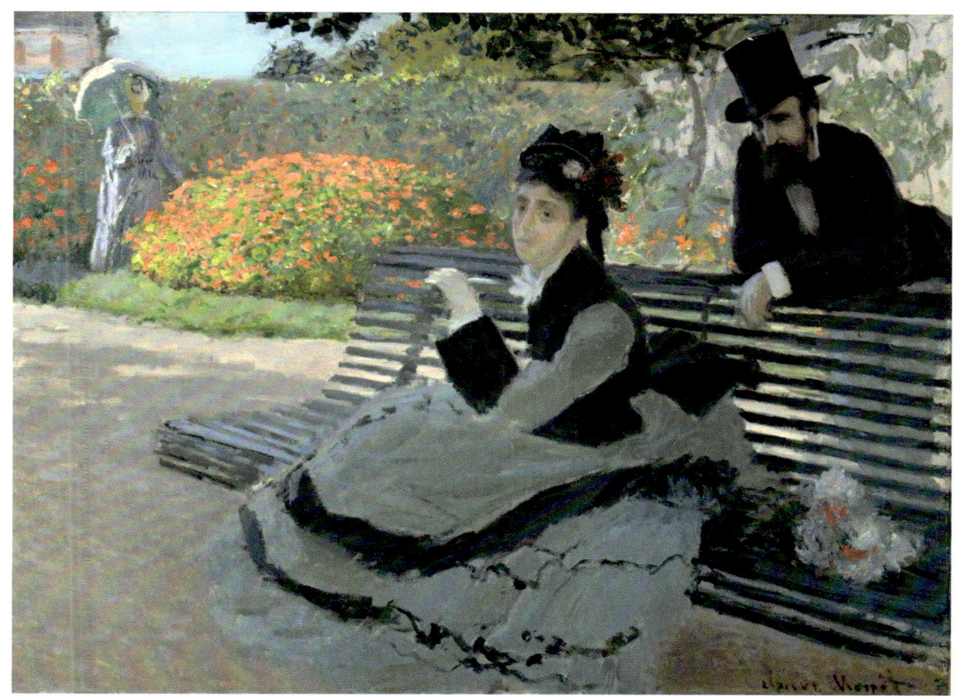

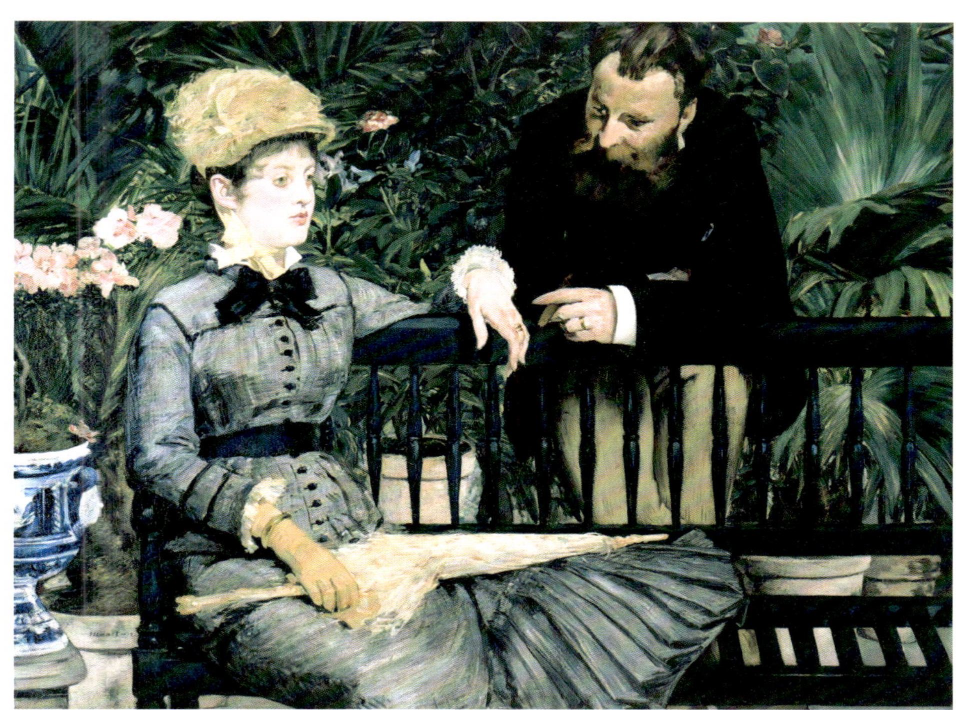

FIG. 111. Claude Monet. *Camille Monet on a Garden Bench*, 1873. Oil on canvas. The Metropolitan Museum of Art, New York

FIG. 112. Edouard Manet. *In the Conservatory*, 1878/79. Oil on canvas. Nationalgalerie, Staatliche Muzeen zu Berlin

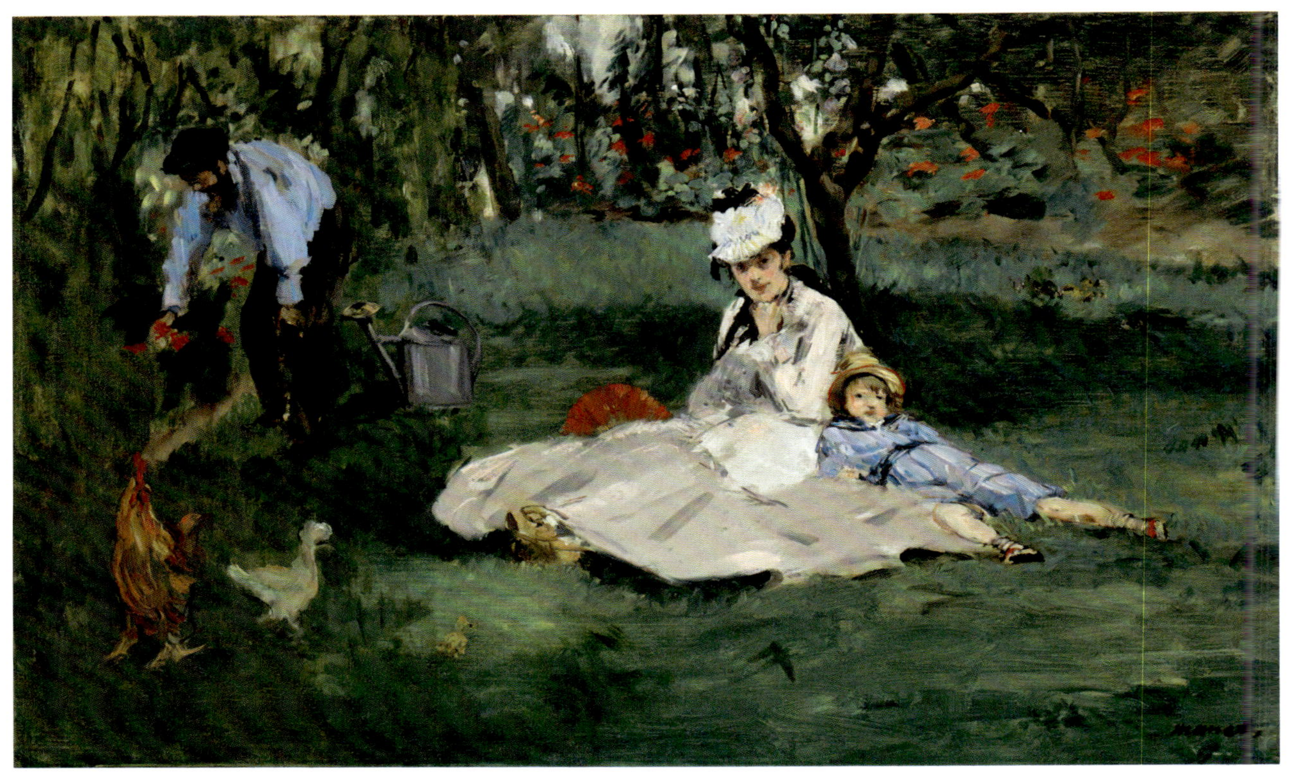

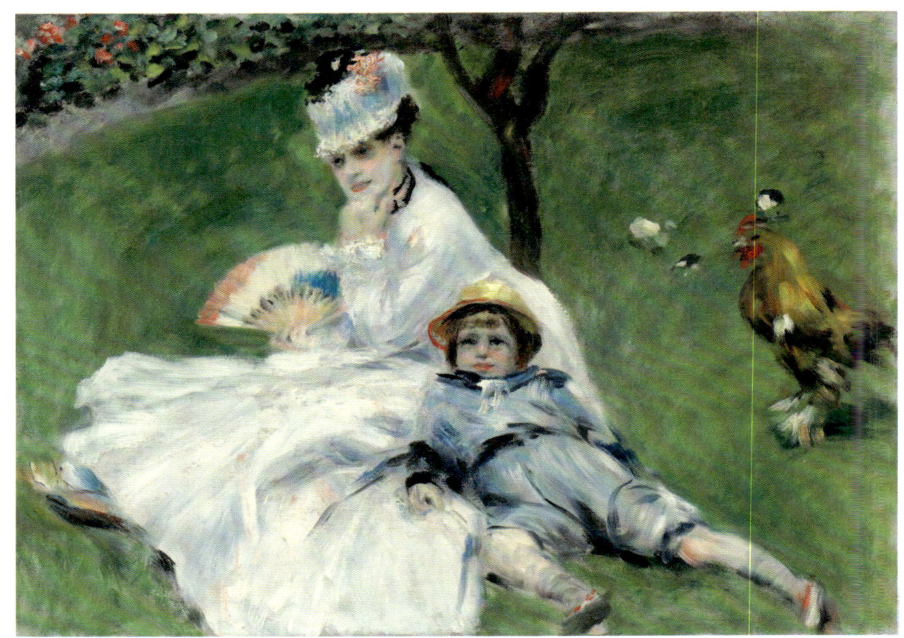

FIG. 113. Edouard Manet. *The Monet Family in Their Garden at Argenteuil*, 1874. Oil on canvas. The Metropolitan Museum of Art, New York

FIG. 114. Auguste Renoir. *Madame Monet and Her Son*, 1874. Oil on canvas. National Gallery of Art, Washington, D.C.

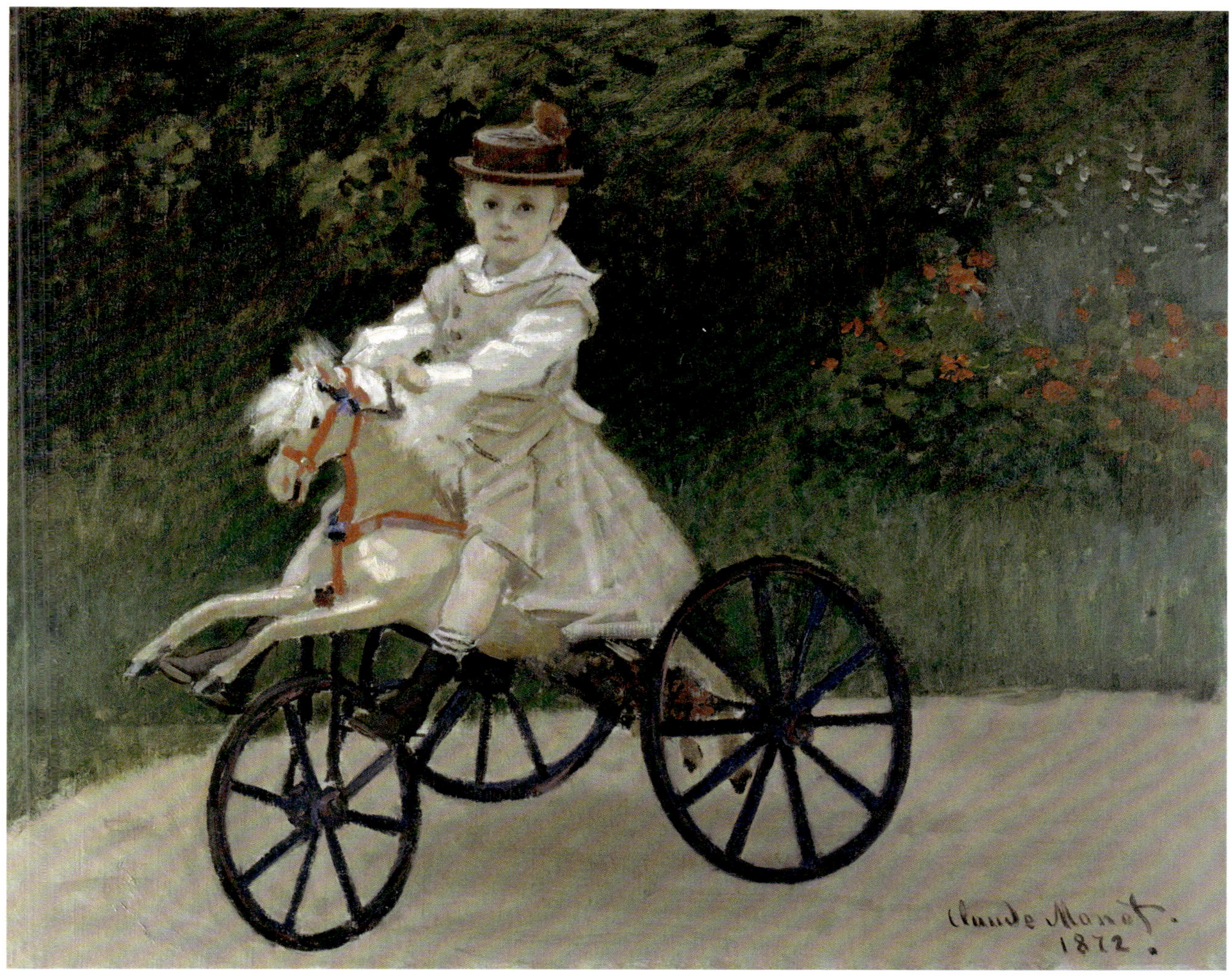

FIG. 115. Claude Monet. *Jean Monet on His Hobby Horse*, 1872. Oil on canvas. The Metropolitan Museum of Art, New York

those by Fragonard and Goya, children were shown with their pets or a favorite toy. Following in this tradition Monet painted his nearly five-year-old son on his hobby horse (fig. 115). Jean appears frequently in Monet's paintings during the 1870s, generally as an accessory and never so formally as he is presented here, a petite equestrian halted while wheeling about the garden.

The garden or the park, while providing an inviting subject to paint, also offers the artist an agreeable place to work and the artist's models a pleasant spot in which to sit. Whereas considerable time and effort are required to outfit and pose a warrior with a spear in the studio, much less is needed when the model is comfortably seated in a garden, where he or she can read or

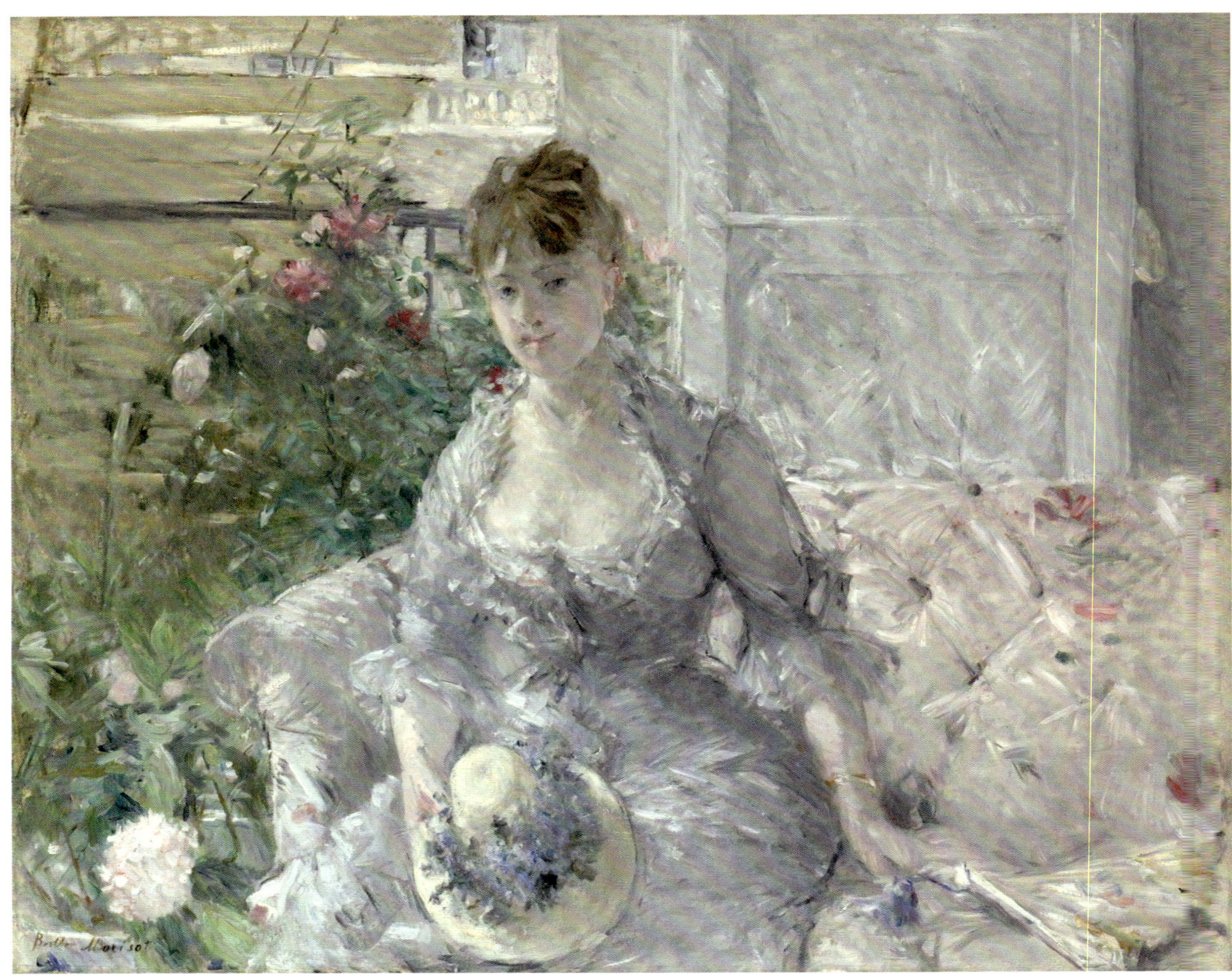

FIG. 116. Berthe Morisot. *Young Woman Seated on a Sofa*, ca. 1879. Oil on canvas. The Metropolitan Museum of Art, New York

knit. The greater challenge for the Impressionists was to render the ephemeral qualities of color and light. By using broken strokes that defied precise delineation they managed to convey the more elusive effects of atmosphere.

The idea of painting in the open air appealed to Berthe Morisot from the start of her career, and, like Monet and other contemporaries, she began a plein-air practice in view of the Forest of Fontainebleau, working at Ville-d'Avray as a pupil of Corot. In 1868 she met Manet, who encouraged her to loosen her brushwork, as she in turn persuaded him to paint out of doors. But where Manet was masterful in the strategic application of black, Morisot was skilled in the application of white. In her watercolors the white of the paper

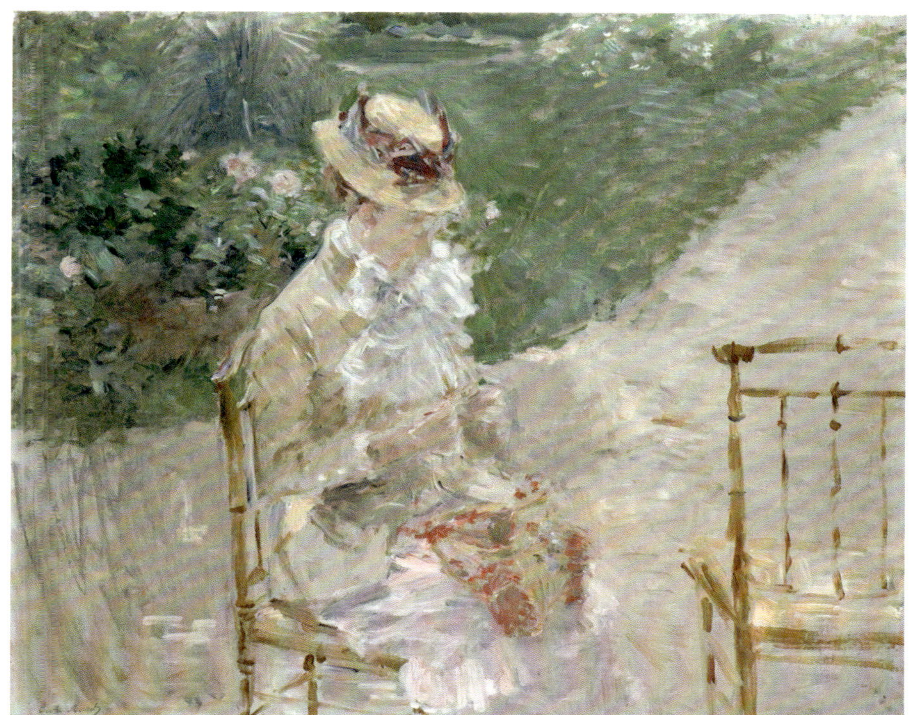

FIG. 117. Berthe Morisot. *Young Woman Knitting*, ca. 1883. Oil on canvas. The Metropolitan Museum of Art, New York

illuminates her subjects; in her paintings she added white to nearly every color in her palette to create pictures with a pearly radiance.

During the years when artists in France were turning out sentimental images of women in gardens for the annual Salons or for sale in the growing art market, Morisot and the other Impressionists were making pictures about new ways of painting. Even when she posed a model in her Paris apartment, Morisot could magically transform the interior into a place out of doors, opening it to her balcony and bringing roses and hydrangeas into the company of a flower-bedecked hat and the floral upholstery of a tufted settee (fig. 116). The art critic Charles Ephrussi may have been looking at such a painting when, in 1880, he wrote of Morisot, "She grinds flower petals onto her palette, in order to spread them later on her canvas with airy, witty touches."[10]

Morisot also painted frequently in the Bois de Boulogne and in the garden her husband made behind their home in nearby Passy. She spent the summers of 1880 to 1884 in a rented house in Bougival, northwest of Paris, which is probably where she painted a young woman—possibly her daughter's nanny—knitting in a garden typical of the period, with a gravel path and flowering roses (fig. 117).

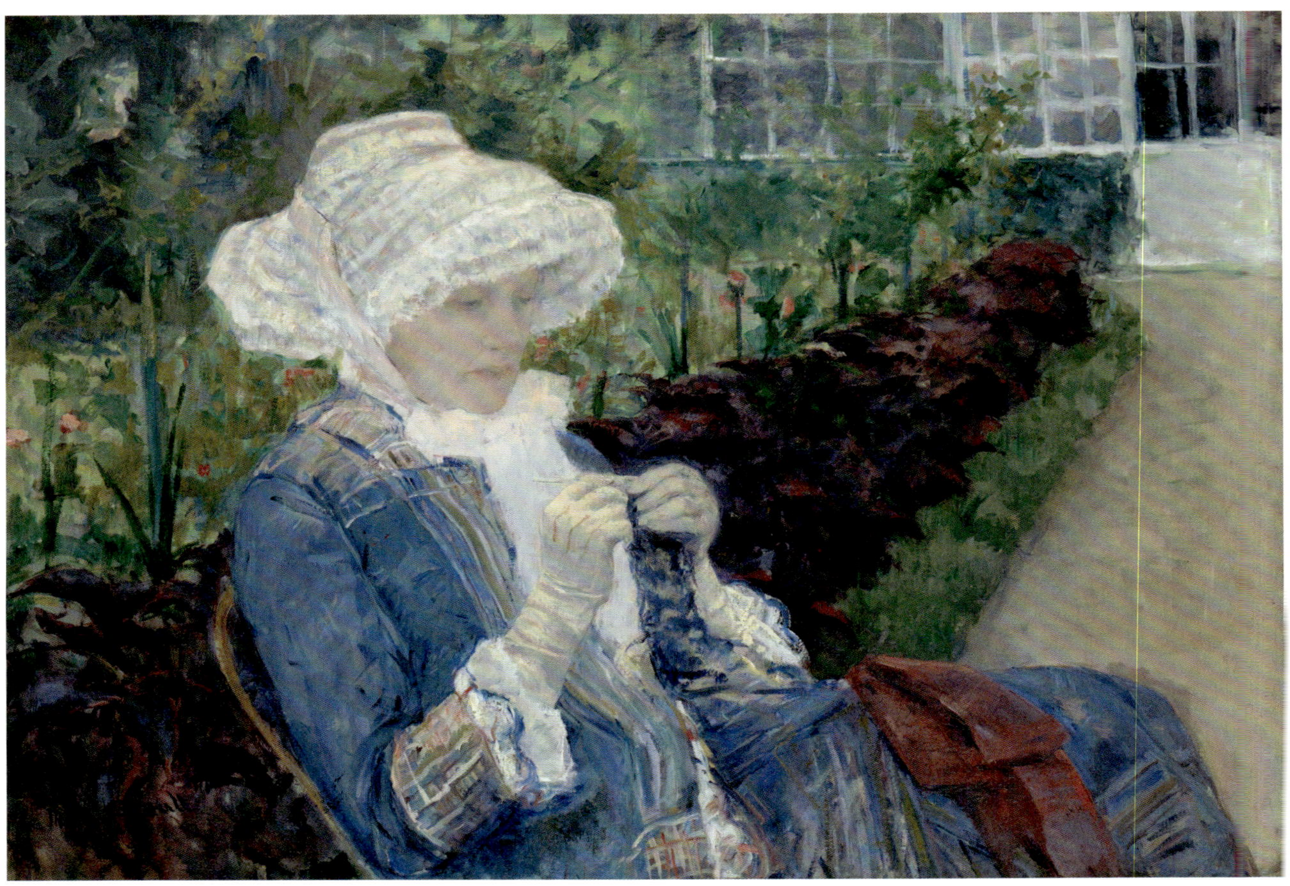

FIG. 118. Mary Cassatt. *Lydia Crocheting in the Garden at Marly*, 1880. Oil on canvas. The Metropolitan Museum of Art, New York

Like Morisot, Mary Cassatt was one of the few women invited to exhibit their work with the Impressionists. An American raised in Philadelphia, Cassatt began studying art in Paris during the 1860s. Her portrait of her sister Lydia (fig. 118), made during the summer of 1880 in the garden of the house that she and her family rented in Marly-le-Roi, is one of the first pictures she painted out of doors. The bold composition, which places Lydia on a diagonally receding walkway and a rising background of greenery, is very close to that of Morisot's somewhat later portrait, which also shows the sitter absorbed in her needlework. Cassatt rendered her frail sister's features realistically and with delicacy, while describing her dress with freer brushwork and handling still more vigorously the foliage of gladioli, roses, and coleus in the border leading to the greenhouse. The painting was displayed in the Impressionist exhibition of 1881 and contributed to the show's success. Cassatt's father was pleased to report, "The things she painted last summer in the open air are those that have been most praised."[11]

Cassatt continued through the years to picture figures in the open air, often depicting women and children circled by haloes of greenery. Portraits dating to circa 1900 provide glimpses of the garden around the château at Mesnil-Beaufresne, which she purchased and renovated in 1894. There, in her fifties, the painter became intensely involved with her garden. Writing to the art collector Ada Pope, she told of the interests she shared with her friend Louisine Havemeyer, another American collector of Impressionist paintings: "Mrs. Havemeyer sent me a book on gardening 'The English flower garden &' which I told her would be my ruin, & now that my lawns have all been properly turned over & levelled & walks designed & made I have gone into roses, & everyday I bend carefully over my delicate 'teas' to watch the shoots, I have over a thousand planted & already fancy myself sniffing the perfume & revelling in the color."[12]

The same summer Cassatt pictured her sister sitting in a garden Manet painted his wife in the sunlit greenery of their seasonal residence in Bellevue (fig. 119). Much of Suzanne Manet's face is hidden beneath the broad rim of her hat, and her figure elides with the background in an accumulation of paint—dashed-off shades of ocher, blue, and emerald green, a color Manet used with unparalleled mastery.

Manet spent five months at the villa he had rented principally for its proximity to the hydropathic clinic where he was receiving treatment. Writing to the artist and critic Zacharie Astruc, he admitted the stay was something of a trial: "Really, the countryside is charming only to those who aren't forced to stay there."[13] Nonetheless, he made the best of the situation by using the garden as his open-air studio. In July, anticipating the visit of his friend Marguerite, whom he planned to paint, he advised, "Bring your needlework and the light-colored summer dress you told me about, and if you have a pretty garden hat don't leave it behind."[14] Marguerite too would be posed in a flowery setting, as were the models Manet profiled in 1881 as *Spring* (J. Paul Getty Museum, Los Angeles) and *Autumn* (Musée des Beaux-Arts, Nancy), further excursions in his continuing alliance of women with flowers. In praise of *Spring*, critics declared the sitter "not a woman [but] a bouquet, truly a visual perfume," "a flower of delicious coloring."[15]

Cézanne portrayed his wife dozens of times, often sphinxlike, as she appears in the greenhouse of his family's estate in Aix-en-Provence (fig. 120). Hortense, who shared her name with the flowering Hydrangea (*Hortensia*),

OVERLEAF:

FIG. 119. Edouard Manet. *Madame Manet at Bellevue*, 1880. Oil on canvas. The Metropolitan Museum of Art, New York

FIG. 120. Paul Cézanne. *Madame Cézanne in the Conservatory*, 1891. Oil on canvas. The Metropolitan Museum of Art, New York

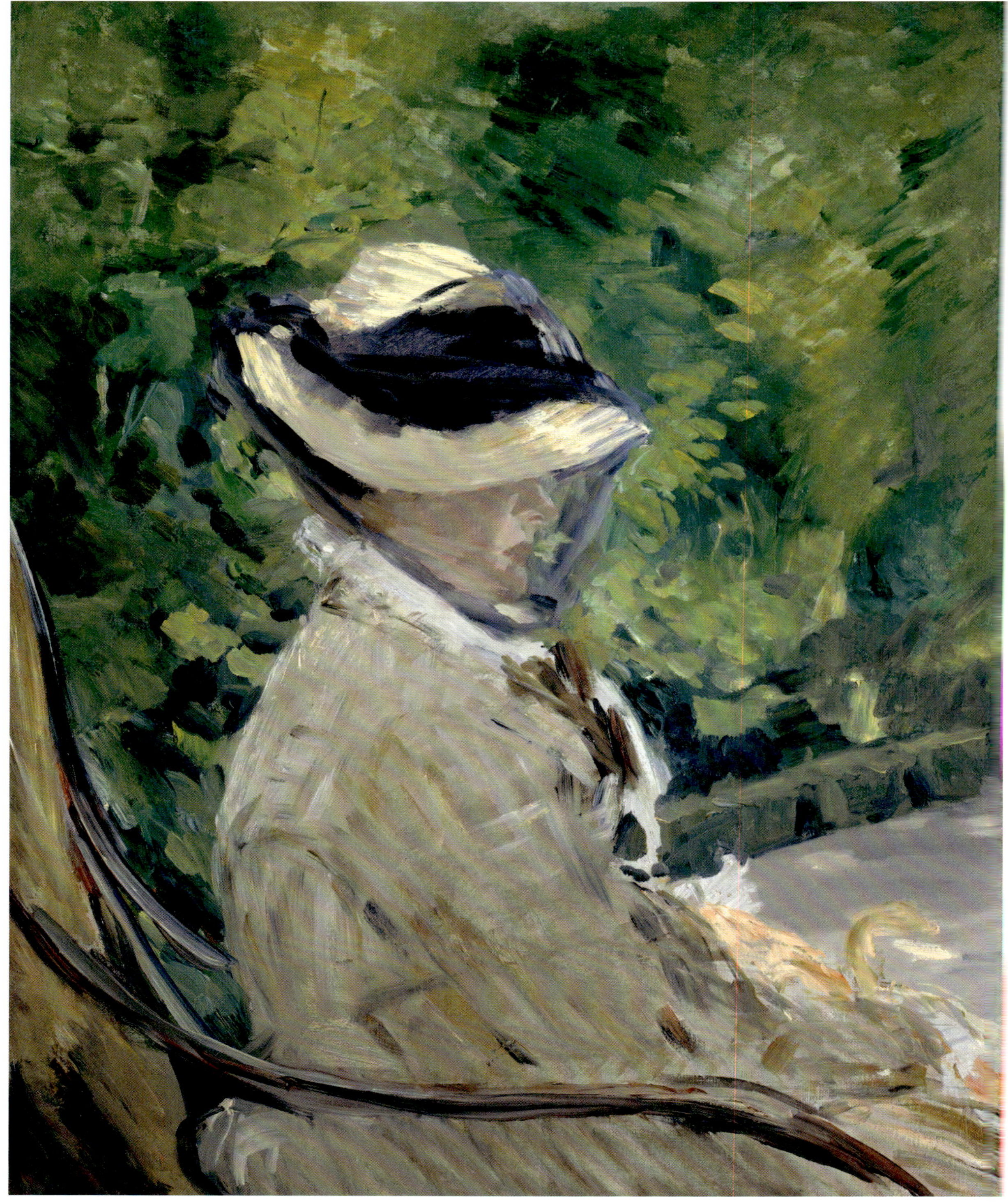

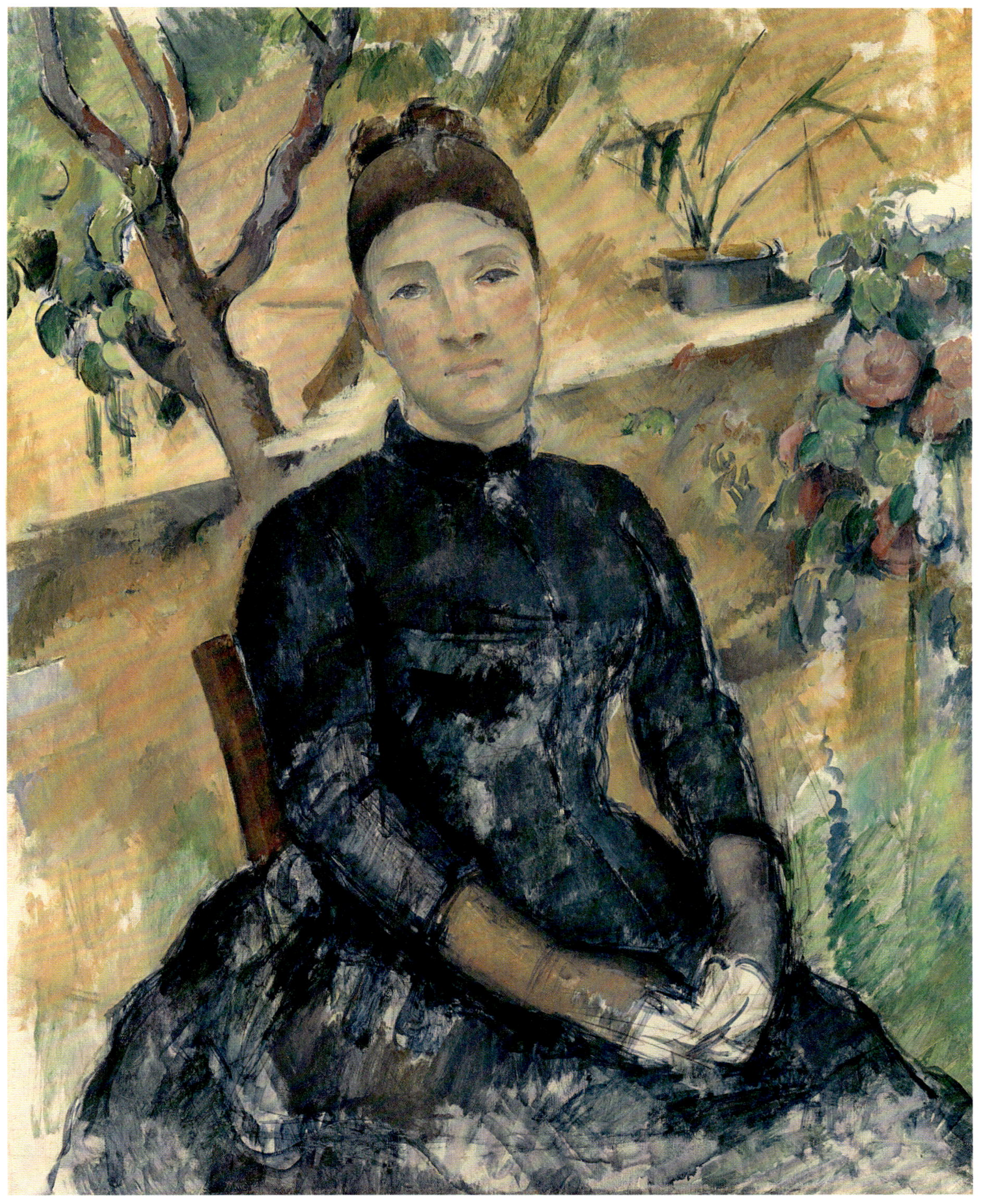

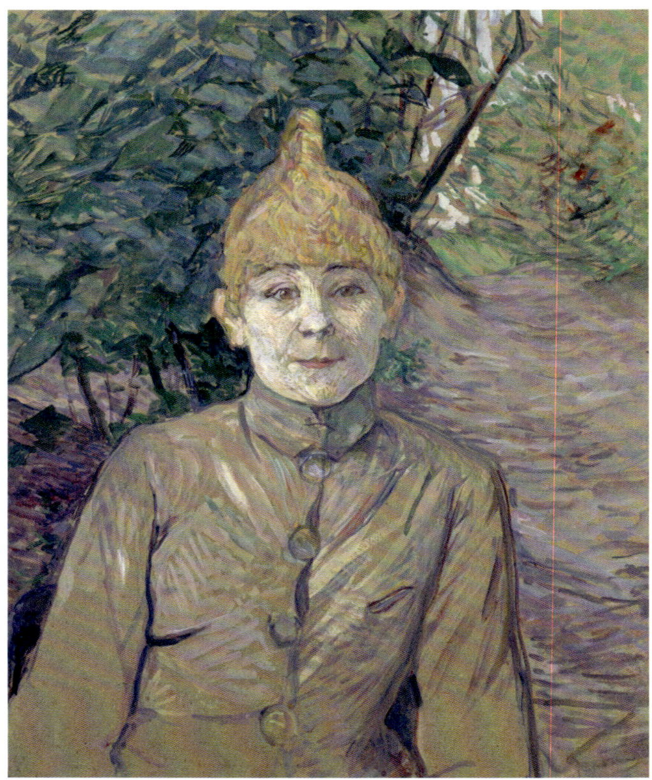

FIG. 121. Henri de Toulouse-Lautrec. *The Streetwalker*, ca. 1890–91. Oil on cardboard. The Metropolitan Museum of Art, New York

is shown seated among the plants of the conservatory. Cézanne found the glasshouse at his family's estate in Provence a convenient place to work in inclement weather and an ideal sheltered space in which to study his most frequent model in a cool, flat light.

One does not expect to find Henri de Toulouse-Lautrec painting women in gardens, as the subjects he generally preferred were denizens of Montmartre's cafés and dance halls, where the artist studied them in the dim shadows of gas lamps or the glare of footlights. Interested in Parisians who were most at home inside crowded night spots, Lautrec had little use for the out-of-doors, considering landscape merely "an accessory . . . [that] should only serve to allow us to better comprehend the character of the figures."[16] Having veered from the path taken by the Impressionists, Lautrec no doubt reveled in the irony of his own plein-air portraits, posing women of ill repute in a garden that was squalid and untended. In a series of portraits he used the neglected area of a garden owned by a well-to-do neighbor, a retired photographer known as Père Forest. Although a large part of the garden was well maintained, the remote area in which Lautrec painted had been "allowed to run wild and was covered with long grass, shrubs, and thickets of bramble."[17] It was here that the artist set up his easel and, summoning local characters to pose for him, proceeded to examine them in the harsh light of day.

The model for *The Streetwalker* (fig. 121) is one who complied, bemusedly peering out from under a mask of white face powder and a crown of brassy hair twisted up in the corkscrew coif then popular among dancers of the cancan. La Casque d'Or, or "Golden Helmet," as she was called, was the *sous-maîtresse* of a brothel and the lover of a notorious killer. Lautrec seated her at the edge of a dirt path amid a tangle of greenery that highlights her pallid complexion and provides a natural foil for her artificial persona. In many ways the painting contrasts with Manet's portrait of his wife (see fig. 119), yet the exuberant brushwork they had both mastered invites comparison.

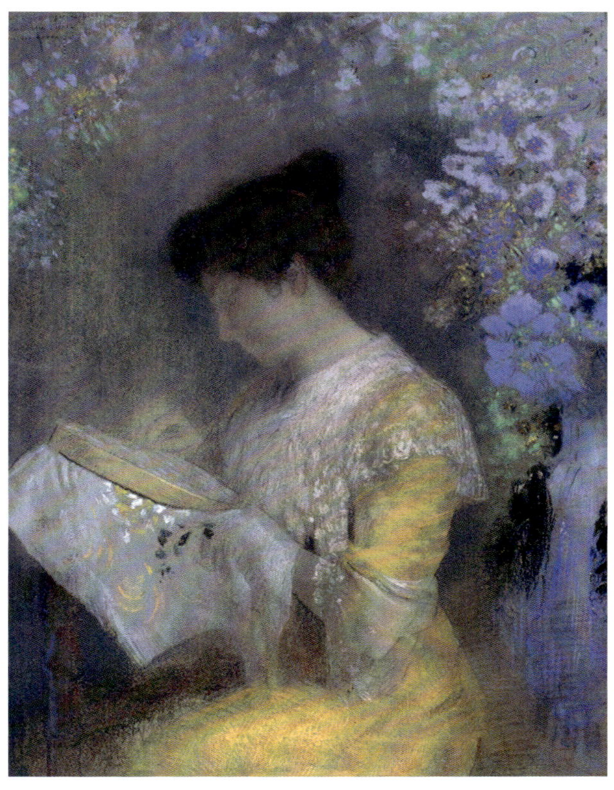

FIG. 122. Odilon Redon. *Madame Arthur Fontaine*, 1901. Pastel on paper. The Metropolitan Museum of Art, New York

Odilon Redon, although he was a contemporary of the Impressionists and exhibited in their final group show of 1886, remained an outsider; he pictured neither the landscape nor the passing occurrences of everyday life. Tutored by his close friend the botanist Armand Clavaud, he had an abiding interest in nature. But his fascination was primarily with hidden forms of life, mysteries conjured in the imagination or visible only under a microscope. Until the 1890s Redon found expression in the blackness of ink and charcoal; then, with the infusion of color into his work, he began to explore a whole new world of brilliant hues. To these he gave the intricate shapes of flowers, both real and imagined, gathering them in still lifes (see fig. 158) or allowing them to float in an ethereal twilight, seen in his portrait of the art patron Marie Escudier Fontaine as she tends her floral embroidery (fig. 122). Although Redon made likenesses of both Madame Fontaine and her industrialist husband, Arthur Fontaine, during their visit to the artist and his wife at the seaside resort of Saint-Georges-de-Didonne, only Madame was realized in full color, haloed by airborne flowers, perhaps the projection of dreams or recollections. Conveying unseen inner worlds that transcended naturalistic depiction, Redon preferred to abandon the garden of reality, instead privileging the imagination, in the words of Baudelaire, the "queen of faculties."[18]

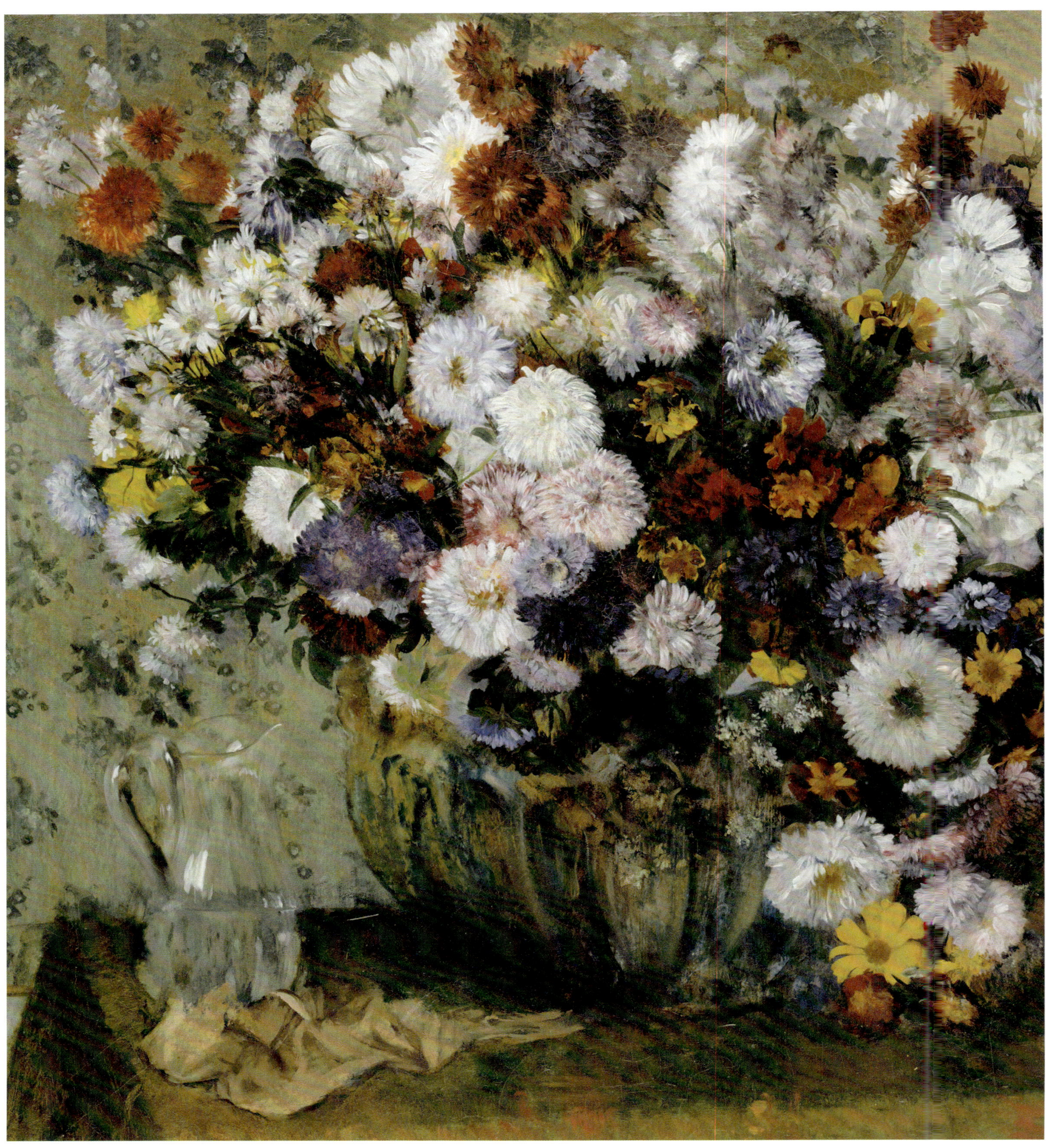

The Revival of the Floral Still Life

By the early nineteenth century shiploads of foreign plant materials were arriving regularly on European shores, especially after the protective glass Wardian cases came into widespread use in the 1840s (see pp. 76–77 and fig. 73). A whole nursery industry grew up to propagate, distribute, and hybridize plants in multiple forms and colors, so that by midcentury urban populations could stroll among a variety of flowers in their public parks, while private landowners, adopting a new style of gardening that embraced an abundance of alluring choices, planted flower beds near to their doorsteps. With the distance narrowed between garden and house, flowers readily found their way into the home, not only to be arranged in bouquets but also to be pictured in paintings and applied as decoration to all manner of domestic goods. The market for cut flowers developed an avid clientele. Highly appreciated as gifts, fresh blooms were lavishly bestowed upon loved ones and presented by fans to their favorite performers. As one Frenchman observed of adored singers and dancers, "Formerly they were paid with money and diamonds; now we heap flowers upon them."[1]

The great botanical discoveries of the late eighteenth and early nineteenth centuries were a source of amazement to those privileged to enter into this hitherto unknown world, in particular the scientists who studied them. But the strange and extraordinary beauty of these new arrivals was appreciated early on and most famously in France by Empress Josephine, who had the passion and the means to collect examples in extravagant quantities. Furthermore, she commissioned knowledgeable botanists and talented artists to

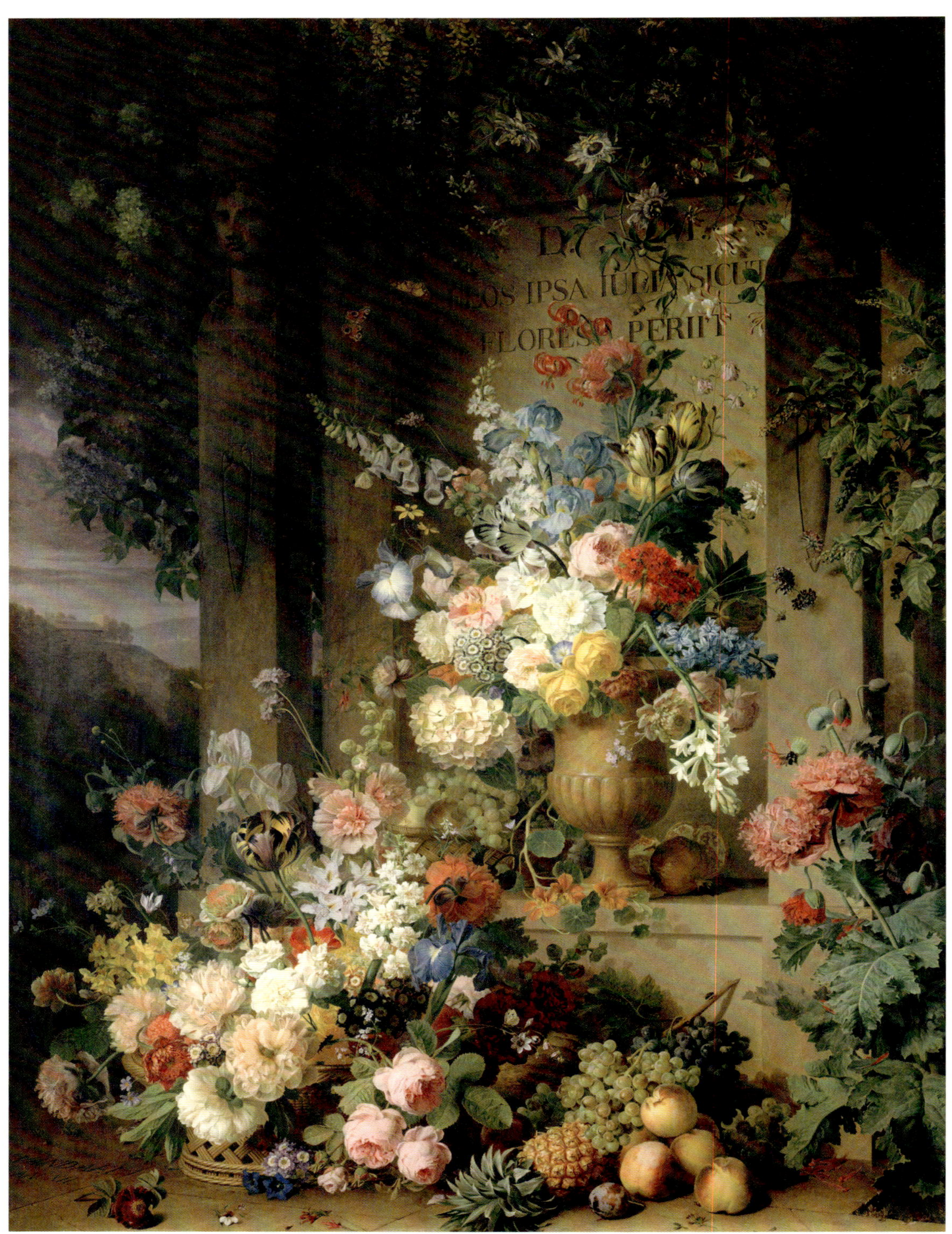

IPSA
FLORES
PERIIT

study and publish them, as demonstrated in the exquisite work of her official painter, Pierre Joseph Redouté (see pp. 20–23 and figs. 17–20). Even after her death in 1814 Josephine's support for botanical research and flower painting continued to be felt at the Jardin des Plantes in Paris, where Redouté established a special school for floral artists, some of whom became designers of porcelain and tapestries. Redouté also continued to publish his watercolors, between 1827 and 1833 issuing a portfolio, *Choix des plus belles fleurs*, of the most popular garden flowers of the day. In a modest format designed for a broader audience than that served by his earlier series, it included the more familiar poppies, pansies, and sweet peas.[2]

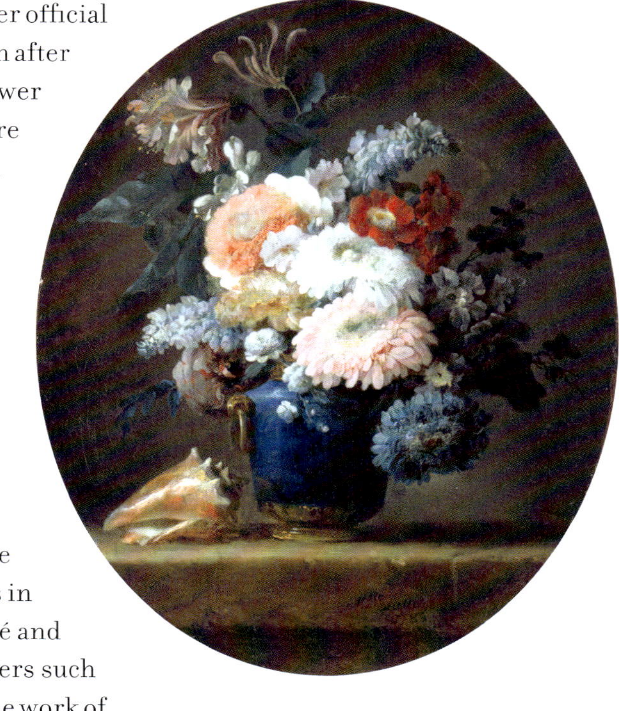

FIG. 124. Anne Vallayer-Coster. *Vase of Flowers and Conch Shell*, 1780. Oil on canvas. The Metropolitan Museum of Art, New York

Official flower painters had been appointed by French kings since the seventeenth century, their watercolors preserved in a special collection known as the Vélins du Roi (King's Vellums) in the royal botanical garden (later the Jardin des Plantes). It was there that the Dutchman Gerard van Spaendonck, a painter of miniatures in the court of Louis XVI (r. 1774–92), taught floral painting to Redouté and others in the meticulously observant manner of northern old masters such as Jan Davidsz. de Heem, Willem van Aelst, and Jan van Huysum.[3] The work of Spaendonck's Belgian colleague at the Jardin des Plantes, Jan Frans van Dael, exemplified the most ambitious efforts of Netherlandish flower painters in France at the beginning of the nineteenth century. Van Dael's monumental canvas purchased by Josephine for Malmaison (fig. 123) pays homage to the tomb of the Romantic heroine of Jean Jacques Rousseau's best-selling *Julie; ou, La Nouvelle Héloïse* (1761), with flowers and fruit from different seasons and climes in a grandiose setting of sculpted stone. Here, according to tradition, flowers symbolized beauty, love, and life, all of which eventually fade away.

During the seventeenth century French still-life painting was accorded the lowest level in the hierarchy of pictorial subjects established by the theorist André Félibien, outranked by history painting, portraiture, and landscape. Nonetheless, succeeding generations of still-life painters, notably Jean Baptiste Monnoyer, then Alexandre François Desportes, and later Anne Vallayer-Coster, continued to enjoy royal patronage and official recognition at the Paris Salon. The delicacy and precision of Vallayer-Coster's painted arrangements of flowers in precious Chinese or Sèvres porcelains won her admission to the Académie Royale in 1770 (fig. 124).

During the nineteenth century Van Spaendonck and Van Dael, too, displayed paintings at the Salon, where their compositions were matched in scale

FIG. 123. Jan Frans van Dael. *The Tomb of Julie*, 1803–4. Oil on canvas. Musée National des Châteaux de Malmaison et Bois-Préau, Rueil-Malmaison

and complexity by showpieces submitted by professors of the so-called school of Lyon. Founded in 1756, the Ecole des Beaux-Arts in Lyon, the commercial center of French textile production, trained students in flower painting and its application to the decorative arts. The school's most influential teachers, Jean François Bony and Antoine Berjon, produced floral works marked by botanical accuracy and subdued color. Both painters encouraged their pupils to copy engravings and paintings by northern artists that had been collected specifically for instruction in the Lyon museum's Salle des Fleurs, a gallery devoted to floral works. Berjon's practice of painstaking detail and high finish was further developed by Simon Saint-Jean, whose five-foot-tall painting *The Gardener* (fig. 125) was awarded a medal at the Salon of 1838 and purchased by the French state. But the devotion to detail that characterized such works had its critics, among them Charles Baudelaire, who, in reviewing the Salon of 1845, condemned the school of Lyon as "the penitentiary of painting."[4]

Baudelaire found greater merit in the work of Eugène Delacroix, who subordinated precision of detail to spontaneity of expression and commanded a palette the critic likened to "an expertly matched bouquet of flowers."[5] A lifelong devotee of flowers and gardens (see p. 80), Delacroix tried his hand at producing a few small unpretentious bouquets in 1833, composing them with broad strokes of color, rapidly and freely brushed.[6] Not until more than a decade later did his ambition to master all genres of painting lead him to revitalize the art of the floral still life. At work on a group of five large flower paintings at Champrosay, his country retreat, Delacroix wrote to his friend the painter and engraver Constant Dutilleux of his efforts to "get away from the convention which seems to condemn anyone who paints flowers to reproduce the same vase with the same columns of fantastic draperies." Determined "to paint bits of nature as we see them in gardens," he gathered in fresh flowers and studied them quickly before they wilted or succumbed to autumn's frost.[7]

The most innovative of the floral compositions that Delacroix presented at the Salon of 1849 displays a bushel of fresh-cut flowers tumbling out of an overturned basket (fig. 126). Above the cascade of brightly colored dahlias, daisies, and rudbeckias, a robust vine of white morning glories reels into the air while stalks of amaranthus and hollyhocks dart skyward, in seeming defiance of floral life's "stillness" and the French term "nature morte." Translated literally as "dead nature," the genre was so named because such compositions often included lifeless animals and fading flowers, recalling the passage of time and the inevitability of death.

FIG. 125. Simon Saint-Jean. *The Gardener,* 1837. Oil on canvas. Musée des Beaux-Arts de Lyon

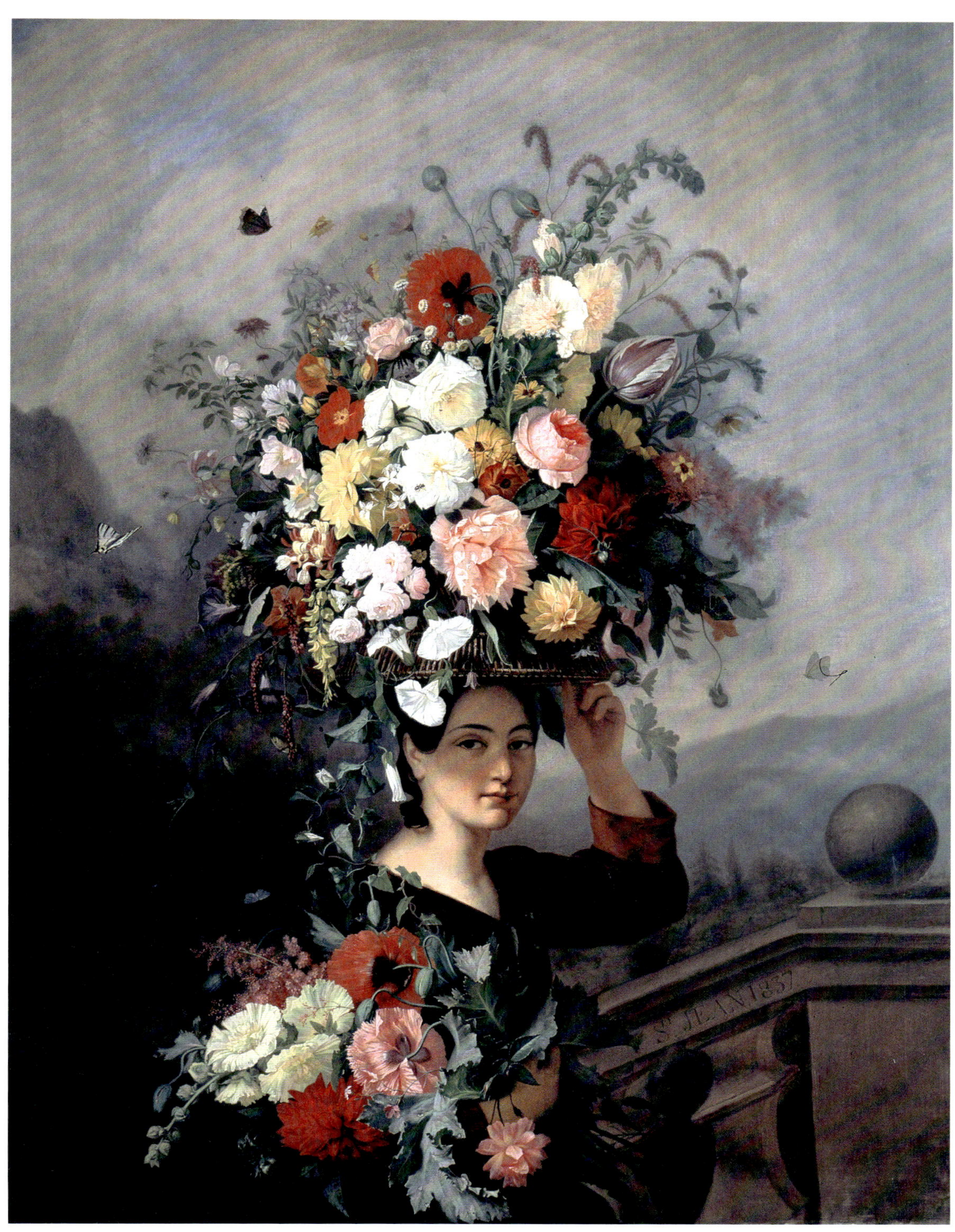
St JEAN 1837

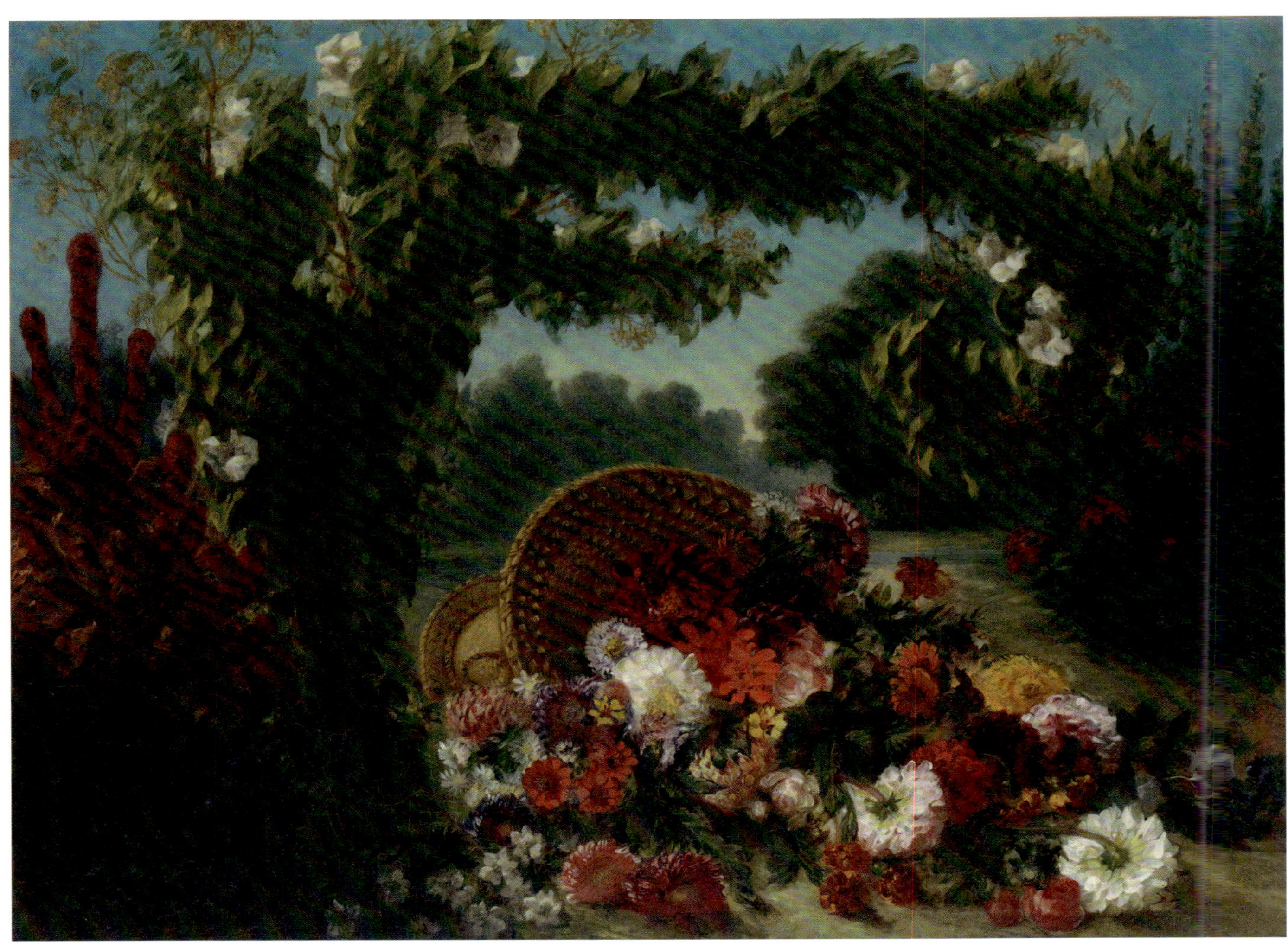

FIG. 126. Eugène Delacroix. *Basket of Flowers*, 1848–49. Oil on canvas. The Metropolitan Museum of Art, New York

An artist better known for picturing the turbulent struggles of mankind and animals, Delacroix imparted an intense vitality to his depictions of flowers. And with more than a passing interest in floral science, which he studied in his youth and on occasion discussed with the head botanist at the Jardin des Plantes, he was keenly attentive to botanical accuracy, achieving a level of realism that was soon to become the province of photographers, among them Adolphe Braun, who made floral studies for the use of artists and designers (fig. 127).

Delacroix's *Basket of Flowers*, displayed at the Salon of 1849 and at exhibitions in 1854, 1855, 1862, and 1864, won admiration especially among painters who were eager to infuse old, overworked themes with new life. Seeing how a high-strung palette and freewheeling paint strokes contributed robust vibrancy to a subject too often daintily treated, younger artists also saw in Delacroix's work how flowers might be used in their experiments with color and brisk brushwork.

One such painter was the Realist Gustave Courbet. During the 1850s Courbet included flowers in his paintings of women, but it was not until the 1860s that he undertook a studied exploration of floral subjects. At the invitation of Etienne Baudry, a writer, art collector, and amateur botanist who maintained vineyards, gardens, and greenhouses at his château in Rochemont, Courbet visited the Saintonge region of southwest France in the summer of 1862. He stayed in the vicinity until the spring of 1863, painting landscapes, portraits, and more than twenty floral subjects, many of them simple, traditional compositions centered on a bunch of assorted blooms crowded into a basket or bowl (fig. 128). Enraptured by the velvety petals, Courbet painted

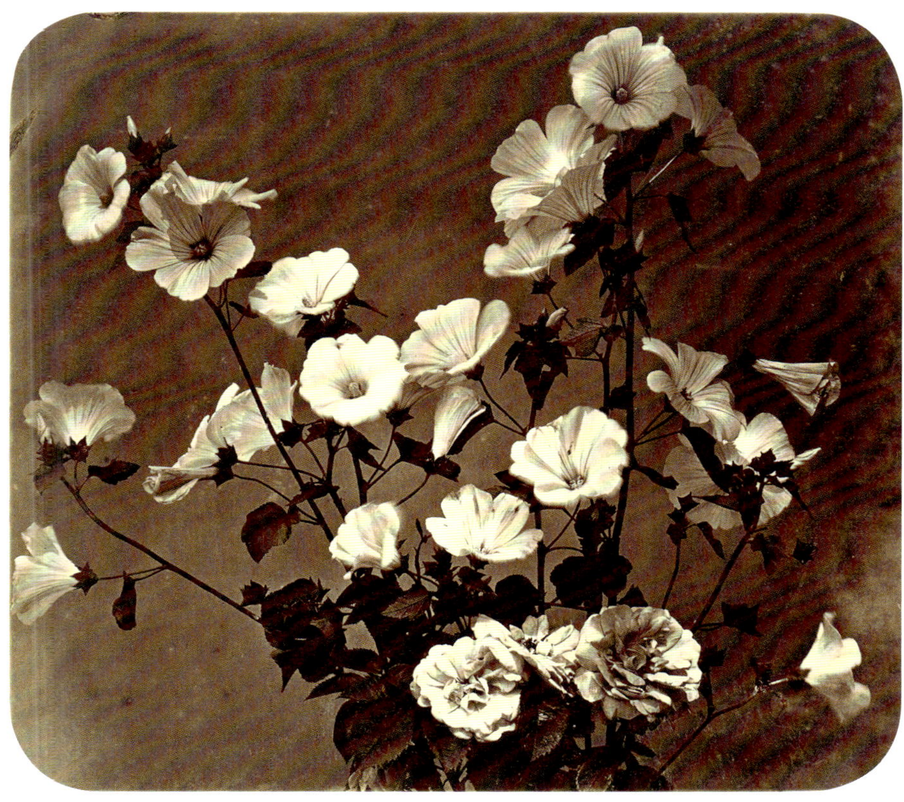

FIG. 127. Adolphe Braun. *Rose of Sharon*, ca. 1854. Albumen silver print from glass negative. The Metropolitan Museum of Art, New York

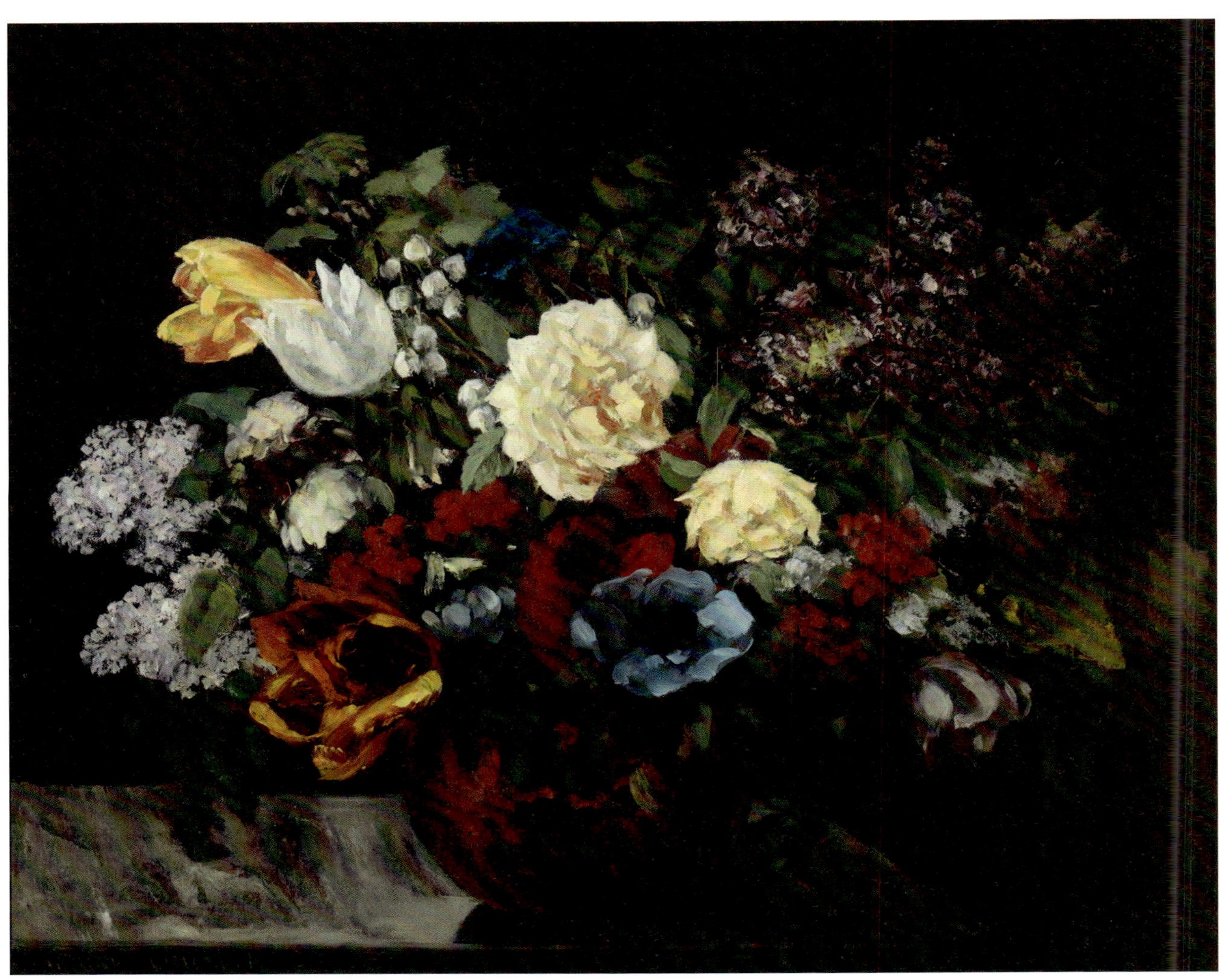

FIG. 128. Gustave Courbet. *Bouquet of Flowers*, 1862–63. Oil on canvas. Private collection

his flowers at close range, illuminated by the kind of torchlight that pierces the darkness in Dutch and Spanish seventeenth-century Baroque pictures. The sprays of lilac and the rich colors of tulips, roses, and various blooms from Baudry's botanical collection led Courbet to expand his generally dark and limited palette. Realized in broad, paint-laden strokes, his bouquets have the luscious look of the fruits and flowers in his only other still-life series, painted between 1871 and 1872.

Eugène Boudin, although best known as the painter of atmospheric Normandy beach scenes, composed a number of still lifes in the early years of his career. His floral studies generally follow his meeting the young Monet in

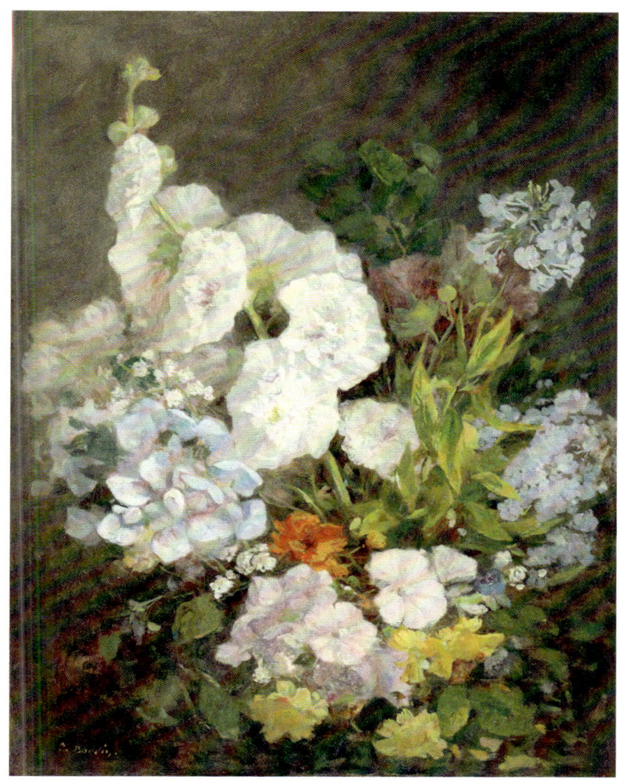

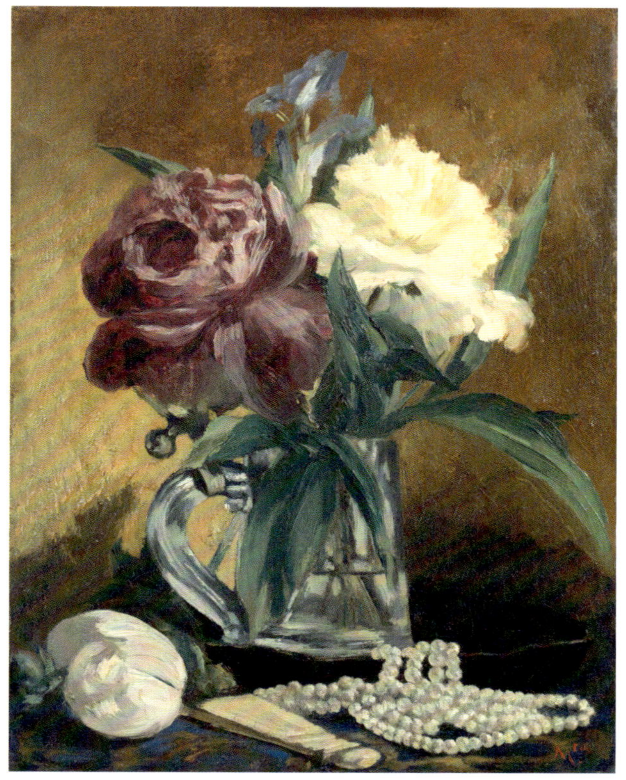

FIG. 129. Eugène Boudin. *Floral Still Life*, ca. 1858–62. Oil on canvas. Private collection

FIG. 130. Edouard Manet. *Still Life with Flowers, Fan, and Pearls*, ca. 1860. Oil on canvas. The Metropolitan Museum of Art, New York

1856 and his contemporary Courbet in 1859, friends with whom he periodically painted in the open air during the early 1860s. Monet credited Boudin with encouraging him to paint out of doors; he may have returned the favor by persuading Boudin to paint flowers. Writing from Honfleur to the artist Frédéric Bazille during the fall of 1864, Monet reported, "Boudin and [the Dutch painter Johan] Jongkind are here; we are getting on marvelously. . . . There are very beautiful flowers at present. . . . I believe it's an excellent thing to paint."[8] Courbet, too, seems to have inspired the exceptionally large and colorful floral works that Boudin composed about 1862, each displaying an armload of assorted flowers thrust into bright light from darkness (fig. 129). Not long after meeting him, Boudin wrote in his notebook, "Courbet has already freed me somewhat of timidity; I shall try some broad paintings, things on a big scale and more particular in tone."[9]

There is perhaps no artist who made painted flowers more seductive than Edouard Manet, who caressed them to life with the strokes of his brush. A master of the incidental still life and attracted to the sensuous qualities of flowers, he found myriad ways to introduce them into his pictures—as florist-wrapped bouquets, simple nosegays, tabletop arrangements, and garden blossoms. In perhaps the first of his floral still-life compositions, Manet employed the sober, saturated colors of the Spanish painting tradition so important to him in his early years. To a handful of peonies and iris placed in a glass tankard he added a string of pearls and a lady's fan, fashionable accessories that evoke the recipient of the flowers, who must have put them in water so hurriedly that one bloom was left behind (fig. 130).[10]

Peonies (*Paeonia lactiflora*), native to central and eastern Asia, were introduced to France in the early nineteenth century and were developed in several varieties. The voluptuous flowers were considered the epitome of luxury, and grew in abundance in the garden of the Manet estate in Gennevilliers. Manet's teacher Thomas Couture in his huge banquet scene *Romans of the Decadence* (1847; Musée d'Orsay, Paris) conspicuously pictured a crimson peony tossed on the floor as a sign of the revelers' extravagance.

Peonies figure prominently in Manet's first series of floral still lifes from the 1860s and again in his second two decades later, when near the end of his life he focused on the ephemeral beauty of flowers by painting bouquets brought to him during his final illness. The artist felt the strong association of flowers with gifts, and he often presented his pictures of them to friends. In the spring of 1864 he began a series of six paintings of peonies, exploring various ways in which they might be portrayed. In two of these, one of which is unfinished (fig. 131), he arranged flowers in a faience vase raised on a pedestal, leaving a maverick blossom below. Other works in this group show the flowers more informally, as cuttings just brought in from the garden, casually placed next to the gardener's shears, rather like hunting trophies displayed with the instrument of their capture (fig. 132). Such works reveal the influence of the eighteenth-century still-life master Jean Siméon Chardin, whose work, nearly a century after his death, was receiving renewed attention. Manet paid further homage

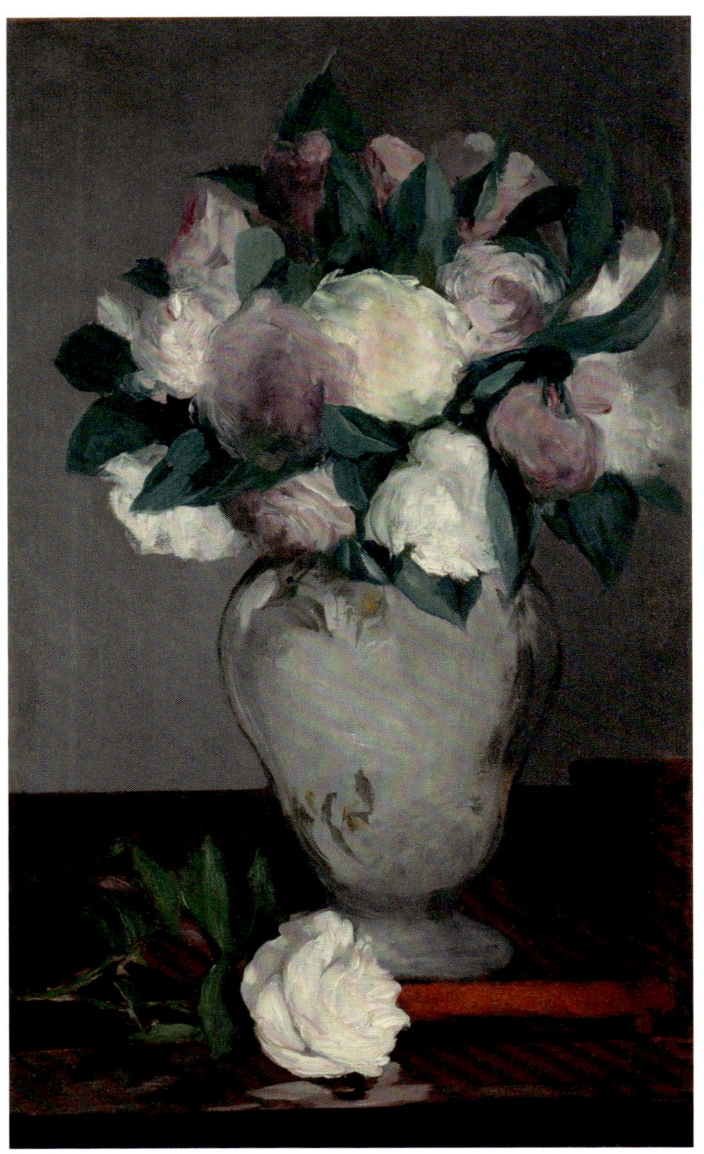

FIG. 131. Edouard Manet. *Peonies*, 1864–65. Oil on canvas. The Metropolitan Museum of Art, New York

FIG. 132. Edouard Manet. *Peonies with Shears*, 1864. Oil on canvas. Musée d'Orsay, Paris

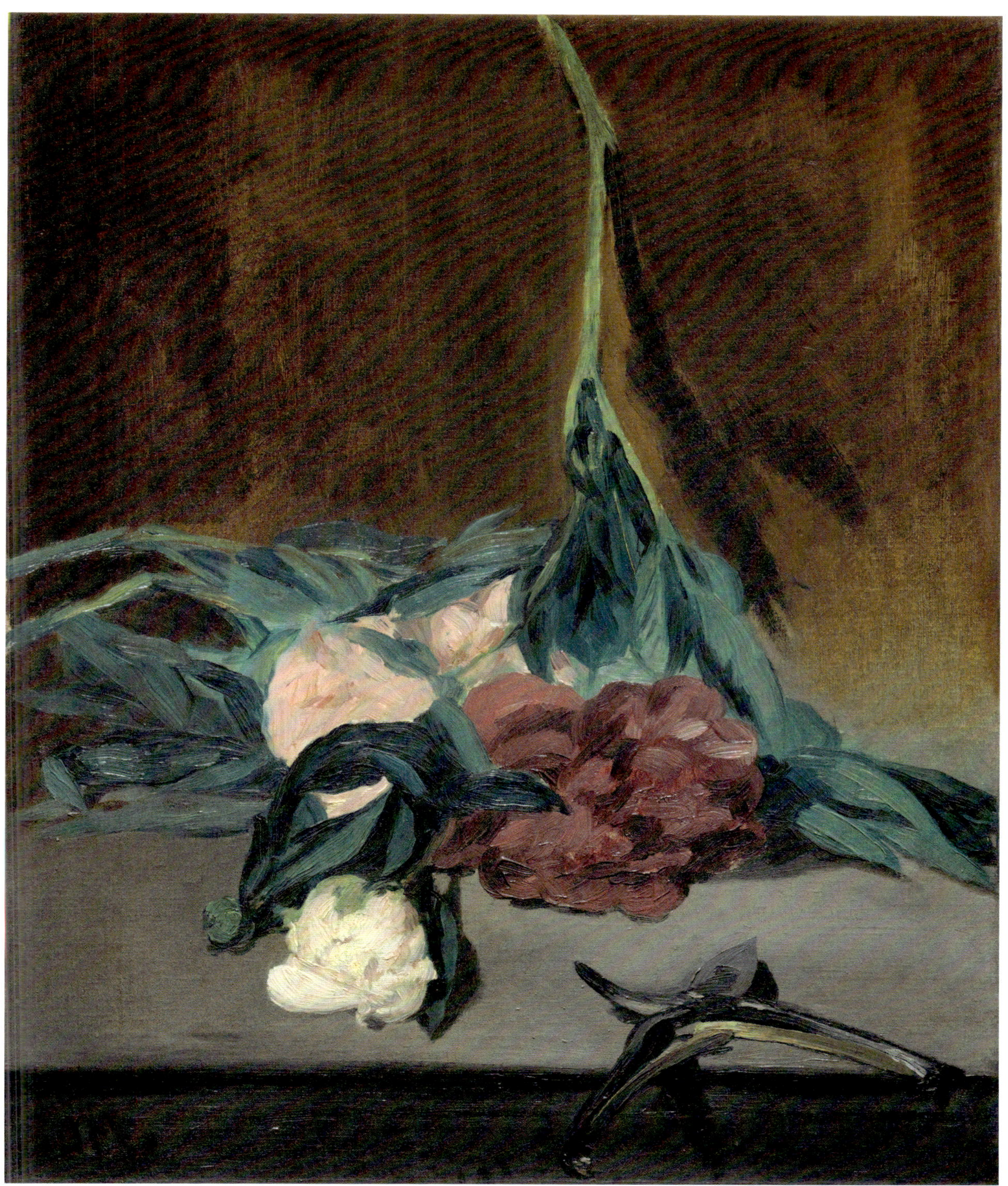

FIG. 133. Jean Siméon Chardin. *The Brioche*, 1763. Oil on canvas. Musée du Louvre, Paris

FIG. 134. Edouard Manet. *The Brioche*, 1870. Oil on canvas. The Metropolitan Museum of Art, New York

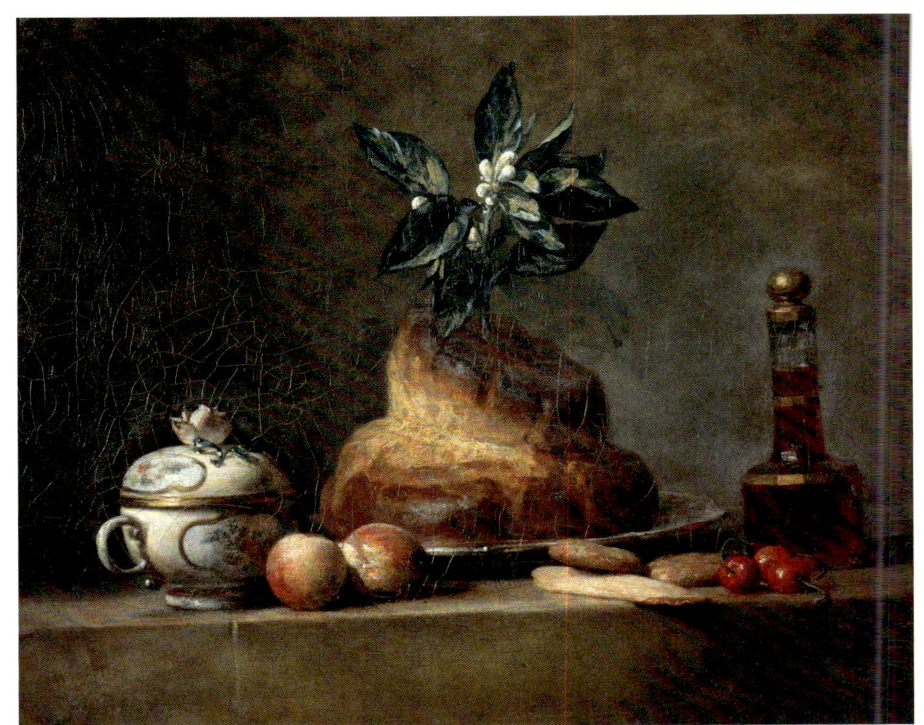

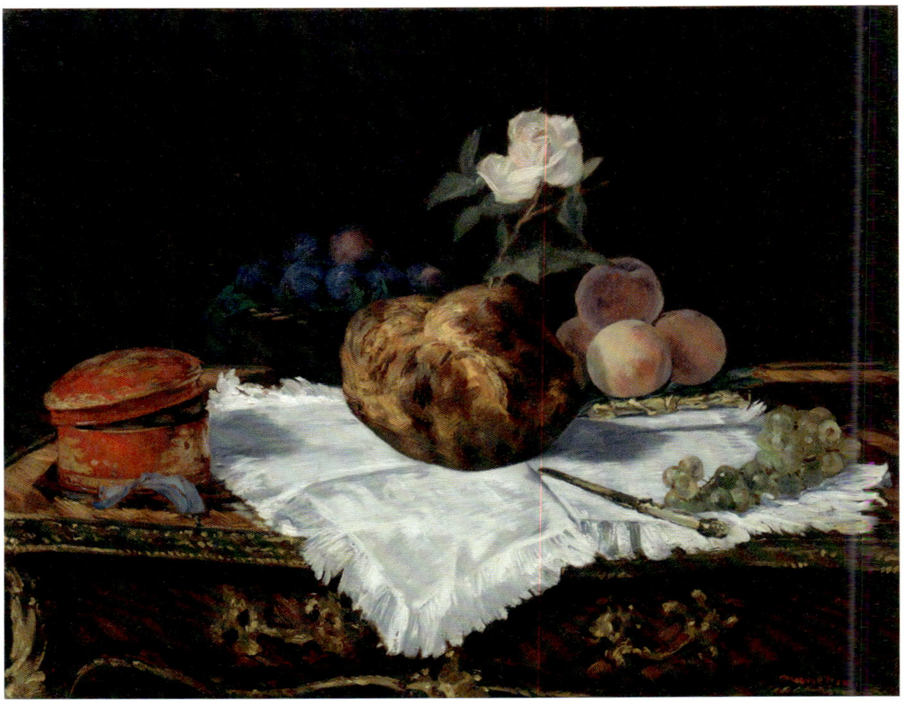

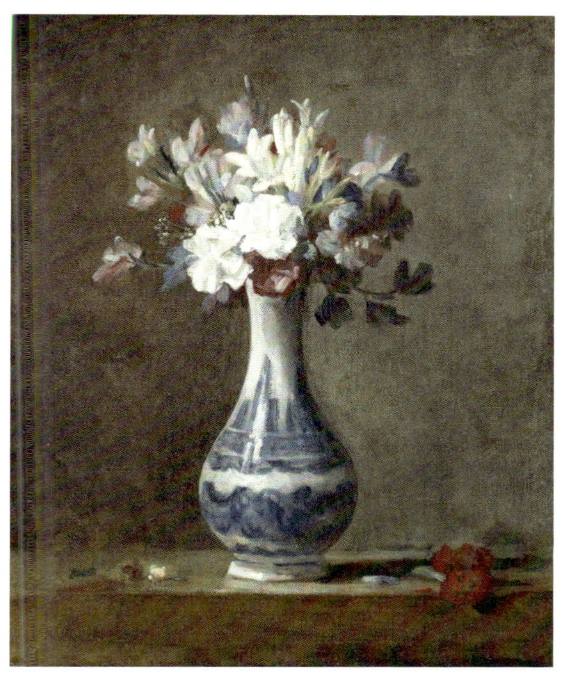

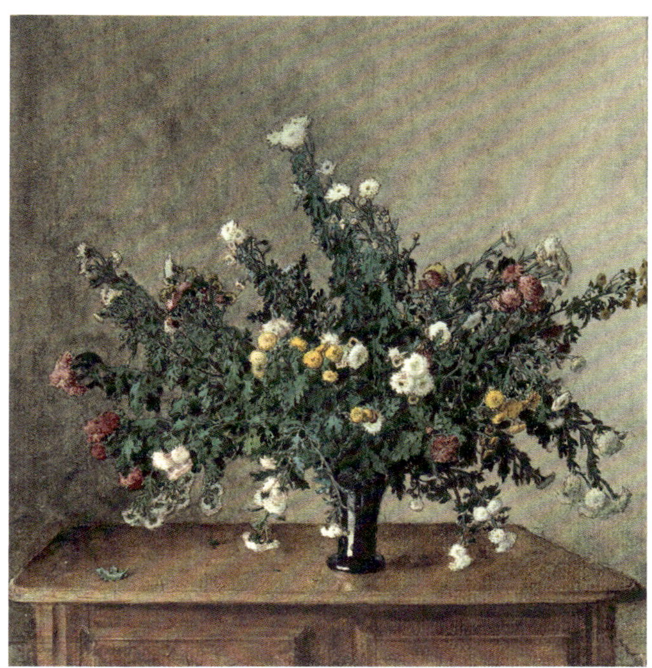

FIG. 135. Jean Siméon Chardin. *A Vase of Flowers*, early 1760s. Oil on canvas. Scottish National Gallery, Edinburgh

FIG. 136. Léon Bonvin. *Bouquet of Small Chrysanthemums*, 1862. Watercolor and gouache. The Metropolitan Museum of Art, New York

to the master when he painted a table arrangement likely based on Chardin's *Brioche* (fig. 133), which had recently entered the collection of the Musée du Louvre. Supplanting the sprig of apple blossom that Chardin had inserted atop his cakelike bread, Manet crowned his brioche with a single rose (fig. 134).

Only one of Chardin's painted bouquets has survived (fig. 135), echoing the perfect simplicity of his still lifes that made modest, everyday objects things to be valued. Rendered in a grainy rather than a glossy finish, they appealed both to the Impressionists and to the Realists, painters like Philippe Rousseau, François Bonvin, and Léon Bonvin, who described unpretentious backcountry flowers with exquisite care (fig. 136).[11]

Although Edgar Degas once expressed his aversion to scented flowers by marching a bowl of roses out of his host's dining room, he too alluded to current fashion by portraying a woman seated beside an enormous bouquet of asters, dahlias, and other late-summer blooms (fig. 137).[12] The sitter, thought to be Marguerite Claire Valpinçon, the wife of Degas's friend Paul Valpinçon, had evidently arranged the flowers after gathering them from the garden, here glimpsed through the window in the background.[13] Her discarded gloves and the water pitcher on the table are the apparent participants in this activity. While it would not have been appropriate for a woman of Madame Valpinçon's

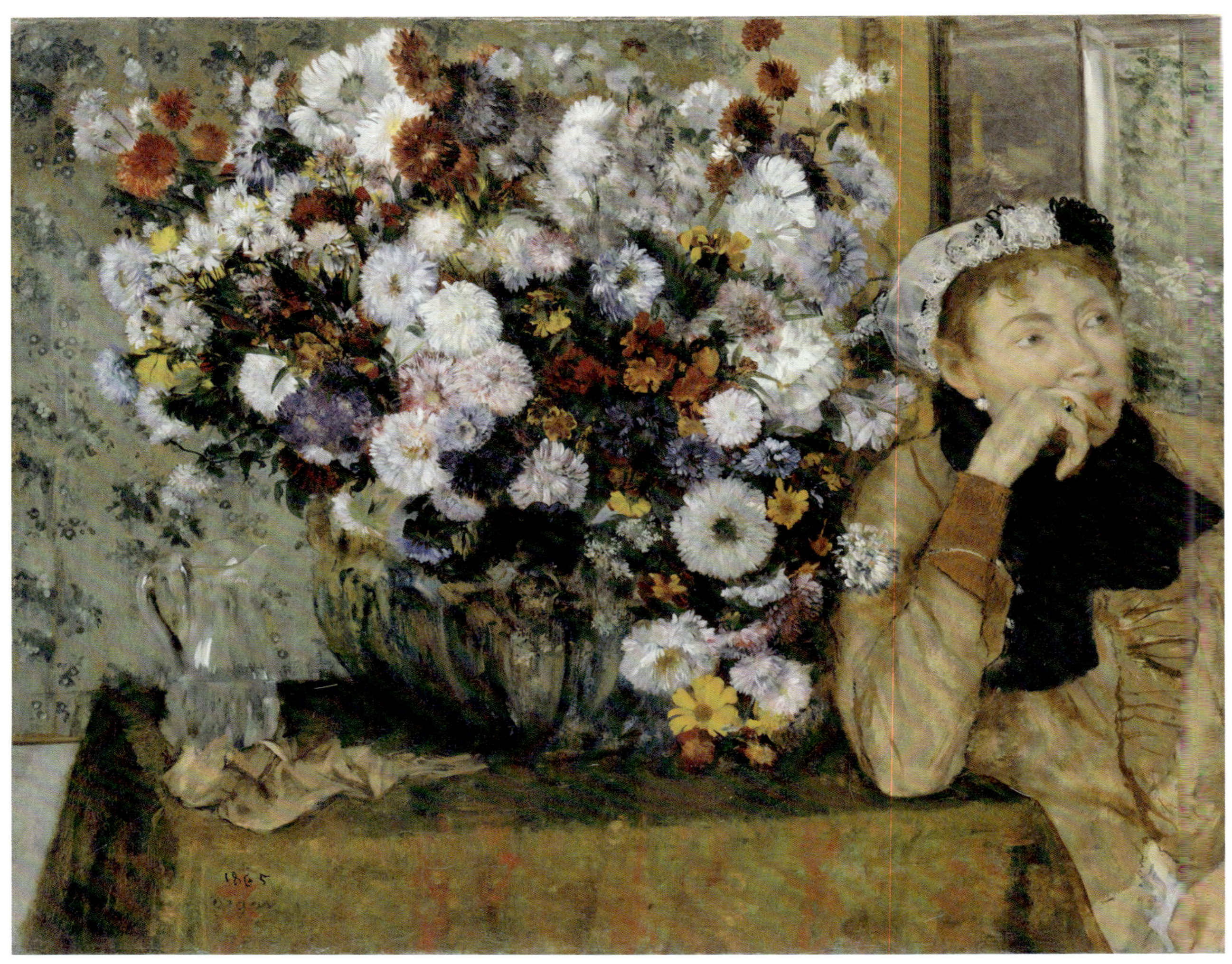

FIG. 137. Edgar Degas. *A Woman Seated beside a Vase of Flowers (Madame Paul Valpinçon?)*, 1865. Oil on canvas. The Metropolitan Museum of Art, New York

social class to wield a trowel or spade, she could have been expected to assume the role of intermediary between house and garden. "Women are the good genii of gardens," it was reported in the *Revue Horticole* in 1859. "It is they who get utilitarian men to bring [gardens] to life, and who show them how much a garden may spread charm over life."[14]

The most striking aspect of Degas's 1865 painting is his conflation of portraiture and still life, in which both sitter and flowers are presented on equal terms, each highly individualized. The artist made three additional paintings of women paired with floral arrangements in the 1870s.[15] While these are less inventive compositions, the scenes are similarly situated within rooms

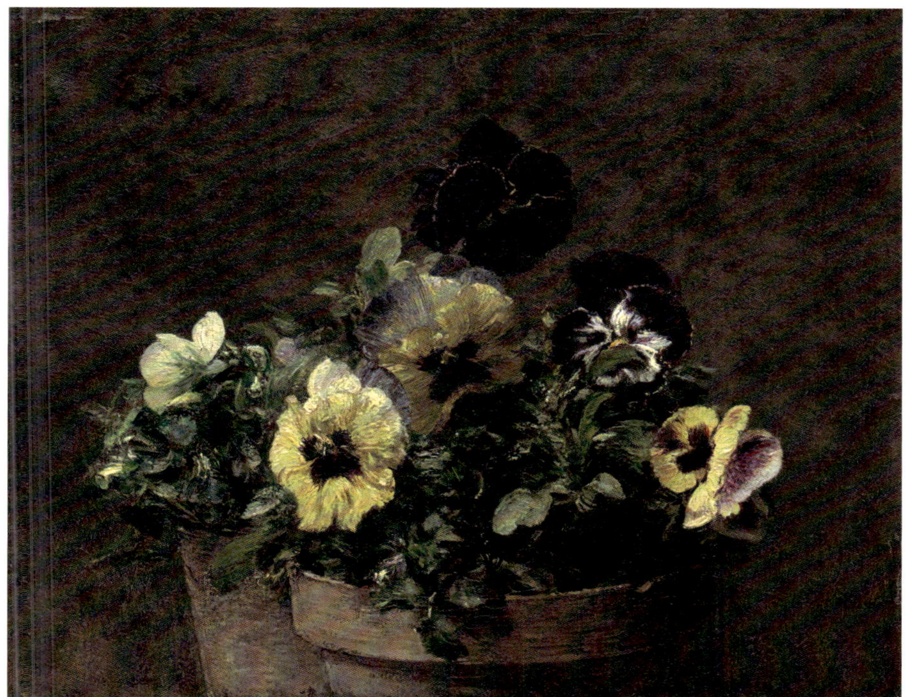

FIG. 138. Henri Fantin-Latour. *Potted Pansies*, 1883. Oil on canvas. The Metropolitan Museum of Art, New York

outfitted with trappings of bourgeois life. In itself an innovation, the contemporary setting seemed to satisfy the entreaties of Charles Baudelaire, whose essay "The Painter of Modern Life," published in 1863, urged artists to paint "the manners of the present," the "modernity" of today, and "the mysterious beauty which human life accidentally puts into it."[16]

Unlike Degas, who cared little for outdoor activities (unless they took place at the racetrack), other Impressionists not only addressed the *pleinairisme* of the garden but showed a real interest in its attendant accoutrements, among them the earthenware containers first designed and produced on an industrial scale during the middle of the century. Filled with popular bedding plants such as the "show pansies" hybridized in France around 1870, the terracotta pot quickly became one of the garden's most useful accessories (fig. 138).

Partners to the expanding corps of rural growers in France were the flower vendors, most often nurserymen's wives and daughters, who brought their products to the urban markets. The tradition of individual street sellers continued throughout the century, although the flower girl's cry, "Fleurissez-vous, Madame!" was less often heard. At midcentury the *bouquetière* might offer her wares from a street corner, a pushcart, a stall, or, at the highest level

FIG. 139. Charles Philipon. *The Pretty Flower Vendor*, ca. 1830. Hand-colored lithograph. Private collection

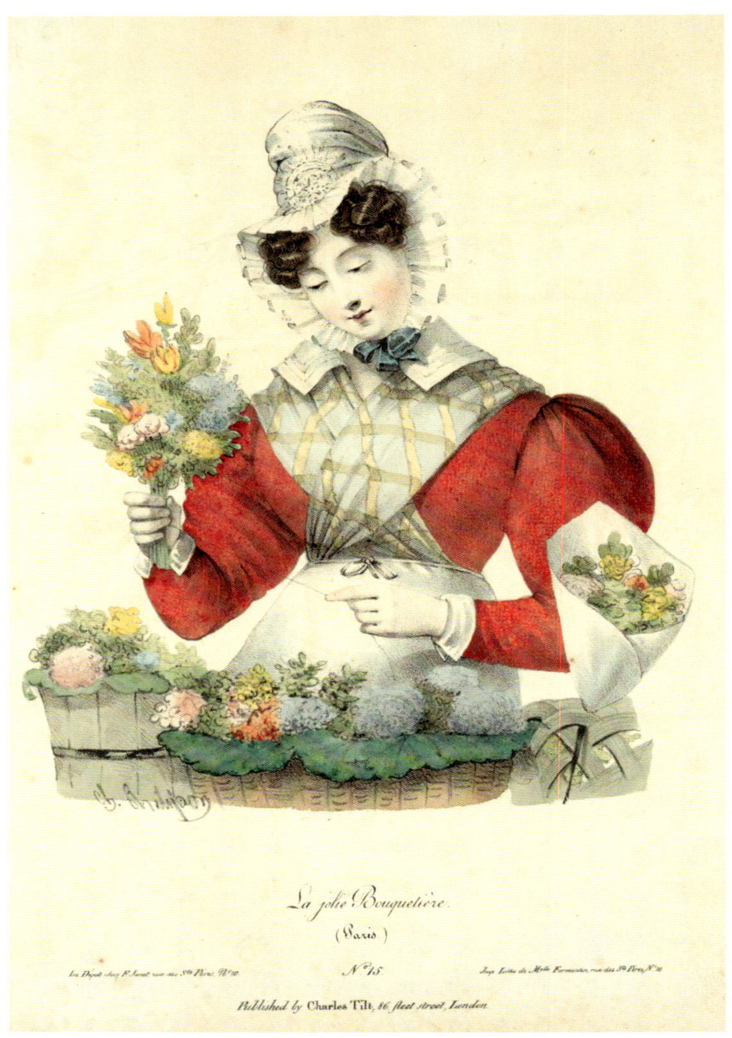

of the trade, a boutique (fig. 139).[17] To accommodate new tastes in interior design, horticultural establishments sprang up to decorate private houses, and the profession of florist was born.[18]

Galignani's New Paris Guide of 1839 gives some idea of the massive consumption of flowers in Paris at this time, noting that "on some particular days, there are exposed for sale in the different markets of the capital 30,000 pots of flowers."[19] Robinson's 1869 guide informed visitors that public flower markets were open twice a week at various locations around Paris: at the Place de la Madeleine, the Château d'Eau, the Quai aux Fleurs, and the Place Saint-Sulpice. At each venue it was reported, "Flowers ready cut for bouquets and

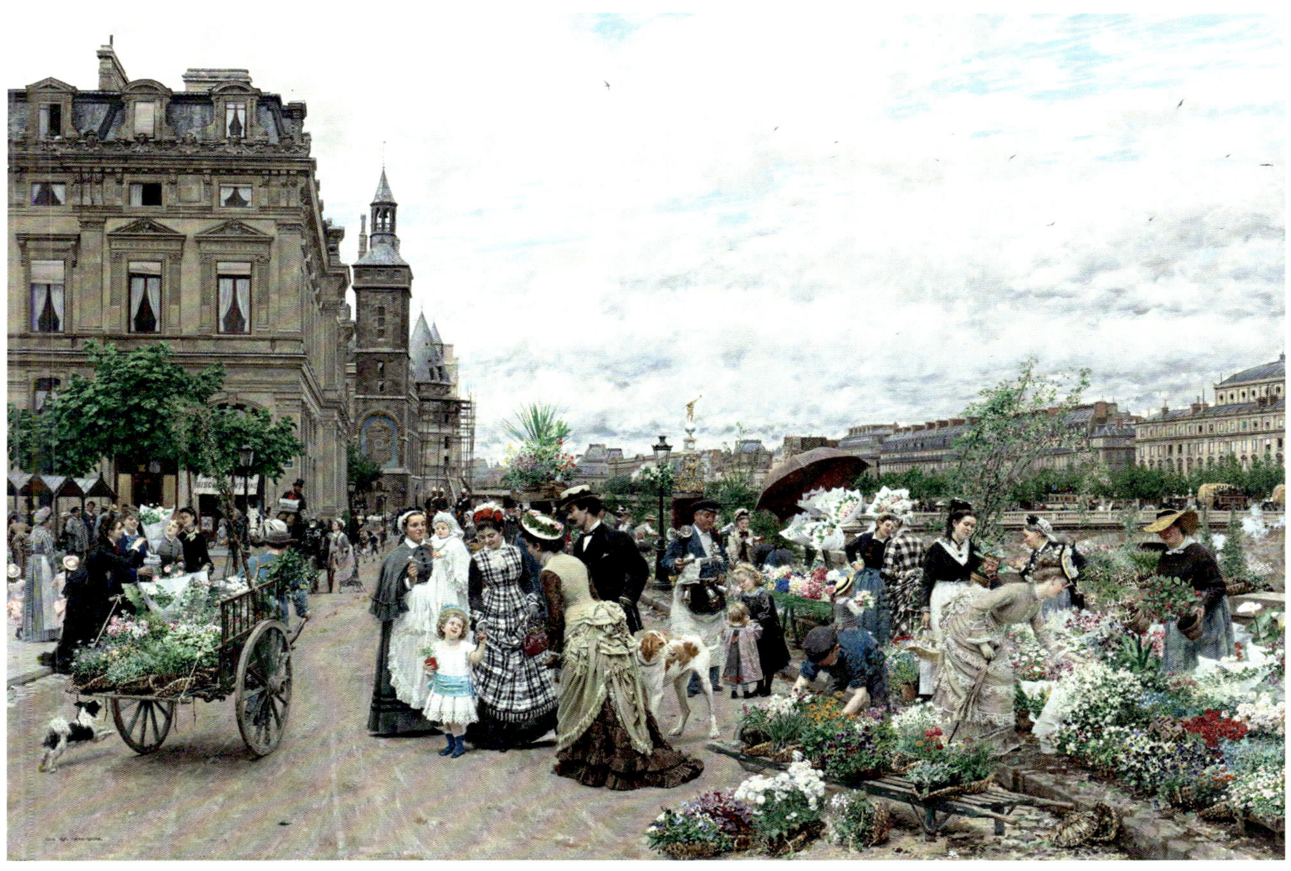

room decoration are particularly well done and very abundant."[20] Indeed, the busy market on the Quai aux Fleurs, as pictured in one of the most popular paintings at the Salon of 1876, by the Realist painter Marie-François Firmin-Girard, is the scene of smartly dressed shoppers and bountiful displays of wrapped bouquets and flower-filled pots and baskets (fig. 140).

FIG. 140. Marie-François Firmin-Girard. *The Flower Market, Paris (Quai aux Fleurs)*, 1875. Oil on canvas. Private collection

A particularly active horticultural industry sprang up in the South of France, and after the opening of the Paris–Nice railway in 1870 Parisians could receive roses sent by rail overnight.[21] The hybrid tea rose, named 'La France,' was developed near Lyon in 1867; the first of the popular modern types admired for their upright growth and repeated bloom, it marked the division between "old" and "new" classes of roses. However, the favorite painter of roses, Henri Fantin-Latour, preferred instead the old-fashioned *Centifolia* group, with their cushions of tightly packed petals, a pink variety of which was named in his honor. With his wife, Victoria Dubourg, also a flower

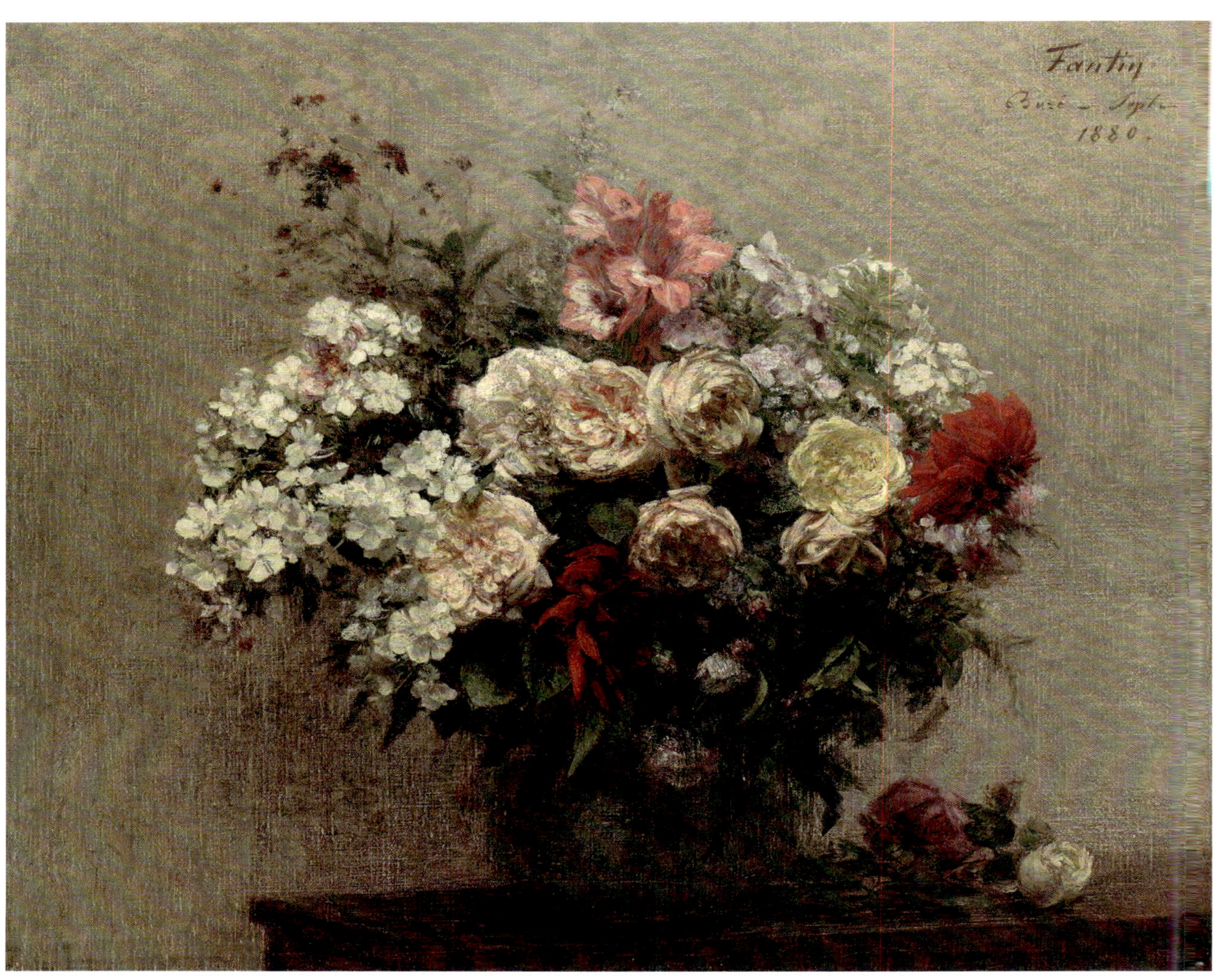

FIG. 141. Henri Fantin-Latour. *Summer Flowers*, 1880. Oil on canvas. The Metropolitan Museum of Art, New York

painter, Fantin spent summers in Normandy gathering blooms from their cottage garden to paint in the undisturbed air of the studio. His restrained bouquets found a particularly supportive audience in England, where they settled comfortably into Victorian parlors (fig. 141).

In the well-appointed French bourgeois household flowers played an increasingly prominent role, perhaps never more lavishly than in the Paris townhouse of Princess Mathilde, niece of Napoleon I and doyenne of a salon for artists and writers, whose guests were invited to dine in her sumptuous winter garden (fig. 142). To the fresh-cut bouquets and potted plants that had become the fashionable enhancements of interior décor were added floral

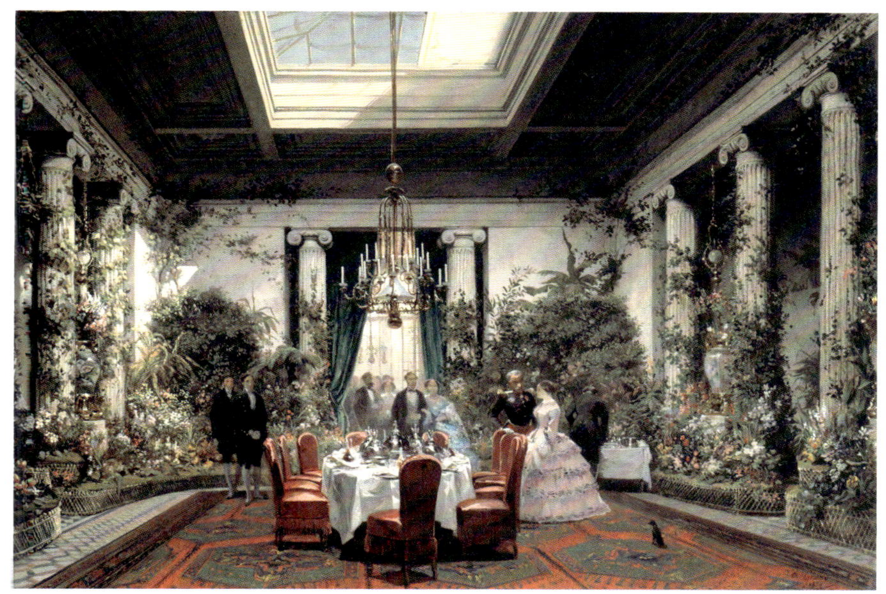

FIG. 142. Sébastien Charles Giraud. *Princess Mathilde's Dining Room*, 1854. Oil on canvas. Château de Compiègne

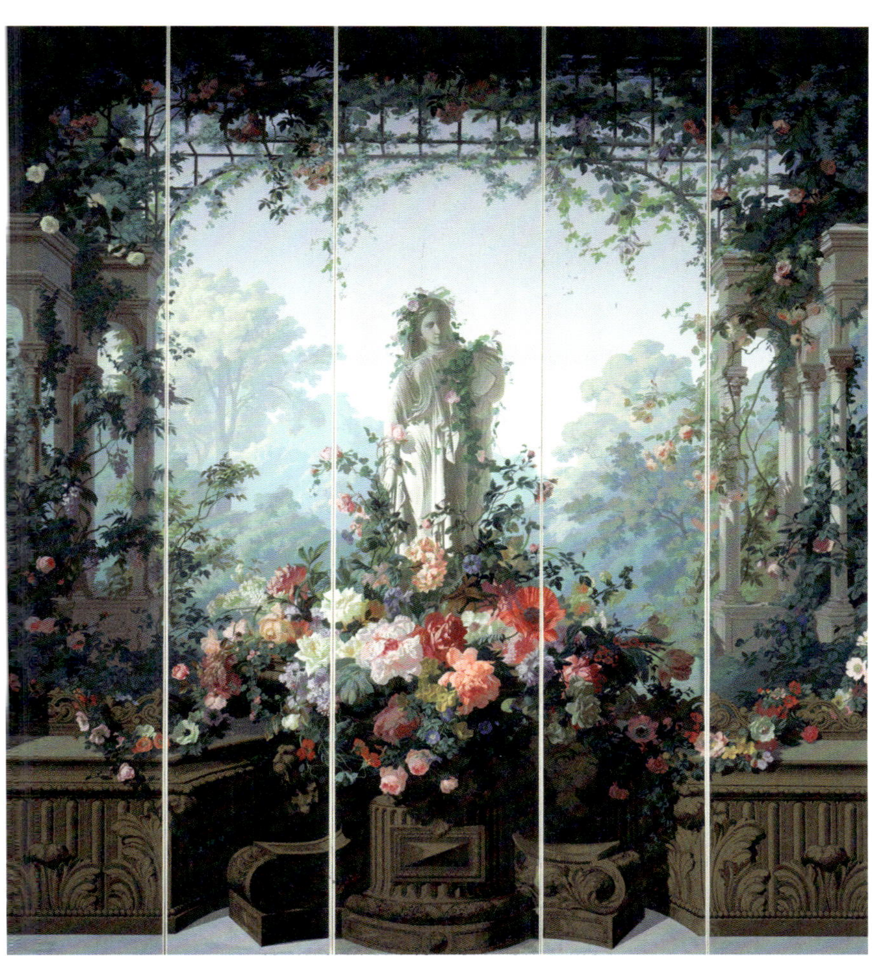

FIG. 143. Edouard Muller, called Rosenmuller. *The Garden of Armida*, 1854. Block-printed wallpaper. Philadelphia Museum of Art

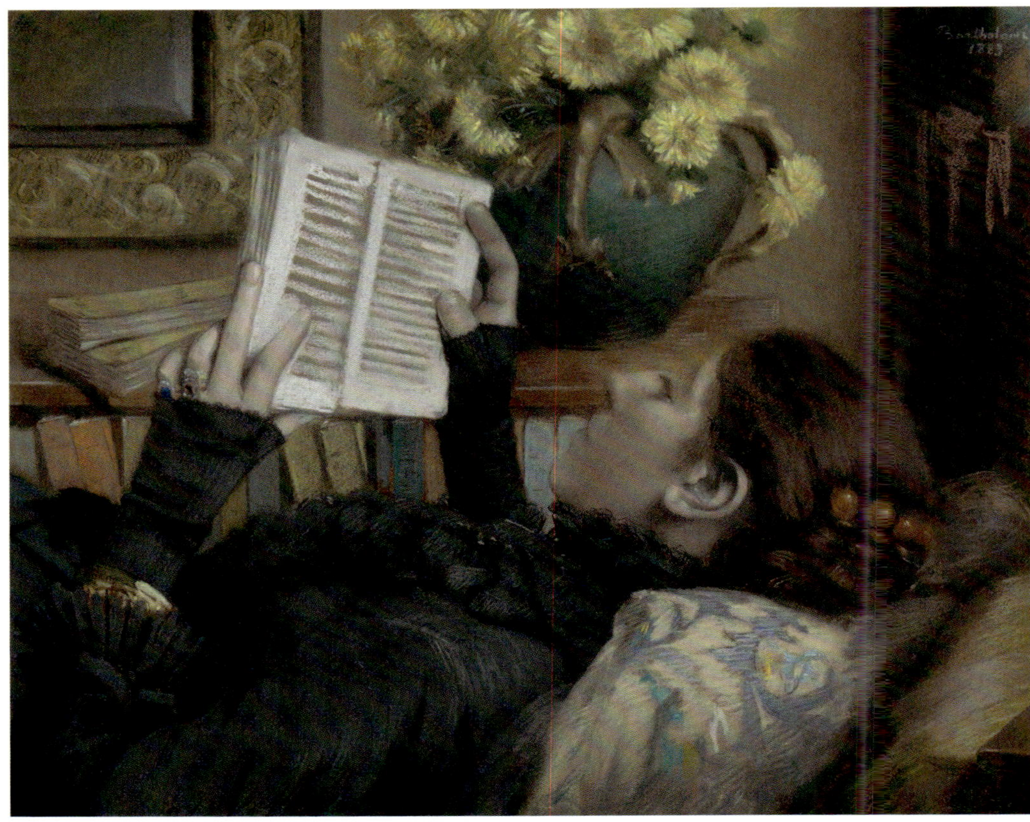

FIG. 144. Albert Bartholomé. *The Artist's Wife Reading*, 1883. Pastel and charcoal on paper, laid down on canvas. The Metropolitan Museum of Art, New York

motifs featured in the patterns of curtains, rugs, upholstery, and wallpapers. A designer of luxurious flowery fabrics, Edouard Muller (appropriately called Rosenmuller) played a leading role in the revival of panoramic wallpapers during the Second Empire. In a naturalistic three-panel tableau, he imagined the palace garden of the magician Armida in Tasso's *Jerusalem Delivered* (1581), presided over by a statue of the goddess Flora (fig. 143). The printed-paper mural, seemingly inspired by Princess Mathilde's garden room, was awarded a first-class medal at the Exposition Universelle of 1855.[22]

In his novel *La Curée* (1871) Emile Zola describes an elegant Parc Monceau mansion whose rooms are adorned with "festoons of roses, topped with tufts of full blown blossoms . . . [above an] Aubusson carpet spread [with] purple flowers . . . porcelain vases standing on the consoles . . . [and] flower-stands placed in the window recesses."[23] In portrait and genre paintings as well, flower-filled vases on parlor tables, consoles, and shelves were a mark of gracious living. Albert Bartholomé's sympathetic portrayal of his frail wife,

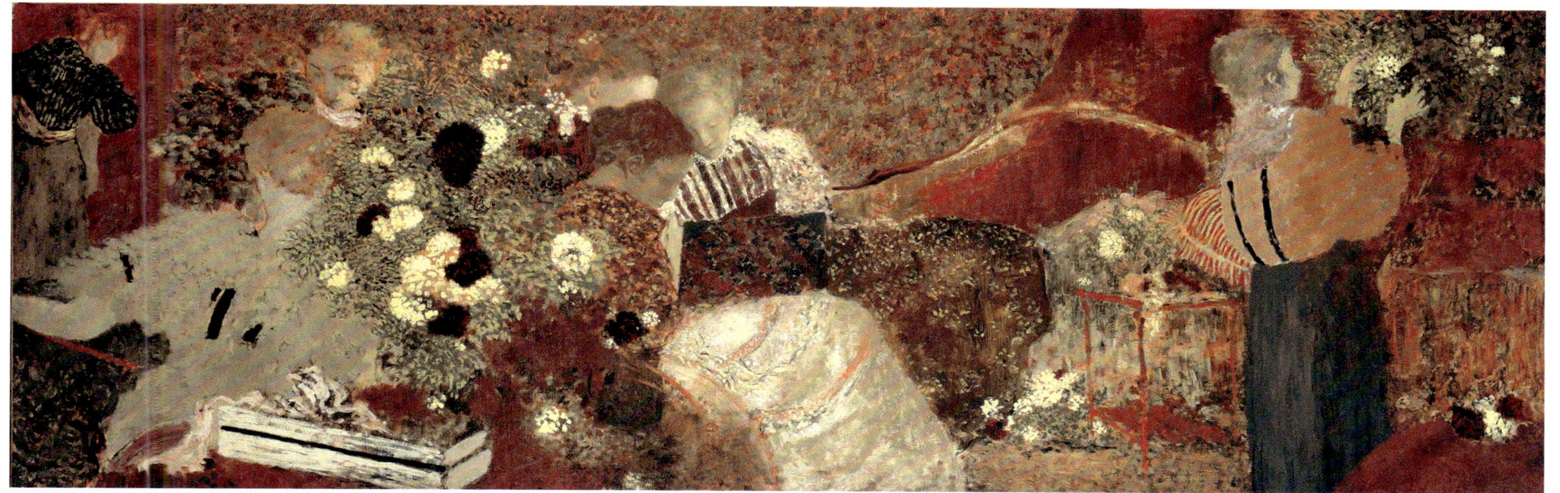

Périe, shows her reading as she reclines on a couch beside a bowl of chrysanthemums (fig. 144), an unusual composition that perhaps pays homage to the close pairing of portraiture and floral still life in the work of his friend Edgar Degas (see fig. 137). A more modern invention is Vuillard's semicinematic depiction of women in an interior arranging armloads of chrysanthemum-like flowers while their companions leaf through the pages of an album. The gaslit sitting room with its densely patterned floral wallpaper evidently mimics the salon of Thadée and Misia Natanson, for whom this picture, one of five panels, was created. The wide-angle view unfurls in an oversized format the artist often favored as a painter of murals and folding screens (fig. 145).

FIG. 145. Edouard Vuillard. *The Album*, 1895. Oil on canvas. The Metropolitan Museum of Art, New York

In such pictures relatively little attention is paid to the containers used for holding flowers. The appeal of decorative porcelain vases and elaborate stone urns had been important to earlier still-life painters, but the Impressionists generally preferred objects of simpler design that quietly deferred to the blossoms. Beginning in the 1860s commonplace ceramic or glass containers found around the house or studio, such as earthenware pots, jugs, and bowls, became the favored vessels.[24]

Departing from a tradition of vases and jardinières that were multicolored and intricate in design (fig. 146), the most forward-looking art potters in late nineteenth-century France, such as Ernest Chaplet (fig. 147) and Auguste Delaherche, expressed their modernity in simple shapes and monochrome glazes inspired by the ceramic arts of East Asia. An important consideration

FIG. 146. Jacob Petit. Jardinière and stand, ca. 1834–48; Fontainebleau Manufactory. Hard-paste porcelain. The Metropolitan Museum of Art, New York

FIG. 147. Ernest Chaplet. Vase, ca. 1889. Porcelain. The Metropolitan Museum of Art, New York

FIG. 148. Emile Gallé. Vase, 1896. Glass. The Metropolitan Museum of Art, New York

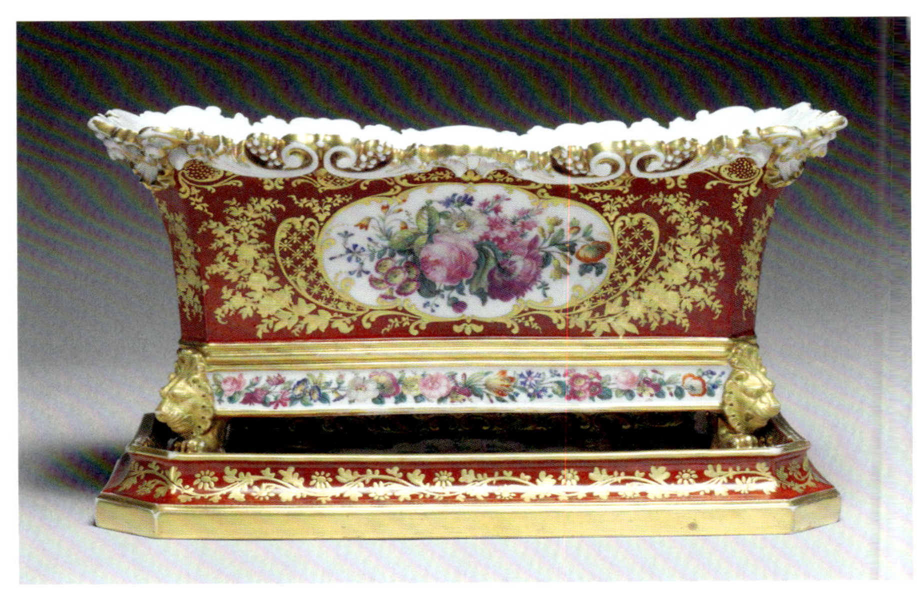

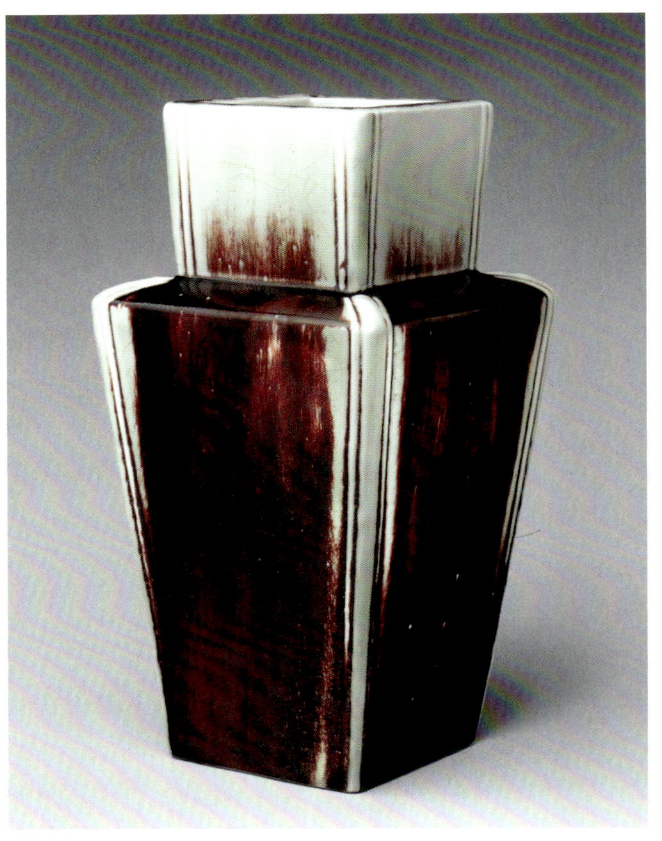

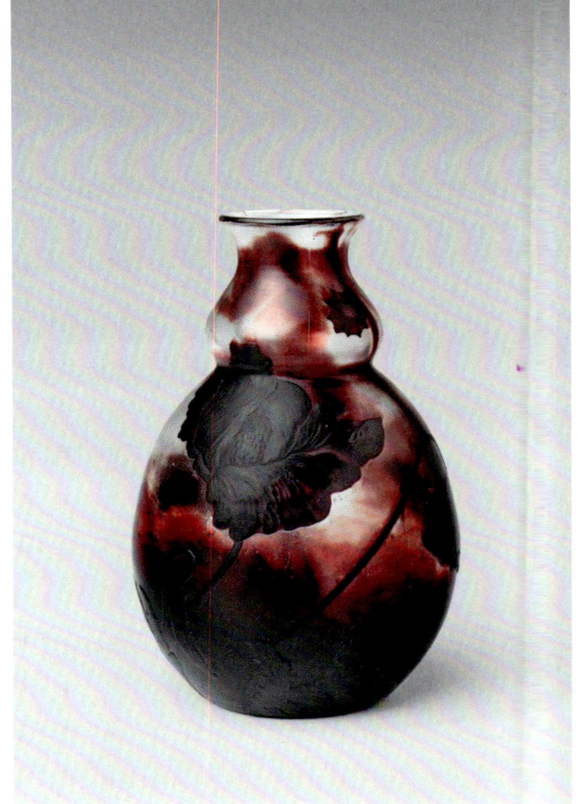

for these artists, as rarely before, was "the true purpose and function of the flower vase . . . of holding and displaying cut flowers to the greatest possible advantage . . . not [to] vie with the flowers placed in them, but rather . . . [to] enhance their beauty."[25] Ironically, the singular allure of these finely crafted ceramics made them desirable as objects in and of themselves, a distinction often afforded vases produced by glassmaking pioneers Eugène Rousseau and Emile Gallé (fig. 148), whose designs frequently incorporated floral motifs.

Although relatively few floral still lifes were accepted for exhibition by the Salon in the seventeenth and eighteenth centuries, their representation more than doubled during the nineteenth century. One journalist called the Salon of 1863, in which fifty-two floral still lifes were exhibited, a veritable "garden" of pictures, with "poppies, peonies, and roses."[26] The popularity of the genre was evident at the Salon of 1880, where 159 floral still lifes were displayed. Of these, approximately one-third were by women artists, with whom the painted subject was traditionally associated. As a journalist advised readers of the *Gazette des Beaux-Arts* in 1860, "Let women have the genres that [they] have preferred in all periods: [among them] flowers, those prodigies of grace and freshness with which women alone can compete in freshness and grace."[27]

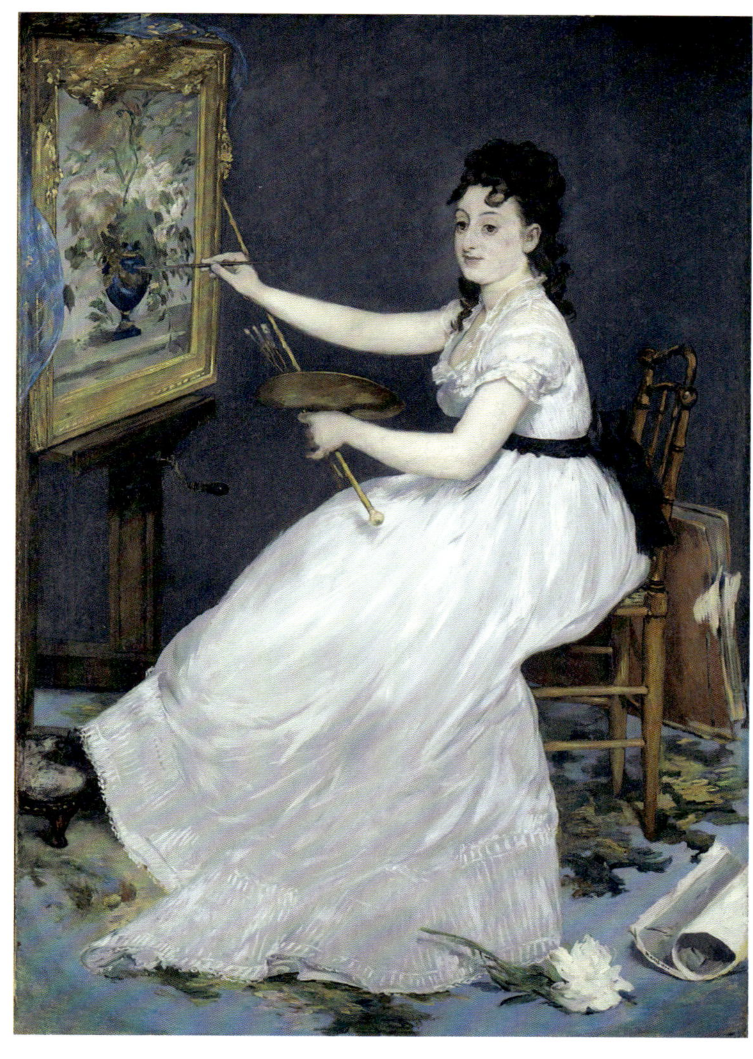

FIG. 149. Edouard Manet. *Eva Gonzalès*, 1870. Oil on canvas. National Gallery, London

In 1870, when Manet portrayed his pupil Eva Gonzalès painting a floral still life, he seemed to be suggesting that her future would be in flowers (fig. 149). In the end she painted very few, preferring instead to demonstrate her skill in studies of the human figure. A woman listed pseudonymously as "M. Jacques François," whose paintings of fruits and flowers were admired for being "bold in a way that is altogether feminine," exhibited with the Impressionists in 1876, but other women artists associated with the group, including Morisot and Cassatt—who depicted garden scenes and incorporated floral motifs in their pictures of domestic interiors—generally steered clear of flower painting.[28] One of Cassatt's rare still lifes, which presents the

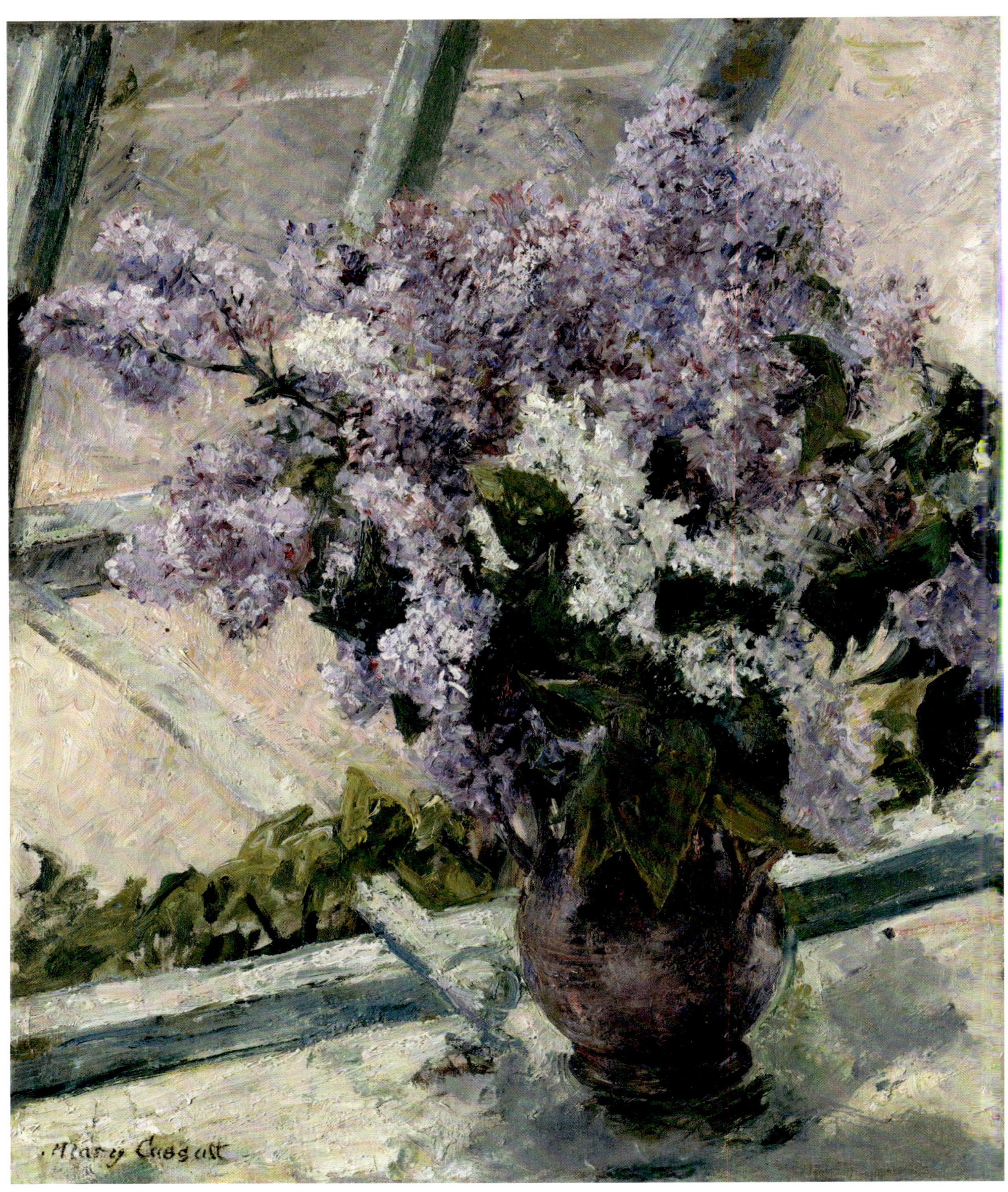
Mary Cassatt

double-flowered lilacs first cultivated in the 1840s (fig. 150), must have been painted at the country house her family rented outside Paris. The artist placed her casually arranged bouquet on the windowsill of the greenhouse, close to the open air, in cool spring light. The container is a simple, unornamented pitcher. Interestingly, about 1902 Cassatt, finding an interest in the vases themselves, took up ceramic vase decoration.[29]

The floral still life, despite the fact that it was an indoor (rather than the often more desirable outdoor) subject, appeared in the work of many painters in the Impressionist circle, notably in ambitious early works of the 1860s. A consistent, if minor, feature of the Impressionist exhibitions held between 1874 and 1886, floral still-life painting received increased attention during the 1880s, no doubt in connection with the artists' experiments with color. Practical considerations also made the subject attractive, as when bad weather drove artists indoors. And, not incidentally, there was the prospect of good sales of this ingratiating, popular subject.[30]

Monet's floral still lifes, although produced in the studio, often evoke fresh air and outdoor light. The artist painted more than twenty flower compositions between 1878 and 1883 before taking up residence in Giverny, where his subject became the entire garden. Instead of painting a bouquet of different varieties, according to traditional practice, Monet preferred a generous display of whatever single flower was then at the height of bloom. A perennial favorite was the exotic "Oriental" chrysanthemum, introduced to France shortly before 1800 but not widely cultivated until midcentury, when it came into fashion. Its popularity was such that in 1854 a journalist reported, "[This] plant raised by the Chinese to a rare degree of perfection, has become all the rage in Europe ever since horticulturists have taken to sowing its seeds and developing varieties with a wide range of hues."[31]

Monet featured chrysanthemums in a series of still lifes he made while living at Vétheuil in 1880 and 1881. Painting the pearly small chrysanthemums of late summer with petal-size dabs and dashes (fig. 151), he created a shimmering effect that is reflected in the polished table. There, the mirrored blooms and their sky-blue background remind us of the artist's infatuation with the watery surfaces of the Seine and, yet to come, his own lily pond.

It was the extraordinary range of hues in which chrysanthemums could now be cultivated that caught the eye of Renoir, who bunched dozens of mums together in a framed display of floral fireworks (fig. 152). Probably gathered from the garden of the artist's patron Paul Bérard at Wargemont, near Dieppe, the flowers themselves must have emboldened the artist to test the overheated

FIG. 150. Mary Cassatt. *Lilacs in a Window*, ca. 1880–83. Oil on canvas. The Metropolitan Museum of Art, New York

OVERLEAF:

FIG. 151. Claude Monet. *Chrysanthemums*, 1882. Oil on canvas. The Metropolitan Museum of Art, New York

FIG. 152. Auguste Renoir. *Bouquet of Chrysanthemums*, 1881. Oil on canvas. The Metropolitan Museum of Art, New York

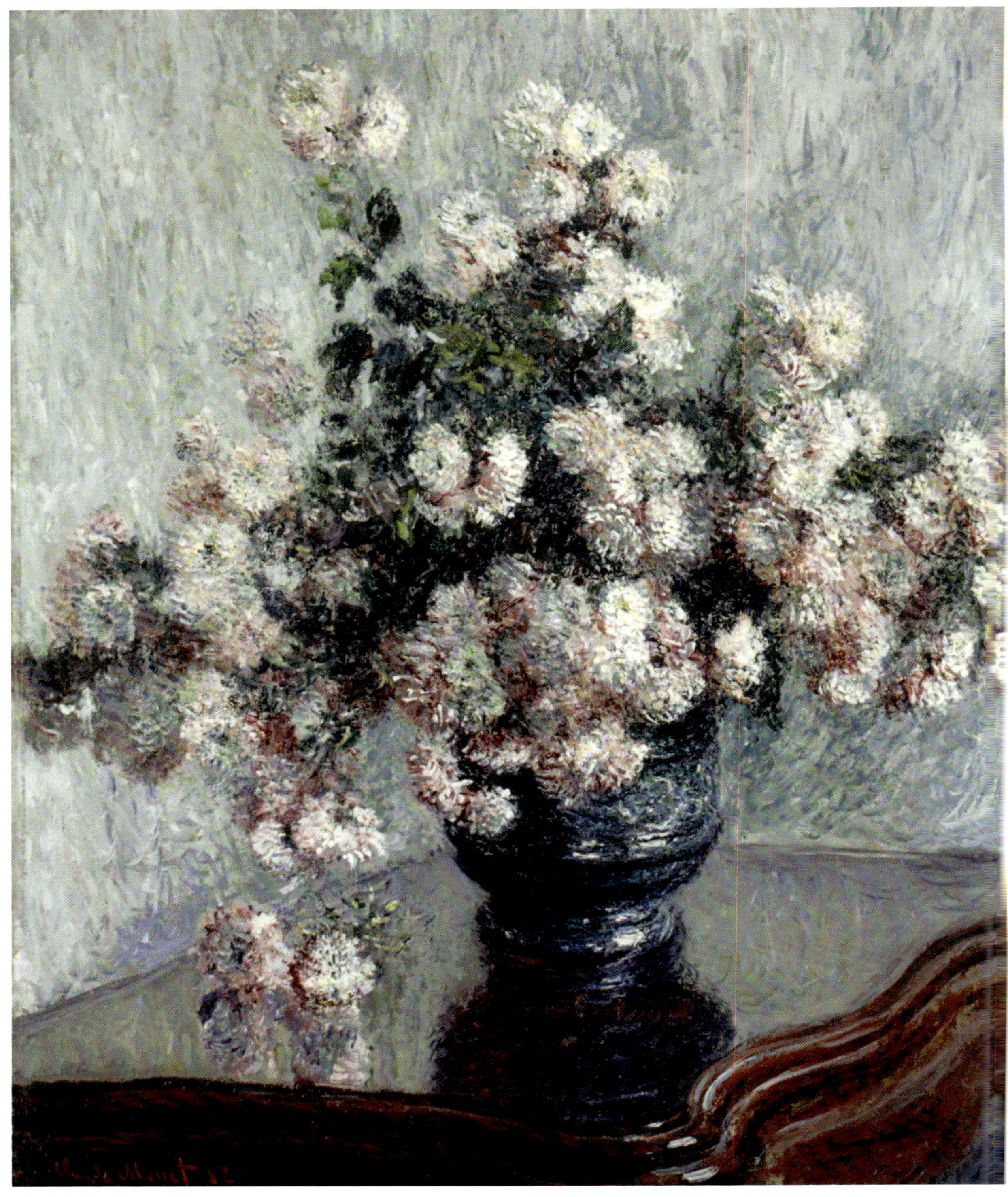

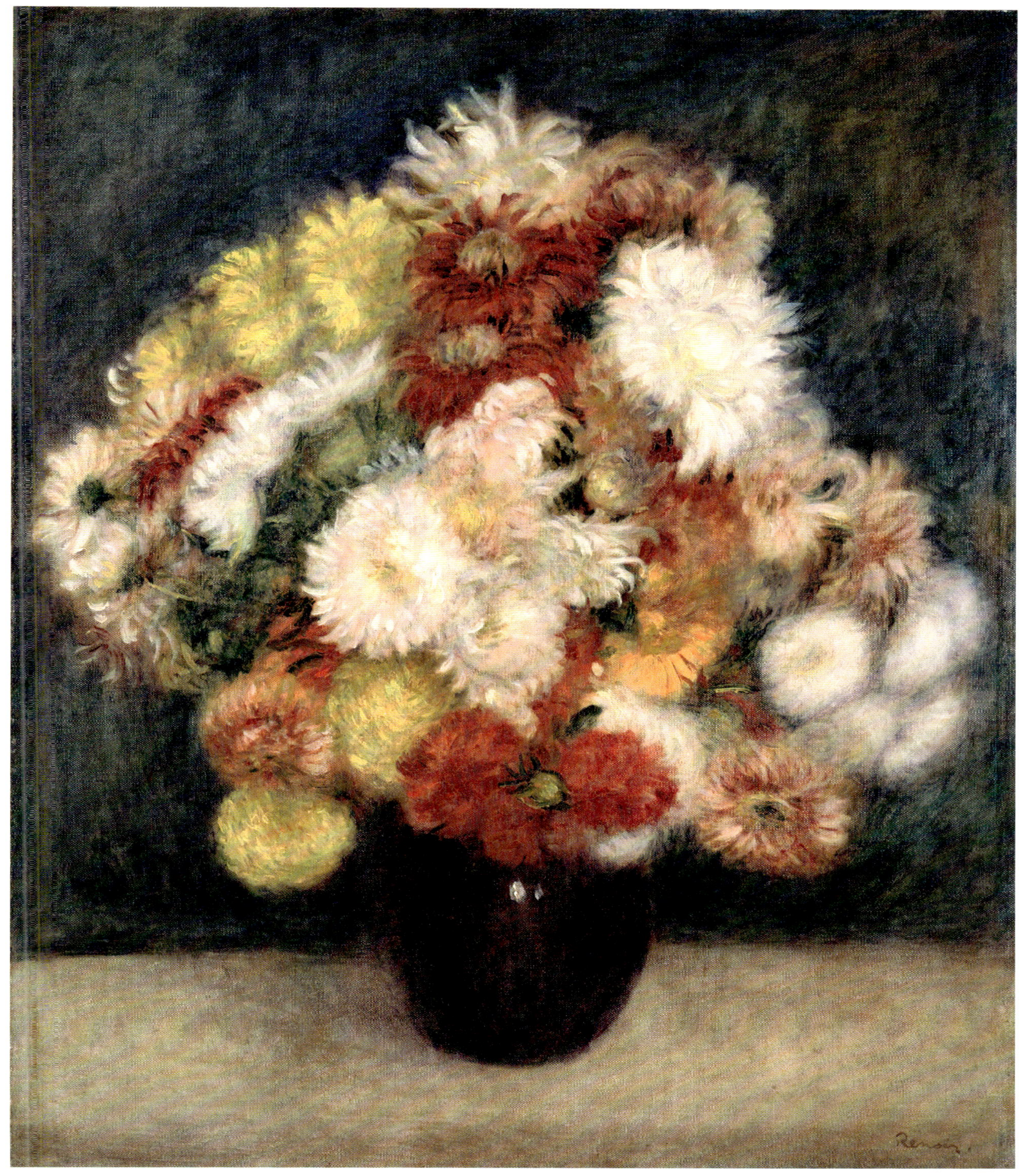

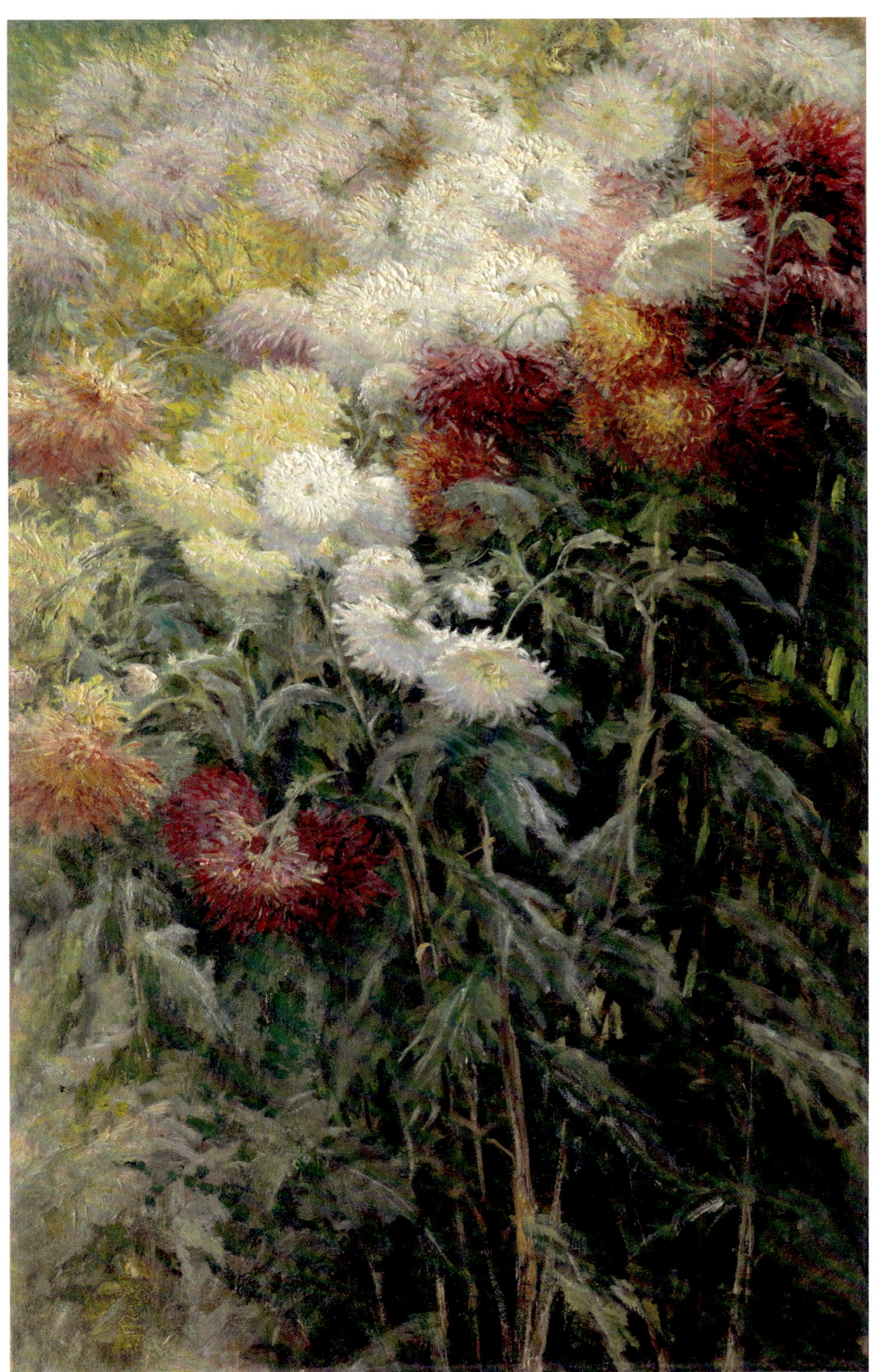

palette he often favored. "When I paint flowers," he said, "I feel free to try out tones and values and worry less about destroying the canvas."[32]

Gustave Caillebotte, too, was enamored of chrysanthemums. Although primarily a figure painter, he began producing floral still lifes in the early 1880s, after acquiring property at Petit-Gennevilliers, where he maintained formal flower beds and, later, an orchid greenhouse. Like Monet, Caillebotte was a passionate gardener, and he exchanged with his friend not only plants and the latest horticultural information but also his floral paintings. He purchased Monet's *Red Chrysanthemums* of 1880 (private collection) around the time of its display at the Impressionist exhibition of 1882 and about a decade later presented Monet with a picture of mums from his own garden (Musée Marmottan Monet, Paris).[33] That same year, 1893, Caillebotte appears to have stationed his easel in the very midst of his garden to paint the tall chrysanthemums right where they grew, rather daringly devoting half the canvas to stems and foliage (fig. 153). This unusual vantage point suggests that Caillebotte was familiar with Japanese ukiyo-e woodcuts like those in Monet's collection, in which such artists as Hokusai and Utamaro depicted flowers at ground level. Although first cultivated in China, chrysanthemums became highly valued in Japan, where they were honored in the imperial crest, celebrated in their season of bloom, and often depicted in works of art.

In another departure from convention Monet, in 1897, painted his own chrysanthemum beds in four decorative panels filled with individual blooms that seem to float like the water lilies on his pond.[34] This application of flowers, unmoored, to the decoration of his home at Giverny followed a commission from the dealer Paul Durand-Ruel to paint thirty-six floral panels for the salon doors of his Paris apartment, completed in 1885, as well as Caillebotte's 1893 embellishment of his dining room with painted orchids from his greenhouse. Renoir, too, had undertaken a similar project in 1879, painting flowers on the doors of Paul Bérard's château at Wargemont. Indeed, many artists included flowers in the decoration of interiors, among them Odilon Redon, who produced eighteen panels, begun in 1900, for a dining room in the fifteenth-century Château de Domecy in Burgundy. When the botanically inspired Art Nouveau style came into vogue, flowers and foliage—often distorted in shape—wrapped themselves around furniture and even entire rooms. For the dining room of an apartment near the Eiffel Tower, Lucien Lévy-Dhurmer incorporated the pendulous blossoms and serpentine vines of Asian wisteria into his designs for tables, chairs, lamps, and carved paneling inset with painted landscapes filled with flowers, herons, and peacocks (fig. 154).

FIG. 153. Gustave Caillebotte. *Chrysanthemums in the Garden at Petit-Gennevilliers*, 1893. Oil on canvas. The Metropolitan Museum of Art, New York

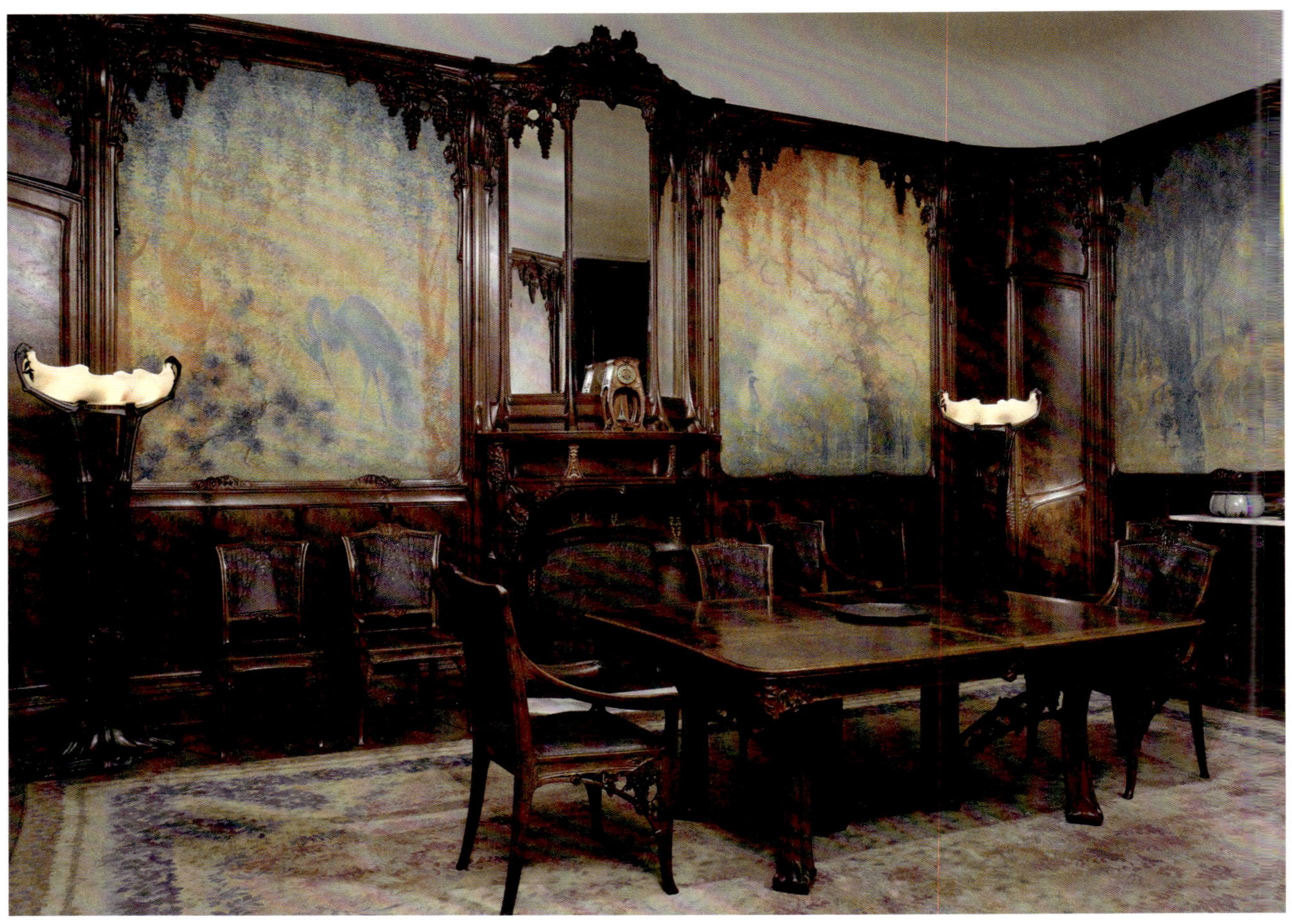

FIG. 154. Lucien Lévy-Dhurmer. Wisteria Dining Room, 1910–14. Carved walnut and amaranth. The Metropolitan Museum of Art, New York

FIG. 155. Claude Monet. *Bouquet of Sunflowers*, 1881. Oil on canvas. The Metropolitan Museum of Art, New York

It was with decoration in mind that Vincent van Gogh created a suite of four sunflower paintings at Arles in 1888. The still lifes were intended to welcome and brighten the room of his much-anticipated visitor Paul Gauguin, who had admired the sunflowers that his host had painted in Paris. To his brother Theo, Van Gogh remarked, "Gauguin was telling me the other day—that he'd seen a painting by Claude Monet of sunflowers in a large Japanese vase, very fine. But—he likes mine better. I'm not of that opinion."[35] Monet's vivid still life of the small sunflowers known in France as *soleils* (*Helianthus chrysanthemum*) is painted with an intensity that surely would have resonated with Van Gogh's sensibility (fig. 155).

While he was in Paris from 1886 to 1888, Van Gogh included sunflowers in the still lifes he painted as exercises to introduce the coloristic brilliance of the Impressionists into his then-drab palette. In walks on the outskirts of

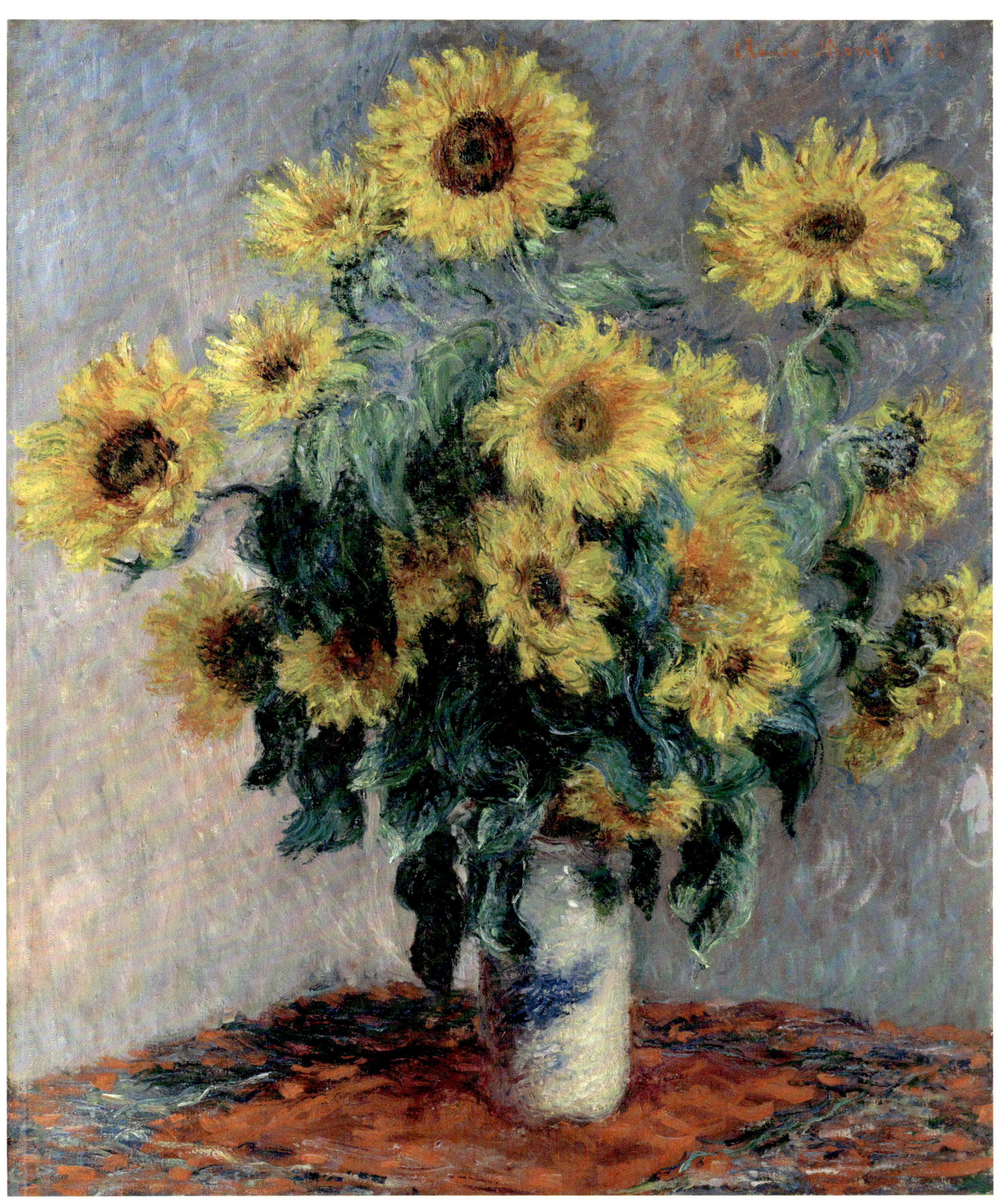

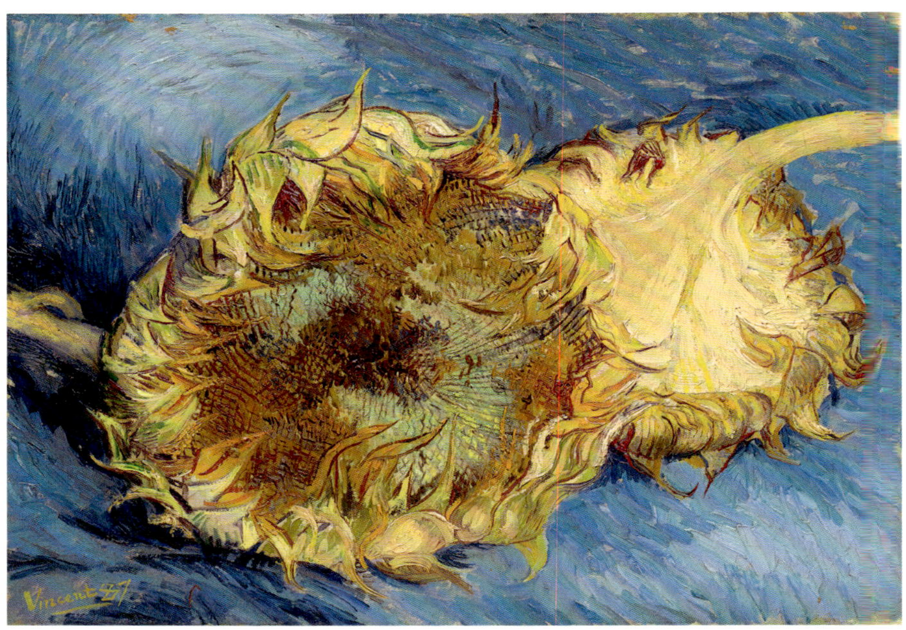

FIG. 156. Vincent van Gogh. *Sunflowers*, 1887. Oil on canvas. The Metropolitan Museum of Art, New York

the city he sketched the sunflowers standing in rustic cottage gardens, the tall *tournesols*, whose big golden faces seemed to follow the daily course of the sun, visible evidence of forces wondrous to this artist who was profoundly attuned to nature.

Late in the summer of 1887 Van Gogh made the dried heads and stalks of sunflowers the focus of four paintings as extraordinary in their subject matter as the artist's still lifes of birds' nests and his own worn-out shoes. Against a background swirling with strokes of sky blue he magnified the *tournesols*' ragged heads, seen from both front and back, where flamelike sepals halo the seeds destined to yield next year's flowers (fig. 156). After exhibiting his sunflower paintings in a Paris restaurant (part of a chain of eateries, one of which featured sunflowers in its decor), Van Gogh parted with two of the canvases (one of which is seen in fig. 156) in an exchange with Gauguin. Gauguin hung both pictures prominently over his bed, perhaps in tribute to what he believed was their shared origin—like sunflowers, he too had been raised in Peru.[36] After settling in the South Seas, Gauguin painted four sunflower still lifes of his own. Becoming something of a gardener in the tropics, he asked that bulbs and seeds be sent to him from Paris, "ordinary dahlias, nasturtiums, various sunflowers . . . I would like to decorate my garden and, as you know, I love flowers."[37]

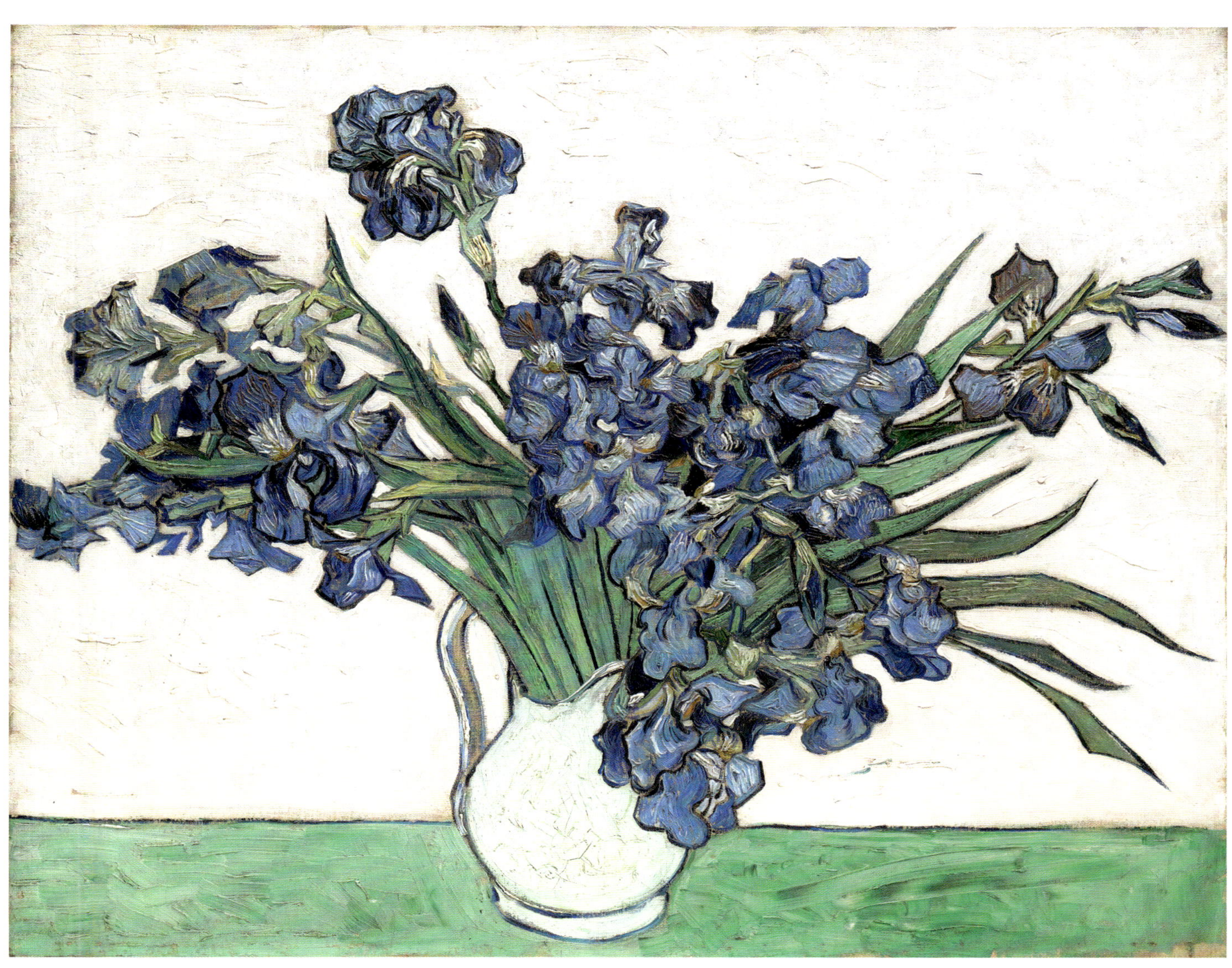

FIG. 157 Vincent van Gogh. *Irises*, 1890. Oil on canvas. The Metropolitan Museum of Art, New York

Wherever Van Gogh traveled he found subjects to paint in gardens, from the wintry trees and shrubs at his father's vicarage in North Brabant, in the Netherlands, to the abundant flowers of spring and summer in Provence, and, finally, the luxuriant greenery of the painter Charles Daubigny's garden in Auvers-sur-Oise. During the year he was confined to the asylum at Saint-Rémy, he produced nearly a hundred paintings and drawings of its enclosed garden. He arrived in May 1889, when the irises were in bloom, and within a week he had painted the seasonal flowers then at their height, welcoming them again a year later, just before his departure.[38]

Van Gogh painted four large floral still lifes that spring of 1890, two of irises and two of roses, in seeming celebration of his release from the asylum and to test his command of color and composition. In contrast to the tall bunch of irises painted on an upright canvas (Van Gogh Museum, Amsterdam), he composed a somewhat looser arrangement in a horizontal format (fig. 157). In both still lifes the blue-violet flowers, crowded together in bud and full bloom, reach out to the edges of the picture. The dark outlines that accentuate the flattened forms of each flower and pointed leaf reveal the artist's fascination with Japanese woodcuts.

While a keen observer of nature, Van Gogh exaggerated and distorted his subjects to convey expressive force. His intoxication with the natural world compelled him not only to closely observe its marvels but to ignite them with his own feelings. In a similar vein, Odilon Redon created a mysterious realm that hovers between the visible and the concealed. His flowers are both real and imagined: "Flowers as they are seen in dreams," wrote one critic in 1905, adding, "They do not flourish under the gardener's hose, under the rays of the sun. Their middays are moonlight."[39] The artist found inspiration in fantasy as well as in the mundane—in flowers arranged by his wife, for example, in a variety of vases, some by their Russian friend the ceramist Marie Botkin (fig. 158).[40] Using the powdery medium of pastel, Redon replaced the dominance of charcoal in his early work with the phosphorescent colors that enriched the efforts of his later years. In small glowing forms that seem to have alighted on the picture's surface, the pastel's compressed dust evokes, as the artist had wished, "simple flowers breathing in their vases."[41]

As the nineteenth century came to a close, artists who made flowers their subject allowed themselves progressively greater freedom to depart from the restraints of botanical accuracy. In their floral still lifes the details of nature were reconfigured to reflect more personal views, allied with modern artistic trends toward expressionism and abstraction.

FIG. 158. Odilon Redon. *Bouquet of Flowers*, ca. 1900–1905. Pastel on paper. The Metropolitan Museum of Art, New York

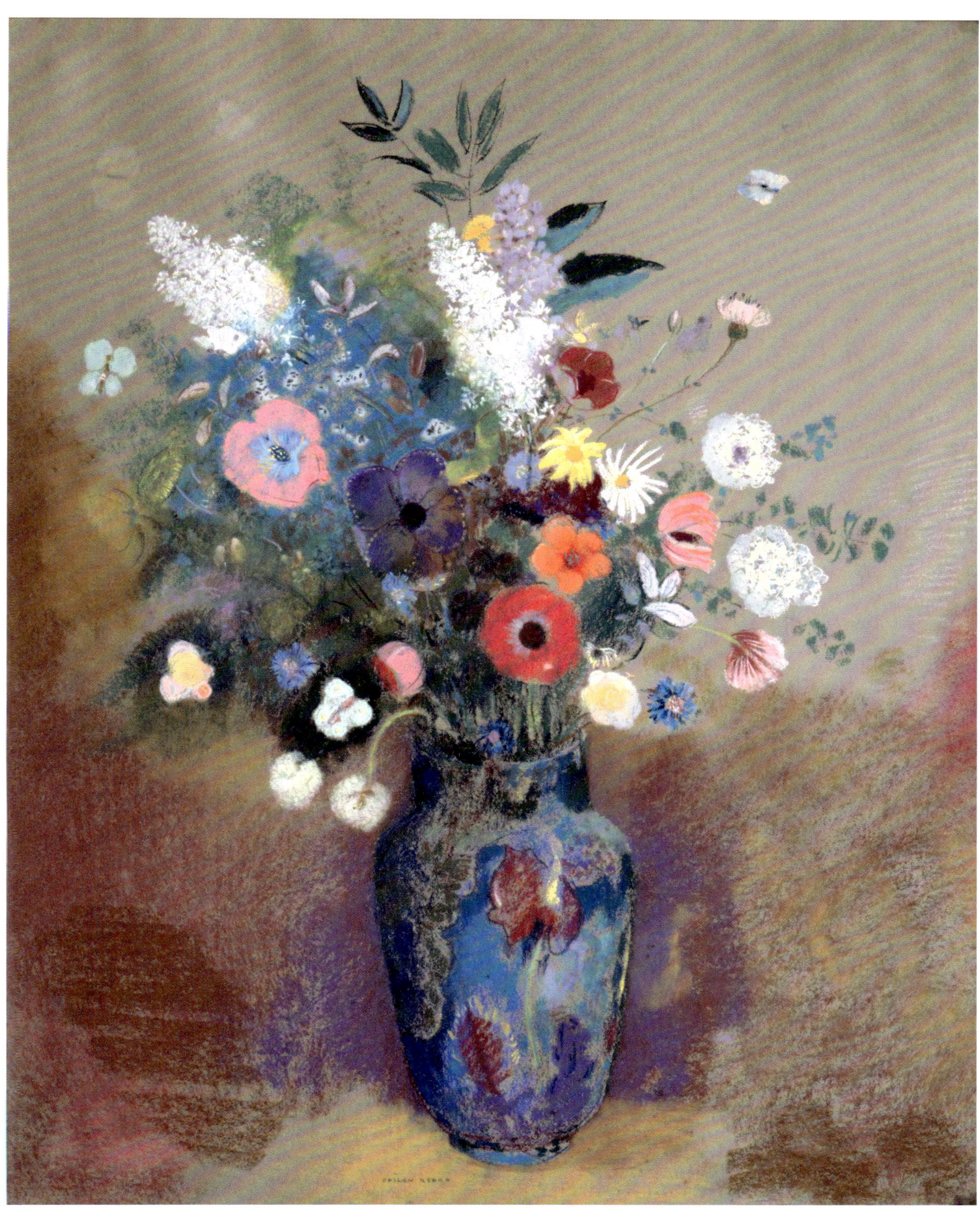

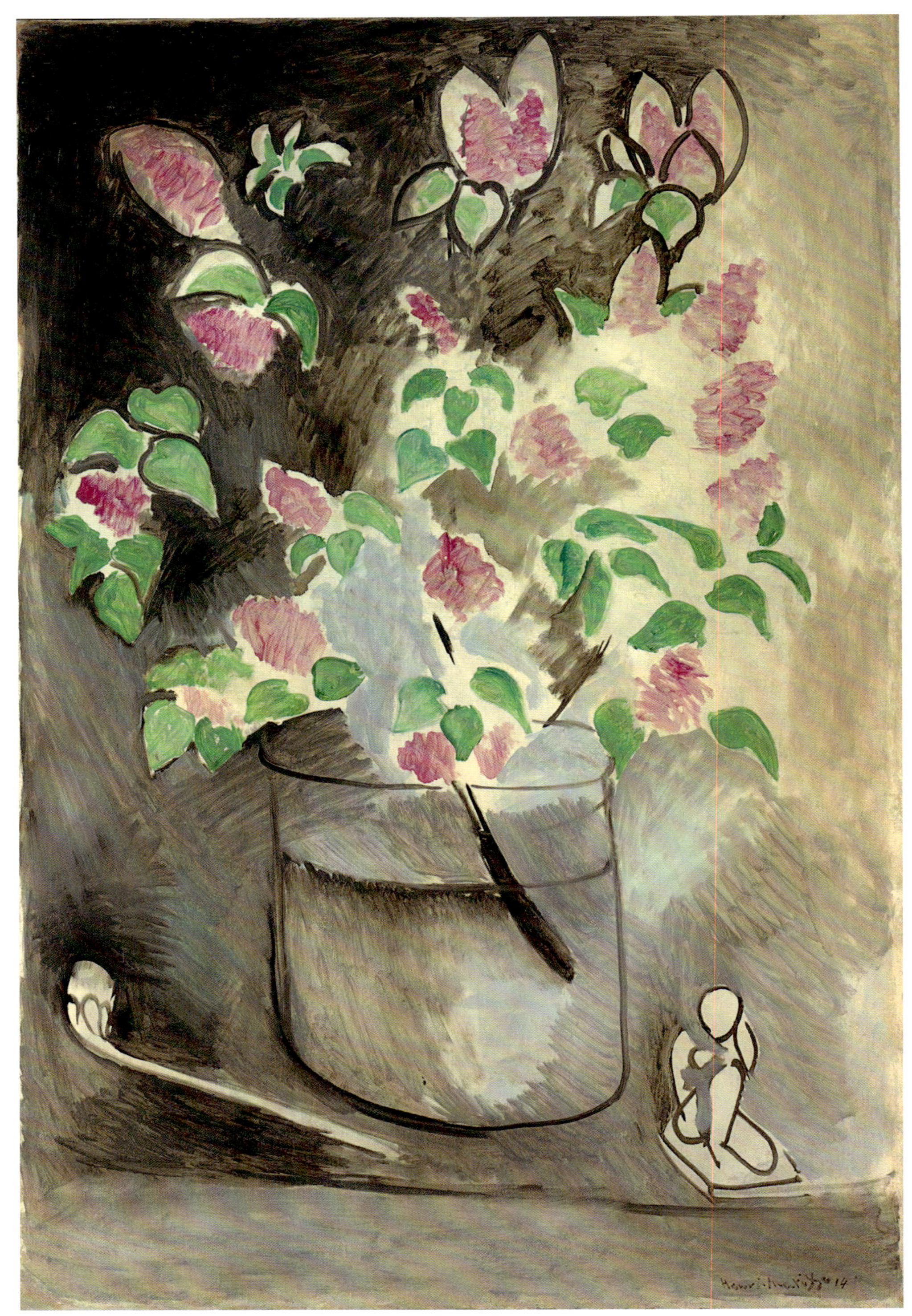

Henri Matisse took up the painting of flower arrangements about the same time that Redon actively embraced the practice. His modernity traveled a different route, but he too unburdened himself of the rules of realistic description to invent flowers that have less to do with earth than with air. The spray of lilacs he painted in his Paris studio appears to spring out of a wintry day, far from any garden (fig. 159). The zigzag blossoms and arabesque leaves seem to have become disconnected from their stems to float above the artist's clay pipe and his little sculpture of a crouching nude. At his home in Issy-les-Moulineaux, on the outskirts of Paris, Matisse and his wife maintained a garden with a lily pond, perhaps inspired by Monet, whom they visited several times at Giverny in 1916 and 1917. In later years, when illness confined him indoors, Matisse called for flowers to surround his bedside, musing, "I made a little garden all around me."[42]

Flowers and foliage are ubiquitous motifs in Matisse's work. They weave through his compositions, often swirling about on textiles, whether apparel, upholstery, carpets, or wall coverings. They are pictured, too, in fresh-cut or potted displays of geraniums, nasturtiums, pansies, daisies, anemones, calla lilies, mimosas, and other garden blooms. Imagined in a palette of pure, bright colors and simple, serpentine contours, these familiar botanicals are appealing yet fancifully abstracted creations. With wonderful shorthand messages of nature's beauty, Matisse, somewhat teasingly, brought the floral still life into the twentieth century.

FIG. 159. Henri Matisse. *Lilacs*, 1914. Oil on canvas. The Metropolitan Museum of Art, New York

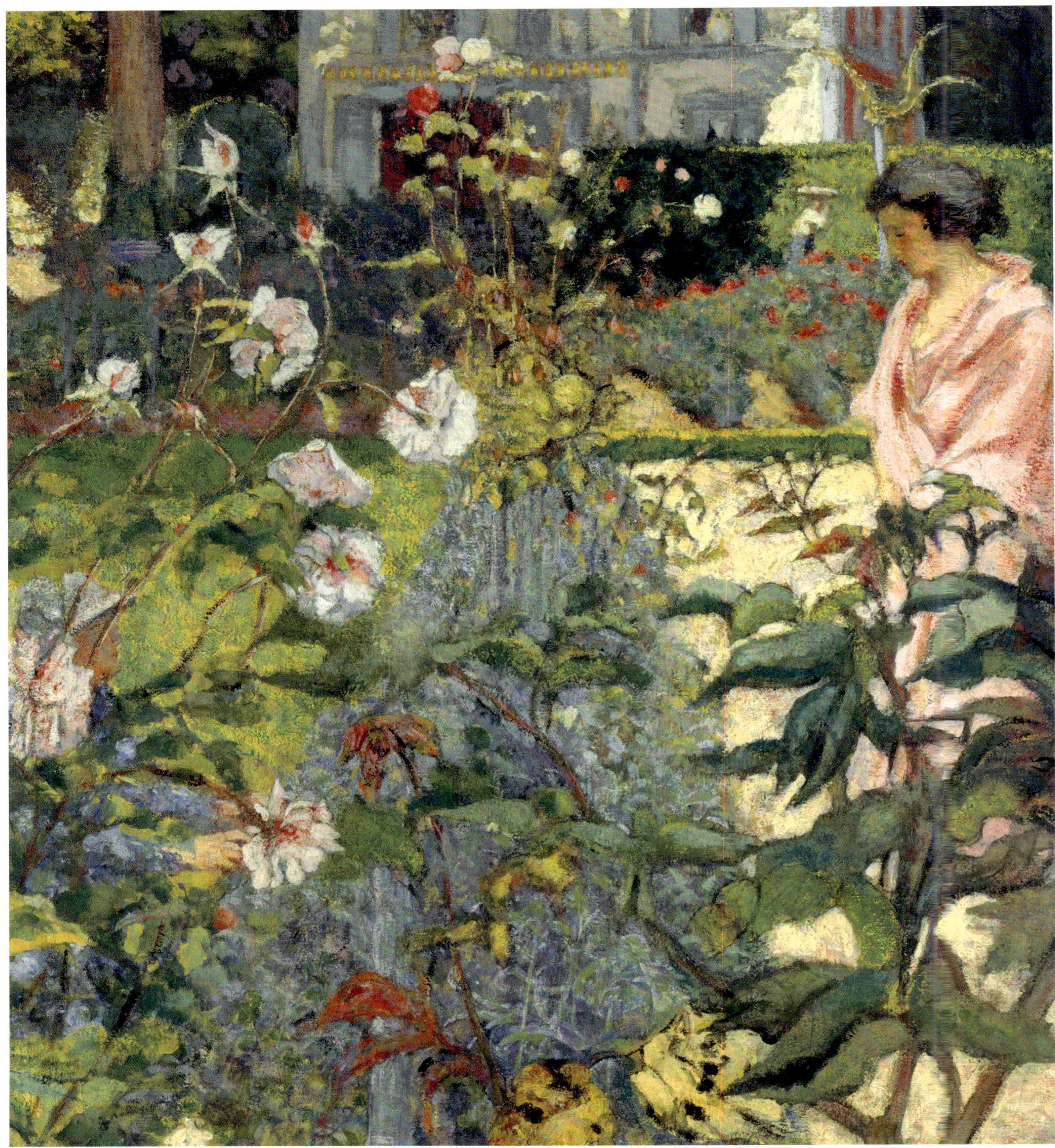

The Garden's Path

THE BIBLICAL STORY of the Garden of Eden, a place of sublime beauty and perfect contentment, undoubtedly has inspired the creation of innumerable pleasure gardens, as well as the idyllic pictures imagining them. Yet it was fact that triumphed over fable during the nineteenth century, when discoveries brought about by global exploration and the advancement of botanical science spurred the development of beautiful gardens large and small, in many parts of the world, often to the benefit of urban populations. It was then that the floral garden came into its own, neither as a fiction nor as an extravagance but as a near necessity. In France the emergence of spectacular parks and gardens brought forth a group of artists who conveyed in a particularly compelling way the spirited response that greeted these new cultural developments.

After the French Impressionists claimed the charms of the garden for their avant-garde art, American Impressionists, among them John Singer Sargent and Childe Hassam, described the growth of gardening in their own country between 1887 and 1920. Their luminous easel paintings of colorful plots and informal yards—like those produced in France—followed in refreshing contradiction to the vast, shadowy landscapes of the Romantics. In America, by the 1870s, the panoramas of Thomas Cole and Frederic Edwin Church had fallen from favor.

Well into the twentieth century gardens continued to appear in paintings, more often in works by European painters outside France, including Gustav Klimt, Joaquín Sorolla, Wassily Kandinsky, and Emil Nolde. But the subject

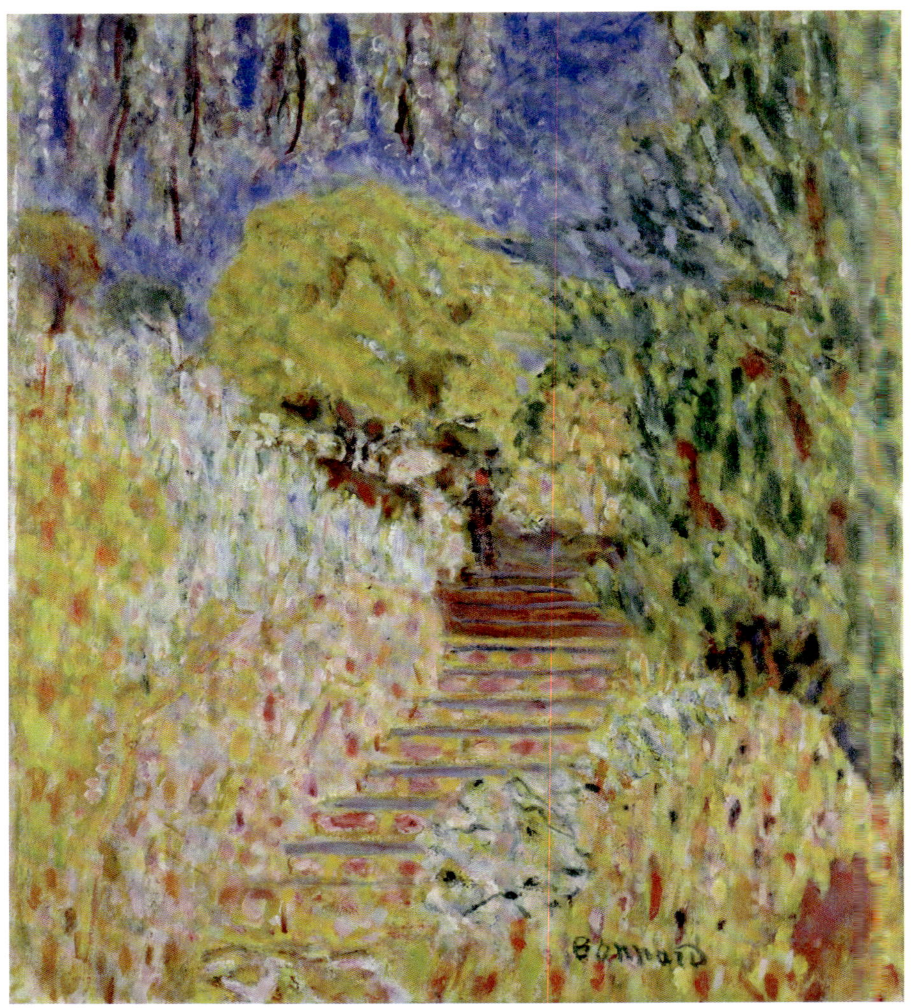

FIG. 160. Pierre Bonnard. *Stairs with Mimosa*, ca. 1940. Oil on canvas. Pola Museum of Art, Hakone

seems to have become less compelling over time as its novelty as a cultural phenomenon faded and the focus of artistic modernity shifted from material reality to the abstract. The late paintings of Monet and Bonnard, in particular, reveal their retirement from mirroring the literal facts of the garden in favor of reflecting perceptions of the mind (fig. 160).

In both horticultural and artistic innovation during the nineteenth century, France proved an outstanding leader, attracting worldwide attention to its cultivated capital. Indeed, the modern design of Parisian parks had a significant impact abroad, in America influencing the thinking of Frederick Law Olmsted and Calvert Vaux, who in 1858 were commissioned to create New York's Central Park. In November 1859 Olmsted spent two weeks in Paris consulting with the principal architect and civil engineer of the city's new landscapes, Jean-Charles Adolphe Alphand, and, as he reported, "examining as carefully as practicable in that time all its pleasure-grounds and promenades."[1] To the then recently inaugurated Bois de Boulogne, an area encompassing two and a half times the acreage allotted for Central Park, Olmsted made no fewer than eight visits. Among the many novel features of the renovated landscape to be admired were the planting designs realized by Jean-Pierre Barillet-Deschamps, the Paris parks' lead horticulturist, which demonstrated the value of botanical diversity and recommended attractive varieties like those introduced to Europe from Japan, Australia, and the Americas.

France continues to make the establishment and maintenance of planted sites a national priority; in Paris alone there are now more than 450 public green spaces. In recent decades the city has been enhanced by the creations of innovative landscape architects and designers, notably the grand Parc André Citroën, which opened in 1992 with monumental glass houses and a panoply of formal and wild gardens, and the Promenade Plantée (now called the Coulée Verte René-Dumont), begun in 1988 and inaugurated in 1993 along an obsolete elevated railway line—the direct forerunner of New York City's High Line, which broke ground in 2006. Such projects offer the salubrious benefits and pleasures that only a garden can provide. Importantly, they serve to strengthen our appreciation for the natural environment and fortify the ecological movement that seeks to ensure that the gardens and parks of today will be here for us tomorrow.

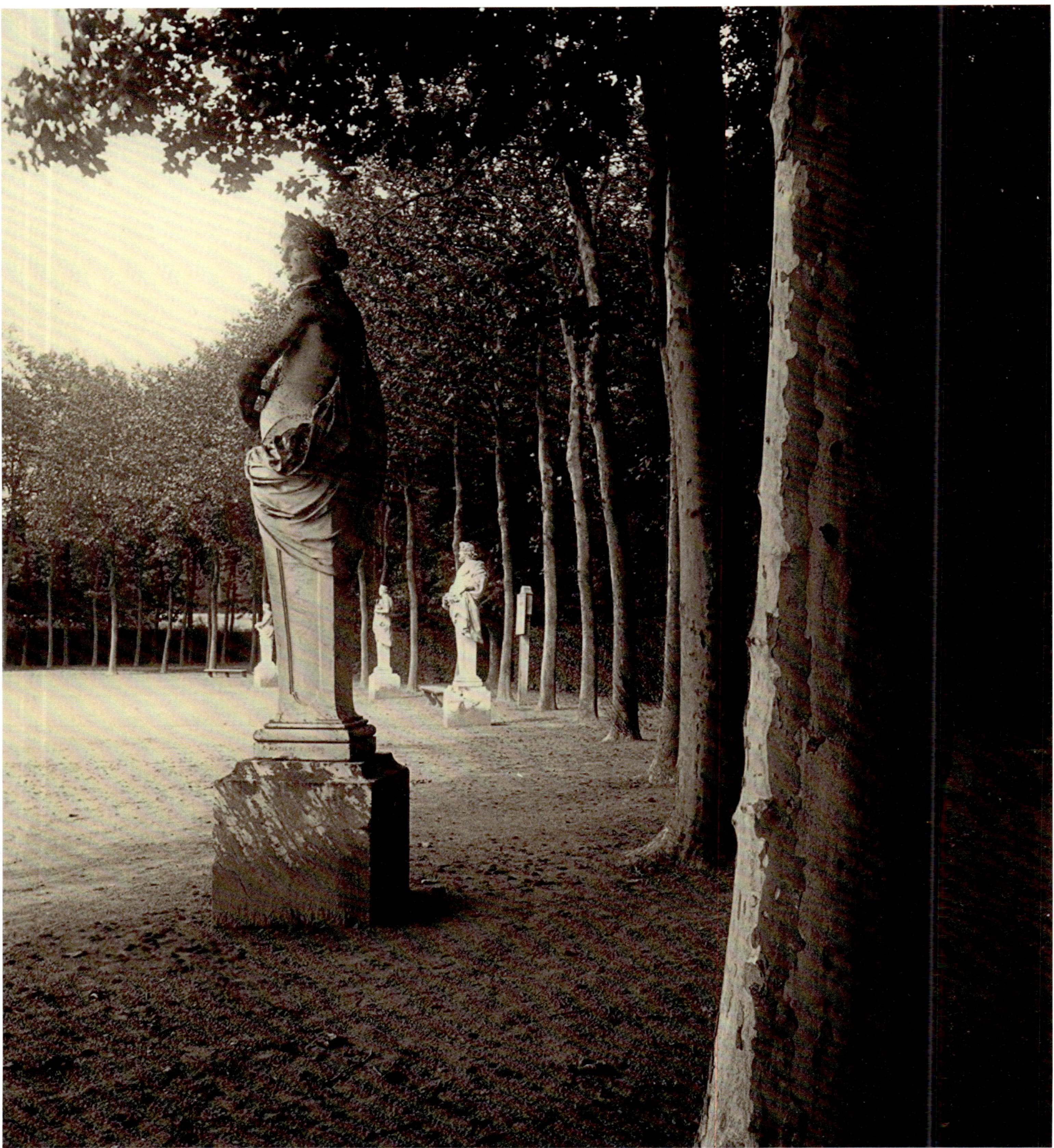

Notes

The Green Wave

1. Andrea Wulf, *The Invention of Nature: Alexander Von Humboldt's New World* (New York: Alfred A. Knopf, 2015), p. 111. In Humboldt's time the Jardin des Plantes was widely esteemed for both its scientific programs and its vast collections.

Revolution in the Garden

1. See Pierre-André Lablaude, *The Gardens of Versailles* (London: Zwemmer, 1995), pp. 134–61 (quote on p. 155).
2. A chronological summary list of eighteenth- and early nineteenth-century French garden publications is included in Catherine de Bourgoing, ed., *Jardins romantiques français: Du jardin des Lumières au parc romantique, 1770–1840*, exh. cat. (Paris: Musée de la Vie Romantique, 2011), pp. 201–2.
3. Le Rouge began publishing the engraved illustrations in his series *Détails des nouveaux jardins à la mode: Jardins anglo-chinois* (Paris: Chez Le Rouge, 1776–87) after meeting the British architect William Chambers, who had visited China in 1744 and 1748 and was the author of *A Dissertation on Oriental Gardening* (London, 1772). Father Jean Denis Attiret, a painter in service to the emperor of China, wrote letters in 1743 describing the emperor's summer residence and other Chinese gardens; quoted in Jurgis Baltrušaitis, *Jardins en France, 1760–1820*, exh. cat., Hôtel de Sully, Paris (Paris: Caisse Nationale des Monuments Historiques et des Sites, 1977), p. 23.
4. See Joseph Disponzio's introduction to Claude Henri Watelet, *Essay on Gardens: A Chapter in the French Picturesque*, ed. and trans. Samuel Danon (Philadelphia: University of Pennsylvania Press, 2003), pp. 1–15; also see Joseph Disponzio, "Jean-Marie Morel and the Invention of Landscape Architecture," in *Tradition and Innovation in French Garden Art: Chapters of a New History*, ed. John Dixon Hunt and Michel Conan (Philadelphia: University of Pennsylvania Press, 2002), pp. 135–59.
5. Antoine Chrysostome Quatremère de Quincy, *Encyclopédie méthodique: Architecture*, vol. 1 (Paris: Panckoucke; Liège: Plomteux, 1788), pp. 85, 518, quoted, in translation, in Georges Teyssot, "The Eclectic Garden and the Imitation of Nature," in *The Architecture of Western Gardens: A Design History from the Renaissance to the Present Day*, ed. Monique Mosser and Georges Teyssot (Cambridge, Mass.: MIT Press, 1991), p. 359.
6. Jean Jacques Rousseau, *Julie; ou, La Nouvelle Héloïse: Lettres de deux amans, habitans d'une petite ville au pied des Alpes* (Geneva, 1761), part 5, letter 1, pp. 21–22, quoted, in translation, in Dora Wiebenson, *The Picturesque Garden in France* (Princeton, N.J.: Princeton University Press, 1978), p. 27.
7. Rousseau, *Julie*, part 5, letter 1, pp. 8–10, quoted, in translation, in Elizabeth Barlow Rogers, "'The Genius of the Place': The Romantic Landscape, 1700–1900," in Elizabeth Barlow Rogers, Elizabeth S. Eustis, and John Bidwell, *Romantic Gardens: Nature, Art, and Landscape Design*, exh. cat., The Morgan Library & Museum, New York (Boston: David R. Godine; New York: Foundation for Landscape Studies, 2010), p. 31.
8. The Scottish plant specialist Alexander Howatson provided the first plan for the Bagatelle gardens, according to Marie-Blanche d'Arneville, "Le Parc de Joséphine à Malmaison," in *L'Impératrice Joséphine et les sciences naturelles*, ed. Marie-Blanche d'Arneville, exh. cat., Musée National des Châteaux de Malmaison et

Bois-Préau (Paris: Réunion des Musées Nationaux, 1997), p. 94n5.

9. The Metropolitan Museum has plans for the exterior and interior floor levels of the Bagatelle drawn by the same artist. Nearly identical in size and appearance is a drawing of the garden plan by one Capitaine Nicolas in the Musée Carnavalet–Histoire de Paris, illustrated in Bourgoing, *Jardins romantiques français*, pp. 82–83, no. 36. This would suggest that both the New York and Paris drawings were made from tracings of the survey by an M. Boucher.
10. Patricia Taylor, "Thomas Blaikie, jardinier anglais paysagiste," in Bourgoing, *Jardins romantiques français*, p. 78.
11. Francis William Blagdon, *Paris As It Was and As It Is; or, A Sketch of the French Capital, Illustrative of the Effects of the Revolution, with Respect to Sciences, Literature, Arts, Religion, Education, Manners, and Amusements; Comprising Also a Correct Account of the Most Remarkable National Establishments and Public Buildings; in a Series of Letters, Written by an English Traveller, during the Years 1801–2 to a Friend in London*, 2 vols. (London: C. and R. Baldwin, 1803), vol. 2, letter LXXXIV, March 23, 1802, pp. 531–32.
12. Bernard Jacqué, "Papier peints panoramiques: L'Oeuvre de P.-A. Mongin chez J. Zuber et Cie. (1804–1827)," *Nouvelles de l'Estampe*, no. 49 (January–February 1980), pp. 6–11.
13. Pierre Henri de Valenciennes, "Idées générales sur les jardins," in *Elémens de perspective pratique, à l'usage des artistes* (Paris: Chez l'auteur, 1800), p. 351, quoted in Luigi Gallo, "Soyons plutôt romains!" in Bourgoing, *Jardins romantiques français*, p. 89.
14. Georges Teyssot, "The Eclectic Garden and the Imitation of Nature," in Mosser and Teyssot, *Architecture of Western Gardens*, p. 367.
15. Pierre François Léonard Fontaine, *Journal, 1799–1953* (Paris: Ecole Nationale Supérieure des Beaux-Arts, 1987), vol. 1, entry for March 3, 1813, quoted by Bernard Chevallier, "Malmaison, parc romantique," in Bourgoing, *Jardins romantiques français*, pp. 134–35; translation by Colta Ives.
16. For detailed accounts of the development of the garden, greenhouse, aviaries, and menagerie at Malmaison, see Arneville, *L'Impératrice Joséphine et les sciences naturelles*; H. Walter Lack and Marina Heilmeyer, *Jardin de la Malmaison: Empress Josephine's Garden* (Munich and New York: Prestel, 2004); and Jennifer Potter, *The Rose: A True History* (London: Atlantic Books, 2010), pp. 178–204.
17. Christian Jouanin, "La Passion de la nature; ou, Joséphine amateur et mécène des sciences de la nature," in Arneville, *L'Impératrice Joséphine et les sciences naturelles*, pp. 24–26.
18. Mary Dorothy George, *Catalogue of Political and Personal Satires Preserved in the Department of Prints and Drawings in the British Museum*, vol. 9, *1811–1819* (London: British Museum, 1949), pp. 346–47, no. 12189.
19. Douglas Brenner and Stephen Scanniello, *A Rose by Any Name: The Little-Known Lore and Deep-Rooted History of Rose Names* (Chapel Hill, N.C.: Algonquin Books, 2009), pp. 263–64.
20. Clare Le Corbeiller in *Recent Acquisitions: A Selection, 1985–1986* (New York: The Metropolitan Museum of Art, 1986), p. 29.
21. See Sue Ann Prince, ed., *Of Elephants & Roses: French Natural History, 1790–1830*, exh. cat. (Philadelphia: American Philosophical Society, 2013), p. 37, fig. 3.1.
22. *Lettres de Napoléon à Joséphine pendant la première campagne d'Italie, le Consultat et l'Empire . . .*, 2 vols. (Paris: Firmin Didot frères, 1833), vol. 2, letter CC (January 1810), quoted, in translation, in Lack and Heilmeyer, *Jardin de la Malmaison*, p. 20.
23. The 120 colorplates of *Jardin de la Malmaison* are reproduced in Lack and Heilmeyer, *Jardin de la Malmaison*, pp. 65–305.

Parks for the Public

1. Georges Riat, *L'Art des jardins* (Paris: Société Française d'Editions d'Art; L.-H. May, [1900]), p. 355.
2. Michel Baridon, *A History of the Gardens of Versailles*, trans. Adrienne Mason (Philadelphia: University of Pennsylvania Press, 2008), p. 226.
3. Georges Teyssot, "The Eclectic Garden and the Imitation of Nature," in *The Architecture of Western Gardens: A Design History from the Renaissance to the Present Day*, ed. Monique Mosser and Georges Teyssot (Cambridge, Mass.: MIT Press, 1991), p. 366.
4. Baridon, *History of the Gardens of Versailles*, pp. 229–31.
5. William Robinson, *The Parks, Promenades & Gardens of Paris Described and Considered in Relation to the Wants of Our Own Cities and of Public and Private Gardens* (London: John Murray, 1869), pp. 239–46.
6. Baridon, *History of the Gardens of Versailles*, p. 228.
7. Pierre François Léonard Fontaine, *Journal, 1799–1853* (Paris: Ecole Nationale Supérieure des Beaux-Arts, 1987), vol. 1, entry for March 3, 1813, quoted, in translation, in Teyssot, "Eclectic Garden," p. 366.
8. For a thorough study of the forest's role in the development of nineteenth-century art, see Kimberly Jones et al., *In the Forest of Fontainebleau: Painters and Photographers from Corot to Monet*, exh. cat. (Washington, D.C.: National Gallery of Art, 2008).
9. The petition is quoted in full, in translation, in Greg M. Thomas, *Art and Ecology in Nineteenth-Century France: The Landscapes of Théodore Rousseau* (Princeton, N.J.: Princeton University Press, 2000), pp. 215–17.
10. See Kimberly Jones, "Landscapes,

Legends, Souvenirs, Fantasies," in Jones et al., *In the Forest of Fontainebleau*, pp. 20–23.

11. See Sarah Kennel, "An Infinite Museum: Photography in the Forest of Fontainebleau," in Jones et al., *In the Forest of Fontainebleau*, pp. 154–67.
12. *Galignani's New Paris Guide* (Paris: A. and W. Galignani, 1839), p. 487.
13. Denencourt's career as the forest's promoter and *conservateur-en-chef* is detailed in Simon Schama, *Landscape and Memory* (New York: Alfred A. Knopf, 1995), pp. 547–60.
14. George Sand, *Agendas*, vol. 1, *1852–1856*, ann. Anne Chevereau (Paris: J. Touzot, 1990), p. 367, entry for March 23, 1856, quoted, in translation, in Jones, "Landscapes, Legends, Souvenirs, Fantasies," p. 19.
15. Two fragments of the completed painting are in the Musée d'Orsay, Paris (rf 1987 12 [center]; rf 1957 7 [left]).
16. Jurgis Baltrušaitis, *Jardins en France, 1760–1820*, exh. cat., Hôtel de Sully, Paris (Paris: Caisse Nationale des Monuments Historiques et des Sites, 1977), p. 118. Two cedar of Lebanon plants were carried to France from the Kew Royal Botanic Gardens in London. One was given to the Jardin des Plantes, the other was planted in Montigny-Lencoup. A hat became the carrying case after the glass one failed. After the Revolution, when the royal menagerie was transferred to the Jardin des Plantes from Versailles, the garden became a zoological center as well.
17. O. Choppin de Janvry, "Les Jardins promenades au XVIIIe siècle," *Revue des Monuments Historiques de France*, no. 5 (1976), pp. 7–15, quoted in Baltrušaitis, *Jardins en France*, p. 168. Joan DeJean points out that early guidebooks to Paris from the late seventeenth and early eighteenth centuries generally recommended a visit to the Tuileries gardens, in which there were cafés "where aristocrats ate and drank in public, even women." She notes that wooden benches were added to the walkways in 1678. Joan E. DeJean, *How Paris Became Paris: The Invention of the Modern City* (New York: Bloomsbury, 2014), pp. 114–15, 118.
18. Louis Sébastien Mercier, *Paris pendant la Révolution (1789–1798); ou, Le Nouveau Paris*, new ed. (Paris: Poulet-Malassis, 1862), vol. 1, p. 322, quoted, in translation, in Denise Le Dantec and Jean-Pierre Le Dantec, *Reading the French Garden: Story and History*, trans. Jessica Levine (Cambridge, Mass.: MIT Press, 1993), p. 160.
19. Robert Hénard, *Les Jardins et les squares* (Paris: Librairie Renouard, H. Laurens, 1911), p. 18.
20. Louis Philipon de La Madelaine, *Le Guide du promeneur aux Tuileries; ou, Description du palais et du jardin national des Tuileries en l'an VI de la République française* (Paris: Hautbout-Dumoulin, Caillot, 1798), pp. 81–82.
21. Catherine de Bourgoing, ed., *Jardins romantiques français: Du jardin des Lumières au parc romantique, 1770–1840*, exh. cat. (Paris: Musée de la Vie Romantique, 2011), p. 163. See also Guillaume Fonkenell, "The Tuileries Garden: Art and Power in the Heart of Paris," in Laura D. Corey et al., *The Art of the Louvre's Tuileries Garden*, exh. cat., High Museum of Art, Atlanta; Toledo Museum of Art, Toledo, Ohio; Portland Art Museum, Portland, Ore. (New Haven and London: Yale University Press, 2013), pp. 29–69.
22. Blagdon reported that it had been "necessary for every person entering this garden to exhibit to the sentinels the national cockade . . . [until] the accession of the consular government [when] the wearing of this doubtful emblem of patriotism has been dispensed with." Francis William Blagdon, *Paris As It Was and As It Is; or, A Sketch of the French Capital, Illustrative of the Effects of the Revolution, with Respect to Sciences, Literature, Arts, Religion, Education, Manners, and Amusements; Comprising Also a Correct Account of the Most Remarkable National Establishments and Public Buildings; in a Series of Letters, Written by an English Traveller, during the Years 1801–2 to a Friend in London*, 2 vols. (London: C. and R. Baldwin, 1803), vol. 1, letter XIII, November 8, 1801, pp. 115, 117–18.
23. Honoré de Balzac, *Lost Illusions*, trans. Kathleen Raine (New York: Random House, 2001), pp. 166–67.
24. In the portion of the Tuileries near the palace reserved for the emperor's private use but "open to the public when he is not at the Tuileries," William Robinson admired "plenty of deciduous flowering shrubs . . . grass plots . . . belted by borders . . . kept pretty gay all the year round . . . [edged with] a beautiful dark green band of ivy." Robinson, *Parks, Promenades & Gardens of Paris*, pp. 12–13.
25. Corey et al., *Art of the Louvre's Tuileries Garden*, p. 109n14.
26. Jennifer Potter, *The Rose: A True History* (London: Atlantic Books, 2010), pp. 371–72.
27. Robinson, *Parks, Promenades & Gardens of Paris*, pp. 77–81.
28. Victor Hugo, *Les Misérables* (Paris: Pagnerre, 1862), vol. 5, *Jean Valjean*, book 1, section 16, quoted, in translation, in Augustus J. C. Hare, *Walks in Paris* (New York, London, and Glasgow: George Routledge and Sons, 1888), pp. 404–5.
29. Guy de Maupassant, "Menuet" (1882), in *Oeuvres complètes illustrées de Guy de Maupassant* (Paris: P. Ollendorff, 1901), vol. 2, p. 81, quoted, in translation, in Stephane Kirkland, *Paris Reborn: Napoléon III, Baron Haussmann, and the Quest to Build a Modern City* (New York: St. Martin's Press, 2013), p. 223.
30. Penelope Hobhouse, *Penelope Hobhouse's Gardening through the Ages: An Illustrated History of Plants and Their Influence on Garden Styles—from Ancient Egypt to the Present Day* (New York: Simon & Schuster, 1992), p. 252.
31. Ch. Lautour-Mézeray in *Journal de*

l'Académie d'Horticulture: Encyclopédie Mensuelle, Pratique et Progressive du Jardinage 1 (April 1831), p. 11.

32. Janine Christiany, "Les Promenades publiques parisiennes au XIXe siècle," in *Jardins d'hier et d'aujourd'hui: De Karnak à l'Eden*, ed. Sydney H. Aufrère and Michel Mazoyer (Paris: L'Harmattan; Association Kubaba, 2012), p. 255.
33. *Mémoires du Baron Haussmann*, vol. 3, *Grands Travaux de Paris* (Paris: Victor-Havard, 1893), p. 173, quoted, in translation, in Le Dantec and Le Dantec, *Reading the French Garden*, p. 171.
34. The original plan is thought to have been lost in the fire at the Hôtel de Ville in Paris in 1871. See David P. Jordan, *Transforming Paris: The Life and Labors of Baron Haussmann* (New York: Free Press, 1995), p. 377n27.
35. Ibid., pp. 34–35.
36. Kirkland, *Paris Reborn*, pp. 18–19.
37. *Journal du Maréchal de Castellane, 1804–1862*, vol. 5, *1853–1862*, 3rd ed. (Paris: Librairie Plon, 1897), p. 51, entry for June 17, 1854. See Jordan, *Transforming Paris*, p. 282.
38. See Renoir's paintings *Riding in the Bois de Boulogne* (1873; Hamburger Kunsthalle) and *Skaters in the Bois de Boulogne* (1868; private collection). For an excellent description of the Bois de Boulogne's renovation and its place in nineteenth-century life, see Robert L. Herbert, *Impressionism: Art, Leisure, and Parisian Society* (New Haven and London: Yale University Press, 1988), pp. 143–70. Winter skating in the Bois is described in Emile Zola, *The Kill (La Curée*, 1871), trans. Brian Nelson (Oxford and New York: Oxford University Press, 2005), p. 167.
39. For more detailed descriptions of Haussmann's park projects, see Christiany, "Promenades publiques parisiennes," pp. 255–65.
40. Quoted in Arsène Alexandre, "La Vie et l'oeuvre d'Henri Rousseau: Peintre et ancien employé de l'octroi," *Comoedia* 901 (March 19, 1910), p. 3.
41. For the history of the Champs-Elysées in the seventeenth and early eighteenth centuries, see DeJean, *How Paris Became Paris*, pp. 2–11.
42. Blagdon identifies the "*Old* Boulevards" as "from the *Rue de la Concorde* to the *Place de la Liberté*, formerly site of the Bastille," and the "*New* Boulevards . . . finished in 1761 . . . from the *Observatoire* to the *Hôtel des Invalides*." Blagdon, *Paris As It Was and As It Is*, vol. 1, letter XXVII, December 3, 1801, pp. 305–6.
43. Pierre François Léonard Fontaine, *Château de Neuilly: Domaine privé du roi* (Paris: Delaforest, 1836), pp. 5–13.
44. Louis Barron, *Les Environs de Paris* (Paris: Quantin, 1886), p. 30, quoted, in translation, in T. J. Clark, *The Painting of Modern Life: Paris in the Art of Manet and His Followers* (New York: Alfred A. Knopf, 1984), p. 261.
45. Emmanuel Pernoud, *Paradis ordinaires: L'Artiste au jardin public* (Dijon: Les Presses du Réel, 2013), p. 7.
46. Zola's damning critique "Les Squares" was first published in *Le Figaro*, June 18, 1867.
47. Robinson, *Parks, Promenades & Gardens of Paris*, p. 103.
48. A thorough study of Vuillard's paintings of the Place Vintimille is found in Gloria Groom, *Beyond the Easel: Decorative Painting by Bonnard, Vuillard, Denis, and Roussel, 1890–1930*, exh. cat., Art Institute of Chicago and The Metropolitan Museum of Art, New York (Chicago: Art Institute of Chicago, 2001), pp. 233–39, 245–47.
49. See Baltrušaitis, *Jardins en France*, pp. 150–63.
50. For documentation on the design of the Jardin Lamartine drawn from the municipal archives of Arles, see Pernoud, *Paradis ordinaires*, pp. 42–44.

The Private Garden

1. J. Lalos, *De la composition des parcs et jardins pittoresques: Ouvrage utile et instructif pour les propriétaires et les amateurs*, 2nd ed. (Paris: L'Auteur, 1824), pp. x–xv.
2. Gabriel Thouin, *Plans raisonnés de toutes les espèces de jardins* (Paris: Imp. de Lebégue, 1820), p. iii (preface), quoted in Michel Conan, "The Coming of Age of the Bourgeois Garden," in *Tradition and Innovation in French Garden Art: Chapters of a New History*, ed. John Dixon Hunt and Michel Conan (Philadelphia: University of Pennsylvania Press, 2002), pp. 160–83.
3. Thouin, *Plans raisonnés*, p. i (preface).
4. Arthur Mangin, *Histoire des jardins anciens et modernes*, new ed. (Tours: Alfred Mame et fils, 1887), pp. 265–66, quoted, in translation, in Colin B. Bailey et al., *Renoir Landscapes, 1865–1883*, exh. cat., The National Gallery, London; The National Gallery of Canada, Ottawa; Philadelphia Museum of Art (London: The National Gallery, 2007), p. 185.
5. Penelope Hobhouse, *Penelope Hobhouse's Gardening through the Ages: An Illustrated History of Plants and Their Influence on Garden Styles—from Ancient Egypt to the Present Day* (New York: Simon & Schuster, 1992), p. 229.
6. See Bernard Marrey and Jean-Pierre Monnet, *La Grande Histoire des serres et des jardins d'hiver: France 1780–1900* (Paris: Graphite, 1984).
7. Flaubert's unfinished novel *Bouvard and Pécuchet* was published posthumously in 1881. The guide referred to is said to be Boitard's *Manuel de l'architecte des jardins* (Paris, 1854), according to Catherine Hug and Monika Leonhard, in Christoph Becker et al., *Monet's Garden*, exh. cat., Kunsthaus Zürich (Ostfildern-Ruit: Hatje Cantz, 2004), p. 155n32.
8. Gustave Flaubert, *Bouvard and Pécuchet*, trans. and intro. by Mark Polizzotti

(Normal, Ill.: Dalkey Archive Press, 2005), pp. 26, 28–30.

9. Reports appeared beginning in 1827 as the *Annales de la Société d'Horticulture de Paris et Journal Spécial de l'Etat et des Progrès du Jardinage.*

10. *Revue Horticole* first appeared in 1826 as a supplement to *Le Bon Jardinier*, an annual publication begun in 1755. By about 1840 it had become a monthly magazine with color illustrations.

11. Opening essay by Ch. Lautour-Mézeray, *Journal de l'Académie d'Horticulture: Encyclopédie Mensuelle, Pratique et Progressive du Jardinage* 1 (April 1831), pp. 5–12.

12. William Robinson, *The Parks, Promenades & Gardens of Paris Described and Considered in Relation to the Wants of Our Own Cities and of Public and Private Gardens* (London: John Murray, 1869), p. 81.

13. André Joubin, ed., *Correspondance générale d'Eugène Delacroix*, vol. 2, *1838–1849* (Paris: Plon, 1936), pp. 175 and 114, quoted, in translation, by Mareike Hennig in *The Painter's Garden: Design, Inspiration, Delight*, ed. Sabine Schulze, exh. cat., Städel Museum, Frankfurt am Main; Städtische Galerie im Lenbachhaus, Munich (Ostfildern-Ruit: Hatje Cantz, 2006), p. 137.

14. George Sand, "Les Promenades dans Paris," in *Paris Guide par les principaux écrivains et artistes de la France*, part 2, *La Vie* (Paris: Librairie Internationale; Brussels: A. Lacroix, Verboeckhoven, 1867), pp. 1196–1203; see Daniel Lejeune, *Edouard André, auteur, acteur, spectateur: Les Clés d'une réussite* (Paris: Société Nationale d'Horticulture de France, 2009), pp. 107–9.

15. *The Journal of Eugène Delacroix*, trans. Lucy Norton (Oxford: Phaidon, 1951), p. 121, entry for May 23, 1850.

16. A document dated 1857 found among the papers of Delacroix's sole legatee, Achille Piron, and now in the Musée National Eugène Delacroix, Paris, describes a series of garden projects, including plantings of all kinds.

17. Michael Pantazzi in Gary Tinterow, Michael Pantazzi, and Vincent Pomarède, *Corot*, exh. cat. (New York: The Metropolitan Museum of Art, 1996), p. 228.

18. Eugène Chapus, "La Vie à Paris: Le Caractère de la société parisienne actuelle; les maisons de la campagne," *Le Sport* 5 (September 1868), pp. 2–3, quoted, in translation, by Paul Hayes Tucker in *Monet at Argenteuil* (New Haven and London: Yale University Press, 1981), p. 125.

19. Clare A. P. Willsdon, *In the Gardens of Impressionism* (New York: Vendome Press, 2004), p. 55.

20. Sylvie Gache-Patin in Andrea P. A. Belloli, ed., *A Day in the Country: Impressionism and the French Landscape*, exh. cat., Los Angeles County Museum of Art; Art Institute of Chicago; Galeries Nationales du Grand Palais, Paris (New York: Harry N. Abrams, 1984), p. 208 (where several other contemporary garden books and periodicals of the time are listed).

21. Alphonse Karr, "L'Horticulteur," in *Les Français peints par eux-mêmes* (Paris: L. Curmer, 1840), vol. 1, pp. 90–96.

22. Willsdon, *In the Gardens of Impressionism*, p. 59.

23. Ibid., pp. 57, 75.

24. Renoir's friend Georges Rivière remembered that Renoir "was charmed by the view of this garden, which looked like a beautiful abandoned park . . . [with] a vast uncultivated lawn dotted with poppies, convolvulus, and daisies." Georges Rivière, *Renoir et ses amis* (Paris: H. Floury, 1921), p. 130, quoted, in translation, by Colin B. Bailey in *The Annenberg Collection: Masterpieces of Impressionism and Post-Impressionism*, ed. Susan Alyson Stein and Asher Ethan Miller, new ed. (New York: The Metropolitan Museum of Art, 2009), pp. 103–4.

25. Christoph Becker in Becker et al., *Monet's Garden*, p. 26.

26. Anne Distel et al., *Gustave Caillebotte, Urban Impressionist*, exh. cat., Musée d'Orsay, Paris; Art Institute of Chicago; Los Angeles County Museum of Art (Paris: Réunion des Musées Nationaux; Chicago: Art Institute of Chicago; New York: Abbeville Press, 1995), pp. 270–72.

27. Saskia de Bodt et al., *Alfred Stevens: Brussels 1823–Paris 1906*, exh. cat., Royal Museums of Fine Arts of Belgium, Brussels; Van Gogh Museum, Amsterdam (Brussels: Mercatorfonds, 2009), pp. 37–39.

28. Elizabeth Robins Pennell and Joseph Pennell, *The Life of James McNeill Whistler*, 6th ed. (Philadelphia: J. B. Lippincott; London: William Heinemann, 1919), p. 313.

29. Charlotte de La Tour [pseud. of Louis-Aimé Martin and his wife, Louise Cortambert], *Le Langage des fleurs*, 3rd ed. (Paris: Audot, 1830), p. vi, quoted in *Jardins romantiques français: Du jardin des Lumières au parc romantique, 1770–1840*, ed. Catherine de Bourgoing, exh. cat. (Paris: Musée de la Vie Romantique, 2011), p. 120. The manual, which was in its twelfth edition by 1876, suggested various symbolic meanings for flowers; see Willsdon, *In the Gardens of Impressionism*, pp. 37–38.

30. Etienne Moreau-Nélaton, *Manet raconté par lui-même* (Paris: H. Laurens, 1926), vol. 2, p. 85, quoted, in translation, by Charles Moffett in Françoise Cachin, Charles S. Moffett, and Michel Melot, *Manet, 1832–1883*, exh. cat., Galeries Nationales du Grand Palais, Paris; The Metropolitan Museum of Art, New York (New York: The Metropolitan Museum of Art, 1983), p. 476.

31. Michel Eugène Chevreul, *De la loi du contraste simultané des couleurs et de l'assortiment des objets colorés* (Paris: Pitois-Levrault, 1839), part 1: section IV and sous-section I, quoted by Isabelle Levêque in Bourgoing, *Jardins romantiques francais*, p. 157. Both Monet and Caillebotte owned copies of Chevreul's book. Monet also owned

the *Manuel de l'amateur de jardin*, 4 vols. (Paris: Didot frères, [1862–66]), by Joseph Decaisne and Charles Naudin, who further elaborated Chevreul's scientific color theories and applied them into the garden. Derek Fell, *The Impressionist Garden* (New York: Carol Southern Books, 1994), p. 70.

32. See Sigolène Tivolle, *Le Jardin d'Albert Kahn: Parcours historique et paysager*, rev. ed. (Nanterre: Conseil Général des Hauts-de-Seine, 2012).
33. Manet to Jean Béraud, as recorded by Antonin Proust in *Manet by Himself: Correspondence and Conversation, Paintings, Pastels, Prints, and Drawings*, ed. Juliet Wilson-Bareau (Boston: Little, Brown, 1991), p. 169.
34. Roger Marx, "Les 'Nymphéas' de M. Claude Monet," *Gazette des Beaux-Arts*, ser. 4, 1 (June 1909), p. 529, quoted, in translation, in Charles Stuckey, ed., *Monet: A Retrospective* (New York: Hugh Lauter Levin Associates, 1985), p. 267.
35. Jean-Pierre Hoschedé, *Claude Monet: Ce Mal Connu* (Geneva: Pierre Cailler, 1960), vol. 1, p. 70, quoted, in translation, by Sylvie Gache-Patin in Belloli, *Day in the Country*, p. 216.
36. Pierre-Louis [Maurice Denis], "Définition du néo-traditionnisme," *Art et Critique* [August 23, 1890], p. 540.
37. Charles Sterling, *Still Life Painting from Antiquity to the Present Time*, rev. ed., trans. James Emmons (New York: Universe Books, 1959), p. 100.
38. See Monique Mosser, "Henri and Achille Duchêne and the Reinvention of Le Nôtre," in *The Architecture of Western Gardens: A Design History from the Renaissance to the Present Day*, ed. Monique Mosser and Georges Teyssot (Cambridge, Mass.: MIT Press, 1991), pp. 446–49.

The Portrait in the Garden

1. Elisabeth de Feydeau, *From Marie-Antoinette's Garden: An Eighteenth-Century Album* (Paris: Flammarion, 2013), p. 13.
2. Robert L. Herbert, *Impressionism: Art, Leisure, and Parisian Society* (New Haven and London: Yale University Press, 1988), p. 1.
3. For an illustration of the photograph dated 1854 by Mayer Frères, see Pierre Apraxine and Xavier Demange, *La Comtesse de Castiglione par elle-même*, exh. cat., Musée d'Orsay, Paris (Paris: Réunion des Musées Nationaux, 1999), p. 57.
4. Florence Austin in a letter to Katharine Baetjer dated July 22, 1999, encloses a photocopy of a photograph of the mid-1860s showing the painted portrait as it hung at Saint-Cloud; curatorial files, Department of European Paintings, The Metropolitan Museum of Art.
5. See James A. Ganz, *Edouard Baldus at the Château de La Faloise* (Williamstown, Mass.: Sterling and Francine Clark Art Institute; New Haven and London: Yale University Press, 2007).
6. Colin B. Bailey provides a thorough discussion of the painting in *The Annenberg Collection: Masterpieces of Impressionism and Post-Impressionism*, ed. Susan Alyson Stein and Asher Ethan Miller, new ed. (New York: The Metropolitan Museum of Art, 2009), pp. 59–69. The gentleman has been identified as Manet's brother Eugène (by Durand-Ruel, in a letter to H. von Tschudi in 1908), as "a neighbor" (by Monet, in a letter to Durand-Ruel, in 1921), and as Manet's brother Gustave, a witness to Monet's marriage in 1870 (by Hugues Wilhelm, in *Women in Impressionism: From Mythical Feminine to Modern Woman*, ed. Sidsel Maria Søndergaard, exh. cat., Ny Carlsberg Glyptotek, Copenhagen [Milan: Skira, 2006], p. 303, no. 13). Complete documentation on *Camille Monet on a Garden Bench* may be found at www.metmuseum.org/art/collection/search/438003.
7. John Dixon Hunt, *Gardens and the Picturesque: Studies in the History of Landscape Architecture* (Cambridge, Mass.: MIT Press, 1992), p. 270.
8. Emile Zola, *The Kill* (*La Curée*, 1871), trans. Brian Nelson (Oxford and New York: Oxford University Press, 2005), pp. 39, 159.
9. See Charles S. Moffett in Françoise Cachin, Charles S. Moffett, and Michel Melot, *Manet, 1832–1883*, exh. cat., Galeries Nationales du Grand Palais, Paris; The Metropolitan Museum of Art, New York (New York: The Metropolitan Museum of Art, 1983), pp. 362–63, no. 141.
10. Charles Ephrussi, "Exposition des artistes independants," *Gazette des Beaux-Arts*, ser. 2, 21 (May 1, 1880), p. 487, quoted, in translation, in *The New Painting: Impressionism, 1874–1886*, ed. Charles S. Moffett, exh. cat., National Gallery of Art, Washington, D.C.; Fine Arts Museums of San Francisco (San Francisco: The Museums, 1986), p. 327.
11. Robert Cassatt to Alexander Cassatt, April 18, 1881, in *Cassatt and Her Circle: Selected Letters*, ed. Nancy Mowll Mathews (New York: Abbeville Press, 1984), p. 161.
12. Mary Cassatt to Ada Pope, Mesnil-Beaufresne, April 7, 1900, quoted in Mathews, *Cassatt and Her Circle*, p. 27.
13. Etienne Moreau-Nélaton, *Manet raconté par lui-même* (Paris; H. Laurens, 1926), vol. 2, p. 68, quoted in Stein and Miller, *Annenberg Collection*, p. 21n3.
14. Jean Guiffrey, ed., *Lettres illustrées de Edouard Manet* (Paris: Maurice LeGarrec, [1929]), quoted, in translation, in Juliet Wilson-Bareau, ed. *Manet by Himself: Correspondence and Conversation, Paintings, Pastels, Prints and Drawings* (Boston: Little, Brown, 1991), p. 252.
15. Maurice Du Seigneur, "L'Art et les

artistes au salon de 1882," *L'Artiste*, ann. 52, no. 2 (July 1882), p. 21; J. K. Huysmans, *L'Art moderne* (Paris: G. Charpentier, 1883), p. 272; both quoted, in translation, in Herbert, *Impressionism*, p. 186.

16. Quoted in Maurice Joyant, *Henri de Toulouse-Lautrec, 1864–1901: Peintre* (Paris: H. Floury, 1926), p. 192; translation by Joseph J. Rishel in Stein and Miller, *Annenberg Collection*, p. 247.
17. Henri Perruchot, *T-Lautrec*, trans. Humphrey Hare (Cleveland: World Publishing, 1960), p. 92.
18. Charles Baudelaire, *Art in Paris, 1845–1862: Salons and Other Exhibitions Reviewed by Charles Baudelaire*, trans. and ed. Jonathan Mayne (London: Phaidon, 1965), p. 155; quoted by Margret Stuffmann in *Odilon Redon*, ed. Raphaël Bouvier, exh. cat. (Riehen/Basel: Fondation Beyler; Ostfildern-Ruit: Hatje Cantz, 2014), p. 69.

The Revival of the Floral Still Life

1. Alphonse Karr, *A Tour Round My Garden*, ed. and trans. Rev. J. G. Wood (London: G. Routledge, 1855), p. 312.
2. Martyn Rix, *The Golden Age of Botanical Art* (London: Andre Deutsch, 2012), p. 136.
3. Ibid., p. 86.
4. [Charles] Baudelaire Dufaÿs, *Salon de 1845* (Paris: Jules Labitte, 1845), p. 60; quoted in "The Salon of 1845," in *The Mirror of Art: Critical Studies by Charles Baudelaire*, trans. and ed. Jonathan Mayne (Garden City, N.Y.: Doubleday, 1956), p. 32.
5. Charles Baudelaire, in a letter to the editor of *L'Opinion Nationale*, 1863; quoted in "Eugène Delacroix," in *Mirror of Art*, p. 313.
6. See Heather MacDonald and Mitchell Merling, *Working among Flowers: Floral Still-Life Painting in Nineteenth-Century France*, exh. cat., Dallas Museum of Art; Virginia Museum of Fine Arts, Richmond; Denver Art Museum (New Haven and London: Yale University Press, 2014), pls. 19 and 20.
7. Letter to Constant Dutilleux, February 6, 1849, in *Eugène Delacroix: Selected Letters, 1813–1863*, ed. and trans. Jean Stewart (London: Eyre and Spottiswoode, 1971), p. 287.
8. Gaston Poulain, *Bazille et ses amis* (Paris: La Renaissance du Livre, 1932), p. 44; quoted, in translation, in John Rewald, *The History of Impressionism*, rev. ed. (New York: Museum of Modern Art, 1961), pp. 111–12.
9. Note of June 18, 1859, in G[eorges] Jean-Aubry, *Eugène Boudin d'après des documents inédits: L'Homme et l'oeuvre* (Paris: Bernheim-Jeune, 1922), p. 39; quoted, in translation, in Rewald, *History of Impressionism*, p. 42.
10. Susan Alyson Stein, "Edouard Manet: *Still Life with Flowers, Fan, and Pearls*," in "Recent Acquisitions: A Selection: 1993–1994," *The Metropolitan Museum of Art Bulletin* 52, no. 2 (Fall 1994), p. 46.
11. See Jo Briggs, "Condemned to Sparkle: The Reception, Presentation, and Production of Léon Bonvin's Floral Still Lifes," *Oxford Art Journal* 38, no. 2 (2015), pp. 247–62.
12. Ambroise Vollard, *Degas: An Intimate Portrait*, trans. Randolph T. Weaver (New York: Crown, 1937), p. 52, also pp. 22, 53, and 64.
13. See Henri Loyrette in Jean Sutherland Boggs et al., *Degas*, exh. cat., Galeries Nationales du Grand Palais, Paris; National Gallery of Canada, Ottawa; The Metropolitan Museum of Art, New York (New York: The Metropolitan Museum of Art; Ottawa: National Gallery of Canada, 1988), pp. 114–16, no. 60; and Gary Tinterow and Henri Loyrette, *Origins of Impressionism*, exh. cat., Galeries Nationales du Grand Palais, Paris; The Metropolitan Museum of Art, New York (New York: The Metropolitan Museum of Art, 1994), pp. 370–71, no. 57.
14. Review of the fourth edition of Madame Millet's *Maison rustique des dames*, in *Revue Horticole*, 1859, p. 619, quoted, in translation, in Clare A. P. Willsdon, *In the Gardens of Impressionism* (New York: Vendome Press, 2004), p. 80. Other notable paintings that treat this subject are Gustave Courbet's *The Woman with Flowers*, 1862 (Toledo Museum of Art, Toledo, Ohio), and Frédéric Bazille's two paintings titled *African Woman with Peonies*, both 1870 (National Gallery of Art, Washington, D.C., and Musée Fabre, Montpellier); illustrated in Willsdon, *In the Gardens of Impressionism*, pp. 44, 48, 49.
15. The three paintings are *Woman beside a Vase*, 1872 (Lemoisne 305; Musée d'Orsay, Paris), *Estelle Musson*, 1872 (Lemoisne 306; New Orleans Museum of Art), and *Mme De Rutté*, 1875 (Lemoisne 369; private collection).
16. Charles Baudelaire, "Le Peintre de la vie moderne," *Le Figaro*, November 26, 1863, pp. 4–5, as translated in *The Painter of Modern Life, and Other Essays*, trans. and ed. Jonathan Mayne (London: Phaidon, 1965), pp. 1, 13.
17. Madame Mélanie Waldor, "Bouquetière," in *Les Français peints par eux-mêmes*, vol. 3 (Paris: L. Curmer, 1841), pp. 129–36.
18. Philippe Prévôt, *Histoire des jardins* (Bordeaux: Sud Ouest, 2006), p. 238.
19. *Galignani's New Paris Guide* (Paris: A. and W. Galignani, 1839), p. 124.
20. William Robinson, *The Parks, Promenades & Gardens of Paris Described and Considered in Relation to the Wants of Our Own Cities and of Public and Private Gardens* (London: John Murray, 1869), p. 544.
21. Willsdon, *In the Gardens of Impressionism*, p. 190.
22. Kathryn B. Hiesinger et al., *The Second Empire, 1852–1870: Art in France under Napoleon III*, exh. cat., Philadelphia Museum of Art; Detroit Institute of Arts; Galeries Nationales du Grand Palais, Paris (Philadelphia: Philadelphia Museum of Art, 1978), pp. 92–93.

23. Emile Zola, *The Kill* (*La Curée*, 1871), trans. Brian Nelson (Oxford and New York: Oxford University Press, 2005), p. 31.
24. Audrey Gay-Mazuel in MacDonald and Merling, *Working among Flowers*, p. 43.
25. Charles Holme, "The Potter's Art—Object Lessons from the Far East," *The Studio* 24, no. 103 (1901), pp. 54–55. Elizabeth Sullivan, curator in the Department of European Sculpture and Decorative Arts at The Metropolitan Museum of Art, kindly brought this article to my attention.
26. Paul Mantz, "Salon de 1863," *Gazette des Beaux-Arts* 15 (July 1863), p. 44, cited by Eliza Rathbone in Eliza E. Rathbone and George T. M. Shackelford, eds., *Impressionist Still Life*, exh. cat., Phillips Collection, Washington, D.C.; Museum of Fine Arts, Boston (Washington, D.C.: Phillips Collection, 2001), pp. 12, 224n2 (French orig.).
27. L. Lagrange, "Du Rang des femmes dans les arts," *Gazette des Beaux-Arts* 8 (October 1860), p. 39, quoted, in translation, by Gloria Groom in Anne Distel et al., *Gustave Caillebotte, Urban Impressionist*, exh. cat., Galeries Nationales du Grand Palais, Paris; Art Institute of Chicago; Los Angeles County Museum of Art (Paris: Musée d'Orsay; Chicago: Art Institute of Chicago; New York: Abbeville Press, 1995), p. 299n2.
28. Pierre Dax, "Chronique," *L'Artiste*, ann. 47, 1 (May 1, 1876), pp. 348–49, quoted, in translation, by Groom in Distel et al., *Gustave Caillebotte*, pp. 298, 299n4.
29. Nancy Mowll Mathews, ed., *Cassatt and Her Circle: Selected Letters* (New York: Abbeville Press, 1984), p. 283n4, with an illustration of one of Cassatt's vases, now in the Petit Palais, Paris.
30. But see Sylvie Patry in her essay "Impressionist Flower Paintings and the Market," where she questions the commercial advantages of the genre; in MacDonald and Merling, *Working among Flowers*, pp. 29–39.
31. A. Ysabeau, *Le Jardinage; ou, L'Art de créer et de bien tenir un jardin* (Paris: Hachette, 1854), p. 14, quoted, in translation, by Sylvie Gache-Patin in *A Day in the Country: Impressionism and the French Landscape*, ed. Andrea P. A. Belloli, exh. cat., Los Angeles County Museum of Art; Art Institute of Chicago; Galeries Nationales du Grand Palais, Paris (Los Angeles: Los Angeles County Museum of Art, 1984), p. 213.
32. Georges Rivière, *Renoir et ses amis* (Paris: H. Floury, 1921), p. 81, quoted, in translation, by Colin B. Bailey in *The Annenberg Collection: Masterpieces of Impressionism and Post-Impressionism*, ed. Susan Alyson Stein and Asher Ethan Miller, new ed. (New York: The Metropolitan Museum of Art, 2009), p. 115.
33. Monet's *Red Chrysanthemums* is reproduced in Joseph Baillio et al., *Claude Monet, 1840–1926*, exh. cat., Galeries Nationales du Grand Palais, Paris (Paris: Réunion des Musées Nationaux; Musée d'Orsay, 2010), no. 88. For the Caillebotte mums, see Groom in Distel et al., *Gustave Caillebotte*, p. 302.
34. Among Monet's other still lifes of chrysanthemums, four from 1897 show flowers, no longer in vases, that fill the entire canvas; see Grace Seiberling, *Monet's Series*, Outstanding Dissertations in the Fine Arts (New York: Garland, 1981), pp. 188–89, 335n2.
35. Van Gogh to Theo, Letter 721, November 19, 1888, available in facsimile and translation at Leo Jansen, Hans Luijten, and Nienke Bakker, eds., *Vincent van Gogh: The Letters* (Amsterdam and The Hague: Van Gogh Museum & Huygens ING, version: December 2010), http://vangoghletters.org.
36. Douglas W. Druick and Peter Kort Zegers, *Van Gogh and Gauguin: The Studio of the South*, exh. cat., Art Institute of Chicago; Rijksmuseum Vincent van Gogh, Amsterdam (Chicago: Art Institute of Chicago; New York: Thames & Hudson, 2001), p. 85.
37. Martin Bailey, *The Sunflowers Are Mine: The Story of Van Gogh's Masterpiece* (London: Frances Lincoln Limited, 2013), p. 125.
38. The irises were probably survivors of the medieval cloister garden, where traditionally irises were raised for use in medicines and ink.
39. Albert Flament, "Le Salon d'Automne," *La Presse*, October 18, 1905, quoted, in translation, by Maryanne Stevens in Douglas W. Druick et al., *Odilon Redon: Prince of Dreams, 1840–1916*, exh. cat. (Chicago: Art Institute of Chicago; Amsterdam: Rijksmuseum Vincent van Gogh; London: Royal Academy of Arts; New York: Harry N. Abrams, 1994), p. 297.
40. Vases by Botkin are found in several pictures by Redon. Those noted by Audrey Gay-Mazuel (in MacDonald and Merling, *Working among Flowers* p. 57n52) are illustrated in Alec Wildenstein, *Odilon Redon: Catalogue raisonné de l'oeuvre peint et dessiné*, vol. 3, *Fleurs et paysages* (Paris: Wildenstein Institute, 1996), nos. 1526–42.
41. Redon's letter to Mme Andries Bonger, May 30, 1902, quoted in Roseline Bacou, *Odilon Redon: Pastels*, trans. Beatrice Rehl (New York: G. Braziller, 1987), p. 17.
42. André Verdet, *Prestiges de Matisse*, facsimile ed. (1952; Tesserete: Pagine d'Arte, 2011), p. 20, quoted in William H. Robinson et al., *Painting the Modern Garden: Monet to Matisse*, exh. cat., Cleveland Museum of Art; Royal Academy of Arts, London (London: Royal Academy of Arts, 2015), p. 27.

The Garden's Path

1. Charles E. Beveridge and David Schuyler, eds., *The Papers of Frederick Law Olmsted*, vol. 3, *Creating Central Park, 1857–1861* (Baltimore: Johns Hopkins Press, 1983), pp. 234–35.

Illustration and Exhibition Checklist

The information on each work is organized alphabetically by artist/author/creator and then by date. Given immediately below the information for each work, (Fig. 00 or Detail, p. 00) indicates that the work is illustrated in this publication; (*) indicates that the work was shown in the exhibition this publication accompanied.

Alphand, [Jean-Charles] Adolphe (1817–1891)

[Artist unknown], "Decorative Ironwork" (detail), in [Jean-Charles] Adolphe Alphand, *Les Promenades de Paris* (Paris, 1867–73)
Engraving, 10¾ x 16½ in. (27.3 x 41.9 cm)
The Metropolitan Museum of Art, New York, Watson Library, Gift in Memory of David W. Langton, 1911
(Fig. 52)

Emile Hochereau, "The Grande Cascade, Bois de Boulogne," in [Jean-Charles] Adolphe Alphand, *Les Promenades de Paris* (Paris, 1867–73)
Engraving, 10⅜ x 13¼ in. (26.4 x 33.6 cm)
The Metropolitan Museum of Art, New York, Watson Library, Gift in Memory of David W. Langton, 1911
(Fig. 50)

*Grandsire, Pierre Eugène (1825–1905), "Route des Buttes, Bois de Vincennes," in [Jean-Charles] Adolphe Alphand, *Les Promenades de Paris* (Paris, 1867–73), vol. 2, pl. 54
Wood engraving, 10½ x 13 in. (26.6 x 33 cm)
The Metropolitan Museum of Art, New York, Watson Library, Gift in Memory of David W. Langton, 1911
(Fig. 54)

*Lancelot, Dieudonné Auguste (1822–1824), "Bois de Boulogne—View of the Grand Lac," in [Jean-Charles] Adolphe Alphand, *Les Promenades de Paris* (Paris, 1867–73)
Wood engraving, sheet 17¾ x 24¹³⁄₁₆ in. (45 x 63 cm)
The Metropolitan Museum of Art, New York, Watson Library, Gift in Memory of David W. Langton, 1911
(Not illustrated)

André, Edouard (1840–1911)

*Garden kiosks and pergolas, in *L'Art des jardins: Traité général de la composition des parcs et jardins* (Paris, 1879)
Lithographs, 11 x 7¾ in. (28 x 19.7 cm)
The Metropolitan Museum of Art, New York, The Elisha Whittelsey Collection, The Elisha Whittelsey Fund, 1963 (63.563)
(Not illustrated)

Atget, Eugène (1857–1927)

**Jardin du Luxembourg (Luxembourg Gardens)*, 1902
Albumen silver print from glass negative, 8¹¹⁄₁₆ x 6¹⁵⁄₁₆ in. (22.1 x 17.7 cm)
The Metropolitan Museum of Art, New York, Gilman Collection, Museum Purchase, 2005 (2005.100.529)
(Fig. 44)

**Versailles—Cour du Parc*, 1902
Albumen silver print from glass negative, 8⁷⁄₁₆ x 7¹⁄₁₆ in. (21.5 x 17.9 cm)
The Metropolitan Museum of Art, New York, Gilman Collection, Purchase, Mr. and Mrs. Henry R. Kravis Gift, 2005 (2005.100.533)
(Detail, p. 168)

**The Palace at Versailles, Late October, Evening, Cloud Effect, View from the North Parterre*, 1903
Albumen silver print from glass negative, 6¹⁵⁄₁₆ x 8½ in. (17.4 x 21.6 cm)
The Metropolitan Museum of Art, New York, Gilman Collection, Purchase, William Talbott Hillman Foundation Gift, 2005 (2005.100.532)
(Fig. 22)

Aubry, Charles Hippolyte (1811–1877)

**Asters*, ca. 1864
Albumen silver print from glass negative, 10 11/16 x 14 7/16 in. (27.2 x 36.7 cm)
The Metropolitan Museum of Art, New York, Purchase, The Horace W. Goldsmith Foundation Gift, through Joyce and Robert Menschel, 1987 (1987.1050)
(Not illustrated)

**Study of Leaves on a Background of Floral Lace*, 1864
Albumen silver print from glass negative, 18 3/8 x 14 7/16 in. (46.7 x 36.7 cm)
The Metropolitan Museum of Art, New York, Gilman Collection, Purchase, Howard Gilman Foundation Gift, 2004 (2004.106)
(Not illustrated)

Baldus, Edouard (1813–1889)

**Group at the Château de La Faloise*, 1856
Salted paper print from glass negative, 10 15/16 x 15 1/16 in. (27.8 x 38.2 cm)
The Metropolitan Museum of Art, New York, Gilman Collection, Purchase, The Horace W. Goldsmith Foundation Gift, through Joyce and Robert Menschel, 2005 (2005.100.50)
(Fig. 108)

Bartholomé, Albert (1848–1928)

**The Artist's Wife (Périe, 1849–1887) Reading*, 1883
Pastel and charcoal on paper, laid down on canvas, 19 7/8 x 24 1/8 in. (50.5 x 61.3 cm)
The Metropolitan Museum of Art, New York, Catharine Lorillard Wolfe Collection, Wolfe Fund, 1990 (1990.117)
(Fig. 144)

Bayard, Hippolyte (1801–1887)

"In the Garden," ca. 1842, in *Bayard: XXV Calotypes, 1842–1850* (Paris, 1965)
Gelatin silver print, 7 3/4 x 6 7/8 in. (19.7 x 17.5 cm)
The Art Institute of Chicago, Restricted gift of Mr. and Mrs. Everett Kovler (1965.556)
(Fig. 76)

Berjon, Antoine (1754–1843)

**Floral Design*, ca. 1820
Gouache, 10 9/16 x 7 7/8 in. (26.9 x 20 cm)
The Metropolitan Museum of Art, New York, Harris Brisbane Dick Fund, 1928 (28.40.12)
(Not illustrated)

Berthault, Louis Martin (1770–1823)

---

*Fruit or flower basket, designed 1812; Sèvres Manufactory, 1823
Hard-paste porcelain, height 14 1/2 in. (36.8 cm)
The Metropolitan Museum of Art, New York, Purchase, Gift of Mr. and Mrs. Charles Wrightsman, by exchange, 1985 (1985.119)
(Fig. 16)

Boitard, Pierre (1789–1859)

---

*[Artist unknown], "Winter Garden," in Pierre Boitard, *Traité de la composition et de l'ornement des jardins*, 3rd ed. (Paris, 1825), pl. 21
Etching, 6 3/4 x 8 1/2 in. (17.1 x 21.6 cm)
The Metropolitan Museum of Art, New York, Gift of Lincoln Kirstein, 1970 (1970.565.185)
(Fig. 75)

*Français, François-Louis (1814–1897), "Cedar of Lebanon," in Pierre Boitard, *Jardin des Plantes* (Paris, 1842), opp. p. 301
Engraving, 10 1/4 x 6 3/4 in. (26 x 17.1 cm)
The Metropolitan Museum of Art, New York, Gift of Lincoln Kirstein, 1979 (1979.600.1)
(Fig. 33)

Bonnard, Pierre (1867–1947)

Arc de Triomphe, ca. 1898
Color lithograph, 16 x 21 in. (40.5 x 53.5 cm)
The Metropolitan Museum of Art, New York, Harris Brisbane Dick Fund, 1928 (28.50.4[12])
(Fig. 62)

**From the Balcony*, 1909
Oil on canvas, 49 x 39 1/8 in. (124.5 x 99.4 cm)
The Metropolitan Museum of Art, New York, Bequest of Charles Goldman, 1966 (66.65.1)
(Fig. 96)

Garden, ca. 1935
Oil on canvas, 35 1/2 x 35 5/8 in. (90.2 x 90.5 cm)
The Metropolitan Museum of Art, New York, The Walter H. and Leonore Annenberg Collection, Bequest of Walter H. Annenberg, 2002 (2003.20.16)
(Fig. 103)

Stairs with Mimosa, ca. 1946
Oil on canvas, 32 x 27 in. (80.8 x 68.8 cm)
Pola Museum of Art, Hakone
(Fig. 160)

Bonvin, Léon (1834–1866)

**Bouquet of Small Chrysanthemums*, 186[illegible]
Watercolor and gouache, 6 1/8 x 5 7/8 in. (15.5 x 14.9 cm)
The Metropolitan Museum of Art, New York, Purchase, Gift of Mrs. Bessie Potter Vonnoh, by exchange, Arthur Ross Foundation Gift, Sarah and Werner H. Kramarsky Gift, Van Day Truex Fund, Ian Woodner Family Collection Fund, and Wildenstein and Co., Inc. Gift, 1996 (1996.296)
(Fig. 136)

Boudin, Eugène (1824–1898)

Floral Still Life, ca. 1858–62
Oil on canvas, 23 5/8 x 18 1/8 in. (60 x 46 cm)
Private collection
(Fig. 129)

Braun, Adolphe (1811–1877)

**Rose of Sharon*, ca. 1854
Albumen silver print from glass negative, $14\frac{3}{4}$ x $16\frac{1}{2}$ in. (37.5 x 41.9 cm)
The Metropolitan Museum of Art, New York, Gift of Gilman Paper Company, in memory of Samuel J. Wagstaff Jr., 1987 (1987.1161)
(Fig. 127; detail, p. 192)

Caillebotte, Gustave (1848–1894)

**The Parc Monceau*, 1877
Oil on canvas, $19\frac{3}{4}$ by $25\frac{5}{8}$ in. (50.2 x 65.1 cm)
Lawrence J. Ellison collection
(Fig. 47)

The Boulevard Seen from Above, 1880
Oil on canvas, $22\frac{5}{8}$ x $21\frac{1}{4}$ in. (57.5 x 54 cm)
Private collection
(Fig. 48)

Roses in the Garden at Petit-Gennevilliers, ca. 1886
Oil on canvas, 35 x $45\frac{5}{8}$ in. (88.9 x 115.9 cm)
Private collection
(Fig. 91)

**Chrysanthemums in the Garden at Petit-Gennevilliers*, 1893
Oil on canvas, $38\frac{5}{8}$ x $23\frac{1}{2}$ in. (98 x 59.8 cm)
The Metropolitan Museum of Art, New York, Gift of the Honorable John C. Whitehead, 2014 (2014.736)
(Fig. 153)

Caranza, Amédée de (1843–1906), attributed to

**Design for a Plate with Cyclamens*, ca. 1875–85
Pen and brown and black ink, watercolor, over graphite, $21\frac{3}{16}$ x $14\frac{13}{16}$ in. (53.8 x 37.6 cm)
The Metropolitan Museum of Art, New York, Purchase, Gift of Joy E. Feinberg of Berkeley, California, 1986 (1986.1179)
(Not illustrated)

Carrogis, Louis, called Carmontelle (1717–1806)

*"View of the Bois des Tombeaux," in *Jardin de Monceau* (Paris, 1779), pl. 12
Engraving, $12\frac{3}{8}$ x $19\frac{1}{4}$ in. (31.4 x 48.8 cm)
The Metropolitan Museum of Art, New York, Harris Brisbane Dick Fund, 1942 (42.142)
(Not illustrated)

"View of the Tatar Tent," in *Jardin de Monceau* (Paris, 1779), pl. 14
Engraving, $12\frac{3}{8}$ x $19\frac{1}{4}$ in. (31.4 x 48.8 cm)
The Metropolitan Museum of Art, New York, Harris Brisbane Dick Fund, 1942 (42.142)
(Fig. 6)

Cassatt, Mary (1844–1926)

**Lydia Crocheting in the Garden at Marly*, 1880
Oil on canvas, $25\frac{13}{16}$ x $36\frac{7}{16}$ in. (65.6 x 92.6 cm)
The Metropolitan Museum of Art, New York, Gift of Mrs. Gardner Cassatt, 1965 (65.184)
(Fig. 118)

**Lilacs in a Window*, ca. 1880–83
Oil on canvas, $24\frac{3}{16}$ x $20\frac{1}{8}$ in. (61.5 x 51.1 cm)
The Metropolitan Museum of Art, New York, Partial and Promised Gift of Mr. and Mrs. Douglas Dillon, 1997 (1997.207)
(Fig. 150)

**Portrait of a Young Girl*, 1899
Oil on canvas, 29 x $24\frac{1}{8}$ in. (73.7 x 61.3 cm)
The Metropolitan Museum of Art, New York, From the Collection of James Stillman, Gift of Dr. Ernest G. Stillman, 1922 (22.16.18)
(Not illustrated)

Cézanne, Paul (1839–1906)

**Entrance to a Garden*, ca. 1878–80
Watercolor over graphite, $18\frac{13}{16}$ x $12\frac{5}{16}$ in. (47.8 x 31.2cm)
The Metropolitan Museum of Art, New York, Gift of C. Douglas Dillon, 1982 (1982.375)
(Not illustrated)

**The Pool at Jas de Bouffan*, ca. 1885–86
Oil on canvas, $25\frac{1}{2}$ x $31\frac{7}{8}$ in. (64.8 x 81 cm)
The Metropolitan Museum of Art, New York, Bequest of Stephen C. Clark, 1960 (61.101.5)
(Fig. 98)

**Madame Cézanne (Hortense Fiquet, 1850–1922) in the Conservatory*, 1891
Oil on canvas, $36\frac{1}{4}$ x $28\frac{3}{4}$ in. (92.1 x 73 cm)
The Metropolitan Museum of Art, New York, Bequest of Stephen C. Clark, 1960 (61.101.2)
(Fig. 120)

Chaplet, Ernest (1835–1909)

*Vase, ca. 1889
Porcelain, height $15\frac{3}{8}$ in. (39.1 cm)
The Metropolitan Museum of Art, New York, Robert A. Ellison Jr. Collection, Purchase, The Isaacson-Draper Foundation Gift, 2013 (2013.477)
(Fig. 149)

Chardin, Jean Siméon (1699–1779)

A Vase of Flowers, early 1760s
Oil on canvas, $17\frac{3}{4}$ x $14\frac{5}{8}$ in. (45.1 x 37.1 cm)
Scottish National Gallery, Edinburgh, Purchased with the aid of the Cowan Smith Bequest Fund 1937
(Fig. 135)

The Brioche, 1763
Oil on canvas, $18\frac{1}{2}$ x 22 in. (47 x 55.9 cm)
Musée du Louvre, Paris, Bequest of Dr. Louis La Caze, 1869
(Fig. 133)

Corot, Camille (1796–1875)

**Fontainebleau: Oak Trees at Bas-Bréau*, 1832 or 1833
Oil on paper, laid down on wood, 15 5/8 x 19 1/2 in. (39.7 x 49.5 cm)
The Metropolitan Museum of Art, New York, Catharine Lorillard Wolfe Collection, Wolfe Fund, 1979 (1979.404)
(Not illustrated)

**Ville-d'Avray: Corot's Father and His Wife in the Garden*, ca. 1845
Oil on canvas, 18 x 12 3/4 in. (45.7 x 32.4 cm)
Private collection
(Fig. 81)

**Fontainebleau: Group of Trees on the Flank of a Rocky Hillside*, ca. 1845–50
Oil on canvas, 16 x 23 3/8 in. (40.6 x 59.4 cm)
Louis-Dreyfus Family Collection
(Fig. 25)

Courbet, Gustave (1819–1877)

**Bouquet of Flowers*, 1862–63
Oil on canvas, 20 1/4 x 24 1/2 in. (51.5 x 62.2 cm)
Private collection
(Fig. 128)

Cross, Henri-Edmond (1856–1910)

**The Artist's Garden at Saint-Clair*, 1904–5
Watercolor, 10 1/2 x 14 1/8 in. (26.6 x 35.8 cm)
The Metropolitan Museum of Art, New York, Harris Brisbane Dick Fund, 1948 (48.10.7)
(Not illustrated)

**Garden of the Painter at Saint-Clair*, 1908
Watercolor over graphite, 6 3/4 x 9 1/2 in. (17.1 x 24.1 cm)
The Metropolitan Museum of Art, New York, Robert Lehman Collection, 1975 (1975.1.590)
(Fig. 103)

Cuvelier, Eugène (1837–1900)

**Fontainebleau Forest*, ca. 1860
Salted paper print from paper negative, 10 3/16 x 7 3/4 in. (25.9 x 19.7 cm)
The Metropolitan Museum of Art, New York, Purchase, The Horace W. Goldsmith Foundation Gift, through Joyce and Robert Menschel, 1987 (1987.1036.1)
(Not illustrated)

**Fontainebleau Forest*, early 1860s
Salted paper print from paper negative, 7 13/16 x 10 3/16 in. (19.8 x 25.8 cm)
The Metropolitan Museum of Art, New York, Purchase, The Howard Gilman Foundation and Joyce and Robert Menschel Gifts, 1988 (1988.1031)
(Fig. 28; detail, p. *xii*)

Dael, Jan Frans van (1764–1840)

The Tomb of Julie, 1803–4
Oil on canvas, 78 x 59 in. (198.1 x 149.9 cm)
Musée National des Châteaux de Malmaison et Bois-Préau, Rueil-Malmaison
(Fig. 123)

Daumier, Honoré (1808–1879)

*"I thought it would be more fun than this to water flowers during a heat wave!" from "Romance of Country Life," in *Le Charivari*, December 29, 1845
Lithograph, 14 1/4 x 9 3/4 in. (36.2 x 24.8 cm)
The Metropolitan Museum of Art, New York, Bequest of Edwin De T. Bechtel, 1957 (57.650.539)
(Fig. 79)

"Tomorrow Is His Wife's Birthday," in *Le Charivari*, June 18, 1846
Lithograph, 11 5/8 x 8 1/8 in. (29.5 x 20.6 cm)
The Metropolitan Museum of Art, New York, Bequest of Howard Carter, 1949 (49.74.41)
(Fig. 77)

"What the Bourgeoisie Call a Minor Distraction," in *Le Charivari*, August 30, 1846
Lithograph, 14 1/8 x 10 3/4 in. (35.9 x 27.3 cm)
The Metropolitan Museum of Art, New York, Rogers Fund, 1922 (22.61.14)
(Fig. 37)

"But I assure you that this is his ball and I am his father . . . ," in *Le Charivari*, February 25, 1847
Lithograph, 11 3/4 x 8 1/4 in. (29.8 x 20.9 cm)
Private collection, New York
(Fig. 38)

*"—No matter what one says, old things are always beautiful.—Yes, my dear, but only in marble," from "As You Like It," in *Le Charivari*, January 21, 1850
Lithograph, 14 1/4 x 9 5/8 in. (36.2 x 24.4 cm)
The Metropolitan Museum of Art, New York, A. Hyatt Mayor Purchase Fund, Marjorie Phelps Starr Bequest, 1980 (1980.1114.[illegible])
(Not illustrated)

*"A Country House near Paris:—Well, my dear . . . it's a good thing we had the idea to plant a house. Without it, we wouldn't have had shade all summer!" from "The Pleasures of a Country Holiday," in *Le Charivari*, May 24, 1858
Lithograph, 10 1/2 x 14 11/16 in. (26.7 x 37.[illegible] cm)
The Metropolitan Museum of Art, New York, The Elisha Whittelsey Collection, The Elisha Whittelsey Fund, 1962 (62.650.[illegible])
(Not illustrated)

*"Well, look here! . . . You also have a boa constrictor in your garden. . . .—Egad! It's indispensable . . . that's why my new plants from Brazil still believe they are in their own country!" from "The Acclimatization Society," in *Le Charivari*, August 18, 185[illegible]
Lithograph, 10 1/2 x 14 3/8 in. (26.7 x 36.5 cm)
The Metropolitan Museum of Art, New York, Bequest of Edwin De T. Bechtel, 1957 (57.650.548)
(Not illustrated)

**A Man Reading in a Garden*, ca. 1865
Watercolor over black chalk, with pen and ink, brush and wash, and lithograph crayon, 13 5/16 x 10 5/8 in. (33.8 x 27 cm)

The Metropolitan Museum of Art, New York, H. O. Havemeyer Collection, Bequest of Mrs. H. O. Havemeyer, 1929 (29.100.199)
(Fig. 82)

Debucourt, Louis Philibert (1755–1832)

**The Public Promenade*, 1792
Etching, engraving, and aquatint printed in color, 14 3/8 x 23 1/4 in. (36.5 x 59.1 cm)
The Metropolitan Museum of Art, New York, The Elisha Whittelsey Collection, The Elisha Whittelsey Fund, 1961 (61.531)
(Fig. 34)

Degas, Edgar (1834–1917)

**A Woman Seated beside a Vase of Flowers (Madame Paul Valpinçon?)*, 1865
Oil on canvas, 29 x 36 1/2 in. (73.7 x 92.7 cm)
The Metropolitan Museum of Art, New York, H. O. Havemeyer Collection, Bequest of Mrs. H. O. Havemeyer, 1929 (29.100.128)
(Fig. 137; detail, p. 126)

Delacroix, Eugène (1798–1863)

**Dahlias*, ca. 1833 or 1847–48
Oil on canvas, 19 x 28 5/8 in. (48.3 x 73 cm)
Private collection
(Not illustrated)

**George Sand's Garden at Nohant*, ca. 1842–43
Oil on canvas, 17 7/8 x 21 3/4 in. (45.4 x 55.2 cm)
The Metropolitan Museum of Art, New York, Purchase, Dikran G. Kelekian Gift, 1922 (22.27.4)
(Fig. 80)

**Arch of Morning Glories, Study for "A Basket of Flowers,"* 1848–49
Pastel on blue paper, 12 1/16 x 18 in. (30.6 x 45.7 cm)
The Metropolitan Museum of Art, New York, Bequest of Miss Adelaide Milton de Groot (1876–1967), 1967 (67.187.4)
(Not illustrated)

Basket of Flowers, 1848–49
Oil on canvas, 42 1/4 x 56 in. (107.3 x 142.2 cm)
The Metropolitan Museum of Art, New York, Bequest of Miss Adelaide Milton de Groot (1876–1967), 1967 (67.187.60)
(Fig. 126)

Delaherche, Auguste (1857–1940)

*Bowl, ca. 1900
Stoneware, height 6 in. (15.2 cm)
The Metropolitan Museum of Art, New York, Purchase, Edward C. Moore Jr. Gift, 1923 (23.176.4)
(Not illustrated)

Delbrück, Jules (1813–1889)

*Belin and Bethmont, "Le Jardinage," in Jules Delbrück, *Les Récréations instructives* (Paris, ca. 1862)
Hand-colored wood engraving, 12 x 16 in. (30.5 x 40.6 cm)
The Metropolitan Museum of Art, New York
(Not illustrated)

Ducel Fils, J. J. (active ca. 1830–50)

*"Cast Iron Garden Accessories," in *Font de Fer J. J. Ducel et Fils* (Paris, ca. 1830–50), pls. 42–43
Lithograph, 10 5/8 x 16 1/8 in. (27 x 40.9 cm)
The Metropolitan Museum of Art, New York, The Elisha Whittelsey Collection, The Elisha Whittelsey Fund, 1949 (49.67.1)
(Fig. 83)

Dugourc, Jean Démosthène (1749–1825)

**The Garden Facade of Bagatelle*, 1779
Pen and black ink, watercolor, over traces of black chalk, 11 1/8 x 15 13/16 in. (28.3 x 40.2 cm)
The Metropolitan Museum of Art, New York, Bequest of Susan Dwight Bliss, 1966 (67.55.17)
(Not illustrated)

**Figures in a Garden*, 1784
Gouache, 12 1/2 x 17 1/4 in. (31.7 x 43.8 cm)
The Metropolitan Museum of Art, New York, Rogers Fund, 1966 (66.54.1)
(Not illustrated)

Dunouy, Alexandre Hyacinthe (1757–1841)

**View in a Park*, ca. 1800–1810
Oil on paper, 8 3/4 x 12 in. (22.2 x 30.5 cm)
The Metropolitan Museum of Art, New York, The Whitney Collection, Promised Gift of Wheelock Whitney III, and Purchase, Gift of Mr. and Mrs. Charles S. McVeigh, by exchange, 2003 (2003.42.26)
(Fig. 10)

Durdent, René Jean (1776?–1819)

Müller, Henri Charles (1784–1846), "View of the Jardin des Plantes," in René Jean Durdent, *Vues et description du Jardin des Plantes* (Paris, 1813), pl. 1
Aquatint, 9 3/4 x 13 in. (25 x 33.2 cm)
The Metropolitan Museum of Art, New York, Gift of Lincoln Kirstein, 1964 (64.505.28)
(Fig. 1)

Durenne, A. (active ca. 1877)

*[Artist unknown], "Garden Benches" and "Iron Supports for Benches," in *Font de Fer A. Durenne, Maître de forges* (Paris, 1877), pls. 442, 443
Lithograph, each plate 10 1/2 x 13 3/4 in. (26.6 x 35 cm)
The Metropolitan Museum of Art, New York, The Elisha Whittelsey Collection, The Elisha Whittelsey Fund, 1953 (53.654.2)
(Fig. 53) and (Not illustrated)

Enfantin, Augustin (1793–1827)

**An Artist Painting in the Forest of Fontainebleau*, ca. 1825
Oil on paper, laid down on canvas, 10 1/2 x 13 1/2 in. (26.7 x 34.3 cm)
Private collection
(Fig. 24)

Ernouf, Alfred-Auguste, Baron (1817–1889), and Alphand, [Jean-Charles] Adolphe (1817–1891)

*[Artist unknown], "Parc des Buttes-Chaumont" and "Bird's-Eye View of the Parc de Montsouris" (after a charcoal drawing by Emile Hochereau and Emile Dardoize), in Baron [Alfred-Auguste] Ernouf and [Jean-Charles] Adolphe Alphand, *L'Art des jardins: Parcs—jardins—promenades*
(Paris, 1886)
Photomechanical reproduction, 11 13/16 x 9 5/8 in. (30 x 24.5 cm)
Private collection
(Not illustrated)

Fantin-Latour, Henri (1836–1904)

**Still Life with Pansies*, 1874
Oil on canvas, 18 1/2 x 22 1/4 in. (47 x 56.5 cm)
The Metropolitan Museum of Art, New York, The Mr. and Mrs. Henry Ittleson Jr. Purchase Fund, 1966 (66.194)
(Not illustrated)

**Summer Flowers*, 1880
Oil on canvas, 20 x 24 3/8 in. (50.8 x 61.9 cm)
The Metropolitan Museum of Art, New York, Gift of Susan S. Dillon, 1997 (1997.347)
(Fig. 141)

**Potted Pansies*, 1883
Oil on canvas, 11 x 13 1/2 in. (27.9 x 34.3 cm)
The Metropolitan Museum of Art, New York, Gift of Susan S. Dillon, 2013 (2013.636)
(Fig. 138)

Fermin-Girard, Marie-François (1838–1921)

The Flower Market, Paris (Quai aux Fleurs), 1875
Oil on canvas, 39 1/2 x 57 in. (100.3 x 144.8 cm)
Private collection
(Fig. 140)

Fragonard, Jean Honoré (1732–1806)

The Swing, 1767
Oil on canvas, 31 7/8 x 25 1/4 in. (81 x 64.1 cm)
Wallace Collection, London
(Fig. 86)

Freeman, W. H.

*"The Water Garden at the Jardin des Plantes," in *Magasin Pittoresque*, 1855
Wood engraving, 8 7/8 x 6 3/16 in. (22.5 x 15.7 cm)
The Metropolitan Museum of Art, New York
(Not illustrated)

Gainsborough, Thomas (1727–1788)

Mr. and Mrs. Andrews, ca. 1750
Oil on canvas, 27 1/2 x 47 in. (69.9 x 119.4 cm)
The National Gallery, London, bought with contributions from The Pilgrim Trust, The Art Fund, Associated Television Ltd, and Mr. and Mrs. W. W. Spooner, 1960
(Fig. 109)

Gallé, Emile (1846–1904)

*Vase, 1896
Glass, height 6 7/8 in. (17.5 cm)
The Metropolitan Museum of Art, New York, Purchase, Edward C. Moore Jr. Gift, 1926
(Fig. 148)

*"Autumn Crocus" Vase, ca. 1900
Glass, height 17 3/8 in. (44.1 cm)
The Metropolitan Museum of Art, New York, Gift of Lloyd and Barbara Macklowe, 1984 (1984.553)
(Not illustrated)

Garneray, Auguste (1785–1824)

Interior of the Hothouse at Malmaison, ca. 1810
Watercolor, 6 1/2 x 9 5/8 in. (16.5 x 24.4 cm)
Musée National des Châteaux de Malmaison et Bois-Préau, Rueil-Malmaison, Don D. David-Weill, 1935
(Fig. 14; detail, p. 6)

Garneray, Auguste (1785–1824), attributed to

**Napoleon and Josephine Strolling in the Garden at Malmaison*, ca. 1809
Gouache over black chalk, 20 1/16 x 26 3/8 in. (51 x 67 cm)
Graham Arader
(Not illustrated)

Gérard, François (1770–1837)

**Allegory of Empress Josephine as Patroness of the Gardens at Malmaison*, ca. 1805–6
Watercolor and pen and black ink over black chalk, 5 3/8 x 8 1/2 in. (13.7 x 21.6 cm)
The Metropolitan Museum of Art, New York, Purchase, Guy Wildenstein Gift, 2003 (2003.134)
(Fig. 13)

Giraud, Sébastien Charles (1819–1892)

Princess Mathilde's Dining Room, 1854
Oil on canvas, 22 x 24 in. (56 x 61 cm)
Château de Compiègne
(Fig. 142)

Gogh, Vincent van (1853–1890)

**Sunflowers*, 1887
Oil on canvas, 17 x 24 in. (43.2 x 61 cm)
The Metropolitan Museum of Art, New York, Rogers Fund, 1949 (49.41)
(Fig. 156)

Entrance to the Public Gardens in Arles, 1888
Oil on canvas, 28 1/2 x 35 3/4 in. (72.4 x 90.8 cm)
The Phillips Collection, Washington, D.C.
(Fig. 68)

**Garden with Flowers*, 1888
Reed pen and ink on paper, 9 7/16 x 12 3/8 in. (24 x 31.5 cm)
Private collection
(Not illustrated)

**Irises*, 1890
Oil on canvas, 29 x 36 1/4 in. (73.7 x 92.1 cm)

The Metropolitan Museum of Art, New York, Gift of Adele R. Levy, 1958 (58.187)
(Fig. 157)

Grandville, Jean-Jacques (1803–1847)

"Rose," in Taxile Delord, *Les Fleurs animées*, new ed. (Paris, 1867), vol. 1
Hand-colored engraving, 10 1/2 x 6 3/4 in. (26.7 x 17.1 cm)
The Metropolitan Museum of Art, New York, Gift of Lincoln Kirstein, 1970 (1970.565.423.1)
(Fig. 106)

Guitry, Sacha (1885–1957), director

*Claude Monet painting in his garden at Giverny, excerpt from *Ceux de chez nous (Those of Our Land)*, 1915
Black-and-white silent film clip
35 mm, Spherical
Archival footage courtesy of Ina Mediapro
(Not illustrated)

Guys, Constantin (1802–1892)

**Meeting in the Park*, ca. 1860
Pen and brown ink, brush and gray, blue, and black wash, 8 9/16 x 11 13/16 in. (21.7 x 30 cm)
The Metropolitan Museum of Art, New York, Rogers Fund, 1937 (37.165.98)
(Not illustrated)

Hals, Frans (1582/83–1666)

Portrait of a Couple, probably Isaac Abrahamsz Massa and Beatrix van der Laen, ca. 1622
Oil on canvas, 55 1/8 x 65 1/2 in. (140 x 166.4 cm)
Rijksmuseum, Amsterdam
(Fig. 110)

Hassam, Childe (1859–1935)

**Luxembourg Gardens*, 1898/1915
Etching and drypoint, 13 13/16 x 12 1/4 in. (35.1 x 31.1 cm)
The Metropolitan Museum of Art, New York, Gift of Mrs. Childe Hassam, 1940 (40.30.26)
(Not illustrated)

Hurtré, Emile (active ca. 1890–1900), and Wielhorski, Jules C. (active ca. 1896–1898)

**Design for a Wall Decoration with Peacock, Cranes, and Sunflowers for the Restaurant in Hotel Langham (Paris)*, 1896–98
Pen and black, blue, and metallic ink, watercolor, over graphite, 18 5/16 x 11 5/16 in. (46.5 x 28.7 cm)
The Metropolitan Museum of Art, New York, Edward Pearce Casey Fund, 1991 (1991.1288)
(Not illustrated)

Laborde, Alexandre de (1773–1842)

Bourgeois, Constant (1767–1841), "The Château of Malmaison, Seen from the Gardens," in Alexandre de Laborde, *Description des nouveaux jardins de la France et de ses anciens châteaux* (Paris, 1808), pl. 4
Engraving, 9 3/8 x 12 1/2 in. (23.8 x 31.7 cm)
The Metropolitan Museum of Art, New York, The Elisha Whittelsey Collection, The Elisha Whittelsey Fund, 1964 (64.518)
(Fig. 11)

Bourgeois, Constant (1767–1841), "The Pond in the Wilderness at Ermenonville," in Alexandre de Laborde, *Description des nouveaux jardins de la France et de ses anciens châteaux* (Paris, 1808), pl. 43
Engraving, 10 1/4 x 15 in. (26 x 38.1 cm)
The Metropolitan Museum of Art, New York, The Elisha Whittelsey Collection, The Elisha Whittelsey Fund, 1964 (64.518)
(Fig. 5)

*Bourgeois, Constant (1767–1841), "Temple of Venus, Garden of the Petit Trianon," in Alexandre de Laborde, *Description des nouveaux jardins de la France et de ses anciens châteaux* (Paris, 1808), pl. 81
Engraving, 12 5/8 x 9 1/2 in. (32 x 24.1 cm)
The Metropolitan Museum of Art, New York, The Elisha Whittelsey Collection, The Elisha Whittelsey Fund, 1964 (64.518)
(Fig. 4)

Lachaise, Jules-Edmond-Charles (died 1897), and Gourdet, Eugène-Pierre (1820–1889)

*Interior Decorator's Account Book of Hours Spent, 1846
Pen and brown ink on ruled paper, watercolors over leadpoint, 14 5/16 x 9 1/16 in. (36.3 x 23 cm)
The Metropolitan Museum of Art, New York, The Elisha Whittelsey Collection, The Elisha Whittelsey Fund, 2013 (2013.496)
(Not illustrated)

**Design for a Ceiling with Lattice Work and Flowering Vines*, ca. 1855–75
Graphite, pen and ink, and watercolor, 14 1/2 x 10 1/2 in. (36.8 x 26.7 cm)
The Metropolitan Museum of Art, New York, Dodge Fund, 1967 (67.827.448)
(Not illustrated)

**A Garden Pavilion in a Forested Landscape*, ca. 1860–70
Oil on canvas, mounted on blue paper, 14 13/16 x 10 7/16 in. (37.7 x 26.5 cm)
The Metropolitan Museum of Art, New York, Dodge Fund, 1967 (67.827.273)
(Not illustrated)

Lapie, Pierre (1777–1850)

**Plan of the Garden of the Château de Bagatelle*, 1817
Pen and black ink, watercolor, 20 1/2 x 36 1/4 in. (52.1 x 92.1 cm)
The Metropolitan Museum of Art, New York, Harris Brisbane Dick Fund, 1924 (24.66.1494)
(Fig. 8)

Le Gray, Gustave (1820–1884)

**Oak Tree and Rocks at Fontainebleau Forest,* 1849–52
Salted paper print from waxed-paper negative, 10 x 14¼ in. (25.4 x 36.2 cm)
The Metropolitan Museum of Art, New York, Gilman Collection, Purchase, The Horace W. Goldsmith Foundation Gift, through Joyce and Robert Menschel, 2005 (2005.100.46)
(Not illustrated)

**Oak Trees and Rocks at Fontainebleau Forest,* 1849–52
Salted paper print from paper negative, $9\frac{15}{16}$ x $14\frac{1}{16}$ in. (25.2 x 35.7 cm)
The Metropolitan Museum of Art, New York, Purchase, Jennifer and Joseph Duke and Lila Acheson Wallace Gifts, 2000 (2000.13)
(Fig. 27)

Lévy-Dhurmer, Lucien (1865–1953)

Wisteria Dining Room, 1910–14
Carved walnut and amaranth, 12 ft. 2 in. x 17 ft. 3 in. x 26 ft. 3 in. (3.71 x 5.26 x 8 m)
The Metropolitan Museum of Art, New York, Harris Brisbane Dick Fund, 1966 (66.244.1–.25)
(Fig. 154)

Lévy-Dhurmer, Lucien (1865–1953), and Massier, Clément (ca. 1845–1917)

*Jardinière, ca. 1893–95
Earthenware with metallic glaze, 9½ x 14 in. (24.1 x 35.6 cm)
The Metropolitan Museum of Art, New York, Purchase, Funds from various donors, The Charles E. Sampson Memorial Fund, and Jerome M. Cohen and The Isak and Rose Weinman Foundation Inc. Gifts, 2005 (2005.220)
(Not illustrated)

Lorrain, Claude (1604/5?–1682)

View of La Crescenza, 1648–50
Oil on canvas, 15¼ x 22⅞ in. (38.7 x 58.1 cm)
The Metropolitan Museum of Art, New York, Purchase, The Annenberg Fund Inc. Gift, 1978 (1978.205)
(Fig. 3)

Lumière, Louis (1864–1948), director

* *L'Arroseur arrosé* (*The Sprinkler Sprinkled*), 1895
Black-and-white silent film
35 mm, Cinématographe
Archival footage courtesy of Historic Film Archive, LLC
(Not illustrated)

Manet, Edouard (1832–1883)

Still Life with Flowers, Fan, and Pearls, ca. 1860
Oil on canvas, 18⅛ x 14½ in. (46 x 36.8 cm)
The Metropolitan Museum of Art, New York, Partial and Promised Gift of Douglas Dillon, 1993 (1993.399)
(Fig. 130)

Music in the Tuileries Gardens, 1862
Oil on canvas, 30 x 46½ in. (76.2 x 118.1 cm)
The National Gallery, London, Sir Hugh Lane Bequest, 1917
(Fig. 39)

Peonies with Shears, 1864
Oil on canvas, 22¼ x 18⅛ in. (56.6 x 46 cm)
Musée d'Orsay, Paris
(Fig. 132)

**Peonies*, 1864–65
Oil on canvas, 23⅜ x 13⅞ in. (59.4 x 35.2 cm)
The Metropolitan Museum of Art, New York, Bequest of Joan Whitney Payson, 1975 (1976.201.16)
(Fig. 131)

The Races at Longchamp, 1866
Oil on canvas, 17¼ x 33¼ in. (43.8 x 84.5 cm)
The Art Institute of Chicago, Potter Palmer Collection (1922.424)
(Fig. 55)

View of the 1867 Exposition Universelle, 1867
Oil on canvas, 42½ x 77⅛ in. (108 x 195.9 cm)
Nasjonalgalleriet, Oslo
(Fig. 59)

The Brioche, 1870
Oil on canvas, 25⅝ x 31⅞ in. (65.1 x 81 cm)
The Metropolitan Museum of Art, New York, Gift and Bequest of David and Peggy Rockefeller, 1991, 2017 (1991.287)
(Fig. 134)

Eva Gonzalès, 1870
Oil on canvas, 75¼ x 52½ in. (191.1 x 133.4 cm)
The National Gallery, London, Sir Hugh Lane Bequest, 1917
(Fig. 149)

**The Monet Family in Their Garden at Argenteuil*, 1874
Oil on canvas, 24 x 39¼ in. (61 x 99.7 cm)
The Metropolitan Museum of Art, New York, Bequest of Joan Whitney Payson, 1975 (1976.201.14)
(Fig. 113; detail, p. 108)

In the Conservatory, 1878/79
Oil on canvas, 45¼ x 59 in. (114.9 x 149.9 cm)
Nationalgalerie, Staatliche Museen zu Berlin
(Fig. 112)

**Madame Manet (Suzanne Leenhoff, 1830–1906) at Bellevue*, 1880
Oil on canvas, 31¾ x 23¾ in. (80.6 x 60.3 cm)
The Metropolitan Museum of Art, New York, The Walter H. and Leonore Annenberg Collection, Gift of Walter H. and Leonore Annenberg, 1997, Bequest of Walter H. Annenberg, 2002 (1997.391.4)
(Fig. 119)

Garden Bench, 1881
Oil on canvas, 25 5/8 x 31 7/8 in. (65.1 x 81 cm)
Private collection
(Fig. 97)

Marville, Charles (1813–1879)

**Bois de Boulogne*, ca. 1858–59
Albumen print, 16 3/8 x 11 1/2 in.
(41.6 x 29.2 cm)
Private collection
(Fig. 49)

Matisse, Henri (1869–1954)

**Pansies*, ca. 1903
Oil on paper mounted on paperboard,
19 1/4 x 17 3/4 in. (48.9 x 45.1cm)
The Metropolitan Museum of Art, New York,
Bequest of Joan Whitney Payson, 1975
(1976.201.22)
(Not illustrated)

**Lilacs*, 1914
Oil on canvas, 57 1/2 x 38 in.
(146.1 x 96.5 cm)
The Metropolitan Museum of Art, New York,
The Pierre and Maria-Gaetana Matisse
Collection, 2002 (2002.456.4)
(Fig. 159)

Melling, Antoine Ignace (1763–1831)

Château de Ris-Orange (detail), 1811
Gouache, 23 3/4 x 37 3/8 in. (60.3 x 95 cm)
Musée de l'Ile de France, Sceaux
(Fig. 69)

Mésangère, Pierre de La (1761–1831)

Jardinière, in Pierre de La Mésangère,
Collection de meubles et objets de goût (Paris,
[1806–18]), vol. 2, pl. 393
Hand-colored engraving, 12 x 7 1/4 in.
(30.4 x 18.4 cm)
The Metropolitan Museum of Art, New York,
Harris Brisbane Dick Fund, 1930 (30.80[2])
(Fig. 15)

Michallon, Achille-Etna (1796–1822)

Beech Tree, by 1817
Oil on canvas, 14 1/4 x 11 3/8 in. (36.2 x 28.9 cm)
Thaw Collection, Jointly Owned by
The Metropolitan Museum of Art and The
Morgan Library & Museum, New York, Gift
of Eugene V. Thaw, 2009 (2009.400.85)
(Fig. 31)

Monet, Claude (1840–1926)

**The Bodmer Oak, Fontainebleau Forest*, 1865
Oil on canvas, 37 7/8 x 50 7/8 in.
(96.2 x 129.2 cm)
The Metropolitan Museum of Art, New York,
Gift of Sam Salz and Bequest of Julia W.
Emmons, by exchange, 1964 (64.210)
(Fig. 30)

Le Déjeuner sur l'herbe, 1865
Oil on canvas, 51 1/8 x 71 1/4 in. (129.9 x 181 cm)
Pushkin State Museum of Fine Arts, Moscow
(Fig. 29)

**Adolphe Monet Reading in a Garden*, 1867
Oil on canvas, 31 7/8 x 39 in. (81 x 99 cm)
Lawrence J. Ellison collection
(Fig. 87)

Women in the Garden, 1866–67
Oil on canvas, 100 3/8 x 80 3/4 in.
(255 x 205 cm)
Musée d'Orsay, Paris
(Fig. 85)

**Garden at Sainte-Adresse*, 1867
Oil on canvas, 38 5/8 x 51 1/8 in.
(98.1 x 129.9 cm)
The Metropolitan Museum of Art, New York,
Purchase, special contributions and funds
given or bequeathed by friends of the
Museum, 1967 (67.241)
(Fig. 88; detail, p. *ii*)

**Jean Monet (1867–1913) on His Hobby Horse*,
1872
Oil on canvas, 23 7/8 x 29 1/4 in. (60.6 x 74.3 cm)
The Metropolitan Museum of Art, New York,
Gift of Sara Lee Corporation, 2000
(2000.195)
(Fig. 115)

**Camille Monet (1847–1879) on a Garden
Bench*, 1873
Oil on canvas, 23 7/8 x 31 5/8 in. (60.6 x 80.3 cm)
The Metropolitan Museum of Art, New York,
The Walter H. and Leonore Annenberg
Collection, Gift of Walter H. and Leonore
Annenberg, 2002, Bequest of Walter H.
Annenberg, 2002 (2002.62.1)
(Fig. 111)

**Camille Monet (1847–1879) in the Garden at
Argenteuil*, 1876
Oil on canvas, 32 1/8 x 23 5/8 in. (81.6 x 60 cm)
The Metropolitan Museum of Art, New York,
The Walter H. and Leonore Annenberg
Collection, Gift of Walter H. and Leonore
Annenberg, 2000, Bequest of Walter H.
Annenberg, 2002 (2000.93.1)
(Fig. 90)

**Landscape: The Parc Monceau*, 1876
Oil on canvas, 23 1/2 x 32 1/2 in.
(59.7 x 82.6 cm)
The Metropolitan Museum of Art, New York,
Bequest of Loula D. Lasker, New York City,
1961 (59.206)
(Fig. 45)

**The Parc Monceau*, 1878
Oil on canvas, 28 5/8 x 21 3/8 in. (72.7 x 54.3 cm)
The Metropolitan Museum of Art, New York,
The Mr. and Mrs. Henry Ittleson Jr.
Purchase Fund, 1959 (59.142)
(Fig. 46)

**Bouquet of Sunflowers*, 1881
Oil on canvas, 39 3/4 x 32 in. (101 x 81.3 cm)
The Metropolitan Museum of Art, New York,
H. O. Havemeyer Collection, Bequest of
Mrs. H. O. Havemeyer, 1929 (29.100.107)
(Fig. 155)

**Chrysanthemums*, 1882
Oil on canvas, 39 1/2 x 32 1/4 in.
(100.3 x 81.9 cm)

The Metropolitan Museum of Art, New York, H. O. Havemeyer Collection, Bequest of Mrs. H. O. Havemeyer, 1929 (29.100.106)
(Fig. 151)

**Bridge over a Pond of Water Lilies*, 1899
Oil on canvas, 36 1/2 x 29 in. (92.7 x 73.7 cm)
The Metropolitan Museum of Art, New York, H. O. Havemeyer Collection, Bequest of Mrs. H. O. Havemeyer, 1929 (29.100.113)
(Fig. 101)

Path in Monet's Garden, 1902
Oil on canvas, 35 1/4 x 36 3/8 in. (89.5 x 92.4 cm)
Österreichische Galerie Belvedere, Vienna
(Fig. 99)

**Water Lilies*, 1905
Oil on canvas, 35 1/4 x 39 1/4 in. (89.5 x 99.7 cm)
Private collection
(Not illustrated)

**The Path through the Irises*, 1914–17
Oil on canvas, 78 7/8 x 70 7/8 in. (200.3 x 180 cm)
The Metropolitan Museum of Art, New York, The Walter H. and Leonore Annenberg Collection, Gift of Walter H. and Leonore Annenberg, 2001, Bequest of Walter H. Annenberg, 2002 (2001.202.6)
(Fig. 100)

Water Lilies, 1919
Oil on canvas, 39 3/4 x 78 3/4 in. (101 x 200 cm)
The Metropolitan Museum of Art, New York, The Walter H. and Leonore Annenberg Collection, Gift of Walter H. and Leonore Annenberg, 1998, Bequest of Walter H. Annenberg, 2002 (1998.325.2)
(Fig. 102; detail, p. 2)

Mongin, Antoine Pierre (1761/62–1827)

**The Progress of Love*, 1803
Brush and brown wash over black chalk underdrawing, 16 9/16 x 21 5/8 in. (42 x 55 cm)
The Metropolitan Museum of Art, New York, Purchase, Harry G. Sperling Fund, Carolyn H. Specht Gift, The Elisha Whittelsey Collection, The Elisha Whittelsey Fund, and funds from various donors, 2011 (2011.203)
(Fig. 9)

Morisot, Berthe (1841–1895)

**Young Woman Seated on a Sofa*, ca. 1879
Oil on canvas, 31 3/4 x 39 1/4 in. (80.6 x 99.7 cm)
The Metropolitan Museum of Art, New York, Partial and Promised Gift of Mr. and Mrs. Douglas Dillon, 1992 (1992.103.2)
(Fig. 116)

**Young Woman Knitting*, ca. 1883
Oil on canvas, 19 3/4 x 23 5/8 in. (50.2 x 60 cm)
The Metropolitan Museum of Art, New York, Bequest of Miss Adelaide Milton de Groot (1876–1967), 1967 (67.187.89)
(Fig. 117)

**The Gate at Bougival*, 1884
Oil on canvas, 23 5/8 x 28 3/4 in. (60 x 73 cm)
Marc and Cathy Lasry
(Not illustrated)

**A Woman Seated at a Bench on the Avenue du Bois*, 1885
Watercolor over traces of graphite, 7 7/8 x 11 in. (20 x 28 cm)
The Metropolitan Museum of Art, New York, Harris Brisbane Dick Fund, 1948 (48.10.8)
(Not illustrated)

Muller, Edouard, called Rosenmuller (1823–1876)

The Garden of Armida, 1854
Block-printed wallpaper, 12 ft. 8 in. x 11 ft. (3.86 x 3.35 m)
Philadelphia Museum of Art, Gift (by exchange) of Julia G. Fahnestock in memory of her husband, William Fahnestock, 1988 (1988-57-1)
(Fig. 143)

Nègre, Charles (1820–1880)

**Lord Brougham and His Family, Cannes*, 1[illegible]
Albumen silver print from glass negativ[illegible]
9 3/4 x 13 3/8 in. (24.8 x 34 cm)
The Metropolitan Museum of Art, New [illegible], Gilman Collection, Purchase, Harriette [illegible] Noel Levine Gift, 2005 (2005.100.264)
(Not illustrated)

Perelle, Adam (1640–1695)

**The Garden of Versailles*, ca. 1664–68
Etching, 6 3/4 x 10 5/8 in. (17.1 x 27 cm)
The Metropolitan Museum of Art, New [illegible], Gift of Louis R. Metcalfe, 1928 (28.57.4[illegible]
(Fig. 2)

**Jardin des Tuileries (The Tuileries Garden*[illegible], 1680
Etching, 6 7/8 x 10 5/8 in. (17.4 x 26.9 cm)
The Metropolitan Museum of Art, New [illegible], Gift of the Estate of Ogden Codman, 19[illegible] (51.644.320)
(Fig. 35)

Petit, Jacob (1796–1865)

Jardinière and stand, ca. 1834–48; Fontainebleau Manufactory
Hard-paste porcelain, height 6 1/8 in. (15.6 cm)
The Metropolitan Museum of Art, New [illegible], Rogers Fund, 1926 (26.223.12a, b)
(Fig. 146)

Philibert, J. (active ca. 1800)

Müller, Henri Charles (1784–1846), "T[illegible] Waterfront Terrace, Jardin des Tuilerie[illegible] J. Philibert, *Promenades de Paris* (Paris, [illegible])
Etching and aquatint, 7 3/8 x 9 3/8 in. (18.7 x 23.8 cm)
The Metropolitan Museum of Art, New [illegible], Gift of Lincoln Kirstein, 1964 (64.505.[illegible]
(Fig. 36)

Philipon, Charles (1800–1861)

The Pretty Flower Vendor, ca. 1830
Hand-colored lithograph, 12½ x 8¾ in.
(30.5 x 20.3 cm)
Private collection
(Fig. 139)

Pissarro, Camille (1830–1903)

**The Public Garden at Pontoise*, 1874
Oil on canvas, 23⅝ x 28¾ in. (60 x 73 cm)
The Metropolitan Museum of Art, New York,
Gift of Mr. and Mrs. Arthur Murray, 1964
(64.156)
(Fig. 67)

**The Garden of the Tuileries on a Spring Morning*, 1899
Oil on canvas, 28⅞ x 36¼ in. (73.3 x 92.1 cm)
The Metropolitan Museum of Art, New York,
Partial and Promised Gift of Mr. and Mrs.
Douglas Dillon, 1992 (1992.103.3)
(Fig. 40)

**The Garden of the Tuileries on a Winter Afternoon*, 1899
Oil on canvas, 29 x 36¼ in. (73.7 x 92.1 cm)
The Metropolitan Museum of Art, New York,
Gift of Katrin S. Vietor, in loving memory of
Ernest G. Vietor, 1966 (66.36)
(Fig. 41; detail, p. *vi*)

Prendergast, Maurice (1858–1924)

**Paris Sketchbook*, 1891–94, leaf 30 verso–31 recto
Conté crayon, pencil, and watercolor,
6¾ x 4½ in. (17.1 x 11.4 cm)
The Metropolitan Museum of Art, New York,
Robert Lehman Collection, 1975
(1975.1.923)
(Fig. 63)

Provost, A. (active 1834–55)

**Panorama of the Champs-Elysées* (detail),
ca. 1845–50
Lithograph, 4½ x 230 in. (11.4 x 584 cm);
exhibited spread 4½ x 88½ in.
(11.4 x 224.8 cm)
The Metropolitan Museum of Art, New York,
A. Hyatt Mayor Purchase Fund, Marjorie
Phelps Starr Bequest, 1980 (1980.1015.2)
(Fig. 61)

Redon, Odilon (1840–1916)

**Bouquet of Flowers*, ca. 1900–1905
Pastel on paper, 31⅝ x 25¼ in.
(80.3 x 64.1 cm)
The Metropolitan Museum of Art, New York,
Gift of Mrs. George B. Post, 1956 (56.50)
(Fig. 158)

**Madame Arthur Fontaine (Marie Escudier, b. 1865)*, 1901
Pastel on paper, 28½ x 22½ in.
(72.4 x 57.2 cm)
The Metropolitan Museum of Art, New York,
The Mr. and Mrs. Henry Ittleson Jr.
Purchase Fund, 1960 (60.54)
(Fig. 122)

Redouté, Pierre Joseph (1759–1840)

*Sweet-Scented Dracaena (*Aletris fragrans*),
in *Les Liliacées* (Paris, 1802–16)
Colored stipple engraving, 20⅞ x 14⅛ in.
(53 x 35.9 cm)
Private collection
(Not illustrated)

*Crown Imperial (*Fritillaria imperialis*),
in *Les Liliacées* (Paris, 1802–16)
Colored stipple engraving, 30½ x 21¼ in.
(77.5 x 54 cm)
Private collection
(Fig. 17)

*Elder Iris (*Iris sambucina*), in *Les Liliacées*
(Paris, 1802–16)
Colored stipple engraving, 21½ x 13⅞ in.
(54.6 x 35.3 cm)
Private collection
(Not illustrated)

Egyptian Blue Lotus (*Nymphaea caerulea*),
in Etienne Pierre Ventenat, *Jardin de la Malmaison* (Paris, 1803–4)
Colored stipple engraving, 22¼ x 28¼ in.
(56.5 x 71.8 cm)
From the collection of the Mertz Library,
The New York Botanical Garden
(Fig. 18)

South African Great-Flowered Heath (*Erica grandiflora*), in Aimé Bonpland, *Description des plantes rares cultivées à Malmaison et à Navarre* (Paris, 1813), pl. 10
Colored stipple engraving, 22 x 28 in.
(55.9 x 71.1 cm)
From the collection of the Mertz Library,
The New York Botanical Garden
(Fig. 19)

*Burgundian Cabbage Rose (*Rosa centifolia burgundiaca*), in Claude-Antoine Thory,
Les Roses (Paris, 1817–24)
Colored stipple engraving, 13¾ x 10½ in.
(34.9 x 26.7 cm)
Private collection
(Not illustrated)

*White Moss Rose (*Rosa muscosa alba*),
in Claude-Antoine Thory, *Les Roses*
(Paris, 1817–24)
Colored stipple engraving, 14 x 10¾ in.
(35.6 x 27.3 cm)
Private collection
(Not illustrated)

*'Empress Josephine' or Frankfort Rose
(*Rosa turbinata*), in Claude-Antoine
Thory, *Les Roses* (Paris, 1817–24)
Colored stipple engraving, 13¾ x 9$^{15}/_{16}$ in.
(34.9 x 25.2 cm)
Private collection
(Fig. 20)

Regnault, Henri-Victor (1810–1878)

Gardens of Saint-Cloud, before 1855
Salted paper print from paper negative,
16⅛ x 14 in. (41 x 35.6 cm)
The Metropolitan Museum of Art, New York,
Gilman Collection, Gift of The Howard
Gilman Foundation, 2005 (2005.100.39)
(Fig. 23)

Renoir, Auguste (1841–1919)

Monet Painting in His Garden at Argenteuil, 1873
Oil on canvas, 18 3/8 x 23 1/2 in. (46.7 x 59.7 cm)
Wadsworth Atheneum Museum of Art, Hartford, Connecticut, Bequest of Anne Parrish Titzell (1957.614)
(Fig. 89)

Madame Monet and Her Son, 1874
Oil on canvas, 19 7/8 x 26 3/4 in. (50.5 x 67.9 cm)
National Gallery of Art, Washington, D.C., Ailsa Mellon Bruce Collection (1970.17.60)
(Fig. 114)

**Figures under a Tree*, 1880–82
Watercolor and graphite, 9 7/16 x 12 5/16 in. (23.9 x 31.2 cm)
The Metropolitan Museum of Art, New York, Robert Lehman Collection, 1975 (1975.1.690)
(Not illustrated)

**Bouquet of Chrysanthemums*, 1881
Oil on canvas, 26 x 21 7/8 in. (66 x 55.6 cm)
The Metropolitan Museum of Art, New York, The Walter H. and Leonore Annenberg Collection, Bequest of Walter H. Annenberg, 2002 (2003.20.10)
(Fig. 152)

**Versailles*, 1900–1905
Oil on canvas, 20 1/2 x 24 7/8 in. (52.1 x 63.2 cm)
The Metropolitan Museum of Art, New York, Robert Lehman Collection, 1975 (1975.1.202)
(Not illustrated)

Robert, Jean François (1778–1832)

*Medici Vase with a Scene of the Château at Saint-Cloud (one of a pair), 1811; Sèvres Manufactory
Commissioned by Napoleon Bonaparte
Hard-paste porcelain, gilt bronze, height 27 1/4 in. (69.2 cm)
The Metropolitan Museum of Art, New York, Purchase, Rogers and 2011 Benefit Funds, and Gift of Dr. Mortimer D. Sackler, Theresa Sackler and Family, 2011 (2011.545)
(Not illustrated)

Robert, Hubert (1733–1808)

The Swing, 1777–79
Oil on canvas, 68 1/4 x 34 5/8 in. (173.4 x 87.9 cm)
The Metropolitan Museum of Art, New York, Gift of J. Pierpont Morgan, 1917 (17.190.27)
(Fig. 7)

Rousseau, François Eugène (1827–1891)

*Vase, 1870–80
Glass, height 12 3/16 in. (31 cm)
The Metropolitan Museum of Art, New York, Gift of James Grafstein, 2001 (2001.656)
(Not illustrated)

Rousseau, Henri (le Douanier) (1844–1910)

Parc Montsouris, ca. 1895
Oil on canvas, 16 x 12 in. (40.5 x 30.5 cm)
Nahmad Collection, Switzerland
(Fig. 57)

Rousseau, Théodore (1812–1867)

**Study for "The Forest in Winter at Sunset,"* ca. 1846
Oil over charcoal with white heightening on paper, laid down on canvas, 9 5/8 x 13 1/4 in. (24.4 x 33.7 cm)
Private collection
(Not illustrated)

**The Edge of the Woods at Monts-Girard, Fontainebleau Forest*, 1852–54
Oil on wood, 31 1/2 x 48 in. (80 x 121.9 cm)
The Metropolitan Museum of Art, New York, Catharine Lorillard Wolfe Collection, Wolfe Fund, 1896 (96.27)
(Fig. 26)

Saint-Jean, Simon (1808–1860)

The Gardener, 1837
Oil on canvas, 63 x 46 1/2 in. (160 x 118.1 cm)
Musée des Beaux-Arts de Lyon, deposit of Centre Nationale des Arts Plastiques
(Fig. 125)

Seurat, Georges (1859–1891)

The Forest at Pontaubert, 1881
Oil on canvas, 31 1/8 x 24 5/8 in. (79.1 x 62.5 cm)
The Metropolitan Museum of Art, New York, Purchase, Gift of Raymonde Paul, in memory of her brother, C. Michael Paul, by exchange, 1985 (1985.237)
(Fig. 32)

Study for "A Sunday on La Grande Jatte," 1884
Oil on wood, 6 1/8 x 9 1/2 in. (15.6 x 24.1 cm)
The Metropolitan Museum of Art, New York, Robert Lehman Collection, 1975 (1975.1.207)
(Fig. 64)

**Study for "A Sunday on La Grande Jatte,"* 1884
Oil on canvas, 27 3/4 x 41 in. (70.5 x 104.1 cm)
The Metropolitan Museum of Art, New York, Bequest of Sam A. Lewisohn, 1951 (51.112.6)
(Fig. 65; detail, p. 24)

Stevens, Alfred (1823–1906)

The Glass Ball, ca. 1875
Oil on canvas, 36 1/2 x 25 1/2 in. (92.7 x 68.4 cm)
Private collection
(Fig. 94; detail, p. 70)

Texier, Edmond Auguste (1815–1887)

Ed. Reinard and H. Valentin, "Winter Garden, Paris," in Edmond Texier, *Tableau de Paris* (Paris, 1852)
Wood engraving, 9 13/16 x 10 3/8 in. (25 x 26.3 cm)
The Metropolitan Museum of Art, New York, A. Hyatt Mayor Purchase Fund, Marjorie

Phelps Starr Bequest, 1990 (1990.1110.1.1)
(Fig. 74)

Thouin, Gabriel (1747–1829)

*"Pleasure Garden," in *Plans raisonnés de toutes les espèces de jardins* (Paris, 1820), pl. 41
Hand-colored lithograph, 13 x 9 3/8 in. (33 x 23.8 cm)
The Metropolitan Museum of Art, New York, Harris Brisbane Dick Fund, 1935 (35.20)
(Fig. 72)

"Romantic Chinese Garden," in *Plans raisonnés de toutes les espèces de jardins* (Paris, 1820)
Hand-colored lithograph, 13 1/4 x 9 1/4 in. (33.6 x 23.4 cm)
The Metropolitan Museum of Art, New York, Harris Brisbane Dick Fund, 1935 (35.20)
(Fig. 71)

"Symmetrical City Garden," in *Plans raisonnés de toutes les espèces de jardins* (Paris, 1820)
Hand-colored lithograph, 13 x 9 3/8 in. (33 x 23.8 cm)
The Metropolitan Museum of Art, New York, Harris Brisbane Dick Fund, 1935 (35.20)
(Fig. 70)

Tissot, James (1836–1902)

Sunday in the Luxembourg Gardens, 1883–85
Oil on canvas, 41 1/2 x 37 1/4 in. (105.4 x 94.6 cm)
Private collection
(Fig. 43)

Toulouse-Lautrec, Henri de (1864–1901)

**The Streetwalker*, ca. 1890–91
Oil on cardboard, 25 1/2 x 21 in. (64.8 x 53.3 cm)
The Metropolitan Museum of Art, New York, The Walter H. and Leonore Annenberg Collection, Bequest of Walter H. Annenberg, 2002 (2003.20.13)
(Fig. 121)

Troll, Johann Heinrich (1756–1824)

**View of the Grand Basin of the Tuileries (behind the statue of Autumn)*, ca. 1803
Etching and aquatint, 10 7/16 x 8 7/16 in. (26.5 x 21.5 cm)
The Metropolitan Museum of Art, New York, The Elisha Whittelsey Collection, The Elisha Whittelsey Fund, 1966 (66.544.14[1])
(Not illustrated)

Vallayer-Coster, Anne (1744–1818)

Vase of Flowers and Conch Shell, 1780
Oil on canvas, 19 3/4 x 15 in. (50.2 x 38.1 cm)
The Metropolitan Museum of Art, New York, Gift of J. Pierpont Morgan, 1906 (07.225.504)
(Fig. 124)

**Two Roses*, ca. 1810
Pen and gray ink, gray wash, over black chalk, 8 1/4 x 13 3/16 in. (21 x 33.5 cm)
The Metropolitan Museum of Art, New York, Purchase, Renée Sacks Bequest, 2005 (2005.237)
(Not illustrated)

Vanderlyn, John (1775–1852)

Panoramic View of the Palace and Gardens of Versailles (detail), 1818–19
Oil on canvas, 12 x 165 ft. (3.6 x 50.3 m)
The Metropolitan Museum of Art, New York, Gift of the Senate House Association, Kingston, New York, 1952 (52.184)
(Fig. 21)

Vigée Le Brun, Elisabeth Louise (1755–1842)

Marie Antoinette with a Rose, 1783
Oil on canvas, 46 x 35 in. (116.8 x 88.9 cm)
Collection of Lynda and Stewart Resnick, Los Angeles
(Fig. 105)

Vuillard, Edouard (1868–1940)

Public Gardens: Conversation, Nannies, and Red Parasol, 1894
Distemper on canvas, 84 1/2 x 122 in. (214 x 310 cm)
Musée d'Orsay, Paris
(Fig. 56)

The Album, 1895
Oil on canvas, 26 3/4 x 80 1/2 in. (67.9 x 204.5 cm)
The Metropolitan Museum of Art, New York, The Walter H. and Leonore Annenberg Collection, Gift of Walter H. and Leonore Annenberg, 2000, Bequest of Walter H. Annenberg, 2002 (2000.93.2)
(Fig. 145)

**Jardin des Tuileries (The Tuileries Garden)*, 1896
Color lithograph, 16 13/16 x 22 1/2 in. (42.7 x 57.2 cm)
The Metropolitan Museum of Art, New York, Harris Brisbane Dick Fund, 1936 (36.11.1)
(Fig. 42)

Place Vintimille, or Berlioz Square, 1915–16; reworked 1923
Distemper on canvas, 64 x 90 in. (162.6 x 228.6 cm)
The Metropolitan Museum of Art, New York, Promised Gift of Anonymous Donor
(Fig. 66)

**Garden at Vaucresson*, 1920; reworked 1926, 1935, 1936
Distemper on canvas, 59 1/2 x 43 5/8 in. (151.1 x 110.8 cm)
The Metropolitan Museum of Art, New York, Catharine Lorillard Wolfe Collection, Wolfe Fund, 1952 (52.183)
(Fig. 95; detail, p. 164)

Ward, Nathaniel Bagshaw (1791–1868)

[Artist unknown], "Wardian Case," in Nathaniel Bagshaw Ward, *On the Growth of Plants in Closely Glazed Cases*, 2nd ed. (London, 1852), p. 35

Engraving, 2 1/2 x 3 in. (6.4 x 7.6 cm)
From the collection of the Mertz Library,
The New York Botanical Garden
(Fig. 73)

Whistler, James McNeill (1834–1903)

**The Pantheon, from the Terrace of the Luxembourg Gardens*, 1893
Transfer lithograph with stumping,
11 1/8 in. x 9 in. (28.2 x 22.8 cm)
The Metropolitan Museum of Art, New York,
Harris Brisbane Dick Fund, 1917 (17.3.193)
(Not illustrated)

**Confidences in the Garden*, 1894
Transfer lithograph, 13 1/8 x 9 11/16 in.
(33.3 x 24.6 cm)
The Metropolitan Museum of Art, New York,
Gift of Paul F. Walter, 1984 (1984.1119.13)
(Not illustrated)

**Tête-à-tête in the Garden*, 1894
Transfer lithograph, 10 1/16 x 8 1/16 in.
(25.6 x 20.5 cm)
The Metropolitan Museum of Art, New York,
Gift of Paul F. Walter, 1985 (1985.1161.4)
(Not illustrated)

Williams, Charles (active 1797–1830), or Cruikshank, George (1792–1878), attributed to

**Imperial Botany—or a Peep at Josephine's Collection of English Exoticks* (detail), 1814
Hand-colored etching, 8 1/2 x 21 3/8 in.
(21.5 x 54.3 cm)
The Metropolitan Museum of Art, New York,
Harris Brisbane Dick Fund,
1917 (17.3.888-334)
(Fig. 12)

Winterhalter, Franz Xaver (1805–1873)

**The Empress Eugénie (Eugénie de Montijo, 1826–1920, Condesa de Teba)*, 1854
Oil on canvas, 36 1/2 x 29 in. (92.7 x 73.7 cm)
The Metropolitan Museum of Art, New York,
Purchase, Mr. and Mrs. Claus von Bülow
Gift, 1978 (1978.403)
(Fig. 107)

Artist Unknown

**Design for Chinois Bench and Planters*,
French, ca. 1870–80
Graphite and watercolor, 7 9/16 x 10 9/16 in.
(19.2 x 26.9 cm)
The Metropolitan Museum of Art, New York,
The Elisha Whittelsey Collection, The
Elisha Whittelsey Fund, 1949 (49.50.133)
(Not illustrated)

**Design for a Porcelain Candelabra with Nine Branches*, French, ca. 1850–70
Graphite, watercolor, gouache, and gold gilt,
18 7/8 x 11 7/16 in. (47.9 x 29.1 cm)
The Metropolitan Museum of Art, New York,
The Elisha Whittelsey Collection, The
Elisha Whittelsey Fund, 1953 (53.675.8)
(Not illustrated)

*The Dubois Pruner (manufacturer's promotional packet), 1886
Engraving, each card approx. 4 5/8 x 3 in.
(11.7 x 7.6 cm)
The Metropolitan Museum of Art, New York,
Purchase, Myra Carter Church Fund, 1957
(57.548a–d)
(Fig. 92: *Dubois Parasol Pruner*, 57.548c)

*Invitation to the Gardeners' Ball, August 30, 1843
Lithograph, 3 1/4 x 4 7/16 in. (8.3 x 11.2 cm)
The Metropolitan Museum of Art, New York,
Museum Accession (x.820)
(Fig. 78)

**View of the Champs-Elysées in 1789*, ca. 1790
Etching and aquatint, 8 x 11 1/8 in.
(20.3 x 28.2 cm)
The Metropolitan Museum of Art, New York,
Gift of the Estate of Ogden Codman, 1951
(51.644.309)
(Fig. 60)

Journals

The Illustrated London News
"Café de la Cascade, Bois de Boulogne,"
August 1866
Engraving, 10 3/4 x 15 7/8 in. (25.4 x 38.1 cm)
Private collection
(Fig. 51)

L'Illustration
*"The Horticultural Establishment of M[illegible]
Linden, Rue de la Paix," December 21, 1[illegible]
Wood engraving, 14 9/16 x 10 13/16 in.
(37 x 27.5 cm)
The Metropolitan Museum of Art, New York
(Not illustrated)

La Maison de Campagne
*Plan for a country house, 1882
Wood engraving, 10 13/16 x 7 1/2 in.
(27.5 x 19 cm)
The Metropolitan Museum of Art, New York
(Not illustrated)

La Mode Illustré
"Women in a Garden," 1865
Hand-colored engraving, 12 x 9 in.
(30.5 x 22.9 cm)
The Metropolitan Museum of Art, New York,
The Irene Lewisohn Reference Library,
Woodman Thompson Collection
(FP.15.1865)
(Fig. 93)

La Science pour Tous
*Hothouse Gardens at the Jardin des Plantes, June 21, 1860
Wood engraving, 12 3/16 x 8 7/8 in.
(31 x 22.5 cm)
The Metropolitan Museum of Art, New York
(Not illustrated)

L'Univers Illustré
*Hothouse Garden at the World's Fair, May 15, 1867
Wood engraving, 15 3/4 x 11 in. (40 x 28 cm)
The Metropolitan Museum of Art, New York
(Not illustrated)

"Le Parc des Buttes Chaumont," ca. 1867
Engraving, 6⅞ x 9 in. (17.3 x 22.8 cm)
Private collection
(Fig. 58)

*"Paris: The New Marché aux Fleurs de la Cité," August 15, 1874
Wood engraving, 10½ x 14 in.
(26.7 x 35.6 cm)
The Metropolitan Museum of Art, New York
(Not illustrated)

Invoices and Trade Cards

*Constantin Magasin de Fleurs Fines, Paris
Invoice for plants and flowers, January 8, 1842
Engraving, pen and ink, 10⁹⁄₁₆ x 8⅛ in.
(26.9 x 20.6 cm)
The Metropolitan Museum of Art, New York,
Gift of Bella C. Landauer, 1926 (26.28.160)
(Not illustrated)

*Ct. Lesueur, horticulture-nursery, Rouen
Invoice for fruit trees, September 9, 1880
Engraving, pen and ink, 6½ x 8¼ in.
(16.5 x 20.9 cm)
The Metropolitan Museum of Art, New York,
Gift of Bella C. Landauer, 1926 (26.28.161)
(Not illustrated)

*Vilmorin-Andrieux et Cie, Paris
Invoice to the Count of Andigné for seed supplies, August 24, 1844
Lithograph, pen and ink, 5⁵⁄₁₆ x 8⁵⁄₁₆ in.
(13.5 x 21.1 cm)
The Metropolitan Museum of Art, New York,
Gift of Bella C. Landauer, 1926 (26.28.162)
(Not illustrated)

*Maison Jacquin Jeune, garden supplier, Paris
Trade card, ca. 1850
Lithograph, 3 x 4½ in. (7.6 x 11.5 cm)
The Metropolitan Museum of Art, New York,
Gift of Bella C. Landauer, 1925 (26.28)
(Fig. 84)

Morier, landscape architect, Paris
Trade card, 19th century
Lithograph, 7¼ x 5½ in. (18.4 x 14 cm)
The Metropolitan Museum of Art, New York,
Gift of Bella C. Landauer, 1926 (26.28.164)
(Not illustrated)

Watering Cans and Garden Implements

French, 19th century
Mark K. Morrison
(Not illustrated)

*Watering can, ca. 1840–55
Copper, height 15 in. (38.1 cm)

*Twin sprinkling rose watering cans, 1860s
Copper, brass, and tin, each height 16 in.
(40.6 cm)

*Nighttime watering can with candle holder, ca. 1870
Copper, height 21 in. (53.3 cm)

*Watering can, ca. 1875
Copper, height 14 in. (35.6 cm)

*Watering can, ca. 1880
Copper, height 12 in. (30.5 cm)

*Watering can, 1880s
Tin, height 14 in. (35.6 cm)

*Watering can, ca. 1885
Copper, height 13 in. (33 cm)

*Hedge shears, 1830s–40s
Hand-forged iron and chestnut,
length 20 in. (50.8 cm)

*Long-handled fork, 1830s–40s
Hand-forged iron and chestnut,
length 20 in. (50.8 cm)

*Hand rake, 1840s
Hand-forged iron and chestnut,
length 21 in. (53.3 cm)

*Aristocratic shears, 1860s
Hand-forged iron and chestnut,
length 22 in. (55.9 cm)

*Three-bladed topiary shears, 1860s
Hand-forged iron and chestnut,
length 18 in. (45.7 cm)

*Seedling waterer, 1860s
Tin, height 18 in. (45.7 cm)

*Cloche, with removable stopper, 1860s
Hand-blown glass, height 11 in. (27.9 cm)

*Cloche, with solid lifting knob, 1860s
Hand-blown glass, height 10½ in.
(26.7 cm)

*Two handmade seedling carriers, 1860s
Zinc-coated steel wire with terra cotta pots,
height 10 in. (25.4 cm)

*Dubois Flower Pruner, with aphid brush, 1870s
Bamboo, length 42½ in. (108 cm)

*Dubois Flower Pruner, with extended reach, 1870s
Bamboo, length 46½ in. (118.1 cm)

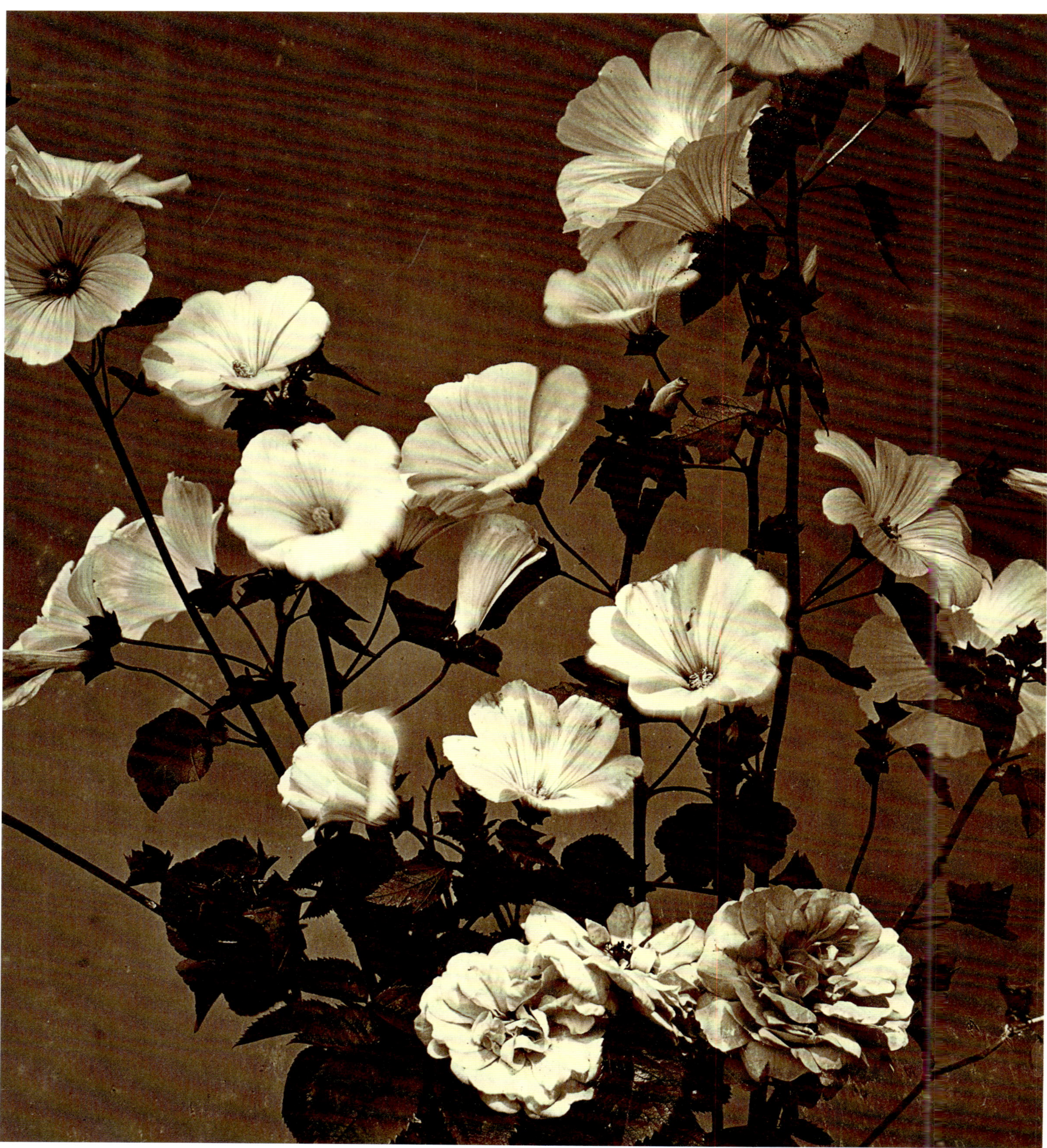

Selected References

Alphand, [Jean-Charles] Adolphe. *Les Promenades de Paris*. 2 vols. Paris: J. Rothschild, 1867–73.

André, Edouard. *L'Art des jardins: Traité général de la composition des parcs et jardins*. Paris: G. Masson, 1879.

Annales de la Société d'Horticulture de Paris, et Journal Spécial de l'Etat et des Progrès du Jardinage. Vols. 1–45 (with slight variations to the title). Paris: Au Bureau de la Société d'Horticulture, 1827–54.

d'Arneville, Marie-Blanche, ed. *L'Impératrice Joséphine et les sciences naturelles*. Exh. cat., Musée Nationale des Châteaux de Malmaison et Bois-Préau. Paris: Réunion des Musées Nationaux, 1997.

Bailey, Colin B., Christopher Riopelle, John House, Simon Kelly, John Zarobell, and Robert McDonald Parker. *Renoir Landscapes, 1865–1883*. Exh. cat., The National Gallery, London; The National Gallery of Canada, Ottawa; Philadelphia Museum of Art. London: National Gallery, 2007.

Bailey, Martin. *The Sunflowers Are Mine: The Story of Van Gogh's Masterpiece*. London: Frances Lincoln Limited, 2013.

Baillio, Joseph, Laurence Bertrand Dorléac, Guy Cogeval, John House, Laurence Madeline, Sylvie Patin, Sylvie Patry, Philippe Piguet, Anne Roquebert, and Richard Thomson. *Claude Monet, 1840–1926*. Exh. cat., Galeries Nationales du Grand Palais, Paris. Paris: Réunion des Musées Nationaux; Musée d'Orsay, 2010.

Baltet, Charles. *L'Horticulture française: Ses Progrès et ses conquêtes depuis 1789*. Paris: Librairie Agricole; Librairie G. Masson, 1892.

Baltrušaitis, Jurgis. *Jardins en France, 1760–1820: Pays d'illusion, terre d'expériences*. Exh. cat., Hôtel de Sully, Paris. Paris: Caisse Nationale des Monuments Historiques et des Sites, 1977.

Baridon, Michel. *A History of the Gardens of Versailles*. Translated by Adrienne Mason. Philadelphia: University of Pennsylvania Press, 2008.

Bazin, Germain. *Les Fleurs vues par les peintres*. Lausanne: Edita; Paris: La Bibliothèque des Arts, 1984.

———. *Paradeisos: The Art of the Garden*. Boston, Toronto, and London: Little, Brown, 1990. First published as *Paradeisos; ou, L'Art du jardin*. Paris: Chêne, 1988.

Becker, Christoph, Catherine Hug, Monika Leonhardt, and Linda Schädler. *Monet's Garden*. Exh. cat., Kunsthaus Zürich. Ostfildern-Ruit: Hatje Cantz, 2004.

Belloli, Andrea P. A., ed. *A Day in the Country: Impressionism and the French Landscape*. Essays by Richard Brettell, Scott Schaefer, Sylvie Gache-Patin, and Françoise Heilbrun. Exh. cat., Los Angeles County Museum of Art; Art Institute of Chicago; Galeries Nationales du Grand Palais, Paris. Los Angeles: Los Angeles County Museum of Art, 1984.

Berrall, Julia S. *The Garden: An Illustrated History*. New York: Viking Press, 1966.

Blagdon, Francis William. *Paris As It Was and As It Is; or, A Sketch of the French Capital, Illustrative of the Effects of the Revolution, with Respect to Sciences, Literature, Arts, Religion, Education, Manners, and Amusements; Comprising Also a Correct Account of the Most Remarkable National Establishments and Public Buildings; in a Series of Letters, Written by an English Traveller, during the Years 1801–2 to a Friend in London*. 2 vols. London: C. and R. Baldwin, 1803.

Bocquillon, Marina Ferretti, ed. *Monet's Garden in Giverny: Inventing the Landscape*. Exh. cat., Musée des Impressionismes, Giverny. Milan: 5 Continents Editions, 2009.

Boggs, Jean Sutherland, Douglas W. Druick, Henri Loyrette, Michael Pantazzi, and Gary Tinterow. *Degas*. Exh. cat., Galeries Nationales du Grand Palais, Paris; National Gallery of Canada, Ottawa; The Metropolitan Museum of Art, New York. New York: The Metropolitan Museum of Art; Ottawa: National Gallery of Canada, 1988.

Boitard, Pierre. *Traité de la composition et de l'ornement des jardins*. 3rd ed. Paris: Audot, 1825.

Le Bon Jardinier: Almanach pour l'année . . . . Paris: Audot; Librairie Agricole de la Maison Rustique, 1755– .

Bonpland, Aimé. *Description des plantes rares cultivées à Malmaison et à Navarre*. Paris: Didot l'Aîné, 1813.

Bourgoing, Catherine de, ed. *Jardins romantiques français: Du jardin des Lumières au parc romantique, 1770–1840*. Exh. cat. Paris: Musée de la Vie Romantique, 2011.

Cachin, Françoise, Charles S. Moffett, and Michel Melot. *Manet, 1832–1883*. Exh. cat., Galeries Nationales du Grand Palais, Paris; The Metropolitan Museum of Art, New York. New York: The Metropolitan Museum of Art, 1983.

Chazal, A[ntoine Toussaint de]. *Flore pittoresque; ou, Recueil de fleurs et de fruits peints d'après nature*. Paris: Chez l'auteur, 1818.

Christiany, Janine. "Les Promenades publiques parisiennes au XIXe siècle." In *Jardins d'hier et d'aujourd'hui: De Karnak à l'Eden*, edited by Sydney H. Aufrère and Michel Mazoyer, pp. 255–65. Paris: L'Harmattan; Association Kubaba, 2012.

Clark, Kenneth. *Landscape into Art*. New York: Harper & Row, 1979.

Clark, T. J. *The Painting of Modern Life: Paris in the Art of Manet and His Followers*. New York: Alfred A. Knopf, 1984.

Conan, Michel, ed. *Bourgeois and Aristocratic Cultural Encounters in Garden Art, 1550–1850*. Washington, D.C.: Dumbarton Oaks Research Library and Collection, 2002.

Corey, Laura D., Paula Deitz, Guillaume Fonkenell, Bruce Guenther, Sarah Kennel, and Richard H. Putney. *The Art of the Louvre's Tuileries Garden*. Exh. cat., High Museum of Art, Atlanta; Toledo Museum of Art, Toledo, Ohio; Portland Art Museum, Portland, Ore. New Haven and London: Yale University Press, 2013.

Decaisne, Joseph, and Charles Naudin. *Manuel de l'amateur des jardins: Traité général d'horticulture*. 4 vols. Paris: Firmin Didot frères, 1862–66.

DeJean, Joan E. *How Paris Became Paris: The Invention of the Modern City*. New York: Bloomsbury, 2014.

Delord, Taxile. *Les Fleurs animées*. Illustrated by Jean-Jacques Grandville; introduction by Alphonse Karr. 2 vols. Paris: Gabriel de Gonet, [1847]. New ed., Paris: Garnier frères, 1867.

Denecourt, Claude François. *L'Indicateur de Fontainebleau: Itinéraire descriptif du palais, de la forêt et des environs*. 17th ed. Fontainebleau: C. F. Denecourt; Paris: Hachette, 1868.

Des Cars, Jean. *Haussmann: La Gloire du Second Empire*. New ed. Paris: Perrin, 1988.

Distel, Anne, et al. *Gustave Caillebotte, Urban Impressionist*. Exh. cat., Galeries Nationales du Grand Palais, Paris; Art Institute of Chicago; Los Angeles County Museum of Art. New York: Abbeville Press, 1995.

Ernouf, [Alfred-Auguste], and [Jean-Charles] Adolphe Alphand. *L'Art des jardins: Parcs—jardins—promenades . . . .* 3rd ed. Paris: J. Rothschild, 1886.

Fell, Derek. *The Impressionist Garden*. New York: Carol Southern Books, 1994.

Feydeau, Elisabeth de. *From Marie-Antoinette's Garden: An Eighteenth-Century Album*. Paris: Flammarion, 2013.

Fowle, Frances, and Richard Thomson, eds. *Soil and Stone: Impressionism, Urbanism, Environment*. Aldershot, England, and Burlington, Vt.: Ashgate, 2003.

Les Français peints par eux-mêmes: Encyclopédie morale du dix-neuvième siècle. Vols. 1, 3, 4. Paris: L. Curmer, 1840–42.

Fryberger, Betsy Geraghty, with essays by Paula Deitz et al. *The Changing Garden: Four Centuries of European and American Art*. Exh. cat., Iris and B. Gerald Cantor Center for Visual Art at Stanford University; Dixon Art Gallery and Gardens, Memphis; University of Michigan Museum of Art, Ann Arbor. Berkeley: University of California Press; Stanford: Iris and B. Gerald Cantor Center for Visual Art at Stanford University, 2003.

Galignani's New Paris Guide, Containing an Accurate Statistical and Historical Description of All the Institutions, Public Edifices, Curiosities, Etc., of the Capital . . . to Which Is Added a Description of the Environs. New and enl. ed. Paris: A. and W. Galignani, 1839.

Le Guide au Jardin des plantes; ou, Description de tout ce que les galeries, serres, etc. du Muséum d'Histoire Naturelle de Paris renferment de plus curieux. Paris: Glisau, 1803.

Hardouin-Fugier, Elisabeth, and Etienne Grafe. *Les Peintres de fleurs en France: De Redouté à Redon*. Paris: Les Editions de l'Amateur, 1992.

Hare, Augustus J. C. *Walks in Paris*. New York, London, and Glasgow: George Routledge and Sons, 1888.

Harrison, Robert Pogue. *Gardens: An Essay on the Human Condition*. Chicago and London: University of Chicago Press, 2008.

Hénard, Robert. *Les Jardins et les squares*. Paris: Librairie Renouard, 1911.

Herbert, Robert L. *Impressionism: Art, Leisure, and Parisian Society*. New Haven and London: Yale University Press, 1988.

Hiesinger, Kathryn B., et al. *The Second Empire, 1852–1870: Art in France under*

Napoleon III. Exh. cat., Philadelphia Museum of Art; Detroit Institute of Arts; Galeries Nationales du Grand Palais, Paris. Philadelphia: The Museum, 1978.

Hobhouse, Penelope. *Penelope Hobhouse's Gardening through the Ages: An Illustrated History of Plants and Their Influence on Garden Styles—from Ancient Egypt to the Present Day*. New York: Simon & Schuster, 1992.

———. *The Story of Gardening*. London: Dorling Kindersley, 2002.

Holme, Charles. "The Potter's Art—Object Lessons from the Far East." *The Studio* 24, no. 103 (October 1901), pp. 48–57.

Hopkins, Richard S. *Planning the Greenspaces of Nineteenth-Century Paris*. Baton Rouge: Louisiana State University Press, 2015.

Horne, Alistair. *Seven Ages of Paris*. New York: Alfred A. Knopf, 2002.

House, Emma, and David Ingram. *Painting Flowers: Fantin-Latour and the Impressionists*. Exh. cat. County Durham, England: The Bowes Museum, 2011.

House, John. "In Detail: Van Gogh's *The Poet's Garden, Arles*." *Portfolio* 2, no. 4 (September–October 1980), pp. 28–33.

Hulsker, Jan. "The Poet's Garden." *Vincent: Bulletin of the Rijksmuseum Vincent van Gogh* 3, no. 1 (1974), pp. 22–32.

Hunt, John Dixon. *Gardens and the Picturesque: Studies in the History of Landscape Architecture*. Cambridge, Mass.: MIT Press, 1992.

———. *A World of Gardens*. London: Reaktion Books, 2012.

Hunt, John Dixon, and Michel Conan, eds., with Claire Goldstein. *Tradition and Innovation in French Garden Art: Chapters of a New History*. Philadelphia: University of Pennsylvania Press, 2002.

Jones, Kimberly, with Simon Kelly, Sarah Kennel, and Helga Aurisch. *In the Forest of Fontainebleau: Painters and Photographers from Corot to Monet*. Exh. cat., National Gallery of Art, Washington, D.C.; The Museum of Fine Arts, Houston. New Haven and London: Yale University Press, 2008.

Jordan, David P. *Transforming Paris: The Life and Labors of Baron Haussmann*. New York: Free Press, 1995.

Jouanin, Christian, with Jérémie Benoit, Marie-Blanche d'Arneville, Bernard Chevallier, Pierre-Jacques Chappero, and Guy Ledoux-Lebard. *L'Impératrice Joséphine et les sciences naturelles*. Exh. cat., Musée National des Châteaux de Malmaison et Bois-Préau, Rueil-Malmaison. Paris: Editions de la Réunion des Musées Nationaux, 1997.

Journal de l'Académie d'Horticulture, Encyclopédie Mensuelle, Pratique et Progressive du Jardinage. Paris: Bureau du Journal de l'Académie d'Horticulture, 1831–36.

Joyes, Claire. *Claude Monet: Life at Giverny*. New York: Vendome Press, 1985.

Joyes, Claire, and Andrew Forge. *Monet at Giverny*. London: Mathews Miller Dunbar, 1975.

Kirkland, Stephane. *Paris Reborn: Napoléon III, Baron Haussmann, and the Quest to Build a Modern City*. New York: St. Martin's Press, 2013.

Krafft, J[ean] Ch[arles]. *Plans des plus beaux jardins pittoresques de France, d'Angleterre et d'Allemagne . . . / Plans of the Most Beautiful Picturesque Gardens in France, England, and Germany . . . / Plaene der schoensten und malerischten Gaerten, Franckreichs, Englands und Deutschlands*. Paris: De l'Imprimerie de Levrault, 1809.

Lablaude, Pierre-André. *The Gardens of Versailles*. London: Zwemmer, 1995.

Laborde, Alexandre de. *Description des nouveaux jardins de la France et de ses anciens châteaux*. Paris: Delance, 1808.

Lack, H. Walter, and Marina Heilmeyer. *Jardin de la Malmaison: Empress Josephine's Garden*. Munich and New York: Prestel, 2004.

Lalos, J. *De la composition des parcs et jardins pittoresques: Ouvrage utile et instructif pour les propriétaires et les amateurs, et orné de planches en noir ou coloriées*. 2nd ed. Paris: L'Auteur, 1824.

Langlois, Gilles-Antoine. *Folies, tivolis et attractions: Les Premiers Parcs de loisirs parisiens*. Exh. cat. Paris: Délégation à l'Action Artistique de la Ville de Paris, 1991.

Lautour-Mézeray, Ch. "Symétrie des jardins." *Journal de l'Académie d'Horticulture* 1 (April 1831), pp. 5–12.

Le Dantec, Denise, and Jean-Pierre Le Dantec. *Reading the French Garden: Story and History*. Translated by Jessica Levine. Cambridge, Mass.: MIT Press, 1993.

Lejeune, Daniel. *Edouard André, Auteur, acteur, spectateur: Les Clés d'une réussite*. Paris: Société Nationale d'Horticulture de France, 2009.

Leribault, Christophe, Stéphane Guégan, and Michèle Hannoosh. *Delacroix, Othoniel, Creten: Des fleurs en hiver*. Exh. cat., Musée National Eugène Delacroix, Paris. Paris: Le Passage Editions, 2012.

Limido, Luisa. *L'Art des jardins sous le Second Empire: Jean-Pierre Barillet-Deschamps (1824–1873)*. Seyssel: Champ Vallon, 2002.

Loudon, J.-C. (Jean Claudius). *An Encyclopaedia of Gardening; Comprising the Theory and Practice of Horticulture, Floriculture, Arboriculture, and Landscape Gardening . . .* . 2 vols. London: Longman, Hurst, Rees, Orme, and Brown, 1822. French translation, *L'Encyclopédie du jardinage*, published in 1830.

Loyrette, Henri. "Still Life." In *Origins of Impressionism*, by Gary Tinterow and Henri Loyrette, pp. 149–81. Exh. cat., Galeries Nationales du Grand Palais, Paris; The Metropolitan Museum of Art, New York. New York: The Metropolitan Museum of Art, 1994.

MacDonald, Heather, and Mitchell Merling, with Audrey Gay-Mazuel, Olivier Meslay, and Sylvie Patry. *Working among Flowers: Floral Still-Life Painting in Nineteenth-Century France*. Exh. cat., Dallas Museum of Art; Virginia

Museum of Fine Arts, Richmond; Denver Art Museum. New Haven and London: Yale University Press, 2014.

Mallet, Robert. *Jardins et paradis.* La Galerie pittoresque 2. Paris: Gallimard, 1959.

Mangin, Arthur. *Histoire des jardins anciens et modernes.* Rev. ed. Tours: Alfred Mame et fils, 1887. Originally published in 1867 as *Les Jardins: Histoire et description*.

Marrey, Bernard, and Jean-Pierre Monnet. *La Grand Histoire des serres et des jardins d'hiver: France, 1780–1900.* Paris: Graphite, 1984.

Mathews, Nancy Mowll, ed. *Cassatt and Her Circle: Selected Letters*. New York: Abbeville Press, 1984.

Mauner, George, and Henri Loyrette. *Manet: The Still-Life Paintings.* Exh. cat., Musée d'Orsay, Paris; Walters Art Gallery, Baltimore. New York: Harry N. Abrams, 2000.

Mosser, Monique, and Georges Teyssot, eds. *The Architecture of Western Gardens: A Design History from the Renaissance to the Present Day.* Cambridge, Mass.: MIT Press, 1991. Originally published as *L'architettura dei giardini d'Occidente*. Milan: Electa, 1990.

Pernoud, Emmanuel. *Paradis ordinaires: L'Artiste au jardin public*. Dijon: Les Presses du Réel, 2013.

Philipon de La Madelaine, Louis. *Le Guide du promeneur aux Tuileries; ou, Description du palais et du jardin national des Tuileries en l'an VI de la République Française.* Paris: Hautbout-Dumoulin, 1798.

Pincemaille, Christophe. *Joséphine: La Passion des fleurs et des oiseaux*. Exh. cat., Musée National des Châteaux de Malmaison et Bois-Préau, Rueil-Malmaison. Paris: Art Lys, 2014.

Pinkney, David H. *Napoleon III and the Rebuilding of Paris*. Princeton, N.J.: Princeton University Press, 1958.

Potter, Jennifer. *The Rose: A True History.* London: Atlantic Books, 2010.

Prévôt, Philippe. *Histoire des jardins.* Bordeaux: Sud Ouest, 2006.

Rathbone, Eliza E., George T. M. Shackelford, eds.; essays by Jeannene M. Przyblyski, John McCoubrey, Richard Shiff, Mary Hannah Byers, Susan Behrends Frank, Jennifer A. Greenhill, and Alexandra Ames Lawrence. *Impressionist Still Life.* Exh. cat., The Phillips Collection, Washington, D.C.; Museum of Fine Arts, Boston. Washington, D.C.: Phillips Collection, 2001.

Revue Horticole; ou, Journal des Jardiniers et Amateurs. Paris, 1829–1974.

Rewald, John. *The History of Impressionism*. Rev. ed. New York: Museum of Modern Art, 1961.

Riat, Georges. *L'Art des jardins.* Paris: Société Française d'Editions d'Art; L.-H. May, [1900].

Rix, Martyn. *The Golden Age of Botanical Art.* London: Andre Deutsch, 2012.

Robinson, W[illiam]. *Gleanings from French Gardens: Comprising an Account of Such Features of French Horticulture as Are Most Worthy of Adoption in British Gardens.* London: Frederick Warne; New York: Scribner, Welford, 1868.

———. *The Parks, Promenades & Gardens of Paris Described and Considered in Relation to the Wants of Our Own Cities and of Public and Private Gardens.* London: John Murray, 1869.

Robinson, William H., Clare A. P. Willsdon, Ann Dumas, Monty Don, James Priest, and Heather Lemonedes. *Painting the Modern Garden: Monet to Matisse.* Exh. cat., Cleveland Museum of Art; Royal Academy of Arts, London. London: Royal Academy of Arts, 2015.

Rogers, Elizabeth Barlow, Elizabeth S. Eustis, and John Bidwell. *Romantic Gardens: Nature, Art, and Landscape Design.* Exh. cat., The Morgan Library & Museum, New York. Boston: David R. Godine; New York: Foundation for Landscape Studies, 2010.

Rubin, James H. *Manet's Silence and the Poetics of Bouquets.* Cambridge, Mass.: Harvard University Press, 1994.

———. *Impressionism and the Modern Landscape: Productivity, Technology, and Urbanization from Manet to Van Gogh.* Berkeley: University of California Press, 2008.

Saule, Béatrix. *Versailles Gardens*. New York: Vendome Press, 2002.

Schama, Simon. *Landscape and Memory.* New York: Alfred A. Knopf, 1995.

Schulze, Sabine, ed.; contributions by Andreas Beyer, Werner Busch, Cornelia Homburg, John House, H. Walter Lack, and Beate Söntgen. *The Painter's Garden: Design, Inspiration, Delight.* Exh. cat., Städel Museum, Frankfurt am Main; Städtische Galerie im Lenbachhaus, Munich. Ostfildern-Ruit: Hatje Cantz, 2006.

Stein, Susan Alyson. "Edouard Manet: *Still Life with Flowers, Fan, and Pearls*." In "Recent Acquisitions: A Selection: 1993–1994," *The Metropolitan Museum of Art Bulletin* 52, no. 2 (Fall 1994), p. [illegible]

Stein, Susan Alyson, and Asher Ethan Miller, eds., contributions by Colin B. Bailey, Joseph J. Rishel, and Mark Rosenthal. *The Annenberg Collection: Masterpieces of Impressionism and Post-Impressionism*. 4th ed. New York: The Metropolitan Museum of Art, 2009.

Sterling, Charles. *Still Life Painting from Antiquity to the Present Time*. Rev. ed. Translated by James Emmons. New York: Universe Books, 1959.

Strong, Roy. *The Artist and the Garden.* New Haven and London: Yale University Press, 2000.

Stuffmann, Margret. "Odilon Redon: Paths to Color." In *Odilon Redon*, edited by Raphaël Bouvier, pp. 66–73. Exh. cat. Fondation Beyeler, Riehen/Basel, Switzerland. Ostfildern-Ruit: Hatje Cantz, 2014.

Texier, Edmond. *Tableau de Paris*. 2 vols. Paris: Paulin et Le Chevalier, 1852–53.

Texier, Simon, ed., with Béatrice de Andia et al. *Les Parcs et jardins dans l'urbanisme parisien, XIXe–XXe siècles*. Paris: Action Artistique de la Ville de Paris, 2001.

Thomas, Greg M. *Art and Ecology in Nineteenth-Century France: The Landscapes of Théodore Rousseau*. Princeton, N.J.: Princeton University Press, 2000.

Thouin, Gabriel. *Plans raisonnés de toutes les espèces de jardins*. Paris: Imp. de Lebégue, 1820.

Tivolle, Sigolène, ed. *Le Jardin d'Albert Kahn: Parcours historique et paysager*. Rev. ed. Nanterre: Hauts-de-Seine Conseil Général, 2012.

Tucker, Paul Hayes. *Monet at Argenteuil*. New Haven and London: Yale University Press, 1981.

——. *Claude Monet: Life and Art*. New Haven and London: Yale University Press, 1995.

Ventenat, Etienne Pierre. *Jardin de la Malmaison*. 2 vols. Paris: L'Imprimerie de Crapelet, 1803–4.

Viart, Amédée de. *Le Jardiniste moderne: Guide des propriétaires qui s'occupent de la composition de leurs jardins, ou de l'embellissement de leur campagne*. Paris: Petit, 1819.

Vitet, Ludovic. *Etudes sur l'histoire de l'art. Quatrième série: Temps modernes*. Paris: Michel Lévy frères, 1864.

Watelet, Claude-Henri. *Essay on Gardens: A Chapter in the French Picturesque*. Edited and translated by Samuel Danon; introduction by Joseph Disponzio. Philadelphia: University of Pennsylvania Press, 2003.

Wiebenson, Dora. *The Picturesque Garden in France*. Princeton, N.J.: Princeton University Press, 1978.

Willsdon, Clare A. P. "'Promenades et plantations': Impressionism, Conservation and Haussmann's Reinvention of Paris." In *Soil and Stone: Impressionism, Urbanism, Environment*, edited by Frances Fowle and Richard Thomson, pp. 107–24. Aldershot, England, and Burlington, Vt.: Ashgate, 2003.

——. *In the Gardens of Impressionism*. New York: Vendome Press, 2004.

——. *Impressionist Gardens*. Exh. cat. Edinburgh: National Galleries of Scotland, 2010.

Wilson-Bareau, Juliet, ed. *Manet by Himself: Correspondence and Conversation, Paintings, Pastels, Prints, and Drawings*. Boston: Little, Brown, 1991.

Wulf, Andrea. *The Invention of Nature: Alexander Von Humboldt's New World*. New York: Alfred A. Knopf, 2015.

Index

Page numbers in *italic* refer to illustrations.

Photograph Credits

From Adolphe Alphand, *Les Promenades de Paris*, 2 vols. (Paris: J. Rothschild, 1868–73). Image © The Metropolitan Museum of Art, photo by Heather Johnson, figs. 50, 52, 54
Archives of The New York Botanical Garden: figs. 18, 19, 73
The Art Institute of Chicago / Art Resource, NY: figs. 55, 76
© Belvedere, Vienna, photo by Johanness Stoll: fig. 99
Photo © John Bigelow Taylor. © 2017 Artists Rights Society (ARS), New York: fig. 66
bpk Bildagentur /Staatliche Museen / Joerg P. Anders / Art Resource, NY: fig. 112
Courtesy Lévy Gorvy, New York, photo by Elisabeth Bernstein: fig. 57
Image © Lyon, Musée des Beaux-Arts, photo by Alain Basset: fig. 125
Image © The Metropolitan Museum of Art: figs. 2, 3, 7, 9, 10, 12, 13, 21–23, 25–28, 30–32, 34, 35, 37, 40, 41, 44, 45, 60, 63–65, 67, 77–79, 82, 84, 88, 90, 92, 98, 100, 101, 103, 107, 108, 111, 113, 115–122, 124, 127, 130, 131, 134, 136–138, 141, 144, 146–148, 150–158
Image © The Metropolitan Museum of Art. © 2017 Artists Rights Society (ARS), New York: figs. 42, 95, 145
Image © The Metropolitan Museum of Art. © 2017 Artists Rights Society (ARS), New York / ADAGP, Paris: figs. 62, 96, 104, 160
Image © The Metropolitan Museum of Art. Artwork © 2017 Succession H. Matisse / Artists Rights Society (ARS), New York: fig. 159
Image © The Metropolitan Museum of Art: p. 168
Image © The Metropolitan Museum of Art, photo by Kathy Dahab: fig. 61
Image © The Metropolitan Museum of Art, photo by Heather Johnson: figs. 38, 51, 58, 93, 139
Image © The Metropolitan Museum of Art, photo by Paul Lachenauer: fig. 16
Image © The Metropolitan Museum of Art, photo by Mark Morosse: figs. 1, 4–6, 8, 11, 15, 33, 36, 53, 70–72, 74, 75, 83, 106
Image © The Metropolitan Museum of Art, photo by Juan Trujillo: figs. 46, 80, 102, 126, 128, 129,
© The National Gallery, London: figs. 39, 109, 149
Courtesy National Gallery of Art, Washington, DC: fig. 114
© The National Museum of Art, Architecture and Design, photo by Børre Høstland: fig. 59
Allen Phillips / Wadsworth Atheneum: fig. 89
The Phillips Collection, Washington, DC: fig. 68
Private Collection / Bridgeman Images: figs. 43, 48, 91
Private Collection / Photo © Christie's Images / Bridgeman Images: fig. 97
Rijksmuseum, Amsterdam: fig. 110
© RMN-Grand Palais / Art Resource, NY, photo by Agence Bulloz: fig. 69
© RMN-Grand Palais / Art Resource, NY, photo by Daniel Arnaudet / Jean Schormans: figs. 14, 123
© RMN-Grand Palais / Art Resource, NY, photo by Jean-Gilles Berizzi: fig. 142
© RMN-Grand Palais / Art Resource, NY, photo by Hervé Lewandowski: figs. 85, 132
© RMN-Grand Palais / Art Resource, NY, photo by Jean Schormans. © 2017 Artists Rights Society (ARS), New York: fig. 56
Scala / Art Resource, NY: fig. 133
Photograph Courtesy of Sotheby's, Inc. © 2014: fig. 140
Photograph Courtesy of Sotheby's, Inc. © 2014, Collection of Diane B. Wilsey: fig. 94
© The Wallace Collection: fig. 86

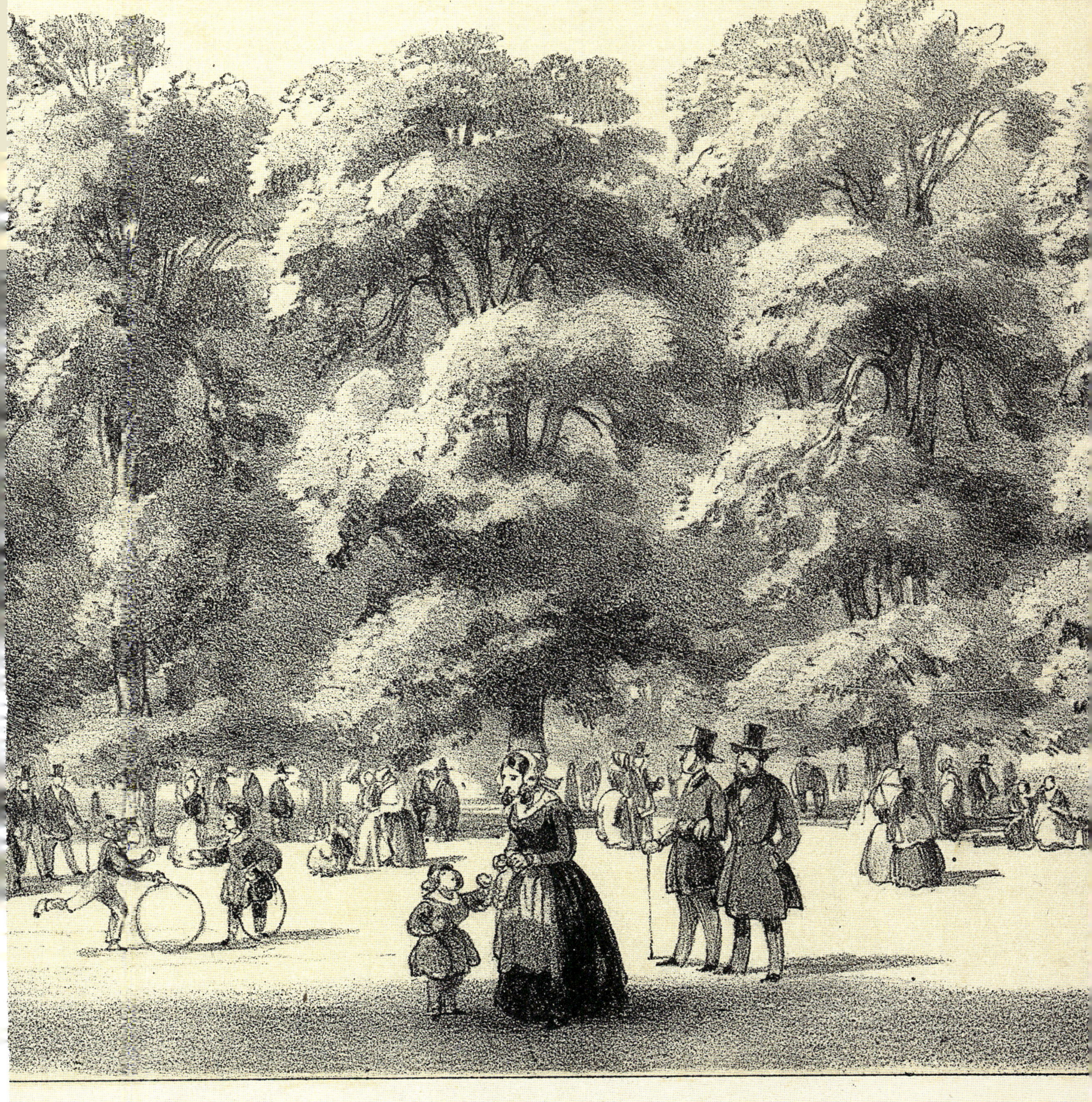

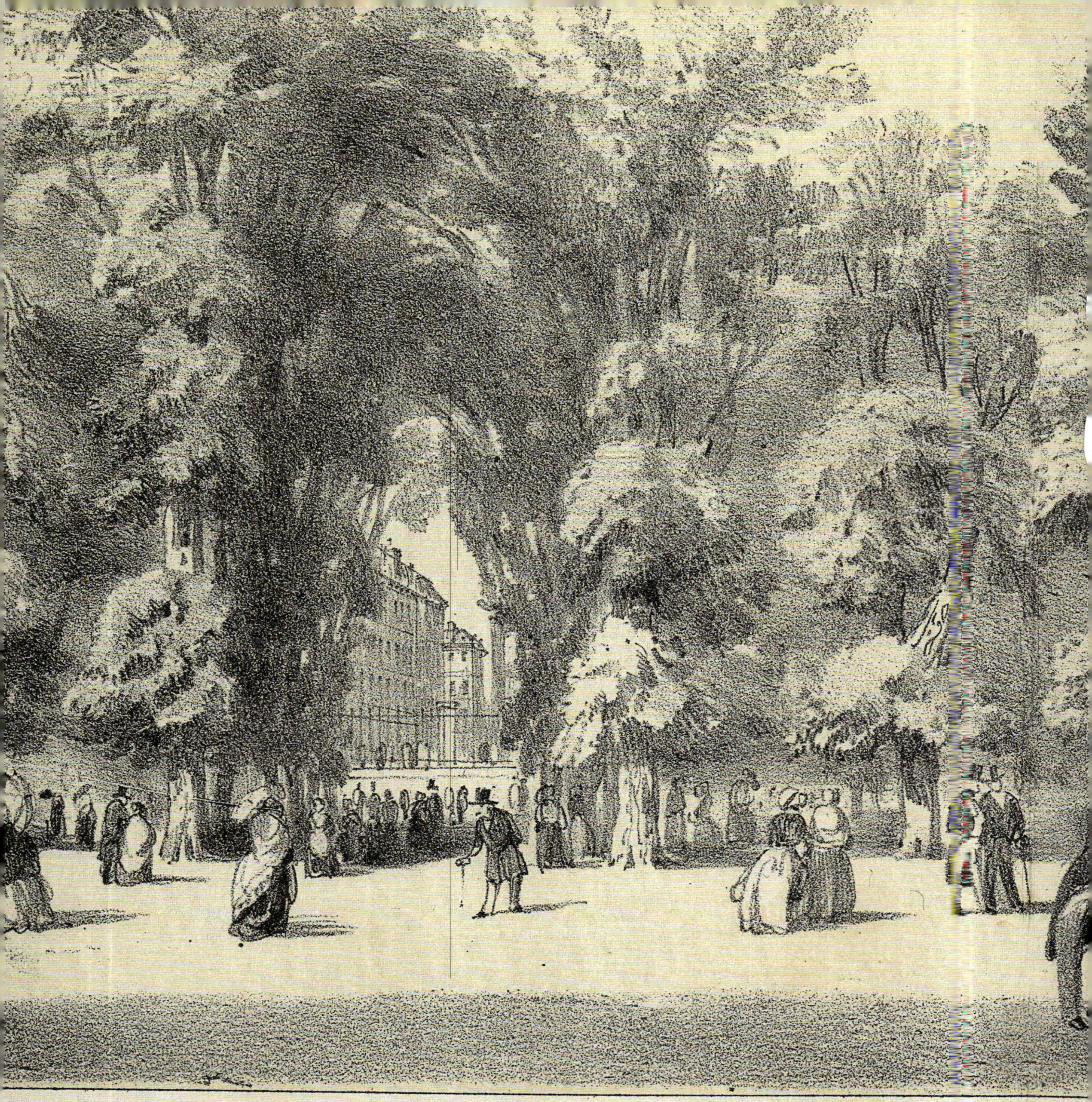

Rue Castighone.